The Social Passion

1

2

3

4

5

6

7

8

9

10

11

12

13

14

15

16

17

19

20

21

22

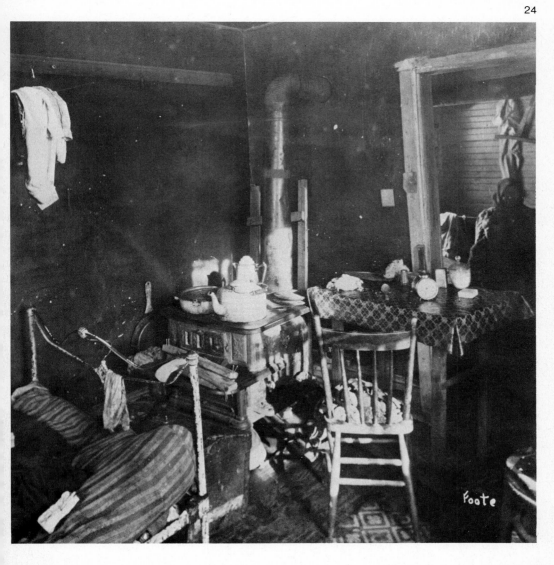

Foote

26

RICHARD ALLEN

The Social Passion

Religion and Social Reform in Canada 1914-28

UNIVERSITY OF TORONTO PRESS

©University of Toronto Press 1971
University of Toronto Press, Toronto and Buffalo
Printed in Canada

ISBN 0-8020-5252-5
ISBN 0-8020-0035-5 (microfiche)
LC 71-151352

TO MY PARENTS
whose living
of the social gospel
began where this book
ends

Illustrations

Unless otherwise noted these photographs are published
by courtesy of the United Church Archives

1 Steel Company of Canada, Hamilton
2 Mining coal near Lethbridge
3 Ernest Thomas
4 Salem Bland (*courtesy Gwendolyn Bland*)
5 International Nickel Company plant, Sudbury
6 Immigrant railway labour
7 Boxcar bunkhouses for railway labour
8 Prairie harvest hands embarking
9 Bumper crop near Scott, Saskatchewan
10 In the Winnipeg slums
11 William Ivens (*courtesy of Manitoba Archives*)
12 W.B. Creighton (*courtesy of Isabel Wilson*)
13 Sweated labour, Toronto
14 Immigrant arrivals, Winnipeg
15 C.W. Gordon, *pseud.* Ralph Connor (*courtesy of Manitoba Archives*)
16 J.S. Woodsworth (*courtesy of Public Archives of Canada*)
17 Immigrant women and children, CPR Station, Winnipeg
18 A Montreal back yard
19 Lane and dwellings, Sydney, Nova Scotia
20 T.A. Moore
21 J.G. Shearer (*courtesy of Canadian Council of Churches*)
22 Charity in the Winnipeg slums
23 Illness strikes down the breadwinner, Toronto
24 Slum quarters, Winnipeg
25 Special police advancing on Winnipeg strikers, June 1919
26 Special police and RNWMP reinforcements, Winnipeg general strike, June 1919
   Frontispiece Labour Day Rally, Winnipeg, being addressed in five languages

Contents

Preface

This book is a study in the history of ideas, specifically with reference to the conjunction of the movements of religion and social reform in Canada in the years 1914 to 1928. The title of the book was a phrase coined by those who figure in it to describe the passion for social involvement which they hoped to instil in the Canadian mind at large and to make a primary characteristic of Canadian Protestantism in particular. The book may be seen as a contribution to the study of the ongoing attempt to relate the religious and ethical demands of the Judaeo-Christian tradition to the conditions of human society. More specifically, its subject is a part of the recent movement of social Christianity. The technically proper title for the movement it studies is the social gospel. In the period in question, it was one of the most significant single features in the complexion of social reform in Canada.

The book catches the social gospel in mid-passage, in a period when its influence was high but its fortunes in crisis. It must be acknowledged that, in the absence of a full study of the rise of the social gospel in Canada, the present work runs the danger of seeming somewhat truncated. This has been partly offset by an introductory sketch and the insertion of considerable background material at appropriate places throughout the book. A fuller introduction could have been supplied but that in turn ran the twin dangers of overextending the length of the work and freezing in print what must still be premature conclusions. A problem remains, and it can only be pleaded that a further book will be forthcoming on the earlier period – and, hopefully, on the later as well. In the meantime, he who wishes to pursue the question will find that there is some writing available to him, the most useful of which can be found in the footnotes to the first chapter.

The social gospel, properly speaking, was a Protestant phenomenon, but an analogous social Catholic movement covered approximately the same years. While it would be tempting to try to weave the social gospel and social Catholic movements in Canada into one account, the winds of ecumenism had not yet, in 1914, begun to blow Canadian Catholics and Protestants together, and despite certain similarities in development, the two movements ran on parallel, but largely unconnected, lines. *Le Devoir*, for instance, might commend the Social Service Congress in 1914, but it was at the time sponsoring its own conference on urban housing problems.

To attempt to document so elusive a matter as the relation of religious attitudes, ideas, and hopes to the actual course of social, political, and economic affairs may seem at times to beg a few questions. Nevertheless, at some points it appeared wiser to be suggestive than to ignore entirely what were important probable correlations. The full effects of such a movement are difficult to assess, but the drama of the social gospel in Canada between 1914 and 1928 was one of high hopes, notable successes, intense encounters, conflicts (both of soul and society), disillusionments, and self-deceptions. Nor was it without elements of intrigue. Its story was one of consequence for some of the deepest issues of self and society, as well as a vital part of a crucial period of transition in Canadian history.

Those whose thought, writing, and action form the basis and context of this book are, of course, acknowledged in the text, the footnotes, and the bibliography. To the making of it, however, many have added their wisdom and skill, and their support, both moral and financial. My first excursion into the history of the social gospel in Canada, a study of the life of Salem Goldworth Bland, owed much to the encouragement of Dr Roger Graham, then at the University of Saskatchewan, now at Queen's University. The present subject was first explored as a doctoral thesis with the assistance of a grant from the Commonwealth Studies Center of Duke University and under the careful supervision of Dr Richard Watson, Jr, chairman of the history department of that university.

The pursuit of the subject has led through the following libraries and archives, always with happy experiences in the assistance provided: the Public Archives of Canada, and of Saskatchewan and Manitoba, the Douglas Library and archives of Queen's University, the libraries of the University of Toronto and its affiliated colleges, the Toronto Public Library, and the Baptist Historical Collection at Mc-Master University. My greatest debt, however, has been incurred in the Archives of the United Church of Canada. Its archivists, first Dr A.G. Reynolds and then the Rev. C.G. Lucas, have together given me immeasurable aid, and its small staff responded patiently to my many requests. I am grateful to Professor A.G. Bedford, University of Winnipeg, for letting me read his manuscript on the history of Wesley College, part of a larger work he is preparing on the university, and for calling my attention to further material pertaining to Salem Bland.

The manuscript has at various stages been read by my father, the Rev. H.T. Allen of Victoria, himself a mine of information on the social gospel in Canada, by Dr John W. Grant, professor of church history, Emmanuel College, Toronto, and by the readers of the University of Toronto Press. Mr Donald Page, assistant professor of history at the University of Saskatchewan, Regina Campus, has read the two chapters on resurgent peace movements and has given me the benefit of his recent research into Canadian internationalism in the 1920s. It has been both my pleasure and my frustration to try to meet their thoughtful criticism, and the book is much the better for it. Mr R.I.K. Davidson, social science editor of the University of Toronto Press, has made my association with the Press a thoroughly pleasant one, and Mrs Rosemary Shipton's rigorous copy editing has added many merits to the style of the book. Publication has been made possible by grants from the Social Science Research Council of Canada (using funds provided by the Canada Council), the University of Saskatchewan, and the Publications Fund of the University of Toronto Press.

As every author – and every author's family – knows, there are times when a book takes possession of his whole household. The bedding and boarding of the creator of such a tyrant, and the typing and other servicing of the tyrant itself, are of an order that makes any expression of thanks gratuitous. Indeed, to summon in one place a few of the many who have made the book possible is to lay one's tribute before the community of man, which, for all the seeming solitariness of scholarship, is both its instrument and its end. The errors and problems remaining in the work are, of course, my own responsibility.

RICHARD ALLEN
Regina, August 1970

Abbreviations

UCA United Church Archives
SW   *Social Welfare*
GGG *Grain Growers' Guide*
CAR *Canadian Annual Review*
CG   *Christian Guardian*
WLN *Western Labor News*
MIR Papers on Methodist Industrial
      Relations, 1920–2
ESS Evangelism and Social Service
SSCC *Social Service Congress of Canada,
      1914*

The Social Passion

1

The Rise of
the Social Gospel
1890-1914

From the 1890s through the 1930s the spirit of reform was abroad in the land. In church and in secular society, in rural and urban life, in municipality and province, and progressively in federal politics, reformers were attempting the awesome task of reshaping Canadian society. When their work was done, both the structures and social outlook of Canada were remarkably altered. Underlying and accompanying the reform movement, and providing an avenue into its many parts, was the social gospel. One of its most important functions was to forge links between proposed reforms and the religious heritage of the nation, in the process endowing reform with an authority it could not otherwise command. At the same time it attempted to mould religious and social attitudes thought necessary for life in a world reformed. Still more fundamentally, it represented the complex of ideas and hopes which lay at the heart of reform, and it did this regardless of whether the social gospel was specifically acknowledged or not. There are many standpoints from which the reform movement can be viewed, but only when it is looked on as a religious expression, striving to embed ultimate human goals in the social, economic, and political order, is the success and the failure of reform fully appreciated. To adopt such a standpoint is not to do violence to the reformers themselves. At one time or another most could be found describing their enterprises in religious terms, and the social passion which marked their lives clearly entered that realm of ultimate commitments usually considered the province of religion. It was no mere coincidence that it was in the conceptions of the social gospel that the social passion of many reformers found its readiest rationalization. For those not already endowed with the passion, the social gospel stood ready to evoke it.[1]

The social gospel was not a uniquely Canadian movement, but was part of a widespread attempt in Europe and North America to revive and develop Christian

---

1 Substantial parts of this chapter have appeared in article form as Allen, 'The Social Gospel and the Reform Tradition in Canada, 1890–1928.' Readers should note that a list of works cited is placed at the end of the book to supplement the author-short title entries in the footnotes.

social insights and to apply them to the emerging forms of a collective society. This task was undertaken under the pressures of positive, organic, and developmental forms of thought arising in Europe and Britain in the wake of Comte, Darwin, and Marx. The social gospel which resulted is usually regarded as an American movement, yet Ritschlian theology in Germany, the 'new theology' of R.J. Campbell in Britain, and the 'new Christianity' of Salem Bland in Canada may all join Walter Rauschenbusch, the classic American spokesman of the movement, in laying claim to the name.

The social gospel rested on the premise that Christianity was a social religion, concerned, when the misunderstanding of the ages was stripped away, with the quality of human relations on this earth. Put in more dramatic terms, it was a call for men to find the meaning of their lives in seeking to realize the Kingdom of God in the very fabric of society. Although there were clear theological implications in such a position, the social gospel did not regard itself as primarily a theological movement. Indeed, it has been observed that its preoccupation with social problems may have been partly motivated by a desire to escape from theological perplexities.[2] Whatever could be disputed in the great systems of theology erected in the course of the nineteenth century, this much was clear, that the gospel mandate required response to concrete human needs. The social gospel was at least as much born of that recognition, combined with a genuine moral enthusiasm, as it was of theological perplexity and escapism. And yet the social gospel could be described as a movement in search of a theology. The social application of the gospel eventually demanded fuller rationalization in theological terms. As the social gospel in Canada was entering its crest, Rauschenbusch was writing a series of lectures to be published in 1917 as *A Theology for the Social Gospel*. While many currents flowed into his book, reduced to its basic concepts it was largely a reflection of the theology of the German scholar, Albrecht Ritschl, who had dominated European Protestant theology in the 1870s and 1880s. Ritschl's thought, usually unsystematically appropriated, provided the implicit theological foundations of much of the social gospel.

In Ritschl's theology, man and God seemed to exist in a single continuum. The decades of arid metaphysical debate had made Ritschl sceptical about the possibility of rational knowledge of God. Not the faculty of reason, but the emotions and, in particular, the experience of divine forgiveness, were the avenue to knowledge of God. Out of Ritschl's emphasis on the forgiving work of God, God emerged simply as love. This was, in effect, a humbler divinity than the Biblical and Reformation attributes of holiness and wrath allowed. Just as the traditional characteristics

2 Nichols, *History of Christianity, 1650–1950*, p. 280

which distinguished God from man were discounted, so the existential alienation between man and God, expressed in the doctrine of original sin, was denied, and man appeared as fundamentally good. Similarly, Ritschl saw no great gulf between mankind and Jesus. Jesus marked the moral perfection that was possible to every man, and His work was to bring the believer into a kingdom of moral ends. The church, it followed, was representative of the universal society that was to come, and was commissioned to be an agent in its fulfilment. Thus, not only man and God, but religious meaning and the social process tended to merge in Ritschl's thought.

The evangelicalism of the nineteenth-century English-speaking world had helped prepare the way for ideas such as Ritschl's, a factor which probably explains the large number of Methodists prominent in the movements of the social gospel in Canada. Evangelicalism was less concerned with theological debate over the nature of God than with the need of man for forgiveness, believed that God's love was available to any man earnestly desiring it and that through repentance he could go on to masterful living, indeed, even to a point of personal perfection or entire sanctification where temptation, if felt at all, no longer held any danger for the soul. This was in sharp contrast to Presbyterianism, and one significant develop-ment in nineteenth-century religious history – especially in North America – was the triumph of evangelicalism over the more sober concepts of Calvinism. The evangelical movement was planted in Canada shortly after the conquest by English Methodist immigrants and soldiers, and by Baptists and Congregationalists from New England. In the course of the next century Methodism became the largest single Protestant body in the nation, and evangelicalism the dominant strain in Canadian Protestantism.[3]

There were, of course, other avenues to the social gospel besides a compound of evangelicalism and Ritschlianism. The Calvinist inheritance of Presbyterianism provided foundations for the reassertion of the social mandate of the Christian gospel. John Calvin in Geneva, John Knox in Scotland, and Jonathon Edwards in New England all conceived of and promoted a society in which social and economic relationships were subject to religious control. If the worlds of commerce and political economy found such conceptions uncongenial, they were not thereby ren-dered irrelevant to the concerns of the new social age of the twentieth century.[4] The Church of Scotland was the major bearer of these earlier Calvinist impulses,

3 See French, 'The Evangelical Creed in Canada'
4 This thesis runs through the work of R.H. Tawney, among others. See McCormack, 'The Protestant Ethic and the Spirit of Socialism'

and although it had become reconciled to its disestablished status in Canadian society, strains of the older social paternalism were still apparent, for instance, in the intimate association of religious and political man propounded by George M. Grant, principal of Queen's University and one of Protestant Canada's most outspoken commentators on public affairs. The social constructions of earlier Calvinism, however, had been intended more to keep society from disintegrating than to provide the staging for the society of regenerated man with which the social gospel was to become enchanted. However, by Grant's time, Canadian Presbyterianism had been first disrupted and then largely transformed by the evangelical influences of the Free Kirk movement. It was within this context that Canadian Presbyterians made their entry into the passionate world of the social gospel.

When Anglicans found their way into the tents of the social gospel, it was not so much by the avenue of evangelicalism as by the traditional ways of the established church. In refurbished form, the paternalism of the church found a new outlet in the social service movement: its corporate concepts provided a basis for countering the sway of economic individualism; and its sacramentalism, its heightened sense that material things could be vehicles of the spirit, contained a clear repudiation of materialism, whether capitalist or socialist. Although such High Church radicalism became the leading edge of Christian social ethics in Britain, its impact upon Canadian Anglicanism was remarkably slight. Evangelicalism, of course, made its own impact on Anglicanism, but this was not to the degree or of such a nature in Canada as to make of Canadian Anglicanism a strong contributor to the social gospel.

The evangelical objective of claiming the land for 'scriptural holiness' encompassed not only an interest in, but the necessity of social reform, as the prominence of evangelicals in the anti-slavery movements of England and America testified. The role of Methodist local preachers in the early trade union movement is common knowledge, and the revivalism of mid-century America, which spilled over into Canada, was accompanied by the slogan 'saved for service.'[5] As evangelicalism became more diffused in the latter half of the century, as more organic forms of social thought emerged, and as awareness of the demands of the social problem became more acute, the underlying individualism of the evangelical way seemed to many to be less and less appropriate.[6] The demand 'save this man, now' became 'save this society, now,' and the slogan 'the evangelization of the world in our

5 See T.L. Smith, *Revivalism and Social Reform in Mid-Nineteenth Century America*, chaps. x and xi

6 For an expression of this transition, see the introduction to Booth, *In Darkest England and the Way Out*

generation' became 'the Christianization of the world in our generation.'[7] The sense of an immanent God working in the movements of revival and awakening was easily transferred to social movements, and hence to the whole evolution of society. Thus Josiah Strong in the United States could speak of the 'great social awakening,' and many could come to view secular social action as a religious rite.

Such combinations of ideas and impulses were apparent in a sermon given to the first Brotherhood group in Canada on 14 April 1895. Speaking on 'Social Resurrection,' J.B. Silcox, a Congregationalist, argued that Jesus' 'resurrection means that humanity shall rise ... into higher, nobler, diviner conditions of life.' He joined several British thinkers, preachers, and writers, he said, in predicting a world-wide revolution for the people in the twentieth century. 'This uprising of the people is divine in its source ... God is in the midst of it ... To the ecclesiastical and industrial Pharaohs of today, God is saying, "Let my people go." ' He concluded by calling for 'a political faith in Jesus' based on the charter of the Sermon on the Mount.[8] C.S. Eby, a Methodist, was somewhat more philosophical in expression: Jesus Christ was the 'type of coming man on this planet'; the Ultimate Reality of which Christ was the revelation was in and through all things – 'the universal spirit of Christ would reconstruct man and mankind'; trade unionism, socialism, and business organization were signs of the development of this reconstructed social order.[9] On this basis Eby built his Socialist church in Toronto in 1909.[10] Slightly more subdued, perhaps, were the ideas of C.W. Gordon, a Presbyterian, in his concept of 'the New Church' delivered to the Social Service Congress in 1914. The 'New Church' would reject the picture of God as 'the stern ruler of the Universe, exacting obedience, and hard on the trail of every sinner,' and would present him 'in the best picture of God we have, a good man with goodness raised to the highest power ... In the New Church Religion and Brotherhood will be synonymous ...' Similarly, the 'New State' would overcome captivity to the 'Big Individual' and 'Big Business,' and would recognize its organic character and serve mankind as a whole.[11] Hu-

7 The distinction was between bringing the message and creating the social reality. For an illuminating discussion of this process, see Meyer, *The Protestant Search for Political Realism, 1919–1941*, chap. 1.

8 United Church Archives, Toronto (UCA), Silcox, *Social Resurrection*

9 Eby, *The World Problem and the Divine Solution, passim*

10 W.S. Ryder, in a paper presented to the Pacific Coast Theology Conferenec, 1920, in *Western Methodist Recorder*, Sept. 1920, pp. 4–5. See also Summers' thesis ,'The Labour Church'

11 Gordon, 'The New State and the New Church,' in *The Social Service Congress of Canada, 1914* (SSCC), pp. 192–8

manity, it seemed, was in the grip of divine currents too strong to be resisted. To submit oneself to these immanent impulses of divinity was to adopt the social gospel and to embrace the social passion which lay at the heart of most of the movements of social reform in Canada in the period 1890–1939.

The Protestant background out of which the Canadian social gospel had to emerge was one overwhelmingly dominated by the Anglican, Methodist, and Presbyterian churches. The similarities and disparities in the social outlook of these churches prior to the onset of the late nineteenth-century depression may be suggested by their reactions to a strike of the Toronto Printers' Union in 1872. The Anglican *Church Herald* condemned the labourers for usurping the role of the employer and blamed the strike upon 'the insidious whimperings of a foreign-born league.' The *Presbyterian Witness* argued that labour's campaign 'strikes at the very root of ... personal independence and perpetuates their social demoralisation ... No man ever rose above a lowly condition who thought more of his class than of his individuality.' The Methodist *Christian Guardian* declared a profound sympathy with all honest working men and a sincere desire for their betterment, but went on to say: 'we seriously question the wisdom and advantage of this movement – especially the strikes to which it is likely to lead.'[12] When news of Henry George's Anti-Poverty Society reached Toronto in 1887, the other two churches would probably have echoed the response of the *Christian Guardian* on 29 June: 'We have no faith in the abolition of poverty by any laws that can be made in legislatures ... The best anti-poverty society is an association of men who would adopt as their governing principles in life, industry, sobriety, economy and intelligence.' Such an individualistic ethic was unable, however, to withstand the combined onslaught of extended depression, the rapid growth of industrial urban centres, and the spread of new social conceptions.

It has been argued that the social gospel in Canada was largely an indigenous

12 These reactions of the church press are cited in Crysdale, *The Industrial Struggle and Protestant Ethics in Canada*, pp. 18–19. It is likely that among the strikers and those who rallied to their support were some who were not prepared to accept the editors' opinions as to their Christian duty. See French, *Faith, Sweat and Politics*. For a fuller account of the social stance of Methodism and Presbyterianism in these years, see theses by Royce, 'The Contribution of the Methodist Church to Social Welfare in Canada,' and E.A. Christie, 'The Presbyterian Church in Canada and Its Official Attitude towards Public Affairs and Social Problems, 1875–1925,' and Magney's article, 'The Methodist Church and the National Gospel.'

development.[13] Although it is possible that a Canadian social gospel might have developed simply in response to domestic urban and industrial problems, it did not in fact happen that way. To be sure, the earliest expressions of the social gospel in Canada may still lie in sources untouched by the historian's hand. And in those sources, the rise of the social gospel may be obscured by the gradual nature of its separation from older forms of Christian social expression characterized by a concern for church-state relations, education, political corruption, and personal and social vice. But almost all evidence regarding the emergence of the social gospel from this tradition points not simply to the challenge of Canadian conditions, but to currents of thought and action which were sweeping the western world, none of which originated in Canada.

The inspiration of the pioneers of the social gospel and the origin of some of its prominent institutions reveal the extent of its indebtedness. Salem Bland, later to become the philosopher and mentor of the movement, is perhaps the best illustration of the debt. He was an omnivorous reader, and in the decade of the 1890s when he seems to have first formulated a social gospel outlook, was especially influenced by Carlyle, Tennyson, Emerson, Channing, and Thoreau, by the historical critics of scripture, and Albrecht Ritschl. At least as significant for Bland was the literature of evolution.[14] The notes for his first socialist lecture, 'Four Steps and a Vision,' acknowledge various works of Darwin, Drummond's *Ascent of Man*, and Kidd's *Social Evolution*, as well as *Fabian Essays*, Arnold Toynbee, Edward Bellamy, and Henry George.[15] A contemporary, W.A. Douglass, in the 1880s expressed his disagreement with individualistic methods of social regeneration by tirelessly campaigning for Henry George's panacea of the single tax.[16] Canadians had attended the three great interdenominational conferences in the United States on social problems in 1887, 1889, and 1893, and one follow-up conference had been held in Montreal in 1888.[17] Institutional vehicles and expressions of the social gospel such as the Brotherhoods, institutional churches, settlements, and Labor

---

13 Crysdale, *The Industrial Struggle*, p. 22 and Magney 'The Methodist Church and the National Gospel,' incline to this position, although neither has explored the alternative.

14 See UCA, Bland Papers, Reading Lists

15 Bland Papers

16 Goodwin, *Canadian Economic Thought*, pp. 32–8; *Toronto World*, 7 Feb. 1898; *Grain Grower's Guide* (GGG), 21 Nov. 1917, pp. 32–3

17 Hopkins, *The Rise of the Social Gospel in American Protestantism, 1865–1915*, p. 114; Berger, *The Sense of Power*, p. 184, 184n

churches derived ultimately from British models, although American mediation and modification took place in some instances. This pattern of influence continued throughout the life of the social gospel in Canada.

The pressures of the last years of depression in the early 1890s precipitated a quickening interest in new forms of social thought and action among a growing group of Christian ministers and laymen. One of the most vital centres of this interest was the Queen's Theological Alumni Conference, instituted by Principal G.M. Grant in 1893. At its annual meetings, the conference discussed papers on such topics as biblical criticism, economic development, the problems of poverty, socialistic schemes, the single tax, social evolution, interpretations of modern life by modern poets, studies of the prophets, Tolstoi, the relation of legislation and morality, and Christianity in its relation to human progress. As a Methodist minority among Presbyterians, Salem Bland was probably the most radical of the regular members.[18]

At least as important, and ultimately a more vigorous source of the social gospel in Canada, was Wesley College, Winnipeg. Set in a community already impressed with the social possibilities of new beginnings on the Canadian prairies, it provided a nucleus of Christian social enthusiasm, not only for some of its faculty and students but for younger clergy of various denominations and socially conscious young men outside the college.[19] Impressed by the unrelieved prospects of farmers who, in the early 1890s, 'sat down beside their unwanted grain and wept,'[20] and influenced by the currents of social thought emanating from the writings of Charles Kingsley, George Eliot, and William Morris, and from the sermons of English preachers like Hugh Price Hughes and Mark Guy Pearse,[21] this group went on to inject the social gospel into all the endeavours of western progressive reform. Tariffs and grain trade, railway rates and direct legislation became vital Christian concerns. In the 1890s, the Rev. J.M. Douglas, a patron member of Parliament for East Assiniboia, symbolized this development,[22] and when in 1903 Salem Bland joined the Wesley College faculty, he became the effective centre of this growing movement in the West.[23]

18 *Kingston Daily News*, 14 Feb. 1894; 13, 20 Feb. 1896; 11 Feb. 1897; *Queen's Quarterly*, v, April 1898, 316–18; vi, April 1899, 314–16; vii, April 1900, 332; viii, April 1901, 388

19 Riddell, *Methodism in the Middle West*, p. 316

20 *Ibid.*, p. 177

21 *Ibid.*, p. 228

22 Johnson, 'James Moffatt Douglas,' pp. 47–51

23 See Allen's thesis, 'Salem Bland and the Social Gospel in Canada,' chaps. i–iii

There were still other signs of a nascent social gospel in the 1890s. At the beginning of the decade a pirated edition of General William Booth's *In Darkest England and the Way Out* was selling fast.[24] Booth's scheme, involving the establishment of labour exchanges, farm colonies, and industrial towns, model suburban villages, paid holidays, and an intelligence service for processing useful social data, was branded by some as socialistic, but encouraged others to view social action as an essential part of true religion.[25] Two Canadian ministers, S.S. Craig and Herbert Casson, taking their cue from John Trevor in Manchester, attempted to found Labor churches. Nothing more is known of Craig's venture in Toronto,[26] but Casson's church at Lynn, Massachusetts, lasted from 1893 to 1898, after which he became a well-known socialist lecturer in Canada as well as the United States.[27] The Congregationalist layman, T.B. Macaulay, in 1894 brought the Brotherhood movement from England to Montreal, whence its combination of 'brief, bright and brotherly' meetings, which mixed gospel songs with social reform, spread across the nation.[28]

Among social problems, those of slums and immigration prompted the larger part of the institutional response of the social gospel within the churches. Again, it was in the last decade of the nineteenth century that the first ambitious innovations were undertaken with the establishment of St Andrew's Institute in 1890 by the Presbyterian, D.J. Macdonnell, and the Fred Victor Mission in 1894 by a Methodist group under the impetus of the Massey family. Together providing facilities for night school, library, savings bank, nursery, clubrooms, gymnasium, medical centre, and restaurant, they reflected ventures pioneered in England, Scotland, and the United States in the previous decade.[29] Further institutional response to urban problems came after 1902 with the development of settlement houses by Miss Sara Libby Carson, working under the Presbyterian church. Miss Carson came to that

24 Sandall, *The History of the Salvation Army.* III: *Social Reform and Welfare Work*, 80

25 Sutherland, *The Kingdom of God and Problems of Today*, p. xiii

26 Bland Papers, Salem Bland, sermon at St James-Bond United Church, 31 Oct. 1937

27 Summers, 'The Labour Church,' pp. 427ff; Hopkins, *Rise of the Social Gospel*, pp. 85–7; French, *Faith, Sweat and Politics*, pp. 129–30

28 *Social Welfare* (SW), Oct. 1923, pp. 14–15; Ward, *The Brotherhood in Canada*. See also Leete, *Christian Brotherhoods*

29 McCurdy, *The Life and Work of D.J. Macdonnell*, pp. 23–4, 289–309; minutes of the Toronto City Missionary Society of the Methodist church, 29 Dec. 1894, 10 Dec. 1895. For the less well-known Scottish side of the story, see Mechie, *The Church and Scottish Social Developments, 1780–1870*

church from the Canadian YWCA, but her real apprenticeship had been served in the American branch and in particular in its so-called 'Americanization' programme. By 1920 there were at least thirteen settlements in Canada, probably all of them formed under the impulse of the social gospel.[30] Where Miss Carson was not involved directly as organizer, she was often associated as consultant, as with the Toronto and McGill University settlements (1907 and 1909 respectively), which grew out of the social concern in the student YMCAS. When the University of Toronto opened its Department of Social Service in 1914, the University Settlement provided the framework for practical work, and Miss Carson and the Rev. F.N. Stapleford of the Neighborhood Workers' Association, among others, were recruited as lecturers.[31] Under J.S. Woodsworth, the settlement approach to the problems of North Winnipeg became a more potent spearhead of social reform, and the beginning for Woodsworth of an ever more radical formulation of the social gospel.[32] Woodsworth's own association with the settlement movement, however, had been initiated by visits to Mansfield House in London's East End during a trip to England in 1899 and 1900. It was from his experience with immigration and the urban slum in Winnipeg between 1907 and 1913 that two of the most important early pieces of social gospel literature flowed, *Strangers Within Our Gates* (1909) and *My Neighbour* (1911).

In the 1890s the churches were deeply involved in a mounting campaign against 'drink.' This was rationalized by leading figures like F.S. Spence as part of the great gospel of liberty.[33] Significantly, however, a rude sort of environmentalism was creeping into the ideology of prohibition, placing it in the context of the strategy of reform Darwinism; that the way to reform the individual was through alterations in his environment. As a wider array of social problems began to engage the minds of clergy and laymen alike, new committees and church structures were required. The Methodist Committee on Sociological Questions from 1894 to 1918 presented to General Conference ever more progressive and comprehensive reports for church guidance. By 1914 committees or departments of temperance and moral reform had become full boards of social service and evangelism. The social task had been placed alongside that of evangelism in the official hierarchy of concerns of the Methodist and Presbyterian churches, and committees of social service were common in the other denominations. In 1913, when Methodists and Presbyterians combined in a programme of social surveys of major Canadian cities and some

30 sw, Feb. 1929, p. 113; sscc, pp. 134–6
31 *Canadian Student*, Oct. 1919, pp. 16–20; sw, Feb. 1929, p. 113; Ross, *The* YMCA *in Canada*, pp. 215–32
32 McNaught, *A Prophet in Politics*, chap. IV
33 See below, pp. 22, 264

rural areas, a systematic attack, chiefly upon the complex environment of the cities, was in the making.[34]

In the background of this escalation of social gospel enterprise was an ambitious effort at institutional consolidation. The Church Union movement, initiated in 1902, was making headway, and in 1907 an alliance of church and labour groups, having won the Lord's Day Act, blossomed into the Moral and Social Reform Council of Canada, jointly headed by J.G. Shearer and T.A. Moore, social service secretaries of the Presbyterian and Methodist churches respectively. Although until the middle of the second decade the provincial units were largely engrossed in temperance campaigns, for several years thereafter they promoted a broad programme of social reform and community action that won the praise of young radicals like William Ivens and William Irvine.[35] In 1913 the national organization changed its name to the Social Service Council of Canada and further broadened its perspectives.[36]

These years were exciting ones for progressive churchmen. Not only were they advancing their campaign to win the churches to what they called sociological conceptions, but they were also making progress in liberalizing the restrictive personal disciplines of their denominations and in reforming theological curricula.[37] During and after 1908 a lively discussion of the relation of Christianity to socialism developed. The subject had been kept alive by a small group among whom was Salem Bland; the Rev. Ben Spence, the socialist-prohibitionist who in 1904 managed A.W. Puttee's campaign in Winnipeg to win a second term as a Labor MP;[38] A.E. Smith, who endorsed labour candidates in successive pastorates at Nelson, Winnipeg, and Brandon;[39] and the Rev. W.E.S. James, general secretary from about 1905 of the Christian Socialist Fellowship in Ontario and organizer in 1914 of a Church of the Social Revolution in Toronto.[40] A wave of millennial socialism in Britain after the election of 1906, the controversy surrounding R.J. Campbell's *New Theology*,[41] and touring lecturers such as Kier Hardie (1908 and 1912) and

34 UCA, Methodist Church of Canada and Presbyterian Church in Canada, *Reports of ... Social Surveys*, 1913–14

35 *Voice*, 8 Dec. 1916, p. 8; *The Nutcracker*, 17 Nov. 1916, p. 8

36 UCA, Moral and Social Reform Council, *Minutes of the Annual Meeting*, 5 Sept. 1913

37 See Walsh, *The Christian Church in Canada*, pp. 290–2

38 A.E. Smith, *All My Life*, p. 33

39 *Ibid.*

40 James, 'Notes on a Socialist Church,' in Summers, 'The Labour Church,' pp. 690–6

41 For an able discussion of these factors in their British context, see Pierson's thesis, 'Socialism and Religion: A Study of their Interaction in Great Britain, 1889–1911.'

the Rev. J. Stitt Wilson (1909 and 1910), the well-known California socialist who preached the message of socialism as applied Christianity, undoubtedly spurred discussion in Canada.[42]

Both socialists and clerics picked up the theme. In 1909 W.A. Cotton, editor of the Canadian socialist journal, *Cotton's Weekly*, developed the notion that Jesus had been the original labour leader.[43] In 1910 a large meeting in Montreal heard an exposition of socialism based on the Bible, and E.T. Kingsley, prominent in the British Columbia section of the Socialist Party of Canada, declared Christianity and socialism to be identical. The current did not run all one way, of course. A group of Toronto socialists in November 1910 devoted at least one evening to the subject, 'Why a Socialist Can Not Be a Christian.'[44]

After 1908 professed socialists in the churches seem not to have been so isolated or so peripheral. The Rev. Dr D.M. Ramsey in Ottawa in 1908 described socialism as 'carrying into economic regions the Christian doctrine of human brotherhood.'[45] The Rev. Elliott S. Rowe organized socialist leagues in Sandon and Victoria, BC.[46] Bryce M. Stewart in his survey of Fort William in 1913 found a considerable number of Christians sympathetic to socialism and observed: 'It is beyond question that in purity of purpose, ethics, and scientific reasoning the socialist position is far beyond any other political organization, and should appeal especially to the Christians.'[47] In the same year, the Rev. Thomas Voaden of Hamilton, in a series of lectures later published, presented the thesis that socialism was the effect of Christianity forced outside the churches.[48] But that socialism was not all outside the churches was becoming more and more apparent. When the Brotherhoods of London, Ontario, surveyed the city in 1913, it was found to be common opinion in the churches that neither unions nor socialist groups threatened or interfered with the church's work, and further, that men of both organizations were found among the church's workers.[49]

42 *Canadian Annual Review* (CAR), 1908, p. 101; 1909, p. 307; 1910, p. 315; 1912, p. 277

43 *Ibid.*, 1909, p. 306

44 These last three incidents are cited in *ibid.*, 1910, pp. 315–16

45 *Ibid.*, 1908, p. 99

46 Paul Fox, 'Early Socialism in Canada,' in Aitcheson, *The Political Process in Canada*, p. 89

47 Methodist and Presbyterian Churches, *Report of a Social Survey of Port Arthur*, p. 10

48 Voaden, *Christianity and Socialism*

49 Methodist and Presbyterian Churches, *Report of a Limited Survey of Educational, Social and Industrial Life in London, Ontario*, p. 43

No major Protestant denomination in the nation escaped the impact of the social gospel, and few did not contribute some major figure to the movement. Baptists and Congregationalists, perhaps owing to their small numbers, seldom found their way beyond secondary leadership positions. Baptists, however, could point to Henry Moyle of the United Farmers of Ontario, secretary of the Social Service Committee of the Ontario and Quebec Convention, and to ministers like M.F. McCutcheon of Montreal or A.A. Shaw in Winnipeg, who did much to keep the social gospel alive for their church. But the struggle was difficult, and many, as was the case with Shaw, ultimately found the more liberal Northern Baptist Convention in the United States more congenial. Some who came from the American church, like D.R. Sharpe, to work with western Canadian Baptists, returned for a similar reason.[50] Congregationalists provided a pioneer of the movement in the person of the Rev. J.B. Silcox who, in pastorates in Toronto, Winnipeg, and Montreal, spoke out against the depredations of the 'industrial pharaohs' of the time. The career of the Rev. D.S. Hamilton took him from graduate studies in social settlement work in Chicago under Professor Graham Taylor, through a number of Congregationalist appointments, and finally to Manitoba, where he combined an ardent advocacy of the single tax with the superintendency of neglected children and then the judgeship of the juvenile court.[51] And in Vancouver, the outspoken Congregationalist minister, A.E. Cooke, provided leadership in the causes of prohibition and Christian socialism. Perhaps the most notable Unitarian in the formative years of the social gospel was A.W. Puttee, editor of the best-known labour paper in Canadian history, the *Voice*. But the smaller denominations worked under obvious handicaps in providing leadership for the new, experimental concerns the social gospel embraced.

Of the larger denominations, the Anglicans found the greatest difficulty in fielding the social gospel, the Methodists the least, and somewhere between them lay the Presbyterians. Dean L.N. Tucker, Canon Vernon, who directed the Anglican Council for Social Service after 1918, and H. Michel, professor of political science at Queen's University, seem to have been the prominent Anglicans in the movement in these years.[52] The Rev. F.E. Mercer in Edmonton and M.J. Coldwell, a Regina high school principal, were somewhat exotic among Anglicans as active labour party proponents. No Anglican, however, by 1928 seems to have played a social gospel role similar to that of the Presbyterian ministers R.C. Henders, who

50 See Albaugh, 'Themes for Research in Canadian Baptist History'; also D.R. Sharpe to the author, 22 July 1963

51 United Church of Canada, *Minutes of the Fifth Manitoba Conference, 1929*, p. 60

52 Judd, 'The Vision and the Dream: The Council for Social Service – Fifty Years,' pp. 76–118

became the president of the Manitoba Grain Growers' Association for a number of years, and W.R. Wood, secretary of the same organization. Both rationalized their activity in terms of the social mandate of the gospel. No denomination harboured a competitor to the Rev. C.W. Gordon, who under the pen-name of Ralph Connor popularized social issues in a series of best-selling novels and who became one of the nation's most successful mediators in industrial disputes. Pre-eminent among a roster of Presbyterian social gospellers was J.G. Shearer, who will figure largely below, but who for a generation after 1900 was considered the 'mouthpiece of the social conscience of Canadian Christianity.'[53]

Methodism became one of the prime providers of leadership for progressive and radical reform: F.S. Spence, Canada's ranking prohibitionist; James Simpson, vice-president of the Trades and Labor Congress and prominent socialist; Louise McKinney of the Non-Partisan League and the Women's Christian Temperance Union; Salem Bland, the major Canadian exponent of the social gospel and contributor to a host of progressive causes; William Ivens, founder of the Canadian Labor churches; A.E. Smith, who became a leading communist; and best known of all, J.S. Woodsworth, the major proponent in Canada of social welfare and democratic socialism. S.D. Chown, general superintendent of the church, urged them all to view the social gospel as 'the voice of prophecy in our time.' They did – and sometimes the results were disconcerting to Chown himself.

This numerical preponderance of Methodists in the social gospel led members of other denominations to complain at times that their contributions were being ignored. Indeed, no one ever accused Baptists, Congregationalists, Anglicans, or Presbyterians of trading the gospel for a social cause or a political panacea. But some later historians who have tried to set the record straight have ended up confirming it.[54]

The trail of the social gospel, however, must be followed as it leads, and the first signpost along the way is the social gospel conviction that Christianity required a passionate commitment to social involvement. For the social gospel the earthbound movements of the disinherited and those who arose to champion them might, in their rough struggle for justice, express some of the profoundest religious yearnings of man, while the hallowed institutions of religion might behave in ways that were not simply unbecoming but worldly and damning. The sacred might be very secular, and the secular sacred. All alike shared in the social guilt of an imperfect world, and the way from death to life, from the present social order to the Kingdom

53 *Canadian Churchman*, 16 April 1925, p. 245
54 See for instance Christie, 'The Presbyterian Church in Canada,' chap. 1 and Conclusion

of God, lay through awakening the 'social consciousness' and harnessing oneself to the social problem with the yoke of social concern. Hence the primary history of the social gospel must take its cue from this master conviction and not from the structure of denominationalism from which its proponents came.

During the generation of its ascent, from 1890 to 1914, the social gospel front had remained remarkably united. Three emphases had begun to crystallize, however, which might be labelled conservative, progressive, and radical.[55] It is in terms of this typology, rather than that of denomination, that the structure and development of the social gospel is best understood. The conservatives were closest to traditional evangelicalism, emphasizing personal-ethical issues, tending to identify sin with individual acts, and taking as their social strategy legislative reform of the environment. The radicals viewed society in more organic terms. Evil was so endemic and pervasive in the social order that they concluded there could be no personal salvation without social salvation. Without belief in an immanent God working in the social process to bring his kingdom to birth, the plight of the radicals would surely have been desperate. Between conservatives and radicals was a broad centre party of progressives, holding the tension between the two extremes, endorsing in considerable measure the platforms of the other two, but transmuting them somewhat in a broad ameliorative programme of reform.

The harmony of these wings was not to last. Between 1914 and 1928 the social gospel enjoyed and endured at one and the same time a period of crest and of crisis. Its growing differentiation in church, interdenominational, and secular organizations multiplied its impact on Canadian society and at the same time initiated interaction between the various modes of its expression. These were the conditions of its potency. They were also the conditions of its crisis, for the encounter with social reality was the true test of social gospel concepts, and the very complexity of that reality and the conflict inherent within it inevitably set one wing of the social gospel in conflict with another. This involved process culminated in the years 1926–8, and the movement generally entered a period of weariness, reaction, and reconsideration.

55 This typology of the social gospel was initially used by Hopkins in the first major treatment of the American movement by an American (see n 17 above), and has been followed in other works such as May, *Protestant Churches and Industrial America,* and Carter, *The Decline and Revival of the Social Gospel, 1920–1940.*

2

The Call of the New Day

By 1914 the social gospel in Canada had been waxing for more than a generation. However much the war which was shortly to come would heighten the social passion of the movement and extend its influence, the pitch of its enthusiasm was already high. Despite differences of emphasis and areas of endeavour, no divisions of note had risen to afflict the social gospel with disunity. Enthusiasm, unity, accomplishment, all combined to underscore the hope of this gospel that social regeneration was historically possible, that personal salvation was won through losing oneself in the social task. Indeed, by 1914 it seemed possible to affirm that even now the times were uniquely open to the impress of the Kingdom of God. Although much remained to be done, much could be done. One of the special times of God, *kairos*, was at hand.

Nowhere was this mood more evident than at the hastily called Social Service Congress meeting from 3 to 5 March 1914 in Ottawa, and nowhere was the range of activity and concern of the social gospel better displayed. The response to this first national Canadian congress on social problems exceeded all expectations. Not only were the provincial units and affiliated organizations of the Social Service Council of Canada well represented, but many others, personally or professionally concerned with what was called 'the social question,' had come at their own expense. Still more, the federal government, several provincial governments, and a number of cities had sent official representation.[1] The day before the congress, the general committee was still processing requests for permission to send delegates. Some, realizing the extent of the platform provided, were petitioning to speak. The latter were rejected; the former permitted.[2] Regular attendants numbering well over two hundred had registered to fill halls at the normal school booked for the

1 Press interview with J.G. Shearer, secretary, Social Service Council of Canada, *Ottawa Free Press*, 2 March 1914
2 *Ottawa Citizen*, 3 March 1914. For example, the Women's Art Association and the local woman suffrage organization were admitted, but E.H. Scammell of the Canadian Peace Centenary Association could not be granted speaking time.

meetings.[3] Special luncheons at the Château Laurier to be addressed by two of the most prominent leaders of the social gospel in the United States, Charles Stelzle and Graham Taylor, were oversubscribed.[4] The response of the public to the evening meetings was still to be measured, but the success of the congress seemed assured.

It was with regret but no deep concern that the organizers learned that Dr Charles S. McFarland, special delegate from the Federal Council of Churches of Christ in America, was snowbound in up-state New York and that Samuel Dwight Chown, the first secretary to a separate Canadian church department on moral and social issues and now general superintendent of the Methodist church of Canada, could not be present.[5] If there had been some anxiety among the organizers as they prepared for the meeting, it was banished in the combination of banter and solemnity with which Albert Carman opened the first session of the congress.[6] Carman had led Canadian Methodism almost since the union of 1884, and still shared the superintendancy with Chown. Unlike Chown, he was not known for his liberal religious views, but in traditional Methodist fashion he was unstinting in support of any movement designed to increase the moral and social righteousness of the nation. He was not a social gospeller, but his presence was clear evidence of the ties of the social gospel with old Methodism. Among those sharing the head table with him were Prime Minister Robert Laird Borden, who cautioned the conferees not to counsel or expect legislation in advance of public opinion, and Wilfrid Laurier, past-prime minister and now leader of the Liberal opposition, who urged delegates on to the conquest of poverty.[7] Introductions and welcomes over, the congress settled down to its heavy agenda of addresses and discussions.

A cursory glance at the programme of the congress revealed a formidable array of subjects and speakers. The main headings stood out: weekly rest day, the Canadian Indian, the church and industrial life, the labour problem, child welfare, the challenge to the church, the problem of the city, the problem of the country, social service as a life work, commercialized vice and the white slave traffic, immigration, political purity, temperance, prison reform, humanising religion.[8] Under each heading was from one to seven subheadings, each denoting a speech of some proportion: forty-six addresses. There was no gainsaying that delegates were to be subjected to a barrage of social statistics, social conditions, social problems, social challenges, and, above all, social exhortation.

3 *Ottawa Evening Journal*, 3 March 1914
4 *Ottawa Citizen*, 3 March 1914   5 *Ibid.*, 6 March 1914
6 *Ottawa Evening Journal*, 3 March 1914
7 *Ottawa Free Press*, 3 March 1914   8 SSCC, pp. vii, viii

Virtually every part of the dominion and every significant area of social endeavour was to be represented on the congress platform. Of forty Canadian speakers,[9] however, only seven came from outside central Canada, and slightly over half were from Ontario. Although the congress considered the rural problem, its speakers overwhelmingly represented the city. Their professions indicated this only too clearly: city politicians, judges, labour leaders, city doctors, college professors, and social workers. The federal members of Parliament involved represented a variety of constituencies. The congress was referred to as a 'free Parliament on Social Questions,'[10] but unlike the other parliament sitting in Ottawa, lawyers played a very modest role! Fully half the speakers were clergy (not all engaged in the pastoral ministry), and of these only two represented the countryside.[11] Of the non-clerical speakers only three had obvious agrarian ties: W.C. Good and E.C. Drury, respectively president and ex-president of the Dominion Grange and Farmers' Association, and Alphonse Desjardins, the founder of the *Caisses Populaires* among Quebec farmers. Emphatically, the conference was centred on the new Canada, on the urban industrial society and its problems. 'Both the men and the subjects are full of interest,' commented the *Free Press*.[12] And the *Journal* observed that 'perhaps never in the history of the capital has there been gathered a more able and eloquent list of speakers.'[13] Conspicuous in their absence, however, were representatives of the world of business ownership and management. This was overwhelmingly a professional man's conference, with a sprinkling of labour representation. Its social sources lay outside and below the centres of power which were forging the new Canada.

Not all speakers gave evidence of the social gospel. All five speakers on child welfare presented aspects of the subject in a professional manner.[14] Mrs Rose Henderson, speaking on mothers' pensions, may have given a hint of social gospel persuasion when she agreed that 'to subsidize the dependent mother to carry out her parental duties, is but putting our beliefs ... into practical form, applying our

9 This number omits brief addresses by chairmen of sessions and similar formal presentations.
10 *Ottawa Free Press*, 2 March, 1914
11 The Revs. John MacDougall and S.F. Sharp
12 2 March 1914
13 4 March 1914
14 J.J. Kelso, 'Importance of Child Welfare'; R.L. Scott, KC, 'The Rights of Children'; Helen MacMurchy, MD, 'Defective Children'; Judge Choquet, 'The Juvenile Court'; Mrs Rose Henderson, 'Mothers' Pensions,' in SSCC, pp. 89–115

Christianity.'[15] And J.J. Kelso, superintendent of neglected and dependent children for Ontario, founder of the Children's Aid in 1891, and a Methodist, revealed a social gospel cast of mind in his claim that 'the world is entering upon an era of social justice ... Before the advancing wave of an enlightened public sentiment' social evils were being met and overcome.[16] The case was similar with five of the speakers on commercialized vice and the white slave traffic, a more recent subject of concerted social action than child welfare. Yet Dr Charles Hastings, for instance, Toronto's medical health officer, was both more religious and more progressive in his inclinations than his address on the consequences of prostitution indicated. He was a Presbyterian elder, had been chairman of the Progressive Club in Toronto, and was a member of the Public Ownership League.[17] Although the broader perspectives in which these speakers saw their work went largely unexpressed, it was possible to view such reformers as representing the social gospel at a low degree of awareness of its religious base.

The speakers on the opening and closing themes, the weekly rest day and temperance, respectively, were, by contrast, deeply conscious of their religious foundation. Neither subject may have seemed a propitious beginning for a national congress on social questions, especially when the Rev. W.M. Rochester of the Lord's Day Alliance urged cities not to compete with the church and the home by keeping playgrounds open on Sunday,[18] and when the Hon. George E. Foster wondered 'if we are not losing something in these more modern times by giving up these good, old-fashioned, effective, public temperance meetings the country through.'[19] It would be wrong to conclude, however, that neither subject contributed to the élan of the congress, let alone of the social gospel. The Lord's Day Act had been won seven years before by an unprecedented alliance of labour and church, which led to the creation of the Moral and Social Reform Council, later renamed the Social Service Council.[20] The alliance was founded on the twin propositions that 'this life of uninterrupted toil is brutalizing' and that leisure was necessary for the growth of

15 *Ibid.*, pp. 112–13. Mrs Henderson was also an active proponent of a labour party for Canada.

16 *Ibid.*, pp. 91–2. See *Canadian Men and Women of the Time*, 1912; see also Baker, 'John Joseph Kelso,' pp. 250–5

17 *Canadian Men and Women of the Time*, 1912

18 'The Weekly Rest Day,' sscc, p. 24

19 sscc, p. 305

20 Eugene Forsey, 'Labour and the Lord's Day Act, 1888–1907' (photocopy of typescript article, nd)

the cultural and spiritual life. Neither work nor leisure was the chief end of man, but rather a personal and social life of quality.[21] The Weekly Rest Day, or the Lord's Day, was both an instrument and a symbol of that high objective.

Like the Lord's Day Alliance, the temperance forces were riding a crest of accomplishment which seemed to bear out their best hopes. A prohibition act had been won in Prince Edward Island, one seemed imminent in Nova Scotia and almost predictable in New Brunswick, Manitoba, and Saskatchewan. The Rev. H.R. Grant, chairman of the Social Service Council in Nova Scotia, quoted the *Charlottetown Guardian* in exultation:

All the evils predicted to result from Prohibition have failed to materialize ... We have reduced the arrests for drunkenness to one-fourth or one-fifth ... trade is better and larger, payments are more prompt, we have better hotels, better streets and sidewalks, better fire and light service than ever before ...

Doubters have been convinced ... The liquor interest has almost ceased to be a political factor in the city or province.[22]

Alderman F.S. Spence of Toronto put the temperance campaign in a still larger context:

We can only have full civil rights, full social justice, full personal liberty, by restraining the vicious and selfish from doing wrong to others. This is the legal embodiment of the golden rule ... We look across the water today and see great parliamentarians working it out, trying to give every man a chance, framing better land laws, providing old age pensions, insuring workingmen against unemployment, sickness and accident ... This great gospel of liberty is the meaning of this temperance movement, this movement for the promotion of good by the suppression of evil.[23]

And Mrs Sara Rowell Wright, president of the Women's Christian Temperance Union, was drawn to conclude from the congress that the WCTU was interested in much more than temperance, and was somewhat surprised to find herself thinking of herself as a Christian socialist.[24]

Indeed, in any area of moral life where men trafficked in the weaknesses of others, reform had been shifting from a moral to a social and institutional base. In terms of motives, the exploiters of moral weakness were being equated with those who exploited the need of the poor for adequate housing, and those in turn with the

21 SSCC, pp. 18–21
22 *Ibid.*, p. 312
23 'Temperance Progress,' SSCC, p. 307
24 'The Women's Christian Temperance Union Program,' SSCC, pp. 324–5

magnates who dominated capitalist industry. As the Rev. A.E. Smith, Methodist minister from Brandon, Manitoba, declared on the white slave traffic: 'All the foes of society have entrenched themselves on the economic plane.'[25] A revolutionary, rather than a reformist, attitude was the requirement of the times: 'We are living in the midst of a great progressive revolution and the inevitable consequence must be the reconstruction of society upon a better basis ... What we need is an epidemic of revolution, or what the chairman called a revival of Christianity.' And, almost as an extension of Spence's thesis, he remarked: 'We believe in destruction truly, but we do not believe in destruction only. We believe also in construction and we are going forward to assist the forces that will reconstruct conditions on this earth ... We have got to assist all the moral and religious forces for good, and whatever other propositions we may consider, we must not forget these ones.'[26] In the midst of what seemed to be the territory of the conservative social gospel, a radical social gospel was beginning to flower.

Almost as startling was the strength of the social gospel in the section on the problem of the country. Here there was a sense of urgency mixed with an element of truculent defensiveness. E.C. Drury, chairman of the section, announced that 'the other [sections] deal only with cleansing the sewers of our civilization; we have to deal with ... the preservation of the springs of our civilization.'[27] The Rev. S.F. Sharp echoed this 'agrarian myth,' and went on to describe the 'present age' in terms Drury was familiar with: 'competition,' 'exploitation,' 'passion for gain through unearned increment,' this age of capitalism 'contrary to the ethical teachings of the Golden Rule.' He continued:

I agree with President L.H. Bailey of Cornell, when he predicts the ushering in of a new era, not through organization only, but mostly through the idealization of the country ... The awful drift [of population to the city] has been because the life of town and city has been idealized as surpassing the country.

He charged the church with complicity in this apotheosis of the city, and, quoting Rauschenbusch, called the church back to the faithfulness of the first three centuries when it 'stood for a Christian social order.'[28] More balanced than Drury and Sharp, the Rev. John MacDougall saw the causes of both urban and rural distress

25 *Ottawa Citizen*, 5 March 1914
26 'Cutting Down An Evil Tree,' sscc, pp. 204–5. Smith was shortly to be elected president of the Manitoba Conference of the Methodist church for an unprecedented two-year term.
27 'The Problem of the Country,' sscc, p. 145
28 'The Church and the Rural Problem,' sscc, pp. 166–70

in the fact that Canada currently led the world in its rate of urbanization, with the cities growing four times as fast as the country in the previous decade. He had hope that social reconstruction would make both more livable. For him the three requirements of rural reconstruction were economic justice and opportunity for the farmer, the increase of 'industrial business efficiency' on the farm, and the building of greater cultural and social satisfactions into rural life. Like Sharp, he concluded with a call to the church to become the 'Institute of the Kingdom – the organization pledged to one special purpose, the establishment of the Kingdom of God in human society.'[29]

It was in the sections on the city and industrial life, however, that the progressive and radical social gospellers were most dominant. This was hardly surprising, for in the dialectical emergence of the social gospel urban and industrial problems had provided the thesis against which sensitive Christians reacted. These were phenomena of the economic order which, for Rauschenbusch, was the only significantly un-Christian order of modern society. The social gospel discerned both problems and hope in the rise of industry and the city. Professor Graham Taylor, guest speaker from Chicago, viewed the rapid growth of the city as the sign of a new social age whose fundamental character would underline the fact that the teachings of Jesus concerned relationships, or man in society.[30] The Rev. J.W. Aiken, of Metropolitan Methodist Church, Toronto, was making the same point with reference to industry when he said that 'it is evident that God intends to use industrial life to bring in His Kingdom on earth.'[31] God seemed to be at work in the very events of the time preparing conditions for the fuller recognition and practice of Christianity. Herein lay the basic conviction of the social gospel, and its exponents hoped that through its preaching the times might become aware of their true meaning. In this sense Aiken could also say: 'It is the light from Jesus Christ which creates the social problem.'[32] Such a vision entailed the end of the slum, the Rev. S.W. Dean believed, and in like spirit Miss Sara Libby Carson had worked for a chain of social settlements under the Presbyterian church from 1902.[33] 'The social conscience is awake as never before,' exclaimed the Rev. R.L. Brydges, social service chaplain for the Toronto Diocese of the Church of England in Canada, as

29 'The Rural Problem,' sscc, pp. 147–57. MacDougall was the author of *Rural Life in Canada, Its Trends and Tasks*.
30 'Social Service as a Life Work,' sscc, p. 185
31 'Jesus Christ and Industry,' sscc, p. 44
32 *Ibid.*, p. 42
33 'The Social Settlement,' sscc, pp. 134–6. See also *Social Welfare*, Feb. 1929, for a sketch of Miss Carson's career.

he outlined ways in which the public school could be developed into social centres for the expression and fostering of the new spirit.[34] 'The social survey,' as the Rev. W.A. Riddell explained it, was both a vehicle for the Brotherhoods to express their mission of social evangelism and a means to systematic social reform across a broad front.[35]

London, Ontario, had been the scene of Riddell's last survey, and the previous year J.S. Woodsworth, Bryce Stewart, and others had conducted five urban and two rural surveys for the Presbyterian and Methodist churches working in conjunction.[36] City governments themselves were becoming interested in social research as a foundation for some of their work. In New York, when various men associated with social work were appointed to head up new areas of civic endeavour, it appeared to Graham Taylor that the city was developing a 'social service' administration.[37] The city of Toronto had recently established a Bureau of Municipal Research, shortly to be headed by Horace Brittain,[38] and a survey of social conditions was just being initiated. In an address delivered with Irish eloquence, Toronto City controller J.O. McCarthy ventured to predict the major findings, and prophesied:

A new day is dawning. Men talk of social welfare, of social Christianity, as though it were a new found religion ... 'Tis not so. 'Tis but a new vision of the old Gospel ... a new birth ... into the kingdom of service established by the Lord and Saviour of mankind ... Because of this new dawn ... municipal governments and departments are able to take up the new responsibilities.[39]

McCarthy was a leading figure in the Canadian Brotherhood Federation, a member of the Methodist Board of Temperance and Moral Reform, and sat on the council of the Canadian Welfare League. With him on the congress platform was his fellow social gospeller and controller, James Simpson.

Simpson had delivered what the *Free Press* considered to be one of the best addresses of the first day of the congress.[40] Regardless of the quality of his address,

34 'Socialization of the Public Schools,' sscc, p. 137

35 sscc, p. 59. Riddell was shortly to be Ontario's first deputy minister of labour.

36 uca, Methodist Church of Canada and Presbyterian Church in Canada, *Reports of ... Social Surveys*, 1913–14

37 'Social Service as a Life Work,' sscc, p. 191

38 Stapleford, *After Twenty Years*, p. 9. See also *Canadian Men and Women of the Time*, 1912

39 'The Municipal Departments,' sscc, pp. 121–2

40 *Ottawa Free Press*, 3 March 1914

Simpson's presence was a matter of note. This was a man to watch, destined to become Toronto City's first socialist mayor in later years. With A.E. Smith, he was probably the best example of the radical social gospel at the congress. Simpson, at forty years, still had some of the ruggedness of feature which had marked him as a younger man. An immigrant from Lancashire in 1888, at first a labourer in a paint factory, then a printer's devil, and later a reporter for the *Toronto Star*, he had risen to be vice-president of the Trades and Labor Congress of Canada, controller in Toronto city government, chairman of the Toronto Board of Education, and a member of the Royal Commission on Industrial Training in 1910. A socialist, he had been temporarily expelled from the Socialist Party of Canada in 1910 for refusing to break his oath as a royal commissioner and purvey information to the party. Simpson was also a vice-president of the Social Service Council of Canada and had been a president of the Methodist youth movement, the Epworth League, many of whose members had stood by him in his political campaigns. He was a Methodist local preacher, a lecturer for the Dominion Prohibition Alliance, and a vice-president of the Toronto branch of the Lord's Day Alliance. His Methodism told him that 'private selfishness is not inevitable'; his socialism assured him that social justice would produce happiness.[41] A radical social gospel and a life-long attack upon capitalism were the results.

Chown, the Methodist superintendant, had wished to give Simpson a special Methodist appointment to interpret labour to the church and the church to labour.[42] It was a task for which he was pre-eminently suited. Why Chown's wish did not become reality is not clear, but the intended role was the one he adopted at the congress in his address, 'The Extension of Social Justice.'[43] He was encouraged to see the conference taking 'a vital interest in some of the problems which are at the same time occupying the interest of the Labor organizations and to which members of the political organizations will have to give increased attention.' The future seemed bright for co-operation. At this juncture in time the church could help 'change a system which is founded upon private selfishness and greed, to one in which public interest will be the chief concern.' As he read the mind of the Congress, it did in fact seem to be inclining in that direction.

No one did more to set the tone of the congress than Charles Stelzle, who delivered three dazzling addresses on the first day. The *Citizen* exclaimed: 'no theatrical

41 SSCC, pp. 40–1
42 Summers, 'The Labour Church,' p. 691. *Canadian Men and Women of the Time*, 1912; *Canadian Forum*, Nov. 1938, p. 229
43 SSCC, pp. 39–41

production that has come to Ottawa in the last few years approached in popularity last evening's session of the Social Service Congress, at which Rev. Charles Stelzle, of New York, was the chief speaker.'[44] Although Stelzle had recently jumped to favour as a speaker, his apprenticeship had been long and extensive. Currently he was a consulting sociologist with the leading denominations of American protestantism. He had begun his career as a machinist, still carried a union card, and regularly attended labour conventions. After a short term in the pastorate he had become head of the aggressive Department of Church and Labor of the Presbyterian church in the United States, and from there had gone on to found a labour church. When the American churches organized a national 'Men and Religion' campaign in 1912, he and Taylor had been prominent in the most successful wing of that drive, the social service division.[45]

The guests of honour at the luncheon at the Château, where Stelzle was to give his first address, were the Hon. Mr Crothers, minister of labour, Judge McTavish, Mr John Fraser, auditor-general, and Mr D.M. Finnie, assistant general manager of the Bank of Ottawa.[46] What they expected of this genial, balding man, with large frank eyes and lips poised ready to smile, may be left to the imagination. He began safely enough on his subject, 'Radical Tendencies Among Workmen.' He had no panacea for the labour problem:

When a man comes forward with a panacea, I am ready to offer a resolution to adjourn the meeting. The labor question will never be solved until the last days work is done. [This is because] we are progressive in our ideals [and] the next generation will not be satisfied with our solution.

Quickly he moved to the causes of labour radicalism, his phrases becoming more incisive. The agitator does not create unrest, it creates him. Not industrial greed alone, but good education, libraries, and churches create social unrest. In a disturbing analogy, he declared that

if the missionaries we are sending [to Africa] are onto their jobs, and I think they are, there will soon be strikes and lockout in the heart of that dark continent ... As they [the Africans] catch the vision of Jesus and all that he may mean to them there will come

44 *Ottawa Citizen*, 4 March 1914. The evening meetings, open to the public, overflowed both the normal school hall and that of a nearby collegiate.

45 *Ottawa Evening Journal*, 4 March 1914; sscc, p. 65; Hopkins, *Rise of the Social Gospel*, pp. 280–3, 296–8. Raymond Robbins, who figured in later social service congresses, was also a member of that division of the campaign.

46 *Ottawa Citizen*, 3 March 1914

among them a healthy spirit of social unrest that will not be satisfied until it breaks the bonds which have bound them through many a century.

The church, he continued, had been the greatest trouble-maker in history, and the critical question was whether 'the Church [will] now step to one side and allow the unscrupulous agitator, as you call him, to come in and usurp the place which right-fully belongs to the Church.' In the struggle between capital and labour, one had to make up one's mind – either their interests were the same or they were not. For his part he supported labour, but the greatest menace to society came from neither of these protagonists who gained such attention, but the 'smug, self-satisfied middle class who have not the courage to face this problem honestly.'[47] Cries of 'hear, hear' had marked the course of the address, and as Stelzle sat down a prolonged deafen-ing applause made it clear that he had hit his mark.[48] Whether the head table was as aroused as the main body of 450 guests is not recorded, but Labour Minister Crothers, rising to perform his appointed task, may have been their barometer. Rather limply he remarked that

Labor's problems have been presented to us in some respects in a manner which we have never heard before ... Perhaps we have not all agreed with him as he went along, but after turning over in our minds the ideas he has expressed to us, we may come to think as he does.[49]

The minister was hardly in tune with the audience. They heard and they agreed.

The course of Stelzle's afternoon and evening speeches followed a similar pat-tern. Having interpreted labour radicalism in a hopeful light, he went on to discuss the problem of 'Capturing the Labor Movement.' This was a critical question for the social gospel. Part of its impetus had originated with a sense that the worker of industrial society was seceding from the church – or that at least the more class conscious were. It was never statistically clear whether this was indeed the case, and Stelzle's opinion was worthy of attention. Apart from his other experience, he had for some time contributed syndicated articles to over three hundred American labour papers.[50] He was in close touch with the labour press and was aware that the evidence from that source was that if labour had been seceding from the church, it certainly was not taking leave of religion, let alone Christianity.[51] This, in any

47 'Radical Tendencies Among Workmen,' sscc, pp. 63–72
48 *Ottawa Citizen*, 4 March 1914
49 sscc, p. 74
50 Hopkins, *Rise of the Social Gospel*, p. 282
51 See the revisionist article by Gutman, 'Protestantism and the American Labor Move-ment: The Christian Spirit in the Gilded Age'

case, was one salient point he made. The question was not simply one of the church saving the masses. They might need better resources to maintain spiritual vision, but without the rugged strength of the common people the church itself would fail. A recent national study indicated that the tendency of the working man was toward the church, but for a successful conclusion of this trend it was essential for the church to be 'genuinely concerned about men' and the condition of life in the twentieth century.[52]

What, then, he asked in his final address, was 'the call of the new day to the old church'? It was not a call to advocate any particular social system, but to 'apply the principles of Jesus Christ fearlessly to the economic and social conditions that we find in these days.' It was a call for the church to be 'broad enough to include all those whose lives are dominated by the spirit of Jesus Christ, and who are seeking to bring in the Kingdom of God, no matter what their economic feelings may be' – socialist, communist, or anarchist (cries of 'hear, hear,' from the crowded hall). Finally, it was a call 'to talk about social salvation.' Individual salvation? 'That is a mighty good thing to talk about,' but Jesus had said, 'He that saveth his life shall lose it.' The fundamental philosophy of the religion of Jesus was evident in the social character of the Lord's Prayer, which could not be prayed except with and for someone else. 'The only way to be saved is to save someone else.' Jesus said: 'Inasmuch as ye do it unto the least of one of these my brethren, ye have done it unto me,' and 'he that loseth his life for my sake, shall find it.' The call of the new day was to have the spirit of Jesus, 'who thought not so much of individual salvation ... but who thought supremely of social salvation.' The religion of Jesus was 'Social Service, and this is the slogan of the great new crusade.'[53]

Stelzle's call to the Social Service Congress was what the delegates were eager to hear. Not only the delegates, but the Ottawa press, were agreed that he was a 'man with a message.'[54] The *Free Press* commented very appropriately, 'there are no international boundary lines in social work, and no tariff is levied upon ideas.'[55] In Stelzle's ideas there was a reciprocity that was warmly welcome, and the response of these Canadians was a measure, if not of the height of the influence of the social gospel in their own thinking, at least of their susceptibility to its message.

Three exhausting days of total immersion in the 'social question,' and the congress was over. When the delegates turned in memory to comparisons of the event, some

52 'Capturing the Labor Movement,' sscc, pp. 35–8
53 'The Call of the New Day to the Old Church,' sscc, pp. 77–87
54 *Ottawa Citizen*, 4 March 1914; *Ottawa Evening Journal*, 4 March 1914; *Ottawa Free Press*, 4 March 1914
55 2 March 1914

recalled the Presbyterian pre-assembly congress on missionary and social questions the year before.[56] Others thought back to the ecumenical conference of Methodism in Toronto, 1911, where the social strides of British Methodism were prominently figured.[57] Anglicans, like the Rev. L.N. Tucker, might recall the Pan-Anglican congress of 1908 in London, England, where the social Christianity of Bishops Temple and Gore had borne off the honours. Those of long memory might remember the great conventions of 1887, 1889, and 1893, called by the Evangelical Alliance in the United States. Canadians had attended the conventions, and one of the conferences following up the first convention had been held in Montreal.[58] Then, as now, the purpose had been to gear Protestantism for progress toward the great social awakening. The Canadian Social Service Congress was to be remembered as the event that marked the beginning of a crest of influence for the social gospel in Canada.

It was a buoyant Social Service Council that met on the morning following the congress to tally financial losses and propaganda gains, and to select the half-dozen most appropriate of the congress' resolutions to lay before the government. In the confidence of fresh victory, the full council then marched to the East Block of the Parliament buildings to place their legislative requests before the ministers of the crown.[59] To a waiting group of reporters, Shearer, as secretary of the council, de-

56 *Pre-Assembly Congress*

57 *Christian Guardian Daily*, Oct. 1911, published to report on the council.

58 Hopkins, *Rise of the Social Gospel*, p. 114. The theme of the conference was 'Vital Questions [affecting the welfare of Montreal].' The other follow-up conference was in New York.

59 Resolutions passed by the congress put it on record as favouring: 'the arbitration of all international disputes; the prohibition of the importation, manufacture, and sale of cigarettes; the securing of total abstinence pledges as regards intoxicants and a national movement for the prohibition of the liquor traffic; the organization of labour; a Royal Commission to deal with the question of unemployment; the establishment of a system of Government employment bureaus; a Royal Commission to examine into the Vancouver Island strike; an old age pension system; the creation of a Canadian Department of Child Welfare; pensions for needy mothers; the extension of the franchise to women; that appointments to the outside civil service be through the Civil Service Commission; the policy of fitting our Indian wards for full citizenship as soon as possible; the submission of the claims of the British Columbia Indians to the Judicial Committee of the Privy Council; the formation of a Canadian Association of Friends of the Native Races; the establishment of a bureau of social surveys and research by the Social Service Council of Canada; the holding of future Social

clared that the congress had far surpassed their hopes, and that it was the council's intention to follow up this success with a further congress the next year.[60] As members waited for their respective trains later in the day they could gauge the impact they had made upon the editors of the city press. The *Free Press* had previously expressed its pleasure with the emphasis on justice, not charity, and found it refreshing to hear social workers urge the priority of public interest over private development and exploitation.[61] Both it and the *Evening Journal* made use of the occasion as a 'splendid illustration of the strength and activity of moral feeling in the community.'[62] The *Citizen*, which had most carefully reported and judiciously commented on the congress, spoke for all three papers in its editorial, 'The Great Social Service Congress Has Ended.' The congress was, to its mind: 'one of the greatest assemblages ever held in Canada to grapple with the social and economical problems confronting all nations of the civilized world. Never in Canada has there been a gathering which attracted so many eminent clerics of all denominations, labor leaders, socialists and champions in a variety of reform movements.'[63]

Probably the last two council members to leave the city were J.G. Shearer and T.A. Moore, the joint secretaries of the Social Service Council and the men most responsible for the planning and execution of the congress. Each was about fifty-five years of age and head of social service work in his church. The outlines of their careers were remarkably similar. Born in Western Ontario, they both held pastorates in that region for a few years. Both had taken up the work of moral and social reform in the 1890s when the new social movement was beginning to grip the Christian imagination. Shearer was the more original of the two, becoming widely recognized as the social conscience of his church. He had been a major force in the creation of the Lord's Day Alliance in 1900, and as its first secretary had been the organizer of the groups that won the Lord's Day Act in 1907. He was the organizing genius and first secretary of the Moral and Social Reform Council in 1907, the organization which, under its new name, had sponsored the congress. A striking

---

Service Congresses when deemed wise' (sscc, p. 358). The council's representation to the government requested legislation or the extension of existing legislation regarding racetrack gambling, raising the age of consent, protection of female employees in factory situations, investigation of labour conditions on Vancouver Island, workmen's compensation, and the distribution and sale of cigarettes (*Ottawa Free Press*, 6 March 1914).

60 *Ottawa Evening Journal*, 6 March 1914
61 4 March, 1914
62 *Ottawa Free Press*, 6 March 1914
63 *Ottawa Citizen*, 6 March 1914; see also editorial of 3 March 1914

speaker, an ardent campaigner, a respected lobbyist, this slight, austere looking man also had the gift of slipping into the background on occasions such as the congress and letting other prophets he had mustered do the prophesying.[64]

Moore followed Shearer, a pace behind. More an administrator than his colleague, he engaged in an incredible amount of high level institutional work which linked him with several international movements of religion and moral and social reform.[65] Both men had first undertaken social tasks which emphasized personal morality: temperance, sabbath observance, gambling, prostitution, and political purity. Industrial and urban growth had created conditions for commercial exploitation, and private vices had become social institutions. As sons of fathers who, following Confederation, sought a Christian nation from sea to sea, they demanded that these institutions which were ruining men and women by the thousand be stopped. In their campaigns they had constructed new institutions – city missions, settlements, rescue homes, institutional churches, interdenominational and non-denominational organizations. Gradually the front of reform had widened, and by 1913 the two men were envisaging co-ordinated attacks upon the complex of institutions comprising the Canadian city. But now the social critique was turning to the social order, 'the system,' itself. The Stelzles and Simpsons might be applauded, but how far would their prescriptions be followed?

While Shearer and Moore sympathized with most of the objectives of the labour movement, the new labour radicalism of the 1910s could well test the limits of their support. As men of faith, their ideas often seemed remarkably open-ended. As men of flesh, the expansion of their ideas and activities had boundaries still, perhaps, to be discovered. They marked the upward course of the progressive social gospel over a generation, the keys to a congeries of reform forces ranging from socialism to temperance. With the stenographic record of the congress bulging their briefcases they left for the train that would take them back to their Toronto headquarters. They and several of the prominent delegates and speakers had lodged in the splendid new Château Laurier across the Rideau locks from Parliament Hill, a tribute to the man who not long before had declared that 'the twentieth century belongs to Canada.' Whether or not Shearer and Moore thought that, they believed that the victory would be hollow were it not also the triumph of the social gospel.

To C.W. Gordon fell the task of writing the introduction to the published report of the congress. Gordon was of Scottish background, educated in Glengarry, Ontario, the University of Toronto, Knox College, and at Edinburgh. He had been a

64 *Canadian Men and Women of the Time*, 1912; *The Canadian Churchman*, 16 April 1925; *Christian Guardian*, 8 April 1925; *Presbyterian Witness*, 9 April 1925
65 *Canadian Men and Women of the Time*, 1912

missionary for three years to coal miners and lumbermen west of Calgary, and in 1894 became pastor of St Stephen's. He became a figure of great distinction and considerable personal wealth through his novels, many of which appealingly fused romance, religion, and social problems. He had several successful experiences of industrial conciliation to his credit. For several years he had been chairman of the Manitoba Moral and Social Reform Council (renamed the Manitoba Social Service Council in 1912), the great objective of which up to 1914 was the winning of prohibition in Manitoba. In 1914 an informal alliance of reformers was on the verge of toppling the Roblin régime in that province and winning, in one sweep, a liberal reform government, women's suffrage, the first use of direct legislation in the province, and prohibition.

Gordon had delivered to the congress a major address which represented the mean position of the social gospel in Canada. Entitled 'The New State and the New Church,' it reviewed the new movements in politics, industry, and religion in the light of the organic unity of society. Evidence abounded, Gordon suggested, that both state and church had failed to develop institutions and attitudes appropriate to the common life of man. The state had come under the spell of the 'Big Individual' and 'Big Business,' while the church had left men quivering as individuals before a perversely conceived God of Wrath, 'hard upon the trail of the wretched sinner.' All of this was a travesty upon genuine social and Christian thought, which contemporary movements of the social conscience were reviving. The primacy of the community, the objective of human development, the spirit of brotherhood, a conception of a God vitally united with humanity ('a good man with goodness raised to the highest power'), and a church pulsating with a 'passion for men,' emphasizing conduct and utility as against creedal orthodoxy: here in brief compass was the progressive social gospel view of God and man, of church and state, of present social problems and the fundamental values that must direct their solution.[66]

The address had left both audience and press in raptures. Surprised that, after the great speeches of the first day, the speakers seemed even to improve, the *Citizen* marvelled at the ability of this 'tall, dark, slim man, with a thick black moustache ... a fringe of a black and iron-grey beard, [and] kindly dark eyes' to capture the hundreds of people before him.[67] The congress, however, had its own impact on Gordon, heightening, in turn, his own rising social expectations. Back in the manse of St Stephen's Church, Winnipeg, whence had flowed so many novels over the pen name of Ralph Connor, Gordon penned an introductory piece for the congress report as boundless in its hope as any produced in the Canadian West:

66 sscc, pp. 192–8
67 *Ottawa Citizen*, 5 March 1914; *Ottawa Free Press*, 5 March 1914

The Congress means that a new day has dawned for Canada. The thoughtful men and women of the country are realizing that both civilization and Christianity are challenged by the economic, industrial and social conditions on which the fabric of our state is erected. It is an immense gain ... for there is in our nation so deep seated a sense of righteousness and brotherhood that it needs only that the light fall clear and white upon the evil to have it finally removed.[68]

Gordon might well be optimistic. And it was an optimism that even the worst of bad news, the outbreak of war on 4 August, could not dampen. 'The failure of the State to eliminate war ... is signal and ghastly,' he had declared to the congress. However, there was no question that a people so possessed of 'a sense of righteousness and brotherhood' should be defended; rather more, should undertaken to assist small nations in their need. Humanity demanded that militarism, another expression of the power that animated the 'Big Individual' and 'Big Business,' be defeated. The war seemed, in essentials, an extension of the spirit of the Social Service Congress. Unhesitatingly Gordon enlisted in the crusade he had always been in, and penned his appeal to his countrymen:

O Canada, What answer make to calling voice and beating drum,
To sword gleam and to pleading prayer of God
For right? What answer makes my soul?
'Mother, to thee! God, to Thy help! Quick! My sword.'[69]

68 SSCC, Foreword   69 CAR, 1914, p. 188

3

The Embattled Years

In their response to the war, it was no uncertain trumpet that the churches of Canada sounded. While they all had histories, long or short, of support for the arbitration of international conflicts, and greeted the war with heavy heart, the struggle was accepted as an honourable defence of liberty. Whether the nation could have carried the war effort to a successful conclusion without the full support of its religious institutions might well be questioned. Under the circumstances, the question did not need to be asked. Clergy and theological students enlisted along with members at large. Churches played an active role in recruiting, organized sewing and knitting circles, used their facilities to provide recreation for soldiers away from home, and promoted victory loans. Clergy spent countless hours in trying to heal the grief that broke the inner life of thousands of homes. Together with the state, the churches promoted a view of the enemy which would justify the terrible deeds of war, and in their own right went on to give the struggle a redemptive quality which would endow every sacrifice with meaning. This was 'God's battle,' and contributing one's energies to help win it was 'a supreme manifestation of faith, a supreme act of decision and of sacrifice for Christ.'[1] To have believed otherwise, 'despair and sorrow would have mounted with the casualties, until the church would have damned the war completely.'[2]

1 *Christian Guardian* (CG), 6 June 1917
2 Bliss, 'The Methodist Church and World War I,' p. 231. Bliss' article, published as this manuscript was nearing completion, gives the historiography of the war a new dimension. I am indebted to it for new information, for confirmation of the thesis of this chapter, and for assistance in further refining my own insight into the relationship between the war, the church, and the social gospel. The rest of this book should help answer Bliss' final query as to how the vision of the new society got lost in the 1920s. For a useful survey of the attitude and action of an other church with respect to the war, see also Christie, 'The Presbyterian Church in Canada,' especially chap. VI, 'The Presbyterian Church and Its Attitude toward War and Peace,' and CAR, 1914–18

With the currents of revision and revulsion over the origins and practices of the war which arose shortly after the close of battle, there were those who were to turn full face and repudiate not only Mars and all his works but also their own words and deeds of the embattled years.[3] This postwar revulsion has provided the orthodoxy that has since prevailed with regard to the war. Hence it has been widely accepted that the war must, at least for the time, have displaced the social problem and sidetracked reform;[4] more particularly, that the churches so compromised themselves during the war, that the honest progressive or radical had no option but to depart their sanctuaries.[5] Yet it has been difficult to ignore entirely the social idealism that accompanied the war years, perhaps itself caused by the national crusade, perhaps by a late wartime extension of Wilsonian idealism.[6] This, after all, had been the war to end war, to make the world safe for democracy. Were the progressive slogans mere hypocrisy?

There is, of course, no simple solution to the complex interrelationship of the war, the church, and the social gospel, nor to the question as to how churchmen, who on the eve of war were ardently pursuing the evils of social misery, could now be firing the awful crucibles of war. Certainly the war played havoc with the lives of a few of the radical social gospellers, like Irvine, Woodsworth, Ivens, and Bland, yet to accept their wartime judgment on the subject (and they were by no means agreed) would be as partial as to base interpretation on the postwar revulsion of progressives.

In fact, the war did not displace the social problem and sidetrack reform – certainly not for the social gospel in any of its expressions. The Social Service Council kept up its pace of development in the buoyant mood of early 1914. It laid plans for a social service bureau with Charles Stelzle as consulting sociologist,[7] which failed to materialize, and launched a series of provincial congresses, which were punctuated with the same flashes of radicalism and enjoyed the same success as the Ottawa congress. The strategy led, first, into the propitious territories of the West, and then into the eastern provinces. The same breadth of social attack was spearheaded, at

3 See below, chap. 20

4 Walsh, *The Christian Church in Canada*, pp. 334–5; Morton, *The Progressive Party*, p. 267

5 McNaught, *A Prophet in Politics*, pp. 66–8, 79, 80, 97, 98

6 Crysdale, *The Industrial Struggle*, pp. vii, 28, 36; Morton, *The Progressive Party*

7 UCA, Methodist Church, General Board of Temperance and Moral Reform, Minutes of the Executive, 21 April 1914

least in the West, by another American, Raymond Robbins, who concentrated his attention on the rights and needs of 'the great industrial army of men, women and children.'[8] At the Manitoba congress, in late 1916, the vigour of social criticism was ensured by the presence of men like F.J. Dixon and Salem Bland.[9] The impressive performance of the Social Service Council was showing fruit in the growing numbers of secular affiliates in its roster of member organizations[10] and in the praise it evoked from young radicals. William Ivens, pastor of MacDougall Methodist Church, Winnipeg, had a few years before considered the council 'a rope of sand,' but now saw the herald of a new day in the council's broad horizons of social reform.[11] William Irvine, in his new publication, *The Nutcracker*, suggested that the churches of tomorrow would, like the council, become co-operative efforts for community welfare. Then, he said, 'there would be no difficulty in answering the question, "What are churches for?"'[12]

Throughout the war the churches, each in its own way, moved steadily in the direction of Irvine's ideal objective. It was in 1915 that the Anglican church transformed its Committee on Moral and Social Reform into a Council for Social Service. A full-time general secretaryship was authorized a year later, and was filled in 1918 with the appointment of Canon C.W. Vernon. Although the council's range of activity was more constricted than that of similar agencies in related churches, Anglicans were continuing to press forward with their social concerns. In 1917 Professor H. Michel of Queen's University began editing a series of bulletins calculated to broaden the social outlook of the church, the early titles ranging over prohibition, alien immigration, children's aid societies, industrial unrest, the church and socialism, the minimum wage, and infant mortality.[13] Although no change took place in the status of Baptist social service work during the war, the pages of the *Canadian Baptist*, as the war years passed, showed an increasing interest in social questions.

That the coming of war had a sobering impact was evident at the Methodist

8 Presbyterian Church, 'Report of the Board of Home Missions and Social Service,' *Acts and Proceedings of the General Assembly* (hereafter cited as *Presbyterian Acts and Proceedings*), 1916–17, pp. 24–5

9 *Voice*, 1, 8 Dec. 1916

10 See below, pp. 64, 240. This was also evidence of the continuing development through 1914–18 of social work at large. See below, pp. 285–6

11 *Voice*, 8 Dec. 1916

12 17 Nov. 1916. See also *The Canadian Friend*, XII, 9, 1917

13 Judd, 'The Vision and the Dream,' pp. 77–82

General Conference in the fall of 1914. Equally obvious was a broader and deeper commitment to the social gospel. In a Manifesto on Peace and War, the conference dedicated itself to efforts to secure an effective international court, a world police force, and a system of sanctions against aggressors once this 'dreadful war' was over.[14] There were signs at the conference that already the war was being viewed as a phase – a regrettable one – of the universal extension of political democracy, but, the conference added, 'kaiserism in industry is yet to be conquered.'[15] In accepting a statement on sociological questions, the conference set the church on a course it was to adhere to throughout the succeeding four years. With economic abundance possible, poverty was now considered a crime and the old political economy out of date. Without revision of the means of distribution, 'wealth captured from the commonwealth' by speculation and unearned reward created a problem of social justice of the first magnitude. Although it did not detail reforms, the report cautioned that paternalism of wealth and stewardship should not obscure the fundamental need for a more just social order. The church was called to an 'irresistible evangelism' that would give rise to a 'new conscience' to make of Methodists once more a 'peculiar people ... in every realm in which Jesus is not recognized as Lord, but especially in ... the realms of business and politics.' The conference therefore merged its social service and evangelistic activities under a single board, and then dispersed until the conference of 1918, at which it would have to redeem a promise to stake out still more advanced policies of social reconstruction.[16] As the war years followed one another in fearful succession, the regular reports of the new Department of Social Service and Evangelism suggested that the promise would not be reneged.[17]

When the Presbyterian Board of Evangelism and Social Service reported to the General Assembly in 1916, it announced with enthusiasm that the great social awakening was beginning and that the war, in unexpected ways, was contributing to the progress of reform and the overturning of privilege and injustice. In Britain, it reported, 'thousands of industries are nationally managed and operated, not for private profit, but for popular protection and benefit.' This nationalization was not simply for military necessity, but for human efficiency and the greatest good of the

---

14 *Methodist Journal of Proceedings*, 1914, p. 404

15 UCA, Methodist Department of Temperance and Moral Reform, *Annual Report*, 1913–14, pp. 55–9

16 *Ibid.*

17 See also the minutes of the General Board and the Executive of the Department, 15–17 Sept. 1915; 30 Aug.–1 Sept. 1916; 13–18 Sept. 1917, which reveal the growing structure, the extensive range of social concern, and some of the leading figures involved.

greatest number. It was small comfort to employers – but also little joy to workers – that the board was happy that the right to strike had been suspended in Britain.[18] A Presbyterian at the helm of the agrarian movement, the Rev. R.C. Henders, president of the Manitoba Grain Growers' Association, also endorsed this enlarging function of the state when he said that the war 'had taught us lessons both in state and industrial control which will stand us in good stead when we come to deal with the rights and liberties of employers and employees in the readjustment which must take place when we come to combat the individualist traditions of the last century.'[19] There were few in the social service centres of the churches who would have disagreed with the Presbyterian board or with Henders' opinion.

The social uses of state control had already been half learned among Protestants in the long years of temperance and prohibition campaigning. In 1888 and 1890, respectively, by granting official support to the political actions of the Dominion Prohibition Alliance, both the Presbyterian and Methodist churches had given sanction to the use of the state to reform individual morality.[20] The upward course of the prohibition cause since 1900 in all provinces, as well as in local option campaigns, seemed to justify that strategy, and by 1914 Methodists, at least, had extended the uses of the state to a radical reforming of society. The greatest prohibition successes were still to come, however, between 1915 and 1918, and while the pre-war trend casts doubt on the proposition that they were simply a result of the war, it did provide additional weaponry for the arsenal of prohibitionist propaganda. National efficiency mated with personal sacrifice was an invincible combination in circumstances where each had been elevated to the highest of virtues. In the course of the war the editor of the Anglican *Canadian Churchman* and Council for Social Service became converts to the cause, arguing, significantly, the value of the reform in peace as well as in war.[21] In 1915 and 1916 Saskatchewan, Manitoba, Alberta, British Columbia, New Brunswick, and Ontario passed prohibition acts, and in early 1918 the federal government terminated all inter-provincial trade in liquor by order-in-council. By the end of the war the oldest moral and social cause of the majority of Canadian Protestants was within a hair's breadth of final success.[22]

However, beyond the victory of prohibition and the social consequences that were anticipated, there was reason to rejoice in new Canadian legislation on wo-

18 Presbyterian Church in Canada, 'Report of the Board of Home Missions and Social Service,' 1915–16, Appendix, pp. 13–14

19 GGG, 4 Dec. 1918, p. 43; 15 Jan. 1917, p. 7

20 Spence, *Prohibition in Canada*, pp. 156–7

21 *Canadian Churchman*, 28 Nov. 1918, p. 763; *Bulletin of the Council for Social Service*, Sept. 1919

22 See below, chap. 17

men's suffrage, workman's compensation, and protective legislation, the beginnings of provincial departments of labour, the government encouragement of fishermen's co-operative societies in Nova Scotia, and the establishment of a Bureau of Social Research under J.S. Woodsworth by the three prairie provinces.[23] The reforms were not confined to provincial legislation. The newly established Toronto Bureau of Municipal Research, for instance, in the years 1914–18 maintained the systematic surveys of social conditions in Toronto initiated in 1913 by the Social Survey Commission.[24] The federal Commission on Conservation continued its research on natural resources and aided efforts at rural and civic reform and public health by engaging in special studies, by sponsoring conferences, and by promoting such organizations as the Civic Improvement League.[25] And the federal civil service was about to be liberated from political partisanship on the recommendations of two royal commissions. With such evidence at hand, progressive churchmen could hardly be persuaded that social idealism had lapsed or that there was some inherent conflict between the war and social reform. Methodists in Vancouver in 1916 awarded first prize in an Epworth League oration contest to one who had spoken on 'The Influence of the War on Social Reform.' After noting such developments as the foregoing, the speaker had concluded: 'We are coming to adopt the Socialists' view of man, according to his worth, according to his service to humanity, the way Christ judges a man.'[26]

Not in its general, its imperial, or its national aspects did the war *per se*, once it was a fact, create fundamental inner conflict for most progressives and radicals. The shibboleths of progressivism in wartime propaganda was a testimony to the height of social reform in the allied world prior to the war. Reform in turn gave new force to the propaganda of progressives. The war to make the world safe for democracy was directed by virtually every identifiable figure of the social gospel to promote the cause of industrial democracy.[27] W.B. Creighton argued that the war seemed 'destined to produce political changes of far-reaching import, and one of them will undoubtedly be a more thorough-going democracy than the world has

23 *Presbyterian Acts and Proceedings*, 1915–16, Appendix, pp. 13–14
24 *Report of the Social Survey Commission; What 'the Ward' is Going to Do with Toronto*. See also above, p. 25
25 Canada, Commission of Conservation, *Conference of the Civic Improvement League for Canada*. See also the annual volumes published by the commission
26 *Youth and Service*, April 1916, pp. 82–3
27 See, for example, W.B. Creighton, CG, 29 Aug. 1917; Ernest Thomas, CG, 7 Nov. 1917; J.G. Shearer, SW, 1 Dec. 1918; R.C. Henders, above, p. 39; and, for a review of Salem Bland's response to the war, Allen, 'Salem Bland,' pp. 103–9

seen, and if capitalism suffers, as it may, it will be because it has shown itself in this hour of national trial, in only too many cases, to be altogether too intent upon private gain to be truly patriotic.'[28] It would be surprising, indeed, if social gospel thinking in Canada had not absorbed some of the conceptions of social imperialism, first consistently formulated by Benjamin Kidd, adopted by a majority of the Fabians at the time of the Boer War, and promoted in a more diluted fashion by such imperial evangelists as Lord Milner. In any case, it was not more difficult for social gospellers to link their imperial sentiments with their reformist programme than it was to tie them to the burgeoning nationalism of the Canadian community.[29] It was not simply from the knapsacks of returning soldiers that a rejuvenated Canadian nationalism was to spring, but from the sense of social solidarity engendered in English-speaking Canada by the war. The social gospel had its own content of reform to pour into the renewed national life that would follow the purging effect of common sacrifice in the common cause.[30] The war, said Salem Bland, was accelerating the forces of regeneration that had been at work before 1914, and to hasten that process he had undertaken in 1917 to organize his 'New Canada Movement.' One of the first functions of the movement was to have been a national convention at which the nation's war aims might be brought more consciously into harmony with the objectives of social reform. Despite initial enthusiasm and press coverage, however, the New Canada Movement seems to have died aborning.[31]

There were high expectations for a rejuvenated national life once the soldiers returned home. The 'Message from the Chaplains' issued at the end of the war was, significantly, couched in terms of the social gospel:

It is of the utmost importance that there should be no doubt about the religious value of the service that the soldiers have rendered ... And it is incumbent upon the whole Canadian Church to realize that her citizen soldiers have been, consciously or unconsciously, moral crusaders ... They have in the last analysis ... been active in the extension of God's Kingdom on earth.[32]

28 CG, 3 Oct. 1917
29 For a convincing demonstration of the confluence of ideas of imperialism, nationalism, and social reform in Canada in the years prior to 1914, see Berger, *The Sense of Power*, especially chap. VII; and for the general subject, also Kidd, *Social Evolution*; Semmel, *Imperialism and Social Reform*
30 See below, chap. IV
31 GGG, 9 Jan. 1918, p. 25; 23 Jan. 1918, p. 38; Bland Papers, Papers on 'The New Canada Movement'; *Nutcracker*, 6 July 1917, p. 5
32 *Presbyterian and Westminster*, 26 June, 3 July 1919

And for the chaplains the 'Kingdom of God [was] a social order as well as a personal gift.'[33] They, along with YMCA workers, had grown close to thousands of men in their four years with the troops. They reported a growing unrest among the men with regard to the established order at home and a concern for the cause of social justice. Moreover, they had been impressed by the reception given to the social gospel in studies and discussions with hundreds of men of such brief but urgent books as Rauschenbusch's *The Social Principles of Jesus*.[34] It would not be enough, the chaplains counselled, for the church to champion the cause of the soldier on his return; it must challenge and harness his new social concern in a moral equivalent of war.

By 1917, then, those concerned with the social mission of the church believed they could see an essential congruity between the more profound effects of the war and the cause of social gospel. The social message continued to be preached, and was listened to; the institutions and legislation of social reform continued to grow; the practice and rhetoric of domestic mobilization added a new respectability to the body of collectivist thought growing in the late prewar years; and the attitudes of the boys overseas suggested that they would be a uniquely regenerating social force on their return.

In the light of all this, it was not surprising that in 1917 the Protestant churches all supported conscription and, with varying degrees of forcefulness, the Union government. The Anglican bishops urged the 'sacred duty' of voting Unionist upon their followers.[35] Presbyterian officialdom left campaigning for Union government to the various journals serving the church,[36] but in June had called for conscription of wealth as well as of men.[37] Methodist leaders echoed the same call, were impressed with Borden's manifesto promising to tax war profits and increase income taxes,[38] and went beyond all others in the pressure they brought on their membership to support the Union government at the polls on 17 December 1917. Both the Presbyterian and the Methodist churches saw in the move toward Union government a possible transcendence of partisan politics whose corruption it had long protested. 'Now is the time,' urged S.D. Chown, 'for Canada to strike for freedom

33 *Ibid.*
34 See CG, 26 March 1919, p. 15
35 CAR, 1917, pp. 629–30
36 Christie, 'The Presbyterian Church in Canada,' pp. 133–4; CAR, 1917, p. 630
37 *Presbyterian Acts and Proceedings*, 1917, p. 37
38 'Manifesto of Sir Robert Borden to the Canadian People,' 17 Nov. 1917, cited in Bliss, 'The Methodist Church and World War I'

from the system of political grafting' and from 'the shackles of blind partisanship.'[39] Radicals like Bland, or outspoken reformers like Nellie McClung, the prairie novelist and suffragette, had no criticism of the church's unprecedented entry into a major political campaign. Bland had been proposing a national non-partisan government since late 1916,[40] and was the willing subject of a citizen's campaign to draft him as a Unionist candidate for Centre Winnipeg. He was unwilling to meet the terms of the Unionist constituency executive, however, and withdrew in favour of a progressive liberal, Major Andrews.[41] On 5 December, just prior to the election, Nellie McClung wrote in the *Guide*: 'The Union Government which is now proposed is an indication of better things. It is a confession, too, of the failure of the party system, which will no doubt die hard, and the wiggling of its tail will be seen in the sulphurous utterances of the party press for many a day. But its time has come ...' A year later, as enthusiasm for the Union government began to wane in the West, an Alberta radical, Will Holmes, suggested that while the church had often attacked political corruption and the party system and was largely responsible for Union government, what it really had in mind was non-partisan government.[42] The minutes of the Methodist Board of Social Service and Evangelism, meeting 13–18 September 1917 as the Union government was taking shape, would seem to bear him out.

If the attitude of the churches toward the war is to be weighed in the balance, it must in fair measure be gauged in terms of their own sense of the issues involved. Probably the finest statement, gathering the threads of church response together, came in the last year of the war from the Presbyterian commission on the war.[43] This commission of clergy, professors, and laymen, some of the ablest in the church,

39 CG, 12 Dec. 1917, cited in Bliss, 'The Methodist Church and World War I,' p. 221; Presbyterian Church in Canada, *The War and the Christian Church*, p. 15
40 See his letters to major Canadian dailies, November 1916, eg, *Toronto Daily Star*, 11 Nov. 1916
41 For a fuller account of the episode with its supporting evidence, see Allen, 'Salem Bland,' pp. 119–22
42 Holmes, 'The Church in Politics,' *Alberta Non-Partisan*, 12 April 1918, p. 7
43 *Presbyterian Acts and Proceedings*, 1917, p. 52. The members of the commission were the Moderator, G.C. Pidgeon, J.G. Shearer, R.P. MacKay, D. McTavish, T.B. Kilpatrick, Professor Shaw, Principal Fraser, W.H. Sedgewick, Principal Baird, M.A. MacKinnon, D.G. McQueen, Principal MacKay, John A. Paterson, Hamilton Cassels, and Dr P.T. Coupland. There is no indication when the report of the commission was delivered to the Assembly or how widely it was circulated.

confessed their sense of 'inability to interpret adequately the appalling catastrophe,' but they believed that God was present in all history, in judgment and in mercy, and it was incumbent upon them to struggle to catch 'some of His meaning ... in the terrors and agonies of this tremendous conflict.' The report gave full evidence of their struggle. If the war offered an opportunity for ministry, it was only because it had exhibited the hollowness of conventional religion. In vain could Christians plead their orthodoxy, liberality, or enterprises, for 'this ghastly thing has happened, which the Church of Christ ought to have prevented and might have prevented.' Not only was the faith of the church judged and its moral feebleness exhibited, but the guilt of western civilization, not only Germany and Austria, but Britain, France, Canada, and the United States, cried to high heaven. The forces creating the holocaust were long endemic in the body politic of the western world as a whole:

The 'claim to world power,' the cynical selfishness, the brutal disregard of the rights and interests of others, the oppression that condemns multitudes to minister to the greed and lust of the dominant class; and the wrongs that we justly condemn and loathe on the part of the German 'war lords' have their analogues in the social system of which we ourselves, even the most pacifically-minded, are a part. These sins the war is judging ... Canada is involved in this sin, and is being comprehended in the judgment ... It is vain to separate ourselves, as individuals, from national transgressions ... *We* are the people. *We* live under the system the war is judging. *We* have profited by it. It is for *us* to repent in dust and ashes ...

The first claim upon the church was to point men to an understanding of their history in which the chains of such sin, corporate and individual, had been broken. Otherwise, the issue lay only with an enveloping fatalism. But it was an equal claim upon the church itself to live out that understanding in actual experience, positively, and in social, worldly terms. Everything which stood between man and the fullness of his humanity was the enemy of God, and was to be fought as such by every servant of God on a battlefront that extended from legislature, court, street, and market to villa and slum. The problems of the peace would undoubtedly prove more severe than any experienced in the war. Now was the time to begin laying up resources of knowledge and determination for the continuing battle.[44]

The commission report was a penetrating document and strong medicine for both church and society in Canada. Here was no easy patriotism or pious prescription. If the report echoed the social and worldly concerns that the social gospel had aroused in the churches, it equally expressed the tragic implications of the social gospel's message of social solidarity. Here again, the total commitment of the

44 Presbyterian Church in Canada, *The War and the Christian Church*

churches to the war effort cannot conceal the intensification of their pledge to social reform. Yet it is not enough to conclude in the usual sense of the words that the war heightened social idealism in the churches. It was a profound observation that unless men, including their corporate structures, accepted their implication in social guilt, and they and their corporate structures were prepared to stand under the radical judgment of God, there was no new way forward. Not through secular conceptions of human perfectibility would a new society be born, but through following in full realism the one whose sacrifice on a cross went beyond all requirements of justice. Whether the church itself, let alone Canadian society at large, could follow that high path only time would tell. If, however, at a later date it could be charged that the social gospel in the churches was in any sense betrayed in the war years by a temporary increase in social purpose occasioned by the war, it was not due simply to hypocritical acquiescence in narrow patriotism but to its best thinking and its more radical hopes.

It was profoundly ironic that, despite the increasing radicalism across the front of the social gospel during the war, crisis struck the movement at the point of the relationship between the radicals and the church. The men primarily involved were William Irvine, J.S. Woodsworth, William Ivens, and Salem Bland. Irvine was a Presbyterian, and the others, Methodists. All four were highly critical of the conduct of the war, although only two, Woodsworth and Ivens, were pacifists. Irvine and Bland were more concerned with the successful prosecution of the war, but for them success required conditions of national unity and equality of sacrifice.[45] Those conditions could be fulfilled, they believed, through a reorganization of the federal government and more social controls on industry. Bland was more optimistic about the possibility of these changes than Irvine. He believed, with the *Free Press* and the *Guide*, that a Union government would conscript wealth on equal terms with manpower, while Irvine and the labour movement had deep doubts that Liberals and Conservatives who had not advocated this separately would now do so together.[46] All four had become heavily committed both to the agrarian and urban reform movements. Bland and Woodsworth, in particular, were already among that small group that was nurturing the associations and ideology for the development of farmer-labour politics.

Together, then, these four represented the various positions of the social gospel left wing in the middle of the war. Whatever the long-run possibility of tensions

45 *The Nutcracker*, 29 Dec. 1916; Allen, 'Salem Bland,' pp. 103–14, 118–23
46 Allen, 'Salem Bland,' pp. 123–5; Smith, *All My Life*, pp. 40–1; Morton, *The Progressive Party*, p. 43

between them and the rest of the movement, it was through the pressures of the war and issues relating to the war that the crisis developed. The outward form of the crisis was simple: each, for various reasons, was separated from his position; each explained his situation in terms of the reaction of 'the interests,' that is, of wealth entrenched in church and state.[47] The most adequate explanation, however, is at once simpler and more complex. The question is an important one, for any judgment on their respective fates at this time inevitably colours the way the social gospel is viewed in succeeding years.

The first to succumb was William Irvine, a vigorous young Presbyterian minister of fresh intellect, but three years ordained. Shortly after coming to Canada from Scotland, he had entered Wesley College, Winnipeg, and studied under Salem Bland. His first and last Presbyterian charge was the Union Church at Emo in the Rainy River district of Ontario. In 1916 he found his position untenable and resigned the charge.

Irvine's problems first arose when the merchants in his church were antagonized by his part in organizing a successful retail co-operative. He had forewarned the board that he intended to preach the social gospel, but apparently made the mistake of doing something about it. Some in the congregation were further irritated by what they believed to be a lack of patriotism in his sermons, and actually engaged a government officer to investigate him. The officer personally exonerated him of any subversive talk or preaching – in fact, commended him for his sermons. A leader of the congregation then laid a heresy charge against him. Irvine himself, on graduation, had wondered whether he should preach, recognized that he held unorthodox views, but the professors of the college had considered these to be minor problems. Now the Presbytery in its turn cleared Irvine of the charge. But, unable to serve any further purpose in the Rainy River post, he resigned. Upon receipt of an invitation to become pastor of the Unitarian church in Calgary, he departed for that city and the beginnings of a notable career in politics.[48] Amid the conscription crisis of 1917, however, he was relieved of his ministry with the free-thinking Unitarians when word filtered to Boston headquarters that he was not loyal to the war effort.[49] By that time, he had become a leading figure in the small but potent Alberta Non-Partisan League, and was editing a crisp little paper, *The Nutcracker*.

47 It was in these terms that I treated Bland's dismissal from Wesley College in my thesis, 'Salem Bland,' and that McNaught interprets Woodsworth's dismissal from the Bureau of Social Research, his resignation from the ministry, and Ivens' case as well in *A Prophet in Politics*, pp. 75–7, 79–87. See also Smith, *All My Life*, pp. 57–8
48 The basis for this account is an interview with Irvine, 15–16 May 1961.
49 *Ibid.* For a more extended sketch and an account of Irvine's parliamentary career, see Stolee's thesis.

The second of the four men to find himself in difficulties caused by the exigencies of war was the more notable figure of J.S. Woodsworth, son of an elder statesman of the Methodist church. Woodsworth had become well-known through the settlement type of mission he had developed in Winnipeg's north end, and through two of the better pieces of early social gospel literature.[50] Studious habits soon made him a Canadian authority in the field of social welfare, and in 1913, when he resigned from All Peoples' Mission, it was to move more directly into pioneering efforts in secular social work. Early in 1916 his hope that governments would undertake responsibility for social research seemed near fulfilment in the prairie region, as the three provincial governments agreed to support a Bureau of Social Research and Woodsworth was appointed as director. Within a year he had resigned and the bureau was closed. The turning point in the development had come with Woodsworth's public protest over the establishment by the federal government of a labour registration plan to facilitate the war effort.

Woodsworth agreed with widespread labour protest that the scheme seemed a prelude to conscription of manpower without conscription of wealth.[51] He had other reasons as well, however, which questioned the likelihood of a fair administration of the plan, and his letter of 28 December 1916 to the *Free Press* concluded, 'as some of us cannot conscientiously engage in military service, we are bound to resist what, if the war continues, will invariably lead to forced service.'[52]

This coincidence of Woodsworth's and labour's objection to the registration plan probably added seriousness to his protest in the eyes of the Norris government of Manitoba. There was an unknown potential in Woodsworth's pacifism. Prior to the war there had been a considerable pacifist movement. Like the anti-war stance

50 The books arose out of his work at All Peoples' Mission; *Strangers Within Our Gates* and *My Neighbour*.

51 Irvine was making the same argument in *The Nutcracker*, a newspaper which he had begun editing shortly after moving to Calgary. See his proposed 'Registration Card for Corporations,' 29 Dec. 1916. 'We are in favor of wholehearted national service. We believe that the manpower of the nation should be unreservedly at the service of the state. The dollar power should also be there.'

52 This episode is on the whole well told in the admirable biography by McNaught, *A Prophet in Politics*, pp. 75–8. However, he plays down this last statement in the letter in order to emphasize the affinity of Woodsworth's position with that of radical labour. Thus, when Woodsworth was 'given a chance to "be good" and "keep quiet," which he refused,' and when he was ordered to close the Bureau of Social Research, it appeared that his radicalism in economic matters was the point at issue and not simply his pacifism or his protest over this one issue. Incontrovertible evidence of this is not given.

of the Second International it had faded with the actual coming of the war. However, a section of the 'international working class' in Canada had revived its protest on grounds suspiciously like the theory that imperialist war was a phenomenon of late capitalism, and that no sensible worker would take part in it. The war had crystallized a new movement of pacifists, the Fellowship of Reconciliation in 1914, in Britain. Would pacifist protest revive in Canada in the same way? Whether or not government officials asked themselves this question, conscientious objection was clearly anathema to most Canadians in 1917. Certainly it could not have seemed conducive to governmental wartime authority for three provinces of the dominion apparently to endorse a prominent and outspoken pacifist.

Woodsworth's dismissal, however, could hardly have been a direct result of his social or economic radicalism. The three governments must have been aware of his views when they hired him to head the newly created bureau a few months earlier. He had become nationally known through his work from 1913–16 with the Canadian Welfare League. In articles and speeches he had not only urged many immediate social reforms like the minimum wage, but he had also spoken for public ownership as 'probably ... the only satisfactory way of protecting the poor and the less able against the exploitation of the rich and clever.'[53] One of his publications pointed to 'increasing social stratification across Canada,' and warned 'that the machinery of production in both country and city was passing into the hands of the few.'[54] The governments must have had no serious qualms about these views of Woodsworth, else they would surely not have entrusted the new post to him. He would seem to have been a victim of wartime attitudes rather than of reactionary influences.[55]

However, Woodsworth's pacifism and his social views both came under attack at

53 *Ibid.*, p. 61

54 *Ibid.*, p. 65, citing *Studies in Rural Citizenship* edited by Woodsworth, with a foreword by R.C. Henders, and contributions by socialist and single taxer F.J. Dixon on direct legislation, and by suffragette Nellie McClung on pacifism.

55 McNaught, in support of the contrary position, refers to the removal of Salem Bland from Wesley College as indicative of an atmosphere in Winnipeg which 'obviously diminished Woodsworth's effectiveness in Manitoba.' He also cites approvingly Woodsworth's view that 'it was unlikely that such a man [as Bland] would survive in a college where the governors cherished the same ideas as those which had caused his own dismissal by the provincial government'. The two situations were in fact quite different (see below, pp. 54–60. McNaught may have been somewhat misled on this by believing Bland likewise a pacifist, which he was not (*ibid.*, pp. 79–81).

Gibson's Landing, the small coastal mission in British Columbia where, after his dismissal, friends in the Methodist Conference arranged that he supply. His situation almost exactly paralleled that of Irvine at Rainy River, and some leading members of the congregation requested that the conference not station him there again. While the British Columbia Stationing Committee had no authority over Woodsworth, it did have responsibility for the Gibson's Landing station and complied with the request.[56] This action can hardly be attributed to lack of social radicalism in the British Columbia Conference, which at that time was preparing radical resolutions and a strong contingent for the General Conference of the Methodist church the following October. Both the leadership of the conference, the Revs. R.J. McIntyre and Ernest Thomas, for instance, and its monthly paper[57] were overt proponents of the social gospel.[58] But what could even a radical stationing committee do with a person of outspoken pacifist views when most circuit leaders all over the country had probably accepted war propaganda at its face value? The British Columbia Conference did not have to answer this question with regard to Woodsworth. Nor was he longer to be a concern of the Manitoba Conference. On 8 June 1918 he presented a letter of resignation from the ministry.

Woodsworth gave three reasons for his action: a continuing sense of his own unorthodoxy, which the conference, however, had not considered serious in 1907; the lack of freedom in the 'institutional' and 'increasingly commercialized' church to promote 'a radical programme of social reform'; and now the rejection and repudiation by the church of what he considered to be the way of Jesus with respect to war.[59] From recent pronouncements of the church he concluded that 'apparently the Church feels that I do not belong and reluctantly I have come to the same conclusion.' However, he wrote: 'I still feel the call of service and trust that I may have some share in the work of bringing in the Kingdom.'

The Manitoba Stationing Committee, some of whom were 'pronounced in their

56 *Ibid.*, pp. 81–2
57 *Western Methodist Recorder*, July 1918, p. 8, for instance
58 *Ibid.*, Jan. 1918, p. 5; Dec. 1918, p. 3
59 The letter is given in full in McNaught, *A Prophet in Politics*, pp. 82–5. Woodsworth cited the *Christian Guardian*, 1 May 1918: '... in time of war the State ... rightly refuses to allow a peace propaganda to be carried on in its midst. Not only so, but the Church has a duty in the matter and that is to prevent unpatriotic speeches in her pulpits. And if the minister who is a confirmed pacifist has a right to speak his mind freely the Church which he serves reserves the right to see that he does not use her pulpits nor her authority to damage or defeat the efforts of patriots who are trying to win a righteous war.'

support of the present war,' regretfully accepted the resignation, stating that 'the feeling of necessity is more insistent in your mind than in ours.'[60] This being Woodsworth's third letter proposing such a course, the committee felt it could not again try to persuade him otherwise.[61] The 'institutional' and 'increasingly commercialized' church was hardly eager to be rid of him! Like Irvine he had encountered petty patriotism and business self-interest in local church officials. The latter he might have contended with successfully; the two issues combined were somewhat formidable, but there is little doubt that he could have maintained his position in the church against such pressures. Although this decision stemmed more from his gnawing sense of unorthodoxy than from the extent of 'commercialism,' the precipitating factor was his pacifist belief in the face of total church commitment to the war. In the higher court of the church, he continued to find understanding until he terminated his ministry.

The same stationing committee that received Woodsworth's resignation also had on its agenda an urgent appeal from McDougall Methodist Church, Winnipeg, that William Ivens not be returned as their pastor.

Ivens, like Irvine, had come from Great Britain to Winnipeg and had studied under Salem Bland, for whom he had great admiration. He had been stationed at McDougall in 1916. This church was the sixth largest of eighteen Methodist churches in North Winnipeg. Apparently it was in dire financial straits and, in an area increasingly inhabited by labourers and immigrants, seemed to face a problem of declining numbers. Congregational membership, which had been 310 in 1915 and dropped to 224 in 1916, climbed during Ivens' first year to 248, but slumped to 171 during the second. Ivens' efforts to recoup the financial position of the church, however, were startlingly successful, increasing revenue for church purposes from $1625 to over $6000 in two years.[62]

Ivens' preaching of the social gospel at McDougall was probably not new to the congregation.[63] He had come to McDougall in hopes of exercising a specialized ministry to working people. Soon he announced his belief that the primary task of the church was to counter the practices and goals of North American capitalism

60 McNaught, *A Prophet in Politics*, p. 86

61 He had suggested this course to the committee in 1902 and 1907.

62 See Methodist Church in Canada, *Year Book(s)*, 1915–18

63 The previous minister, R.A. Scarlett, seems to have had marked social gospel sympathies (see Bland Papers, Scarlett to Bland, 25 Nov. 1907) and an earlier minister had been A.E. Smith (see above, pp. 13, 16, 23).

with those of prophetic teaching. Democracy, especially in the industrial sector, was the challenge of the day. If the church led the people in this struggle she would hold labour, he concluded; if not, 'Labor will win her own battles and the Church will have lost the opportunity of the Century.'[64] His first year at McDougall did not lead him to alter this conviction, or the belief that his work could be accomplished in and through the church.[65]

With the introduction of conscription of manpower in mid-1917 and the subsequent failure of the Union government to conscript wealth in the same measure, labour's rapidly growing ranks increased in radicalism. So did Ivens' views and his direct relationship with organized labour. It was not Ivens' radicalism, however, but his pacifism that was the nub of his problem. Conscription implicitly placed conscientious objection outside the law. Through the winter of 1917–18 the *Voice* carried articles about the abuse of conscientious objectors and the deprivations of civil liberties. Among these were a few by Ivens on 'The War and Its Problems.' Ivens had early decided that it would be improper for him to express his views on the war from the pulpit, but considered himself free of obligation on this point outside it.[66]

On 19 March 1918 Ivens gave notice to his congregation of a move afoot among the officials of the church to have him removed as their minister. At least nine letters and a petition from twelve choir members descended on W. Wilson, the secretary of the Board of Management, protesting any such action and defending Ivens' effectiveness as a pastor.[67] A heated meeting of the quarterly board was held on the following Thursday.[68] Whether it resulted in any further action is not clear, but Ivens, on the next Sunday, speaking on 'The Crown Rights of Conscience,' declared: 'I am a man first, a pastor second. In this pulpit I will speak only as I understand God. You can have me as your minister or not, but outside the Church I am a man and will not be interfered with in my speech on public questions.'[69] Almost immediately thereafter he undertook a tour of eight prairie centres, speaking on 'Commerce, Diplomacy, and the War.'[70]

Ivens was a supporter of the recently organized Dominion Labor party, and active on its propaganda and publicity committee. His tour was in some degree an attempt to interrelate incipient groups of the party in the prairie region. In several

64 *Voice*, 8 Sept. 1916, p. 3   65 *Ibid.*, 14 Sept. 1917, p. 5
66 *Ibid.*, 29 March 1918
67 UCA, Ivens' file, Papers, 'Attitude of the Methodist Church to the War'
68 *Voice*, 29 March 1918   69 *Ibid.*
70 *Ibid.*, 19 April 1918

centres he found fellow ministers associated with the 'progressives.' In Swift Current, where 'everyone must first visit J.G. Laycock's drug store and get linked up with the progressives right away,' the Baptist minister, the Rev. Speller, was 'a pusher for the Forum.' In Calgary, of course, Irvine was 'a great force,' and in Edmonton, the Rev. F.E. Mercer, secretary of the Labor Representation League, was an 'enthusiast and eminently practical.'[71]

On his return, Ivens found that the Trades and Labor Council had called a 'strike for the right to strike' in support of civil employees seeking bargaining rights. Ten unions were officially reported on strike, although at a meeting on 22 May it was claimed that forty unions were out.[72] On the 24th the strike was settled with the recognition of the civic employees union. Certain other benefits were won, and an agreement concluded to arbitrate disputes in future and use the strike weapon only as a last resort.[73] Ivens had immediately plunged into the struggle and assumed editorship of the strike newspaper.

Early in these events the official board of the church met again, and voted eleven to two to 'request Conference not to send Mr Ivens as Pastor of McDougall Church, and that we abide by their decision, or the policy be accepted on a vote being taken thereon.'[74] Legally, the board could not repudiate any decision by the stationing committee of conference. Neither could the minister, although each could present reasons and appeal a decision to the Court of Appeal if there seemed a clear case of abuse of rights.

When the stationing committee met it had fifteen letters of support for Ivens (in addition to the nine of March), and two petitions totalling 331 names of which 31 were duplicates. Of these, 99 were full members out of a total congregation of 171 members. Most of the letters and the petition referred to Ivens' effective extrication of the church from financial difficulty. Some of them declared his ministry to people who had suffered loss overseas to be a helpful one.[75] All claimed, some by personal

71 *Alberta Non-Partisan*, 24 March 1918. Mercer came from Canterbury, England, was a Labour party supporter, and wrote occasional articles for the *Edmonton Free Press* (later *Alberta Labor News*), edited by Elmo E. Roper who seemed very sympathetic to the social gospel.
72 *Voice*, 24 May 1918
73 *Ibid.*, 31 May 1918
74 Ivens' file, Papers, 'Attitude of the Methodist Church to the War'
75 However, the Rev. Haw's later defence of Ivens before the Court of Appeal refers to this ministry as naturally a difficult one for a person of his views to exercise. See UCA, Papers, Court of Appeal, 1919. Both views may be true, depending on who the bereaved person was – conservative ultra-patriot or labour reformer.

testimony, that Ivens had an unusual appeal to working people, considerable numbers of whom were attaching themselves closely to his church. As a witness to this, F.G. Tipping, president of the Trades and Labor Council, had written an appreciation of his 'thoughtful sermons and addresses,' and, although he did not entirely agree with Ivens and was 'not particularly interested in Methodism,' he argued that the church could scarcely afford to lose 'men like him.'[76] Tipping's letter was further backed up with a petition from the Labor Temple with 2000 names.[77]

By the end of the strike, the McDougall board considered the situation much more urgent, and authorized a committee of three to take its case to the stationing committee.[78] At the same time the board put out feelers on the possibility of uniting with Wesley Church for a period of time. The stationing committee, weighing the evidence and faced with a badly split congregation, followed what was a fairly standard procedure. It removed Ivens from McDougall in the hope that a new man might restore unity, and offered him another circuit in Winnipeg if he so desired.[79] This was not a bold and radical decision, but it had its wisdom given the circumstances, and could in any case hardly be construed as capitulation to wealthy interests. Ivens had not simplified matters by making it a condition of restationing at McDougall that he 'be allowed to work out a workers' church.'[80] Clearly, this could not be done without further congregational disruption.

In offering Ivens another station in Winnipeg it was apparent that the committee as a whole was making no adverse judgment on Ivens' character, religious views, ability, or recent public speeches and activities. The committee was perhaps risking further contention in such an offer, but may have been hoping, as one letter had suggested, that an early conclusion of the war would deliver them from part of the problem at least. Ivens' own reply to this offer, that his pacifist views would cause difficulty in any congregation, was probably wiser but less daring than the proposal of the committee.[81] When he refused the offer and requested to be left for a year without station, the committee was obliged to give him his wish only if he produced satisfactory reasons. Apparently his desire to establish a labour church in which to continue his ministry to the working class was acceptable, even including the likelihood suggested by recent experience that he would fully identify with labour's struggle. Had the committee found this unacceptable (and the move had manifestly sectarian possibilities quite apart from its radicalism), it could have

76 Ivens' file, Papers, 'Attitude of the Methodist Church to the War'
77 *Voice*, 14 June 1918
78 Ivens' file, Papers, 'Attitude of the Methodist Church to the War'
79 *Voice*, interview with Ivens, 21 June 1918
80 *Ibid.*   81 *Ibid.*

forced him to accept a station or locate him forthwith if he refused.[82] Apparently Ivens' special ministry was acceptable both to most of the committee and to the Manitoba Conference.

Taken as a whole, the conference decision hardly represented the fresh wine of social radicalism, but neither was it acting under the domination of narrow patriotism, the influence of wealth, or the control of institutional conservatism.[83] Having refused a station, Ivens was less than correct in stating to the press that Methodism no longer stood for a free pulpit, that it put political connections before religous convictions.[84]

It is notable that in this cluster of cases, Bland's is the only instance up to the end of 1918 of an actual dismissal from a church position. Irvine, Woodsworth, and Ivens, although subject to the harrying of congregational factions, received a remarkable degree of support from the higher courts of the church, and to the degree that they were separated further from the churches, it was on their own initiative. Bland, by contrast, held tenaciously to his position in the church. Was the Bland case, perhaps, a more obvious instance of vested interests in church and society plotting to be rid of the stormy petrel of social gospel radicalism in the West?

Bland was fifty-eight years old, and had been teaching church history for fourteen years at Wesley College when he was informed on 5 June 1917 that because of a reorganization of staff necessitated by financial problems, his services would no longer be needed. Another man, A.J. Irwin, professor of New Testament, suffered the same fate. In the spring of 1917 the Board of Directors of the college faced a

82 Methodist Church of Canada, *The Doctrine and Discipline, 1914*, pp. 65–6, paragraphs 120, 121. Location meant denying a minister the right to function as a minister of the church. It was normally done after a year's notice, but not necessarily.

83 McNaught, *A Prophet in Politics*, pp. 97–8, suggests the conference 'was even more cautious and conservative than the Church as a whole.' But he has confused the June 1918 circumstances with those of June 1919. Ivens was not located until 1919, when circumstances had changed considerably. In 1918 the conference fulfilled the terms of the Rev. John Haw's eloquent defence of Ivens before the Court of Appeal, which McNaught cites approvingly. His judgment was probably also influenced by the mistaken impression that the Manitoba Conference in 1917 had supported the dismissal of Salem Bland (p. 80). See, however, Bland and Irwin to CG, 7 Nov. 1917, pp. 2, 20–2

84 See also his final sermon at McDougall, 'Would the Church Today Crucify Christ?' *Voice*, 14 June 1918, in which he described the church as now the most conservative institution on earth. For a summary, see below, p. 84.

bank overdraft of $28,000, the result of increasing yearly deficits since the begin-ning of the war. On the one hand the deficits had been incurred by a board decision to re-establish an Arts programme in the fall of 1915, and on the other hand they were affected by wartime inflation increasing operating costs, while enrolments and hence revenue from fees declined. Grants from the government helped to maintain the arts programme, but the theological programme was caught between a larger proportional drop in student enrolment and a complete lack of grants from any secular sources. Financial pressures on congregations had made unlikely more than a modest increase of funds from the supporting conferences. Retrenchment was necessary. As early as 23 June 1916, the board authorized Principal Crummy 'in consultation with the faculty to arrange to free one of the theological staff for work in the field.' Apparently, no action was taken, and to cope with the problem the Board of Directors struck a special committee to determine ways and means.[85] A review of the college's affairs indicated that some staff would have to be released and other adjustments made. It was known in April that one of the men would likely be Salem Bland. Apparently to give itself a free hand, the board followed a recent device of the University of Manitoba and on 31 May put all faculty and other employees on notice. It was clear that many would be retained, but on 5 June it was also clear that the axe had fallen on Salem Bland and A.J. Irwin.[86]

Bland had earlier launched a counter attack, charging ulterior political motiva-tion. Irwin had not been marked for release at first, but when the dismissal of both men was announced, they together issued a strong protest based on a number of charges: that the form of dismissal was invalid; that it was done at a time which precluded their conferences from stationing them; that the board was organized in a way that violated church disciplines and the college charter, a factor which con-tributed to the improper action; that the dismissal caused professional harm; that the action was taken without just cause; that the reason alleged was not genuine, and that, if it were, was still not a necessary or sufficient reason.[87] S.D. Chown, general superintendent of the church, wrote to Bland that he hoped the case would

85 The committee was composed of J.H. Ashdown, Dr Popham, Dr Halpenny, Dr Hughson, Dr Darwin, the Rev. A.E. Smith, and E.L. Taylor.
86 This account is based on a number of sources, including McNaught, *A Prophet in Politics*, p. 80; *Voice*, 8, 21 June 1917; GGG, 27 June, 15 Aug. 1917; CAR, 1917, pp. 739–40, and 1918, p. 680; Papers, Court of Appeal, 1917; Minutes of the Board of Directors and the Executive of Wesley College, 1915–18, University of Winnipeg; Proceedings of Commission of Saskatchewan Conference re Wesley College Affairs, Sept. 1918, University of Winnipeg.
87 Papers, Court of Appeal, 1917

clear up several murky areas of discipline.[88] But the key question to Bland and Irwin was that the real reasons were not given. In their minds this was a manoeuvre to remove Bland from the college.

The announcement of dismissal caused a furor in the press of the West, in the Saskatchewan and Manitoba conferences, and among the students of Wesley College. The *Grain Growers' Guide* on 27 June declared Bland suffered because of 'his outspoken condemnation of political corruption and his unswerving championship of social reform,' and the Winnipeg *Tribune* observed that he was feared by the corporations because 'for years every movement for the common weal that had made headway in the West has been helped and pushed forward by Dr Bland.'[89] The *Voice* trumpeted:

Wesley College is sacrificing the strongest man west of the Great Lakes on the altar of obedience to vested interests and political pull ... Such an institution has no place and no function in the free West ... They plead poverty. Yet they own millions. Shame on the Church. Shame on the men, millionaires, men of brains and business who put up such a plea.[90]

The issue put the Manitoba Conference in an uproar. The public had to be excluded from sessions discussing the case,[91] and the conference urged the full board to review the decision in the light of conference discussion, which was strong in favour of reinstatement. The Saskatchewan Conference was more perturbed still. This had been Bland's home conference since coming to the West in 1903. Many members proposed suspension of support of the college. The conference as a whole declared: 'The truest economy would be to strengthen rather than weaken the theological department of Wesley College and in view of the unquestioned ability of Dr Bland and the excellence and loyalty of his services for the past fourteen years, we trust every effort will be made by the Board to retain his services.'[92] The students of Wesley College followed a similar course, and concluded that the reasons adduced by the board were not in accord with the facts. According to Bland, they stuck to this position 'in spite of a whole day of third degree examination by the Board.'[93] Bland obviously had widespread support, and most of it was prepared to believe that, put most charitably, powerful and wealthy men had taken advantage

88 Chown to Bland, 9 Nov. 1917, Papers, Court of Appeal, 1917
89 Cited by *Toronto World*, 25 June 1917
90 8 June 1917, cited in McNaught, *A Prophet in Politics*, p. 80
91 GGG, 27 June 1917, p. 22
92 McNaught, *A Prophet in Politics*, p. 80
93 Bland to the *Toronto Daily Star*, 21 March 1931

of a financial crisis in the college to remove him from its staff. In reviewing the news of the year on the case, the *Canadian Annual Review* presented both factors as reasons.[94]

However, this interpretation has some severe problems. In the first place, not all the board members represented 'vested interests.' One notably did not, the Rev. A.E. Smith, then president of Manitoba Conference and a radical exponent of the social gospel. He was not a man easily manipulated and was a friend of Bland. Naturally, he was hesitant to see Bland go, but both in the committee of the board to reorganize staff and in the later September meeting of the full board, he moved from early opposition to either support or abstention.[95] He was sensitive to the possible influence of other than financial motives, but if he had seen the move primarily as an attack on Bland, surely he would have taken an obdurate stand in opposition.

Second, why was A.J. Irwin removed? A friend on the board apparently told Bland later that it had been to cover the attack on Bland.[96] But this explanation was patently untrue, for while Bland had known since April that he was a probable sacrifice if reorganization of the staff were carried through, Irwin's removal was not contemplated until the last minute when J.H. Riddell was hired as principal. Irwin's field was New Testament, and since Riddell taught New Testament subjects, Irwin was no longer necessary on the staff.[97]

Third, Dr S.D. Chown, general superintendent of the church, was an old and close friend of the Bland family who on various occasions professed to hold similar social views.[98] He was the chairman of the Court of Appeal which heard the case. If he had any reason to suspect ulterior motives in Bland's dismissal, surely he would have taken pains to satisfy himself of the validity of such suspicions. There is no evidence that he felt this necessary.

Fourth, if Bland was considered a nuisance in the college because of his political views and activities, why had he not earlier been censured or reprimanded? In

94 See pp. 739–40. McNaught, *A Prophet in Politics*, pp. 79–81

95 See McNaught, *A Prophet in Politics*, p. 80, and letter from the board to the CG, 31 Oct. 1917, pp. 12–13, published alongside a letter from Bland and Irwin. A.E. Smith's own account of this in his autobiography, *All My Life*, pp. 57–8, is quite faulty. See minutes of a meeting of the principal committee of the Wesley College Board, 4 June 1917

96 Bland to the *Toronto Daily Star*, 21 March 1931

97 Proceedings, *passim*. Letter of the board to the CG, 31 Oct. 1917

98 Bland had served as pastor to the Chown family during his Kingston ministry. Chown was, in fact, rather less radical.

1907 when a powerful group numbering among them Sir Rodmond Roblin and Sir James Aiken, smarting from an attack by Bland, endeavoured to secure his dismissal, and at least a ban on faculty participation in public controversy, political or religious, the attempt had foundered on the obduracy of the board.[99] More recently, in 1913 or 1914, the chairman of the board counselled him to tone down the temper of his public statements, but neither party suggested at any time that the conversation was other than friendly.[100] Indeed, the nearest the board had ever come to restraining the faculty was in 1910 when, following Professor Osborne's contest for public office, it declared it an inadvisable course of action.[101]

Fifth, who were those suspected of trying to remove Bland? The chief suspect was J.H. Ashdown, chairman of the board for many years, past mayor of the city, and wealthy owner of a chain of hardware stores. Ivens was so convinced of Ashdown's guilt that he 'bearded' him in his office on the subject.[102] It is more than probable that Ashdown's views did not coincide with Bland's, and he had frankly had some concern about the impact Bland was having on college finances.[103] Yet Ashdown had been prominent in shielding Bland in 1907, and in proposals Bland made in 1916 and 1917 for a nationally representative non-partisan federal administration, J.H. Ashdown was one of the able and upright men he suggested as a member of it.[104] Ashdown's offer in April of the next year of one-third of the debt of $30,000 and $100,000 toward an endowment fund of $400,000 has sometimes been cited as evidence, if not of his guilt, at least of his hypocrisy regarding the financial crisis.[105] The $100,000, however, had been a standing offer for several years, awaiting the accumulation of the rest of the fund.[106] His willingness to cover a portion of the debt was similarly predicated on the action of others, and on best business principles was not offered until the college budget had been brought into line with regular revenue possibilities and the new principal had demonstrated that fact by eliminating the deficit for 1917–18. Other members of the board and the

99 Bland and Irwin to the *Free Press*, 21 Sept. 1917

100 Proceedings, pp. 170 f

101 Letter from the board to CG 31 Oct. 1917. The board felt this way even though Osborne had taken a year's leave to run for office.

102 *Voice*, 21 June 1918

103 Proceedings, pp. 170 f

104 Bland to the *Toronto Daily Star*, 11 Nov. 1916; Bland to the *Manitoba Free Press*, 9 Dec. 1916

105 Allen, 'Salem Bland,' p. 117; Dennis L. Butcher, 'Rev. Dr Salem G. Bland, 1903–19,' honours paper, University of Manitoba, 1970, p. 22

106 Proceedings, pp. 97–8

committee on staff reorganization might be shown on various grounds to be un-likely sympathizers of Bland. Among them, Dr Hughson, pastor of Grace Method-ist Church, had of late been spoiling for a showdown with the *bête noir* of Wesley College.[107] A more likely opponent was E.L. Taylor, a lawyer with financial connections, and a Conservative member of the legislature who had sat for a con-stituency with notorious patronage practices. Yet when Smith suggested in the committee on staff that Taylor's known affiliations might give rise to rumours of partiality, he readily admitted the possibility and withdrew.[108] In testimony before the Saskatchewan Conference Commission investigating the case he candidly ad-mitted that there were a number of men who did not subscribe to Wesley College because of Bland and had since begun to contribute, but insisted that none of these was close to the board or had exercised any direct or indirect influence, and for his part declared to Bland, 'I have stayed with the College all these years and anything you have ever said about anything never affected me in the slightest degree as you know ...'[109]

The case was very complex. It was plagued by a number of unfortunate mis-understandings, and obscured by the personal circumstances of Principal Crummy. Whether the situation can now be satisfactorily resolved may be doubted, but only by the most circumstantial of evidence and questionable argument can the action of the board be construed as either a direct or covert attack on Bland by the wealthy and the conservative in Winnipeg.[110] The case takes on a much more straightfor-ward aspect if it is viewed as a genuine means of coping with a difficult financial situation which, though caused by the war, was of unpredictable duration. This makes intelligible Smith's behaviour, Irwin's dismissal, Chown's 'failure' to come to Bland's defence, the board's failure ever to reprimand Bland, and Bland's respect for J.H. Ashdown. It was the view taken by the Court of Appeal in Decem-ber 1917.[111] The whole action, however, had been unfair to the two men, and had been carried out in a rather summary manner. The court ruled that the general dismissal of 31 May was not an adequate ground for the two professors to seek alternative employment through their respective stationing committees, that the final notice of 5 June came too late for that course to be followed, and that notice

107 Interview with the Rev. Dr F. Passmore, 13 Dec. 1960; Minutes of the Winnipeg
   Methodist Ministerial Association, 8 Feb. 1915; *Manitoba Free Press*, 15 Feb. 1915
108 Proceedings, pp. 203–4
109 *Ibid.*, pp. 129–30
110 The case will be dealt with in full detail in a biography of Bland being prepared by
   the author.
111 Papers, Court of Appeal, 1917

should have come from the full board. Such notice, of course, had since been given. The court further obligated the board to compensate the men in lieu of proper notice.

Bland never changed his belief as to the real reasons for his dismissal, and the Saskatchewan Conference was not thoroughly satisfied. In 1918 it asked an investigating committee under Chief Justice Brown of Saskatchewan to bring in a report on the matter. Its thorough report to the session of 1919 acknowledged the reality of the need for retrenchment, was surprised at the lack of consideration shown to Bland, but 'in the light of the evidence as a whole [was] not prepared to hold that the suspicion referred to [was] well founded.'[112]

There were good reasons why conservative interests in political, economic, and religious life should fear Bland's influence, and they may well have been relieved at his departure. He himself was obviously aware that the radical cause of the social gospel could not be pursued without tension and struggle. In his proposals from 1913 on for a party based on farmer-labour interests, he continually held that 'history teaches us that real reforms and big changes do not come from settled organizations but from distinct cleavages in political alignment.'[113] His interpretation of the war also reflected his acceptance of the progressive uses of conflict and opposition. Despite its horrible aspect, the war was a fact and, somehow, had to be put in a meaningful perspective. In his mind, the struggle became a bloody dialectic which would purge the worst extremes of statism and individualism. 'Opposition is the path to peace,' he wrote, 'and the sharper and deeper the opposition, the more complete and lasting is the peace. That is the law of human progress.'[114] Bland was not only prepared for opposition, but in his world-view gave it a vital function in the engines of progress and might well infer its existence as a material cause where there were few grounds in fact. It seems likely that his view of the underlying reasons for his dismissal from Wesley College was a case in point.

Even as the war years passed, however, he became increasingly hopeful as signs multiplied that the war was indeed hastening the acceptance of social reforms and larger social conceptions. Perhaps the terrible experience of war might spare Canadians the experience of deep internal social conflict. His New Canada Movement had been an expression of that hope. As for the church, he found little cause, either in the trend of its social attitudes or in its wartime role, for expecting, let alone

112 CAR, 1919, p. 571

113 Address to the People's Forum, *Manitoba Free Press*, 24 Feb. 1913, and *Winnipeg Tribune*, 24 Feb. 1913

114 GGG, 9 Jan. 1918, p. 25

promoting, a rupture of the forces within it. Shortly after learning of Woodsworth's dismissal he wrote a letter to him, regretting his decision, and expressing the height of his hopes:

I am sure you have done what you felt you must do. I could have wished you could have remained in the Church until the regeneration. I think the regeneration is going to come to pass. Perhaps it may involve a division, but I hope not, and think not. The practical Christians will capture the Church from the sentimental and dogmatic Christians.[115]

Increasing radicalism was a mark of all sectors of the social gospel. The large majority of the movement, including some radicals, moved leftward partly as a positive response to the wartime experience itself. A very small minority, all radicals, did so in reaction to what were essentially wartime issues, and developed a closer alliance with the more radical centres of Canadian society in labour and socialist groups. In the skirmishes of 1916–18 the radicals were apt to exaggerate and mis-interpret what had happened to them. The labour press urged them on. The *Voice* expected an increasing flood of ministers to leave the church for service in labour's ranks.[116] Dr W.J. Curry, writing in the b.c. *Federationist*, expected Dr Ernest Thomas to join the martyred after a powerful sermon in his Vancouver west-end church attacking social oppression and pointing to the enlarged role labour would play in Canadian social life following the war.[117] But labour had its own myth about the role of the church in society, and it is a testimony both to the inadequacy of that myth and to the continuing force of the social gospel in the churches that neither the prediction of the *Voice* nor that of Curry came to pass.

The deepening of radicalism on the left may in significant measure have been a function of the leftward movement of the social gospel as a whole. That peculiarly wartime issues, for the most part, led to a separation of some of the leading radicals from the main body of the social gospel movement was a tragic occurrence that might, however, have resulted from any later crisis of deep proportions. But to conclude that the separation was due to a late wartime development of caution, social conservatism, and the influence of wealthy interests in the churches, which in turn led to a decline of social gospel fortunes, would be not only mistaken but a reversal of the case. 'If ever I feel anxious,' Bland wrote to Woodsworth, 'I reflect on the revolutionary times that are at hand and the assurance always wells up that

115 5 July 1918, pac, J.S. Woodsworth Papers, Correspondence ii, 611–13
116 21 June 1918
117 'Ye Cannot Serve God and Mammon,' 12 July 1918

there will be a place and a work for me somewhere ... And so it will be with you.'[118] And so indeed it was. For the radicals, the years 1918 and 1919 were active and influential ones, both inside and outside the churches. Their impact in neither sphere was diminished.[119]

118 5 July 1918, J.S. Woodsworth Papers, Correspondence II, 611–13
119 A.R.M. Lower's statement that Methodism fathered a large proportion of Canada's radicals (*Colony to Nation*, p. 499) remains truer than McNaught's comment that it expelled rather than fathered them (*A Prophet in Politics*, p. 98).

4

A Complete
Social Reconstruction

The year 1918 began for Canada with the spurious unity of Union government and closed with the superficial unity of victory in war. The truce that in November began to lengthen into a peace called for the application of the flow of talk about reconstruction that had swelled to a flood over the previous months. The war effort had required a propaganda which utilized the social idealism that had been rising prior to the war. That this language became the common currency of reconstruction speeches and schemes helped hide from many the deep and growing divisions in Canadian society. But although this unity of language may have made many in the social gospel movement over-sanguine in their hopes – and they were perhaps too optimistic in the first place – it did not alter their prospectus for Canadian development. By the year's end the programmes they advocated seemed to be in much sharper focus. At least one of these programmes, that of the Methodist General Conference of 1918, was to attract more interest and acclaim both at home and abroad than perhaps any other Canadian reconstruction manifesto.

The two key problems faced in one way or another by most of these manifestos were, first, the place of the farmer in the national structure and, second, industrial conflict. The solutions proposed by the various wings of the social gospel depended to some degree on their position with regard to the various contending interests in Canada, and perhaps even more on the scope of their social responsibility. Thus the wing of the social gospel most alienated from the organized church, whose emergent leaders were Irvine, Woodsworth, and Ivens, were developing their positions in a much closer dialectic with the western labour movement than ever before, respectively in Calgary, Vancouver, and Winnipeg. They were able to be quite specific in their proposals of reform. Conversely, the churches, involving many community interests, had to eschew detailed programmes for broader principles. The Social Service Council, more removed from the church membership, could occupy a somewhat middle ground. But its association with the conservative wing of the labour movement made it more reformist than radical. If there were a keystone in this arch of social gospel expression it was Salem Bland, highly regarded by a large number of his colleagues and national church leaders, revered by the Grain Growers, respected by labour, and on close personal terms with Irvine, Woodsworth, and Ivens. Throughout 1918 he was not only actively related to all these wings of the social gospel, but in the *Guide* and on the Chautauqua platform he probably delivered his mind on 'Canada at the Crossroads' to a bigger constituency than any of them.

If there were variations in the social gospel expressions of 1918 there was also a remarkable consistency of both attitude and programme. There was, after all, a consensus as to the fundamental evil – competitive individualism; the appropriate solution – industrial democracy; and the general answer – the Kingdom of God conceived as a co-operative commonwealth.

In 1918 the Social Service Council had reached a new peak of influence and a new extent of organization and means of expression. Like Salem Bland, its leaders were dreaming of a new Canada in which they expected to play a prominent part in the building. The *Canadian Annual Review* observed that the council was now a federation of many great organizations for social work,[1] made up, as it was, of fourteen dominion-wide affiliates and eleven provincial units.[2] Dr J.G. Shearer was secured as full-time general secretary over the protests of the Presbyterian church, which did not wish to lose its foremost leader in the work of social service.[3] The projected budget for the year was increased from just over $2000 to $10,000, and plans were initiated for a regular publication.[4] The provincial councils had full-time staffs totalling fourteen persons,[5] and some of the units were devoting special

1 CAR, 1918, p. 598
2 'Report of the Board of Home Missions and Social Service,' *Presbyterian Acts and Proceedings*, 1918, Appendix, p. 15; 1919, Appendix, p. 10. The organizations were: Church of England, Presbyterian church, Methodist church, Baptist church, Congregational church, Evangelical Association, Dominion Grange and Farmers' Association, Salvation Army, Canadian Purity-Education Association, Christian Men's Federation of Canada, National Council of the YMCA, Dominion Council of the YWCA, Dominion Women's Temperance Union, Canadian Council of Agriculture, National Council of Provincial Sunday School Associations. The provincial units included Newfoundland and Bermuda.
3 CAR, 1918, p. 598
4 Social Service Council of Canada, *Minutes*, Annual Meeting, 1918 (January), pp. 8–9, 15
5 *Presbyterian Acts and Proceedings*, 1919, Appendix, p. 10

attention to certain subjects. The Saskatchewan council, for instance, under the Roman Catholic Archbishop of Regina, was in 1918 making a special study of labour and class questions.[6] By the end of the year the council's new publication *Social Welfare* had a circulation between four and six thousand.[7] In jubilation the council exclaimed that 'there is no problem, economic, social, moral or political, whether local, provincial or federal, that cannot be solved by a union of this kind ...'[8]

The enthusiasm of the council illustrates the continuity of conservative and progressive social gospel attitudes within the organization. Recent amendments to the Criminal Code recommended by the council to the government had been enacted,[9] and the government had issued an order-in-council prohibiting both the importation of alcoholic liquors for beverage purposes into provinces which had enacted a prohibitory law and the manufacture of alcoholic beverages after 1 April 1919.[10] The council considered that 'the wonderful success that has attended our efforts ... demonstrates what can be done by such an organization.'[11]

The first several issues of *Social Welfare* elaborated the principles and programme of the national Social Service Council. Out of eighteen declared objectives, only four, however, dealt in any way with the traditional concerns of moral reform. Six concerned industrial matters, seven dealt with social questions such as housing, abolition of poverty, social insurance, and one declared for universal peace.[12] During 1918–19 the publication maintained this balance, with fifty-five articles on social questions, thirty-six on industrial matters, and twenty-three on moral reform. The only change over the subsequent decade was a growing predominance of social issues over all others (three-to-one over industrial), and the steady decline of concern for the moral issues of drinking, gambling, and sexual vice. Organizational articles stayed at a low level, except in the first year and in 1926–8 when the founding of the Canadian Conference of Social Work and the Canadian Association of Social Workers took place. Except in the first two years, with a total of thirty-eight articles, there was seldom discussion of social gospel theory, while political and international issues appeared only rarely.

6 CAR, 1918, p. 598   7 SW, 1 March 1921; 1 March 1922
8 SW, 1 Oct. 1918
9 These regarded the protection of wards from seduction by step-parents or foster parents, the ampler definition of bawdy houses, and the prohibition of racetrack gambling for the duration of the war. *Minutes*, Annual Meeting, 1918, p. 5
10 *Ibid.*, p. 31   11 *Ibid.*, p. 5
12 1 Oct. 1918

The social objective of the council was expressed in the interpretation of the Lord's Prayer that it offered its readers:

We are one and all to 'Hallow our Father's name' and to pray and work for the new social order in which His will is done 'as in Heaven'; in which His children have 'bread' (all needed material good), shared on a basis of brotherhood which will be according to the need of each, love – not selfish competition – governing the distribution; in which each shall be so disposed to all, that he shall seek forgiveness from God and grant it to his brethren; in which each shall prayerfully seek to shield all from temptation and evil; in which there shall be 'universal righteousness and social justice through the evangel of Christ.'[13]

The fulfilling of this prayer meant the espousal of specific objectives. It was not enough to declare for 'perfect people in a perfect society.'

The specific social objectives of the council were numerous. Its declaration 'for the right of the child to be well born, well developed, well educated' involved a host of proposals which soon became the special work of an offshoot of the council, the Child Welfare Council, under Charlotte Whitton. The Social Service Council not only generally stood for the 'abatement and ultimate abolition of poverty,' but pressed for mothers' pensions, adequate care for dependents, defectives, and delinquents, proper housing and health measures, and a system of social insurance against accidents, sickness, unemployment, and old age. Among its other objectives were more enlightened measures for the 'prevention of crime and the redemption of criminals,' and more adequate recreational facilities.

Although the council did not consider political questions its field, it did have a political attitude. It believed in a democracy in which special privilege was eliminated, in which men and women were equal, and in which the test of all institutions was the degree to which they served the highest good of all the people. It specifically declared itself against the patronage system and against partisan priorities. In brief, it said, 'politics is the science of social welfare.'[14] If there were tension between this last proposition and the normal procedures of democracy, the council seemed unaware of it. On the one hand, it encouraged the application of scientific means to the discovery and solution of problems of social welfare, and, on the other, promoted community organization and decision making. Symbolic of these two emphases were, first, the offer of the Social Service Council to take over the work of the Bureau of Social Research of the three prairie provinces after Woodsworth's dismissal,[15] and second, its campaign following the war for the erection of community

13 1 Nov. 1918   14 SW, 1 Nov. 1918
15 *Minutes*, Annual Meeting, 1918, p. 7, which apparently repeated the offer made a

centres in place of traditional memorials to the fallen. It assumed that there would be no serious disharmony between individual or community desires and the social good as revealed by scientific research. In this, the political attitude of the council was of a piece with the progressive politics of the age.

This is not to say that the Social Service Council was unaware of social conflict. It viewed industrial life as a 'war between two organized camps ... with a third camp of consumers, the public, helplessly but anxiously looking in.'[16] This 'pagan' state of affairs was the result of a competitive industrial system in which machinery was of greater concern than men, for the capitalist had to pay for mechanical replacement while men could be replaced at no cost to him at all. Radical changes were obviously necessary 'in the system, control, and governing principles of industry'[17] before anything resembling a Christian industrial order would be possible.

In addition to social insurance schemes to remove fear of unemployment, illness, and accident from the minds of workers, the spirit and practice of autocracy in industrial organization would have to be eradicated. Employees and the public had a vital stake in every industry. The editor of *Social Welfare* was not convinced that employees had a right to share in the financial management of a plant, but they did 'have a right to share in the operating management, in fixing wages, hours, operating conditions.' But sharing in operating management, of course, meant sharing in financial management if it were to be done responsibly. As a means of securing this 'democratic' management, the council recommended establishment of the joint industrial councils of the Whitley Report in Great Britain. The public interest was best served by the widest possible use of conciliation and arbitration procedures, but the right to strike, 'being the one and only ultimately effective weapon' of the employees, 'must be conserved.' Finally, in this industrial programme, public control of natural resources and ownership of utilities and transportation were to be recovered from the 'highwaymen' who too often in Canada 'have been publicly honoured and their praises loudly sung.'[18]

For the new postwar Canada, then, the Social Service Council proposed a broad progressive programme of social welfare and industrial democracy. It would probably be truer to describe it as liberal rather than socialist reform. Yet it was symptomatic of the leaning of the officers of the council that the first few issues of *Social Welfare* carried detailed and approving accounts of the new programme of the British Labour party. In this they were in the company of J.S. Woodsworth, who

year earlier. If any provincial council was equipped to undertake such a task it was the Manitoba council.

16 sw, 1 Jan. 1919   17 *Ibid.*
18 *Ibid.*, 1 Feb. 1919

admired the 'painstaking preparation, education and planning of the kind advocated by the British gradualists ...'[19] More important, however, was the way the council's programme related to those of the major organizations and churches which comprised it, and from which came all its financial help. Not that the council was careful to defer to the feelings of the churches, for when the editor of *Social Welfare* asked rhetorically on 1 December 1918 whether 'kaiserism' was unknown in Canada, he was prepared to cite the 'domineering attitude of some Church officials' among the several instances constituting the answer to his question.

The smaller nonconformist churches failed to offer any significant programme or prospectus for Canadian society following the war. There were signs, however, that here and there the social gospel was being preached within them. In the Presbyterian and Methodist churches, by contrast, interest in the social gospel was high and rising, and was to issue in comprehensive and advanced statements of their social position. Somewhere between lay the Anglican church.[20]

Concern for social gospel issues was inhibited in the smaller churches by pressures of denominational survival and a congregational type of polity which kept attitudes localized. However, one sign of a vigorous social gospel in Congregationalism in 1918–19 came from A.E. Cooke at First Congregational Church, Vancouver, who tried to persuade both his church and Vancouver socialists of the validity and necessity of the social gospel for the postwar world.[21] Baptist reading on the social gospel in 1918 was heavily padded with reprints in the *Canadian Baptist* from American publications.[22] At McMaster commencement exercises in May 1919, the Dean of the Divinity School at Colgate University, New York, advised students not

---

19 McNaught, *A Prophet in Politics*, p. 95
20 Number of articles pertaining to social gospel concerns:

PUBLICATION	*1918*	*1919*
Christian Guardian (Methodist weekly)	38*	87
Western Methodist Recorder (monthly)	15	11
Presbyterian & Westminster (weekly)	24*	49
Canadian Churchman (Anglican weekly)	13	41
Canadian Baptist (weekly)	31†	13
Canadian Congregationalist (monthly)	1	3
Canadian Disciple (monthly)	1	3

*calculated on one-half year
†largely American contributions

21 *Canadian Congregationalist*, 9 Jan. 1919, p. 7; B.C. *Federationist*, 13 May, 1921
22 See *Canadian Baptist*, 3 Jan. 1918, pp. 3–4; 9 Aug. 1918, p. 3

to be afraid of the modern social movement, because even though some of its representatives might be anti-religious, it was 'born of the Gospel of Christ.'[23] Young American clergy sometimes worked for a period with the Western Baptist Union in particular. One of these who tried to arouse the social passion among his fellows was the Rev. D.R. Sharpe, first as a minister in Edmonton from about 1910 to 1918 and then as the provincial superintendent of the church in Saskatchewan. He found that the persistent attacks of fundamentalists and the failure of liberally minded Baptists to break silence on social issues frustrated his efforts, and in 1924 he returned to the United States. There he later wrote a biography of Walter R. Rauschenbusch, the outstanding American social gospeller.[24]

While there were occasional signs of social gospel impact in the Ontario and Quebec Baptist Convention,[25] there was little official encouragement. For instance, although the Social Service Committee was appointed year after year by the convention, unlike other agencies of the church it was given no definite piece of work to do.[26] If it took the proposal of the Methodist, S.D. Chown, to bring the committee to birth in 1907, it took a Presbyterian, J.G. Shearer, to call the convention's attention to the recent work by the American Baptist, Dr S.Z. Batten, *The Social Task of Christianity*.[27] The Baptist Book Room dutifully secured a supply and displayed it side by side with Conwell's *Acres of Diamonds*![28] Although in the course of the next few years an occasional strong voice, such as that of Dr M.F. McCutcheon of Montreal or of Professor A.L. MacCrimmon at McMaster, was raised on behalf of the social implications of the gospel, the mounting fundamentalist-modernist controversy in the convention kept the proponents of the social gospel at a low level of activity for the subsequent decade.[29]

23 *Ibid.*, 15 May 1919, pp. 2–4

24 See his superintendent's report, *Western Baptist Year Book*, 1920, pp. 64–9. In a letter to the author 22 July 1963, Sharpe stated that these circumstances drove many young Baptists with a social reform outlook from the Canadian church.

25 For instance in sermons of Charles R. Duncan in Ottawa. *Canadian Baptist*, 27 Feb. 1919, p. 2; 3 April 1919, pp. 2–3. See also 'The Present State of Religion,' *ibid.*, 8 Aug. 1918, pp. 3–4

26 The Baptist Convention of Ontario and Quebec, *Baptist Year Book for Ontario and Quebec and Western Canada*, 1920, p. 218

27 *Canadian Baptist*, 13 Feb. 1919, p. 1

28 *Ibid.*, 5 Dec. 1918, p. 16

29 *Ibid.*, 17 May 1923, p. 1; 20 May 1926, p. 1, for articles by McCutcheon and MacCrimmon. The Fundamentalist controversy came to a head at the Ontario and Quebec Convention of Baptists, 12–18 Oct. 1927. See *ibid.*, 20 Oct. 1927

As with the Congregationalists, the chief evidence of the social gospel in the Baptist church in 1918 lay in the West. On the east coast the United Baptist Convention was beginning to awaken to the existence of a social problem,[30] but was not to advance very far in expressing it before 1929. Conversely, by 1918 the social gospel had a decade of history behind it among western Baptists.[31] The Rev. H.C. Speller at Swift Current in 1918, for instance, was a leading figure in the People's Forum and an admirer of D.R. Sharpe.[32] The BC Convention in 1918 heard Dr George I. Webb's address on 'Christianity as a Social Religion,'[33] a term he preferred to 'social service,' believing that the latter had become rather worn with overuse.

While a Baptist like Speller brought to the interpretation of the social gospel the concept of 'the immanence of God in His own world,'[34] Anglicans who became aroused to social questions utilized hierarchical concepts which often seemed the antithesis of the social gospel passion for democracy and brotherhood. Dean L.N. Tucker, for instance, found the lack of the "steadying influence of an upper class' the primary reason for the lack of integrity in American society. Social service agencies, he observed, helped supply this lack.[35]

The year 1918 finally saw a general secretary, Canon Vernon, heading the Anglican Council for Social Service. The first task of the council was to persuade the church at large of the validity of the task it had undertaken. To the extent that this task was done through the Social Service Notes in the *Canadian Churchman* and the *Bulletin* of the council, it was largely the work of Professor H. Michell of Queen's University. One problem that seemed to block the council's propaganda was the difficulty of breaking into or using imaginatively the fixed calendar of worship in the church. Nevertheless, there was a potential dynamo for social reform in the corporate concepts of Anglicanism, as could be seen in the work of Temple and Gore in England. The question in 1918 was whether the Council for Social Service would be able to mobilize the Canadian church in the same way.

The prospect was not altogether bleak. The Bishop of Huron, for instance, in his charge to the Synod of 1918, observed that 'the old individualism is passing away

30 United Baptist Convention, *United Baptist Year Book of the Maritime Provinces of Canada*, 1918, p. 134
31 See *Western Baptist Year Book*, 1908, pp. 117–36
32 *Canadian Baptist*, 21 Feb. 1918, p. 9
33 *Ibid.*, 25 July 1918, p. 15. See also 'The Kingdom of God,' *ibid.*, pp. 2–3, by the Rev. D.J. Rowland, Vancouver
34 *Ibid.*, 21 Feb. 1918, p. 9
35 *Canadian Churchman*, 31 Jan. 1918, p. 68

and a kind of socialism is replacing it. It is our duty to see that the new order, whether called socialism or not, be built up in harmony with Christian ideals.'[36] The occasonal letter from laymen to the *Canadian Churchman* eagerly endorsed the spirit of social change and urged the church to do its prophetic work among and with the forces of change.[37] Such persons were probably pleased to see 'co-partnership in work and profit' endorsed in the 'Social Service News and Notes,' and a 'more brotherly type of religion' and some form of church union proposed.[38] But these things were suggested as part of a campaign to avoid a 'backwash' from the war effort, and to 'preserve social unity.' What would be the reaction of the council and the church, should the backwash come anyway?

The General Synod of the church in September 1918 further spelled out the background of such proposals in a statement which condemned 'the individualistic ideal' as being 'in open conflict with the laws of God and Society,' and rejected the competitive and materialistic spirit of economic life. But the statement made no reference to social alternatives. In fact, it seemed to consider this unimportant, since 'the Church has to do with men rather than institutions, and many of the abuses and evils that grow rank in our midst are the result of false ideals and conceptions of life and society in the minds of men.'[39] Despite the fact that the statement was couched in careful terms, it could provide a basis for a progressive work by the Council for Social Service, interpreted in the more specific programme of the Social Service Council of Canada.

Hard on the heels of the Anglican statement and in the dying days of the war, the Methodist General Conference, meeting in Hamilton, declared its mind on the social and economic goals of the nation. Its call for 'nothing less than a complete social reconstruction' is the most radical statement of social objectives ever delivered by a national church body in Canada. It not only provoked a much more widespread discussion of the social gospel in the church itself and in the press across the nation, but also secured considerable attention abroad. The *Canadian Annual Review* ignored all other church gatherings during the year, but of the Methodist conference stated that 'this meeting was of such general, political, national importance that it must be referred to here ...'[40]

The General Conference had not met since the early days of the war, and al-

36 *Ibid.*, 16 May 1918, p. 312
37 W.F. Clarke, MD, 'The Spirit of Revolution and How to Meet it,' *ibid.*, 13 Feb.
    1918, pp. 102–3; also letter from 'Central Canadian,' 14 Nov. 1918, p. 732
38 *Ibid.*, 21 Nov. 1918, p. 747; 28 Nov. 1918, p. 763
39 SW, 1 May 1919, pp. 185–6   40 CAR, 1918, pp. 602–3

though the tide of progressivism in the church was apparent, its strength had not been tested recently in a national forum, and there was much conservatism in the church at large. The *Hamilton Spectator* listed the greatest questions before the conference: closer co-operation of churches, conservation of food and the rehabilitation of soldiers, the attitude of labour to the church, the rush of the feminist movement, cleansing Canadian political life, the reform of the educational system, and a constructive response to modern thought.[41] Although the *Spectator* was aware of the spirit of modernism and progressivism that would characterize at least the western delegates, it was not convinced that the Methodists would clearly face up to these issues. An Alberta Conference resolution urged the church to shift its theological foundations from metaphysics to the 'spirit and ethics of Jesus,' and asked:

Shall the program of reconstruction we have in view be apocalyptic or developmental? Shall we look for the Lord to come in clouds with a shout and the holy Angels, or shall we assume the responsibility for bringing about our own millennium, to will and to work His good pleasure?[42]

The *Western Methodist Recorder* was not sure that this approach would carry the conference, since 'conservative persons' and 'designing men of the commercial capitalistic class' would attempt to denounce such apparent 'departures from the Old Gospel' and 'prevent the Church's sympathetic [to labour] leadership in the direction of equalizing human conditions ...'[43] In the early days of the conference, such fears were mixed with assurances that the war had dethroned commercialism, and herein lay 'one of the reasons it is going to be easier for the church to do her work.'[44]

The progressives and radicals need not have feared, for they carried the conference, from Chown's opening powerful statement of the social and moral position of Methodism to the radical report of the Committee on the Church in Relation to the War and Patriotism. Delegates for whom the Bland case was still a live issue heard the General Superintendent denounce plutocracy and declare that there was not 'a single instance in the administration of the affairs of Canadian Methodism with which he has been identified in which money has had controlling power.'[45] This statement may have oversimplified the influence of wealth in the church, but

41 *Hamilton Spectator*, 30 Sept. 1918
42 *Ibid.*, 30 Sept. 1918   43 July 1918, p. 8
44 Chief Justice McKeown to a meeting, 2 Oct., *Hamilton Spectator*, 3 Oct. 1918. See also Editorial, *ibid.*, 2 Oct. 1918
45 *Ibid.*, 2 Oct. 1918

the intent was clear, and delegates chose Salem Bland over strong alternates such as Chancellor Bowles of Victoria College as fraternal delegate to the Methodist Episcopal church (South).[46] Conservative leaders in the church were unable to prevent alterations in 'doctrine and discipline' whereby 'conversion' became 'a vital Christian experience,' and the phrase 'witness of the Spirit' was deleted in questions for examining students for ordination. The ecclesiastical *status quo* only barely held the line in having a decision on the ordination of women deferred to the next conference.[47] The crucial questions for the social gospel, however, lay in the reports of the committees of Social Service and Evangelism and the Church in Relation to the War and Patriotism.

In early September the annual meeting of the General Board of Social Service and Evangelism had met to give final consideration to the proposals it would lay before the General Conference. The reports of its several committees combined an assertion of high social objectives, a sense of the complexity of the issues involved, and the use of relevant statistical data. Their work was more detailed than that of the General Conference Committee. However, both the statement of the annual meeting that 'the task of Social Reconstruction should involve the building up of a new social order' whose standard is 'the conservation, development and enrichment of human life' and the board's major specific objectives were reflected in the report of the Conference Committee on Social Service and Evangelism.[48]

This report was essentially the same as the programme of the Social Service Council. It condemned special privilege, autocratic business organization, profiteering, and all unearned wealth. It called for the development of democratic forms of industrial organization which would make labour a co-partner in management, profit, and risk, and at the same time urged the nationalization of natural resources industries, means of communication and transportation, and public utilities. It further recommended such legislative controls on industry as were necessary to secure labour a wage adequate to a reasonable living, business a profit adequate to its continuance, and 'the public all returns in excess of these.' Although the board had urged social insurance for illness, accident, unemployment, mothers, and old age, the conference committee referred only to the last. But its proposed pension was an 'annuity based upon the average earnings of the country, each year of a man's effective life.' The report concluded with an adroit expression of sympathy

46 *Ibid.*, 16 Oct. 1918. Bland's name figured prominently in the newspaper accounts of conference debates.

47 *Ibid.*, 3 Oct. 1918; 18 Oct. 1918

48 UCA, *Minutes,* Annual Meeting of the General Board of Social Service and Evangelism, 3–5 Sept. 1918

for the aims of labour, which could be defended as saying less than it seemed should conservative social critics protest.[49] In summary, the new industrial order contemplated by the committee was to be a mixed economy, with close controls on the private sector. This sector was to be encouraged, by unspecified means, to become more democratically organized so as to engage the abilities of labour in as many aspects of plant operation as possible. Where the economy so organized was unable to meet the needs of all citizens, insurance and welfare provisions were to be undertaken as the responsibility of society.

This Methodist programme was further to the left than that of any party of consequence before the emergence of the CCF in 1933. Its social provisions were more ample than those of the Progressive party elaborated in the 1919 National Farmers' platform, and its industrial provisions regarding national ownership and social controls entered a field hardly touched by the Liberal 'chart' of 1919. However, this was not the report referred to in later months as 'the resolution of the Methodist General Conference,' although it was important that such a document lay in the background. The Army and Navy Board of the church had called for a general conference committee on the church in relation to the war and patriotism. From this apparently unlikely source came the most radical social statement of the conference. It said what the foregoing report had left unsaid. It was, indeed, a manifesto: it nailed the colours to the mast.

This committee's rejection of capitalism was almost complete: 'the present economic system stands revealed as one of the roots of war.' The evangelical emphasis on changing society by changing individual minds or spirits was abandoned in the face of the 'moral perils inherent in the system of production for profits ... The system rather than the individual calls for change.' In a key paragraph, the committee declared that

the triumph of democracy, the demand of the educated workers for human conditions of life, the deep condemnation this war has passed on competitive struggle, the revelation of the superior efficiency of rational organization and co-operation, combine with the undying ethics of Jesus, to demand nothing less than a transference of the whole economic life from a basis of competition and profits to one of co-operation and service.

The committee believed that experience had now proved such a system practicable. As an interim programme it proposed joint industrial councils, which implied full participation of employers and employees in their own separate organizations until co-operative organization and public ownership were attained. Labour seemed

49 *Methodist Journal of Proceedings*, 1918, pp. 341–2

ready for such a development, and the committee called on the national government to enlist the organizational capacity of corporation leadership.

That the church should reject such a policy was inconceivable to the committee, for 'it presupposes, as Jesus did, that the normal human spirit will respond more readily to the call to service than to the lure of private gain.' Further, nothing less than the goal outlined would 'retain for the Church any leadership in the testing period that is upon them.' Since such a reconstruction was a complex task, the committee urged the calling of a national convention of the churches on the subject. It proposed that the church at large become conversant with such documents as the 'report of the United States Commission on Industrial Relations, the Inter-Allied Labor Press' Memorandum on War Aims, the British Labor Party's Programme of the new social order and the British Governmental Commission Reports on Industrial Relations.'[50]

The resolution was tabled in the middle of the conference, and as the days wore on and an influenza epidemic began to thin its numbers, there was some doubt whether the resolution would reach the floor of the conference.[51] When on the last day it did, it was subject to immediate vehement opposition, which faded as discussion progressed. The only amendment which was passed was one changing the word 'revolution' to 'reconstruction' as less liable to misinterpretation. Cyrus W. Birge, a Hamilton manufacturer, was adamant in arguing that the resolution would add to the flames of discontent, but only three others joined him in opposition in the final vote.[52] It was soon to be argued that only a rump conference passed the resolution and that it did not represent the mind of the whole.[53] However, a committee of forty laymen and forty clergymen had considered the main lines of the report and later passed on it. A sub-committee of twenty had done the actual composition under the Hon. W.H. Cushing. It was probably true, however, that some one or two were responsible for the penultimate drafts in committee. The statement was referred to as the 'Bland resolution' at the time,[54] and some years later Bland

---

50 *Ibid.*, pp. 290–3. This was only part of the larger report of the committee. The balance of the report was not controversial and quickly passed the conference. This section was entitled 'Church Leadership in the Nation.'

51 *Hamilton Spectator*, 12 Oct. 1918; 16 Oct. 1918

52 *Ibid.*, 17 Oct. 1918, has a record of the main outline of the debate.

53 Bland Papers, S. Bond to the *Toronto Daily Star*, nd, claimed there were only seventy-four persons present, and went on to attack the resolutions from a very conservative theological standpoint.

54 *Hamilton Spectator*, 12 Oct. 1918

acknowledged that he 'had some little share in the drafting.[55] Ernest Thomas, shortly to become responsible for interpreting the document to the church at large, presented the resolution as secretary of the committee, and probably assisted in preparation of drafts. He later reported that drafting was done 'by such men as Dr Salem Bland, Hugh Dobson, Professor A.J. Irwin, and Dr W.B. Creighton.'[56] However, three further stages of processing prevented arbitrary domination by a few men's ideas.[57] Although the total vote in plenary session was not recorded, an election on the same day involved 231 votes. If the whole conference of 374 had been present it would probably have made little difference to the outcome.[58]

The Methodist statement immediately became the subject of widespread reporting and comment. Some attacks were sharp and from highly placed sources, but deep controversy did not occur until the Winnipeg general strike and the preparations for the round of Methodist conferences in 1919 combined to make the resolution an issue which called for decision.

Some papers, like *The Globe*, simply reported the conference action in detail but without comment.[59] The *Hamilton Spectator* was enthusiastic about this 'clear indication of the trend of thinking men today.'[60] The *Winnipeg Tribune* praised the church's courage in declaring that 'political democracy means little without economic democracy.'[61] The *Grain Grower's Guide* approved the resolution,[62] and the *Vancouver World* believed it to be 'one of the most momentous in Church history in Canada,' linking up 'a great organization to a program of social and economic reform that will take decades to accomplish ...'[63] Not all papers accorded such fulsome praise. One 'prominent paper' charged that the statement 'endorsed the social and industrial system conceived by Marx, Engels and Lassalle, atheists all.' W.B. Creighton, editor of the *Christian Guardian*, replied calmly that the day had passed when that was grounds for libel, and that while some might call it socialism it 'means Christianity in practice.'[64]

Bland himself publicized the statement in reports to the *Guide* and to the *Western*

55 Letter to the editor, *Toronto Daily Star*, 21 March 1931
56 *Western Methodist Recorder*, March 1919, pp. 5–6
57 Chairman of the committee was A. W. Briggs, KC, secretary of the Court of Appeal.
   Another member was Mr J.O. McCarthy, national chairman of the Canadian
   Brotherhood Federation.
58 *Toronto Daily Star*, 9 May 1919, T.A. Moore defending the resolution.
59 17 Oct. 1918   60 18 Oct. 1918
61 Cited in the CG, 6 Nov. 1918, p. 17   62 6 Nov. 1919
63 Cited in the *Western Methodist Recorder*, Oct. 1918, p. 8
64 13 Nov. 1918

Labor News.[65] He had attended the Trades and Labour Congress in Quebec, and reported that among the delegates the conservative-radical ratio was five-to-two, with the bulk of the radicals coming from the West. He thought that at the General Conference the east-west line was not so clear, and the conservatives relatively fewer. Not all who voted for the resolution, he observed, were radical, though he did not say what his criteria were at each gathering. William Irvine considered the church too compromised to be able to lead the new social movement, and put his finger on a major flaw in the statement – its expectation that government might enlist the services of industrial leaders in such a venture: 'The trouble with this is that ... these great leaders and corporations have enlisted the government in their service and it is the duty of Methodist ministers who pass such resolutions to reverse this order.'[66] Irvine, however, considered the conference action a hopeful sign. After a month of press comment, the *Guardian* assessed the resolution to be almost universally and often enthusiastically endorsed.[67] Apparently this was true also of the church press. The *Christian Register* in Boston thought it 'without parallel as a formal religious pronouncement.'[68] And the *New Republic*, 8 February 1919, stated that the resolution placed 'the Canadian Methodist Church, with its million members, in the extreme forefront of the modern democratic movement.'[69]

Methodist church officials and periodicals seemed satisfied with the conference and its aftermath.[70] In December, in the relatively calm aftermath of the conference, a joint executive meeting of the Board of Evangelism and Social Service and the Army and Navy Board reconsidered their reports in an approving spirit, and declared it to be the duty of church and state to find 'a happy mien [*sic*] between Bolshevist ideals and methods and those of autocracy and capital.'[71] But the church was not without its dissenting members. An 'observer' writing in the *Western Methodist Recorder* badly misinterpreted much of the statement, but made the

65 GGG, 6 Nov. 1918, p. 35; *Western Labor News* (WLN), 8 Nov. 1918
66 *Alberta Non-Partisan*, 6 Nov. 1918
67 CG, 27 Nov. 1918   68 Cited in *ibid.*
69 Cited in *ibid.*, 5 March 1919, p. 6
70 See *Western Methodist Recorder*, Nov. 1918, for numerous comments, including S.D. Chown and BC delegates such as Professor A.E. Hetherington, the Rev. Frank Hardy (who commented on the 'representatives of predatory wealth' at the conference 'who were as purple in their wrath as they were impotent in debate'), the Rev. J.H. White (who interestingly observed that radicalism at the beginning soon tempered and the conference as a whole was conservative); and a further list in December.
71 *Minutes*, the joint executive, 10 Dec. 1918

valid point which some, though not necessarily the drafters of the resolution, ignored: 'that a system allows the display of the evil in men's hearts is no necessary condemnation of it.' If there were to be more national control, this critic felt, it should be more theocratic than democratic.[72]

It was not long before the ideals of 'capital' were raised within the Methodist community itself to combat the social declaration of the church. Shortly after the conference, S.R. Parsons, past-president of the Canadian Manufacturers' Association, speaking in Central Methodist Church, Hamilton, initiated a campaign against the resolution. Undoubtedly he spoke for many businessmen when he said that 'while he was willing to take his theology and religious instruction from his "ministerial brethren," he would not accept instruction from them in economics.' In a remarkable piece of self-disclosure, he went on:

Because it had failed to deliver the true gospel the Church had lost the active support of the working masses. Its latest venture into the realm of economics made it probable that it would lose the support of the men of wealth, from whom the Church drew its whole support. Many, many laymen ... were to-day seriously asking, is the Church economically worthwhile.[73]

It would have made little difference to Parsons to be shown the relatively small proportion of Methodist finances the wealthy probably contributed. He believed, like Burke, that equality existed when the man with ten shillings and the man with ten pounds were equally secure in their unequal wealth, and that democracy obtained when 'rich and poor, high and low, strong and weak, learned and unlearned, employer and employed [co-operated] for the benefit of each and all.' Furthermore, it was interference with 'the plan of divine Providence ... through the machinery of the state and in the name of liberty [to] undertake to create an equality between those who are naturally unequal.'[74]

Parsons' views on reconstruction were those of the Canadian Manufacturers' Association and the Canadian Reconstruction Association. Proffers of goodwill to labour and agriculture from these groups were accompanied by adamant refusal to concede either a place of equality in the national system or the structure of industry. They were prepared to accept industrial councils, but in terms of the benevolent autocracy condemned by the Methodist conferences,[75] and without conceding

72 Dec. 1918, pp. 5, 6; Jan. 1919, pp. 7, 8. For replies see March 1919, pp. 5, 6
73 Quoted in GGG, 6 Nov. 1918, Editorial
74 S.R. Parsons, 'Industrial Reconstruction,' sw, 1 April 1919, pp. 151–4
75 See *ibid.*, for an account of Parsons' unilateral approach to the question in his own firm. See also the attitude of the Canadian Manufacturers' Association at its annual convention as reported in the *Hamilton Spectator*, 10 June 1919

effective labour organization beyond the boundaries of the single firm. They were willing to admit the need to humanize industry, but not by any general plans or measures which might protect the workers of marginal industries. No plan, Parsons said, could meet the variety of conditions in different plants. It was then quite easy for him to comment: 'Personally, I am not afraid to trust representatives of our workmen to join in plans of co-operation in the interests of all concerned.'[76] Every source of countervailing power available to labour had been cut!

But were social gospel clergymen trying to teach economics? The *Vancouver World* held that the best retort to Parsons was that they were only trying to teach the manufacturers Christianity.[77] The science of economics concerned not how a thing ought to be done, the *World* suggested, but the actual forces in the economic order. In this sense, the report did not deal with economic man at all, but with the demands of the Christian life and the organization of industry most in accord with its spirit. With similar arguments, T.A. Moore, general secretary of the Board of Evangelism and Social Service, interpreted the Methodist statement to those of Parsons' mind. The church had not identified itself with any detailed theory of economic organization, he said, but had tried to articulate the spiritual dynamic necessary to whatever system replaced the current one.[78] Moore was not simply trying to persuade Parsons, but also to still a mounting newspaper debate between Parsons and Bland, which was to climax in a dramatic confrontation at the Toronto Methodist Conference in June 1919 when it came to consider the General Conference pronouncement.[79]

In April of 1919, the Presbyterian Board of Home Missions and Social Service seemed to be preparing a parallel statement for the coming General Assembly in June. In analysis and proposals, its work followed closely the lines of the Methodist committee report on evangelism and social service. It referred to the serious divisions that had 'developed in the nation with regard to the large questions relating to wealth, industry and commerce,' and delivered the opinion that 'to-day in Canada the only alternatives are revolution or radical reform.'[80] The statement represented an advance, but no sharp break, from previous expressions of the board. The Rev. W.R. Wood, secretary of the Manitoba Grain Growers' Association, thought it 'a stimulating and inspiring manifesto,' but asked whether the church was ready

76 sw, 1 April 1919, pp. 151–4. The editor of the *Presbyterian and Westminster* was quite taken in by this. See 23 Jan. 1919, p. 75
77 10 May 1919, cited in cg, 21 May 1919, p. 2
78 *Toronto Daily Star*, 9 May 1919
79 See below, pp. 123–4, 129–30
80 *Presbyterian and Westminster*, 10 April 1919, p. 351

to stand by the man who in legislature and parliament would 'espouse these objectives and be villified for it.' Did the church realize how much such a programme would require 'wealthy corporations to disgorge?' What did the church have to say to the able young minister who wrote to Wood about his decision to resign from the ministry in June?

Our Church seems to be absolutely in the grip of the big interests ... Several of the old party men here have left the Church because of my active association with the Grain Growers' movement. I feel that I am not leaving the Church. It is a clear case of the Church leaving me.

While it was easy to criticize such remarks, they pointed up the importance of the church meaning what it said. It was not enough, Wood claimed, to permit such men to espouse reform; it was necessary to call them to the 'remaking of our social, political and economic life, until there is no shadow of excuse for any saying the Church was "a capitalistic institution." '[81]

Wood's letter was not only a biting critique of the board's statement, it was also an expression of growing farm radicalism that pointed up the alternatives of 'revolution or radical reform.' As he was writing, the superficial unities of late wartime Canada were in dissolution. The farmers he represented had decided to engage in direct political action to secure the New National Policy, placing the old parties in a still further exposed position. Labour, caught up in the groundswell of industrial unionism, had just precipitated the largest industrial demonstration in Canadian history. Soldiers, in the midst of dfficult personal readjustments, found a nation inadequately prepared for their rehabilitation. Some, bitterly reflecting that 'the War for Christ was over,'[82] began to vent resentment upon recent immigrants and 'Bolshevists' and even to storm factories in efforts to secure the jobs that were their due.[83] Canadian society was in crisis. It was both to meet the problem of an inequitable social order and to avoid the crisis in the making that the bold expressions of the social gospel had been made in 1918 and early 1919. What course would its exponents take with the crisis upon them?

81 *Ibid.*, 8 May 1919, pp. 457–8   82 *The Searchlight*, 13 Aug. 1920, p. 3
83 WLN, 31 Jan. 1919, p. 1

5

Labour's Great Day

While the radical social gospel was winning its victories in the formulation of Protestant social policies in 1918 and early 1919, the radicals were to be found relating themselves ever more closely to their favourite constituencies, the agrarian and the labour movements. J.S. Woodsworth addressed meetings of the Federated Labor party in Vancouver, wrote in the BC *Federationist,* and in the spring of 1919 embarked upon a lecture tour of the prairie region. William Irvine had become editor of the *Alberta Non-Partisan,* the official organ of the Non-Partisan League in Alberta which was to emerge a year later as the *Western Independent* and voice of the United Farmers of Alberta Political Association. Salem Bland, in 1918, had for the past year written a regular column for the *Grain Growers' Guide.* During that summer, together with Henry Wise Wood, he addressed tens of thousands of westerners from the Chautauqua platform. In February 1919 he delivered the key-note address to the annual convention of the Saskatchewan Grain Growers' Association, helping to propel the organization into political action. William Ivens stepped from his Methodist ministry to the high priesthood, as the *Voice* put it,[1] of labour forces at Winnipeg, founding a thriving Labor church in June, and becoming editor of the *Western Labor News* for the Trades and Labor Council. Of all these activities, perhaps Ivens' Labor church symbolized best what the radicals believed themselves to be about, and illustrates most clearly the nexus between the creative figures of Canadian radicalism.

The Canadian Labor churches of 1918–24 were a variant of the Labour churches founded in England in 1890. There they had an early rapid expansion, but by the second decade of the new century were in a state of severe decline, with few left by 1918.[2] The Labour church had been founded to appeal to those with whom the church had lost touch, and had a tendency to become captive to a variety of forms

---

1 21 June 1918, p. 4

2 For a full account, see Summers, 'The Labour Church,' and for a short but substantial chapter, Inglis, *Churches and Working Classes in Victorian England,* chap. 6, 'Labour Churches.'

of contemporary heterodoxy. Similar feelings and ideas pulsed through the British Labour churches and their Canadian successors: that they had a peculiar insight into the implications of primitive Christianity; that a world of justice and brotherhood for which Jesus lived and taught and died was in the making, and that the labour movement was a bearer of this 'will' in history. In many respects, the Labour churches were a modern expression of a subterranean current of belief within Western culture which has often provided a Christian basis of social revolt.[3]

But the Canadian Labor churches had a more particular role in their brief life than was encompassed by the foregoing observations. The sympathetic strikes and labour unrest of 1919 were to act as a catalyst in their development, and for a highly fragmented labour and socialist movement Labor churches in a few centres preserved the memory and something of the practice of the essential unity of those demonstrations of labour revolt. The churches thus prefigured the constellation of forces of a Canadian labour party. At the same time they expressed the religious impulses of the social gospel that had become part of the motivation and mood of the Winnipeg strike and were to remain an inescapable part of subsequent political reform movements on the left during the next generation.

Canadian socialists and labouring people, in reacting to the enterprises of such persons as Bland, Woodsworth, Ivens, and Irvine, often betrayed the large residue of Christian teaching that was a part of the motivation of their own social action. They distinguished between a false and a true Christianity. The former was represented by the institutional church which had formalized and dogmatized the religion of Jesus out of all recognition, and by and large was a tool of the vested interests of society.[4] True Christianity identified itself with the oppressed, as these men were doing. This formula took a Marxist colouring with socialists like Dr W.J. Curry in British Columbia, who saw in the actions of the radical social gospel a sign that the theological wing of the social super-structure was shifting with its economic base. A great 'spiritual earthquake' paralleling the Protestant Reformation was about to occur, which would 'shatter the tomb of theology and result in the real resurrection of Him who has been crucified by the ruling class priesthood for fifteen long centuries.'[5] At the time that Curry was writing, a Labor church was arising out of the ashes of William Ivens' pastorate at McDougall Methodist Church in Winnipeg.

3 Morris, *The Christian Origins of Social Revolt*
4 See, for instance, *The Searchlight* (Calgary), 25 June 1920
5 'Ye Cannot Serve God and Mammon,' B.C. *Federationist*, 12 July 1918. See also above, p. 14 for other expressions of 'true Christianity.' For a recent study revising accepted views as to the relationship of American labour radicalism to its Protestant heritage, see Gutman, 'Protestantism and the American Labor Movement.'

Behind such a development lay a history propitious for the emergence of a Labor church in Winnipeg. In 1910, J.S. Woodsworth had established people's forums, whose blend of education, religion, and entertainment was proven popular in their spread across the nation.[6] He had sometimes referred to these as 'People's Churches.' The power of the forums as a substitute church was attested in at least one community where citizens had issued an ultimatum to four competing churches to unite or face the competition of a People's Forum.[7] Not only Woodsworth, Bland, and Ivens had looked with hope upon the social and spiritual promise of the labour movements, but others such as the Rev. Dr Horace Westwood, minister of the First Unitarian Church, Winnipeg, had for several years urged on labour its religious role. Speaking at the Labor Temple in 1915, Westwood observed that he had 'sometimes been irreverent enough to say that while the church represents religion in institutions, the labour movement represents it in motion.'[8] And on another occasion he asked a labour audience: 'Why not by the sheer weight of your numbers make [the church] the great sword in your hands, [and thus make it] the real dwelling place of the Most High?'[9] That his brand of Christian socialism found favour with Winnipeg socialists was evident in the frequent printing of his sermons in the *Voice* and the decision of that paper in 1917 to publish one of his sermons per month at a subscription cost of a dollar per year.[10] It was not irrelevant that the editor, A.W. Puttee, was a member of Westwood's congregation, many of whom were soon to abandon it for the Labor church.[11]

During these same few years, Winnipeg Social Democrats had shown evidence of desiring a religious form of expression. In December 1916 a Socialist Sunday School was created 'to impart the idealistic and religious conception of our noble cause ... that the kingdom of love and happiness must be set up here on this earth, based on just social and economic conditions ...'[12] Forty students at the first meeting had grown to one hundred by the next May. It was out of these elements of experience with people's forums, social gospel preaching, and religious socialism, that William Ivens forged his Labor church in late June 1918.

6 McNaught, *A Prophet in Politics*, p. 44   7 *Voice*, 21 April 1916
8 *Ibid.*, 1 Sept. 1916, p. 6   9 *Ibid.*, 27 Oct. 1915, p. 5
10 *Voice*, 9 March 1917; for examples, see issues of 12 May 1915, 17 Sept. 1915, 29
    Oct. 1915, 3 Dec. 1915, 2 June 1916, 9 Feb. 1917, 2 March 1917. His sermon
    series 'Prophets of Modern Times' was published in the GGG.
11 The Rev. P.M. Petursson, former minister of the church to the author, 21 July 1970
12 *Ibid.*, 11 Feb. 1916. See Watt, 'The National Policy, the Working Man, and Prole-
    tarian Ideas in Victorian Canada,' pp. 1–26 for a few remarks on millennial social-
    ism in early twentieth-century labour journals.

Ivens' final sermon at McDougall Church, in mid-June, provided the keynote for his new ministry. In effect, he argued, the progress of Christianity had by-passed the church, a development in keeping with the spirit of its founder, Jesus Christ, who could not be orthodox, but was always putting aside old ways and thoughts. The Church's most hopeful fields of endeavour in the modern world were the realms of 'politics, commerce, industrialism, and internationalism,' but so long as it was controlled by men of wealth, 'she will be compelled to refrain from Christianizing the present civilization.' While 'the great need of the hour [was] that the Church herself should be Christian,' it was clear that this would not happen without an infusion from the common people, who in Jesus' time had heard him gladly. The masses were not attending church, said Ivens, but they were still interested in Jesus. The message was clear: only through the common people, the world of labour, would the re-Christianization of the church and the Christianization of society take place.[13]

When the first exciting meeting of the Labor church was held on 30 June at the Labor Temple, some two hundred of those present signed cards declaring: 'I am willing to support an independent and creedless Church based on the Fatherhood of God and the Brotherhood of Man. Its aim shall be the establishment of justice and righteousness among men of all nations.'[14] S.J. Farmer, chairman of the Dominion Labor party in Manitoba and future leader of the CCF in that province, was in the chair. Many who had been attracted by Ivens' preaching and ministry at McDougall Church were undoubtedly present. A committee was formed to tackle the problem of future organization, and the church was on its way. A.W. Puttee, editor of the *Voice*, predicted they had created 'the first purely democratic and distinctly labor church, we think, in existence.'[15] It would be an instrument 'to voice the teachings of Christ as they affect the lives and happiness of the great struggling humanity.'[16]

13 *Voice*, 14 June 1918
14 Provincial Archives of Manitoba, Winnipeg, Ivens' Papers. In the preparation of this chapter, two dissertations have been of general use. Summers, 'The Labour Church,' while primarily a study of the British Labour churches, gathered together some of the material on their Canadian counterparts, and Pratt, 'William Ivens and the Winnipeg Labor Church.' However, this chapter and chapter x are based on a much wider study of Canadian primary sources than either of the foregoing.
15 *Voice*, 5 July 1918. It is intriguing that although many Winnipeg residents of British background, including Ivens, must have known of the British churches, none of the documentary material examined contains the slightest allusion to them.
16 *Ibid.*, 12 July 1918

The Labor church made considerable progress during its first year. By October crowds were being turned away from the Labor Temple, necessitating a move to the Dominion Theatre.[17] Women's Sunday at the church, 12 January, packed the Columbia Theatre.[18] The practice was early established of donating a large proportion of church collections to labour causes.[19] This feature greatly impressed returned soldiers who were given a forum for their complaints and hopes by the church in early February 1919.[20] Their presence in the pulpit marked another policy of the church, its open pulpit. Ivens was, of course, its most common occupant as preacher, speaking on a considerable variety of themes such as divorce, the home, and the problems of religion and the church. Most common were social subjects: The League of Nations, The Immorality of the Profit System, Reconstruction and the Reconstructionists, The Resurrection of Democracy.[21] But other persons frequently supplemented Ivens. Salem Bland delivered the Labour Sunday sermon, September 1918, on 'Labor's Great Day.'[22] In March, William Irvine was the preacher several times. His addresses on 'The Coming Upheaval' were warmly received, while a talk by W.R. Wood, MPP for Beautiful Plains, on 'The Farmer and the Working Man' was apparently too conservative for the audience's taste.[23] Visiting church, labour, and socialist notables were usually asked to say a few words to the church. Although this policy of openness was later to cause misunderstanding, it was not abused by extremists during the first year of the church.

Both the open pulpit and the possibility of its abuse, however, were essential to the religious outlook of Ivens and his followers. Men, Ivens believed, were not only practical, but fundamentally mystical, pondering over creation and destiny and forming philosophies whether they intended to or not. Thus all participated to some degree in the search of the ages for a universal religion, one which could not be expressed in terms of any orthodoxy of creed, since it would need a flexibility accommodating differences of time and place. The churches of the past, he believed, had autocratically demanded absolute obedience on pain of hell, and had

17 WLN, 11 Oct. 1918, p. 1; 15 Nov. 1918, p. 1

18 *Ibid.*, 17 Jan. 1919, p. 1 19 *Ibid.*, 9 Aug. 1918, p. 1

20 *Ibid.*, 14 Feb. 1919, pp. 1, 8

21 *Ibid.*, 9 Aug. 1918, p. 1; 16 Aug. 1918, p. 1; UCA, 'Notes on the Labor Churches,' 'Papers on Methodist Industrial Relations, 1920–2 (hereafter cited as MIR). These notes were compiled from reports of Royal North-West Mounted Police – RCMP secret agents and sent to T.A. Moore for the information of the Methodist Department of Evangelism and Social Service (hereafter cited as ESS).

22 *Alberta Non-Partisan*, 12 Sept. 1918, p. 12

23 'Notes on the Labor Churches'

been dominated by strong central figures. The Labor church could have none of this, but by the dictates of its essential belief must be creedless, allow individual expression of experience and thought, and, dominated by none, give all a 'share in the formulation of and working out of the best conceptions.' Such a democratic expression of universal religion, Ivens felt, was in harmony with the mind of Christ who taught of a God concerned with the problems of his people.[24]

Ivens may not have believed that one man's religious testament was as valuable as any other's, but this was the tendency in his thought. In his rebellion against the authoritarianism of 'dogmatic religion' (which Methodism was not), Ivens' grip on any principle of authority was dangerously weakened. The symbol of the church was an open Bible inside a ring, upon which was inscribed: 'If any man will not work, he shall not eat.'[25] The latter sentiment was laudable, but hardly the basis for a new religious movement. The open Bible would probably not have provided an adequate basis when interpreted by persons who ignored its message of human faithlessness, the scandal of particularity it implied, and who believed the religious consciousness of man to be reliable because God was faithful to his people. Such, however, were the essential religious resources the Labor church brought to its task.

What would have happened to the Labor church had not the Winnipeg General Sympathetic Strike intervened dramatically at the end of a first year of steady growth and accomplishment is a question for which history does not provide an answer. At the end of April 1919, just prior to the strike, a congregational meeting formulated a bold programme of advance. This included not only the establishment of a new church in Weston and a $50,000 building fund, but also proposals for a people's university and a 'progressive convention' in Winnipeg during the following summer.[26] The great strike, however, immediately changed the prospectus of Labor church expansion.

In June 1919 labour unrest in Canada reached a climax. A constellation of factors, negative and positive, combined to produce this result. On the positive side was the progress abroad of labour and radical efforts, and the rapid growth at home of trade union membership during the war, reaching almost 380,000 in 1919. The negative causes of unrest were several, comprising a growing disparity between the cost of living and wages, problems of soldier and economic rehabilitation, continuing reaction to late wartime acts and orders-in-council imposing conscription, tightening censorship, and the apprehension of conscientious objectors. The ban on

24 WLN, 16 Aug. 1918, p. 1   25 CG, 6 Nov. 1918, p. 17
26 WLN, 2 May 1919, p. 1

strikes, imposed in October 1918, left a particularly bitter taste. Strikes had been few during the war, and even conservative commentators and responsible dailies considered the ban unnecessary. Labour had just cause for concern, was in a mood to seek redress, and approached its problems in 1919 in a spirit of aggressive self-confidence.[27]

Canadian labour faced its problems with broken ranks, however, in 1919. Especially in the West a radical form of industrial unionism, the One Big Union (OBU) movement, was consolidating sentiment for a syndicalist programme of direct action. Its success was measured by the impact such views had in a meeting of the Trades and Labor Congress (TLC) held in Quebec in September 1918, attended by Bland, and in the secession of 41,150 workers from the TLC to form the OBU in Canada in 1919.[28] It is significant that the OBU was not responsible for initiating the Winnipeg general strike,[29] and, further, that in its chief centres of activity, Vancouver, Calgary, and Winnipeg, its major organization and influence generally followed, rather than preceded, sympathetic strikes and threats (though never the use) of general strikes.[30] However, it was important that the new idea of the OBU was in the air, exciting the minds of a number of labour leaders over the prospects it seemed to hold for an advance in labour's cause.

The climax of the unrest came in May and June 1919, with the outbreak of the Winnipeg General Sympathetic Strike. By early June strikes in sympathy with the Winnipeg workers were called in Brandon, Calgary, Vancouver, Edmonton, Prince Albert, Regina, and Saskatoon, and partly related strikes were in progress in To-

27 See CAR, 1917, pp. 416ff; *The Globe*, 18 Oct. 1918, p. 8, and 21 Oct. 1918, p. 4; B.C. *Federationist*, 18 Oct. 1918

28 Logan, *Trade Unionism in Canada*, pp. 77, 306

29 This term is a misnomer. The strike officially had none of the purposes of a 'general strike' in the syndicalist (and proper) use of the term. It was rather a general sympathetic strike, which is the term used hereafter to refer to it.

30 The BC Federation of Labor held a referendum in 1917 to secure the mind of the membership on a proposed general strike to protest conscription. See *Voice*, 6 July 1917, p. 3. See also WLN, 25 Oct. 1918, p. 1, for a similar feeling among Winnipeg workers. The Vancouver Federation of Labor used the device for a day-long demonstration over the shooting of 'Ginger' Goodwin, the labour organizer and conscientious objector; the Winnipeg TLC had called a sympathetic strike in May 1918, and twice considered using the weapon again before the big strike of 1919; and in Calgary, Aug. 1918, a sympathetic strike developed in support of striking railway workers.

ronto, Amherst, and Sydney. The walkouts were so widespread that there was some pressure for a dominion strike committee.[31]

The strikers had no pretensions of securing any kind of political or comprehensive industrial control.[32] The fundamental issue was the right of the metal workers to bargain collectively through agents of their choice. Despite assurances to the contrary, three of the largest firms among the Ironmasters persisted in interpreting this demand in the sense that the Labor Council or other outside parties would have to pass on the validity of any contract signed with their employees. The *Free Press*, which otherwise seemed to have a sound view on the question of collective bargaining, also laboured under this misapprehension.[33] The *Western Labor News* went out of its way to affirm the strikers' agreement with the *Free Press* view of legitimate collective bargaining,[34] but the three Ironmasters' firms turned a blind eye to such assurances, hoping, it would seem, to defeat the demand for collective bargaining itself.

Although the major issues seem clear in retrospect, the public statements of strike leaders often appeared to betray grander designs. On 21 May, Ernest Robinson, secretary of the Winnipeg TLC, wrote to Mayor J.H. Gray stating three objectives of the strike to be: 1) recognition by the employers of organized labour through representatives of the unions concerned; 2) recognition of the Building Trades Council and the Metal Trades Council; and 3) reinstatement of all employees on strike.[35] But the previous day he told a mass meeting of strikers: 'We are winning the strike because we are going about it properly. We are out to win what labor produces. We may have to change the system but we will get what we are after.'[36] And on 22 May, the day after the letter, both he and Persident Winning, in public address, presented the broader purpose of cleaning up all the demands of all the unions with all the employers at this one time.[37]

In any case, with 30–35,000 men on strike in sympathy with the Ironworkers, probably representing 100,000 people in Winnipeg alone, alarmists sent up the cry of 'aliens,' 'bolsheviks,' and 'revolution.' The Mayor of the city, who at first had a

---

31 Logan, *Trade Unionism*, p. 318. See also *The Soviet*, 10 June 1919, p. 4, for a doctrinaire Marxist interpretation of this course of events.

32 Masters, *The Winnipeg General Strike*, is the best extensive account of the strike. But see also McNaught, *A Prophet in Politics*, chap. 8, 'The Winnipeg Strike'

33 *Manitoba Free Press*, 28 May 1919, cited in WLN, Special Strike Edition #12, 30 May 1919

34 WLN, Special Strike Edition #12, 30 May 1919

35 *Toronto Daily Star*, 21 May 1919, p. 1

36 *Ibid.*, 20 May 1919, p. 1   37 *Ibid.*, 22 May 1919, p. 1

balanced perspective on the strike, came progressively under the influence of such elements.[38] The latter had early in the strike organized a 'Citizens' Committee of One Thousand,' and became steadily more influential with public authorities at all levels. Although the strikers maintained perfect order on a 'do nothing' policy, the civic administration took advantage of the situation to sever the police union's connections with the organized labour movement. On the Strike Committee's advice, the police, though in favour of a walkout, had stayed on the job and had done a good job of maintaining order. When they refused to sign a new agreement severing their connection with the labour movement, they were fired and replaced with special constables on 11 June. From that date on maintaining civic order became more and more difficult, although the strikers remained unprovocative.[39] On 17 June the federal government, under cover of darkness, arrested ten men – six strike leaders, and, apparently to give credence to charges of alien influence, four persons with alien sounding names – and searched labour headquarters for evidence. On 1 July, a further dominion-wide search occurred with midnight raids by police across the nation. Measures for the suppression of the strike were stepped up following 17 June, and on 25 June the committee sent Manitoba Premier Norris a message that the strike would end the following day.

Undoubtedly the most dramatic event with which the social gospel was associated in Canada was the Winnipeg General Sympathetic Strike of May and June 1919. The leaders of the radical social gospel were all involved, in one way or another, in the strikes of those months.[40] Ivens, in the *Western Labor News* (Winnipeg), followed OBU progress with considerable interest. The paper carried a complete verbatim account of the Western Canada Labor Conference in Calgary in March, whose purpose was to consolidate western labour efforts and where the OBU spirit was very much in evidence.[41] In an article on 9 May 1919 he presented a history of

38 See the copy of Mayor Gray's telegram to the federal government early in the strike, WLN, 4 July 1919, p. 3. See also the account of the confrontation of 'citizens'' representatives and A.J. Andrews, the federal government's agent in the Winnipeg situation, on the one hand, and labour aldermen on the other, at a meeting called by the Mayor (WLN, Special Strike Edition #8, 26 May 1919).

39 See *ibid*., Special Strike Edition #23, 12 June 1919, for first reports of disorder.

40 A closer account than the following of the involvement of Ivens and Woodsworth is to be found in McNaught, *A Prophet in Politics*, pp. 91–131, and in Masters, *The Winnipeg General Strike*.

41 Morton, *Manitoba, A History*, p. 364, says that Ivens and Bland attended the conference. However, the best evidence suggests that Bland was then taking up the

the OBU's rise among unskilled workers in Australia five years earlier. He was obviously aware that, three years before, an OBU general strike in that country had been vigorously suppressed, but when the Edmonton Trades Council expelled locals dominated by the OBU in April 1919, Ivens observed that again that council 'made good its reputation of being the most reactionary of all the labour councils in Western Canada.'[42] Ivens, as a member of the Winnipeg Strike Committee itself, and editor of the *Western Labor News* and the daily Special Strike Edition, was one of the men arrested on 17 June. Woodsworth, who terminated a prairie speaking tour in Winnipeg in early June, took Ivens' place as editor, and was in turn arrested on a charge of seditious libel.[43] Ivens' Labor church virtually became the assembly of the strikers, with huge meetings of 5–10,000 people, the collections from which largely went to the strike fund.[44] As a consequence, the one Labor church soon proliferated to nine, and spread to other centres. Salem Bland, now resident in Toronto, returned to Winnipeg in August to terminate his affairs there, and addressed a mass meeting of the churches in Victoria Park.[45] However, he had also had some association with the strike in Toronto as a speaker at labour meetings at the Labor Temple and in Queen's Park, a fact which helped precipitate a struggle with some of the leaders of his new congregation.[46] A.E. Smith in Brandon openly supported the strikers and shortly established a People's church there. He also seems to have been the editor of *The Confederate*, organ of the Dominion Labor party in Brandon.[47] Although no evidence is at hand, it is difficult to believe that William Irvine in Calgary was not involved in the short-lived strike in that city.

---

duties of his new Toronto charge. Ivens' attendance is possible, but he is not referred to in either the list of accredited delegates or the recorded discussions, nor can one infer his attendance from his editorials.

42 WLN, 2 May 1919, p. 2

43 McNaught, *A Prophet in Politics*, p. 128

44 WLN, Special Strike Edition #3, 20 May 1919; 9 June 1919

45 WLN, 8 Aug. 1919, p. 1. CAR, 1919, p. 461, erroneously reports that in staging the strike Ivens was 'assisted by certain "intellectuals" of the type of Rev. Dr S.G. Bland, who afterwards moved to Toronto.' A.E. Smith, in his autobiography also suggests Bland was in Winnipeg during the strike, addressing a meeting with Smith, see *All My Life*, p. 57. Smith addressed various meetings with Bland at other times, but not during the strike itself.

46 *The Globe*, 12 May 1919; *Hamilton Review*, 18 July 1919. See below, pp. 148–9

47 Summers, 'The Labour Church,' Appendix, p. 380, suggests this, but no perusal of the paper itself confirms it or otherwise names an editor.

There was little in the views of such men, if carefully studied, to warrant the villification they received in the conservative press or their persecution by the government. However, few at the time made such a study, and not many had the relevant information at hand on the occasions when they were pressed for a decision. There was probably adequate evidence to conclude reasonably that the strike was not an effort to topple the Canadian, or even Winnipeg, political structure, but reason was not the order of the day in 1919 in North America. Furthermore, it was difficult to gauge the actual force of syndicalist ideas in the motivation as distinct from declared objectives of the strike. This confusion can be seen in the statements of the radicals of the social gospel who were most directly involved. Ivens has been reported as telling a labour-socialist meeting in February 1919 that to take over an industry it was simply necessary to walk in, tell the owner, 'and it is done.'[48] He was also quoted as proclaiming a soviet rule in Winnipeg early in the strike,[49] and as citing the Methodist call for a 'complete social reconstruction' as justification for overturning the social order.[50]

Such reports emanated from hostile sources. However, although it is impossible to find anything overtly seditious in Ivens' writing, there is little doubt at all that his enthusiasm frequently ran away with his reason. His editing of the Special Strike Edition of the *Western Labor News* was characterized by a light-heartedness, most apparent in his 'strikelets': 'Happy is the strike that the sun shines on.'[51] Such a mood, however, and Ivens' reassurances as to the specific objectives of the strike and his good advice on how the strikers might avoid public disorder, stood at once in a strange harmony and contrast with a millennial optimism regarding the strike and its purposes: 'We have not passed this way before. It is the path of the pioneer that we tread today in the general strike. The new venture has its thrills, its fears, its enthusiasm ... The new harbor of safety can be reached only by a bold sailing into the unknown.'[52] The sympathetic strike seemed a demonstration of the triumph of brotherhood.

In a short time there would be no need to use the weapon of the strike. We shall not need to strike when we own and control industry, – and we wont [*sic*] relinquish the fight until we do control. This is not revolution. The workers are docile, as President

48 CAR, 1919, p. 461
49 *The Citizen* (organ of the anti-strike Citizens' Committee), cited in *Toronto Daily Star*, 21 May 1919, p. 1
50 *Hamilton Herald*, cited by the *Toronto Daily Star*, 22 May 1919, p. 6
51 WLN, Special Strike Edition #2, 19 May 1919
52 *Ibid.*

Winning [of the Winnipeg TLC] has said. But the workers realize their importance and they see no reason why they should not own and enjoy, since they produce all. Today, now their labor power was withdrawn there was no production.[53]

Ivens' views were a heady mixture of prophecy, platform rhetoric, and industrial tactics. Although his remarks may well have been subject to interpretation in terms of a long-term programme aiming at public ownership of industry by constitutional means, they were easy even for the unwilful to interpret in quite other ways.

The public pronouncements of A.E. Smith were afflicted with the same problem. There is very little evidence on which to base an estimate of his views on the sympathetic strike or many other subjects. Politically, he may already have been more radical than Ivens. During the previous summer, when asked to make some impromptu remarks while visiting the Labor church, he had commented that 'the theory of evolution is very comforting, yet the great strides in history had mostly been made by revolution.' Apparently he had begun to feel ill at ease in the church – at least, as he put it: 'When I have to choose between an institution and the cause of humanity, I shall not hesitate to back humanity.' When the Brandon and the Winnipeg sympathetic strikes took place, Smith's support was quite obvious, and expressed in terms not unlike Ivens. 'The sympathetic strike,' he declared, 'was just as religious a movement as a Church revival ...'[54] As with certain remarks of Ivens, Smith's were open to serious misinterpretation by 'outsiders' and to misuse by thoughtless followers.

Woodsworth, like Ivens and Smith, was a supporter of industrial unionism and wrote 'bitingly about Gomperism,' but no evidence prior to the strike indicates that he was a proponent of the general strike or OBU direct action.[55] In British Columbia he seems not to have fallen in with the extreme radicals in the labour movement. In his editorials in the Special Strike Edition following Ivens' arrest, he struck a moderate note, and tried to calm the tempers of returning soldiers who were threatening to take events into their own hands. Behind the issue of the sympathetic strike, he believed, was that of the democratic control of industry. While he looked on the British government proposal of industrial councils with some skepticism, it at least to his mind provided a temporary *modus vivendi*.[56] But these expressions came after the sobering arrest of the strike leaders. In the midst of the strike a somewhat more extreme attitude crept into his writing and speaking. Woodsworth's analysis of the

53 *Ibid.*, Special Strike Edition #3, 20 May 1919
54 *Ibid.*, 9 Aug. 1918, p. 1; Special Strike Edition #26, 15 June 1919
55 McNaught, *A Prophet in Politics*, p. 96
56 *Ibid.*, pp. 126–8

strike in a letter to the *Western Labor News* of 12 June seemed in most respects the work of a moderate. His theme, which had many sound observations about the causes of unrest, was that it was justifiable for the public at large to suffer because it was guilty of the sin of indifference.[57] Like Ivens and Smith, Woodsworth was carried off his feet by what seemed a grand demonstration of brotherhood, which to them was the real religion of Jesus. On 15 June in the Labor church he endorsed the OBU and 'One Big Church' as well, declared old forms of religion inapplicable today, and stated that the 'real test [of true religion] was brotherhood. The one requirement was the forward look.'[58] His later description of the Labor church strike rallies in terms of a religious revival was more than a figure of speech.[59]

It may be that these more rhapsodic and undisciplined comments of Ivens, Smith, and Woodsworth should be judged with the latitude normally given platform oratory. They were statements of consequence, however, since they were not only seized on by hostile parties, but widely disseminated by the Special Strike Edition of the *Labor News* itself. Also, even after allowances are made, such remarks reflected aspects of the motivation of these men which more considered statements might not reveal. At the very least, they must be looked on as commentaries on the mood and hopes which surrounded the specific objectives of the strike. But it is not surprising that, especially outside the major scene of battle, they were often read as more than that, in fact as constituting statements of the immediate objectives themselves. The millennialism of the radical social gospel clearly played a notable role in the strikes of May and June.

The expressions of Bland and Irvine on the sympathetic strike were, by contrast, quite moderate. Bland had expressed his views on this subject in connection with the Winnipeg strike of a year earlier. In brief, he believed that such a strike should be engaged in with great care, and only in defence of a vital principle. It could in many circumstances be an unjust and tyrannous action, but in some cases it might be quite necessary to the maintenance of justice and democracy. If utilized, it could most safely be carried through where labour considered itself in the broadest possible terms and was aware that 'in history [there had been] not yet one class that had the power that did not use it selfishly.'[60] At an address to a labour audience on 11 May 1919, he had questioned the ability of labour to cause a revolution, but, he said, 'they could involve the country in great misery.'[61]

57 Cited in *ibid.*, pp. 115–16
58 WLN, Special Strike Edition # 26, 15 June 1919
59 Woodsworth, *The First Story of the Labor Church*, p. 8
60 Bland Papers, Salem Bland, 'Thoughts About the Strike,' and 'Labor's Great Day'
61 *The Globe*, 12 May 1919

Bland had occasion to speak on the Winnipeg strike itself before the Toronto People's Forum on 25 May 1919, after the Winnipeg strike had been in progress for ten days. At that time he concluded that the strike had driven a lot of people to declare support for collective bargaining, and observed that labour 'had appealed to our sense of justice but had got no response. They assailed our comfort and their wrongs were righted.'[62] On the subject of the syndicalist programme, he did not hesitate to condemn 'immediate seizure [of industry] a dream and an evil dream. [It was] not possible and not just. Neither capitalists nor workers [were] ready. The attempt would result in disaster and set-back for the progress of Labor.' Government would have 'to put down the resulting disorder or abdicate. That is its function. If it misgoverns, of course there will come revolt and sooner or later revolt it cannot put down.' But, although he criticized such recent repressive measures of the government regarding freedom of the press, he did not consider revolution necessary in a democracy.[63]

Later in the year he further elaborated his views. The Carpenters' Unit of the OBU wished him to address the Workers' Educational League, preferably, the communication said, on a subject opposed to OBU principles.[64] In an address to the league on 4 December he undertook a critique of the direct action theory. Many of the foregoing points were reiterated, but in addition he made a strong plea for political action which effectively closed the curtain on at least the more ambitious form of direct industrial action. 'If any class is not strong enough to secure their aims by regular political action, they are not strong enough to realize them permanently by force. If strong enough to win and hold power by force, they are abundantly strong enough to obtain them without force.'[65] Salem Bland may have had deep sympathies with the leadership of the Winnipeg strike, but on the subject of the concept of the general strike his voice was that of reason itself.

Irvine's view of the sympathetic strike was based on the experience of the Calgary strike in August and September 1918 on behalf of the CPR freight handlers. He was impressed by the weakness of labour organization to prosecute such an effort and by the readiness of the rest of the community to close ranks in opposition.[66] Like another writer in his paper he may have had doubts about the value of the sympathetic strike as such, but did not express them. He made no comment about the relatively weak Calgary strike in sympathy with the Winnipeg workers in 1919. In his debates with Wood, which preoccupied him at this time, he obviously believed industrial

62 The quote is from a remark of Dr Jowett, a British nonconformist leader.
63 Bland Papers, MSS, Salem Bland, 'The Outlook for Labor'
64 *Ibid.*, M.D. Armstrong to S.G. Bland, 26 Sept. 1919
65 *Ibid.*, MSS, Salem Bland, Address to the Workers' Educational League
66 *Alberta Non-Partisan*, 16 Nov. 1918

action a more effective tool for labour than for the farmer. But his arguments against it applied equally well to labour: it increasingly disregarded constituted government and finally resulted in the general strike or sabotage, a state Canada seemed close to at that moment.[67] However, he believed the Winnipeg cause a just one. Although he observed that 'Canada has no government,' this was not a result of the labour action so much as the lack of vision of the government and its slavery to moneyed interests. This demonstration of the power of labour seemed to assure Irvine that whatever trials may be ahead, one thing was certain, the coming of a new social order.[68] When news of the breaking of the strike reached Calgary, he commented that 'if ... strikes, the OBU, etc., are dangerous, the government has assuredly created them,' and quoted Ruskin: 'We still crucify our Christs but we have forgotten to crucify our thieves with them.'[69]

The tones of the social gospel radicals who were not directly involved in the strike in Winnipeg were understandably more objective than the impassioned views of Ivens, Woodsworth, and Smith. It was notable, however, that they were all tarred with the same brush in the press campaign which accompanied and followed the strike.

The radical social gospel, which felt itself identified with the strikes of May and June, had ranged in attitude from the millennial optimism of some of Ivens' statements to the sobriety of Bland's reflections. Sometimes their voices were not heard with patience by some of their more radical labour associates. For the most part, they were heard by the rest of the Canadian community only in terms of One Big Union radicalism further distorted by strange fears and ignorance.

The *Hamilton Review* declared that the 'general doctrine expounded by Dr Bland was that all agitators who profess to speak for labor are above the law.' Commenting on an attack by Bland on the extraordinary and dubious treatment of the strike leaders, it added that such measures were necessary because it was the 'first time we have had to deal with Canadians who openly sought to overthrow our entire government and economic system.'[70] The *Toronto Times* noted that Bland was apparently not unfavourable to the OBU 'and the overturning of society by general strikes.'[71] The *Hamilton Spectator*, which had applauded the Methodist resolutions in the previous October, unquestioningly repeated alarmist reports from the United States regarding Bolshevism and bombs.[72] It succumbed to the national hysteria and approved rush legislation at Ottawa to strengthen provisions for de-

---

67 *Ibid.*, 5 June 1919, pp. 5–6
69 *Ibid.*, 7 July 1919, pp. 12–13
71 28 July 1919
72 9 June 1919, 'I.W.W. alleged to have bombs'
68 *Ibid.*, p. 6
70 18 July 1919

porting trouble-makers: 'A general clean-up is long overdue.'[73] The Canadian Manufacturers Association roundly condemned western agitators as men with 'half-baked economic ideas' and declared that 'the sooner the Dominion Government ... placed them where they belong, the better ...'[74] In Winnipeg a vigilante state of mind was evident in the *Telegram* of 20 June 1919, which accused the government of being 'yellow' in releasing the six strike leaders on bail, and urged the 'citizens' to take new resolution. 'They, not the authorities, have won this strike. Let them, therefore, resolve that they, and not the authorities shall dictate the terms of peace.'[75] The ears of many had been stopped that they might not hear!

It was of less significance to the social gospel, however, that conservatives and manufacturing interests were alienated by the strike in Winnipeg, than that it might completely isolate labour from the various bearers of the social gospel, the agrarian movements, the clergy, and the denominational and interdenominational press.

The farmers themselves and the small town population of the West seemed solidly opposed to the strike.[76] The *Guide*, which had championed the identity of interest of farmer and labour and supported collective bargaining, interpreted the strike in terms of a few radical leaders taking advantage of general unrest, and attempting to set up an autocratic government in Winnipeg. It declared the strike a failure because its 'leaders preached the worst doctrines of Bolshevism – confiscation and rule by force.'[77] In September, when Woodsworth requested an interview with the directors of the Saskatchewan Grain Growers' Association as a representative of the Defence Committee of the arrested strike leaders, he was received coolly.[78] In two short years, it seemed, he had lost all his capital with the association. The strike was largely to blame.

However, the situation was more complex than those facts alone indicate. Woodsworth, with Mrs F.J. Dixon, was invited to address a farmers' picnic on 9 July at Watrous, Saskatchewan, and found a 'decidedly encouraging' and sympathetic response.[79] The *Guide* was not deflected from its policy of promoting the identity of farmer and labour interests.[80] It continued Bland's column uninterrupted, and in Ontario, where his chief field of activity now lay, he was *persona grata* to the United Farmers of Ontario.[81] Irvine's paper shortly became the publication of the

73 *Ibid.*, 7 June 1919, Editorial. See cartoon 'The Foreign Agitator in Our Midst,' 13 June 1919

74 *Ibid.*, 13 June 1919

75 Cited in the WLN, Special Strike Edition #32, 23 June 1919

76 See H.D. Ranns report in CG, 4 June 1919, p. 14

77 GGG, 2 July 1919, p. 5   78 *Ibid.*, 19 Sept. 1919

79 WLN, 18 July 1919   80 GGG, 2 July 1919, pp. 5, 70–1

81 See below, pp. 216n, 217

UFA political association and, like Bland, he continued not unsuccessfully his efforts to promote farmer and labour political action. Nevertheless, the task of those of the social gospel striving for farmer-labour co-operation was made much more difficult by the Winnipeg strike and the extreme propaganda surrounding it. Whether the coming months would mitigate or multiply that difficulty only time would tell. In the meantime, the awesome power of united labour – or, as the radicals (and not a few progressives) saw it, the awesome power of sympathy and brotherhood – which only the political power of the state could break, lived vividly in the radicals' minds. This had virtually been for them a religious experience, and the new deity had apparently chosen as its vehicle in the new era the Labor church.

From the first the church was a rallying point for the strikers. Crowds of up to ten thousand gathered in Victoria Park on Sunday afternoons for inspiration to carry on their struggle.[82] The labour millennialism fostered by the church and its ante-cedents became part of the mystique of the strike, and this religious sense of purpose undoubtedly contributed to its high degree of discipline. When the strike ended, one Labor church had grown to eight separate congregations in Winnipeg,[83] and similar churches were in the process of organization in several other centres. The Labor church now had not only a general religious attitude to propagate, but an epic event and martyred leaders to celebrate.

Such a development was evident on the day following the arrest of Ivens and the other strike leaders, when Woodsworth wrote that 'The enemy has enthroned the men they desire to overthrow ... The world has always been compelled to discover the fountains of inspiration and guidance in the strong personalities whom God seemed to have abandoned for the time, but who in reality were being shaped by events into the very scheme of things.'[84] When the Defence Committee drew up its history of the strike, it described Ivens as one 'who loved mankind better than the worn out creeds and rituals of a church which existed only to cover the nakedness of the exploiters of his fellow men. Today he is pastor of the largest church in Winnipeg, with more adherents than any other on the continent ...'[85] Occasionally the ultimate comparison of the strike leaders with Jesus Christ, 'who was one of the best known agitators,' was made.[86]

The religious conceptions of the church were spread by the touring of Ivens,

82 See above, p. 90; also Woodsworth, *The First Story of the Labor Church*, p. 8

83 WLN, Special Strike Edition #31, 21 June 1919. Another congregation was to be added shortly.

84 *Ibid.*, Special Strike Edition #28, 18 June 1919

85 Defence Committee, *The Winnipeg General Sympathetic Strike*, p. 153

86 MIR, 'Notes on the Labor Churches'

Smith, Woodsworth, and others during the fall of 1919 on behalf of the Defence Committee. Labor churches elsewhere took up collections for the saints in Winnipeg, and labour papers reported to readers Ivens' inspiring words as he learned of his conviction and sentence:[87] 'Ideas cannot be crushed; principles never die. When one man falls, the heavier task falls on the shoulders of those who remain free. Let us all be true to God, true to humanity and true to ourselves and all will be well.'[88] Woodsworth was later to describe the experience of the Labor church during the strike in terms of 'the spirit of a great religious revival,'[89] and an experience of 'solidarity and enthusiasm which it will take more than the later divisions to abolish.'[90] It was this religious experience which the augmented church now existed to perpetuate and interpret.

This perpetuation was not an easy task, nor was it simply conservative in its implications. The labour and socialist movements had been deeply divided before the strike. In it they had found a common means of expression. Soon afterward the divisions reappeared. The industrial unionism of the OBU and the conservative craft unionism of the TLC parted company in the course of 1919. There were, further, differences between the Dominion Labor party, largely backed by more orthodox trade unionists, the doctrinaire Socialist Party of Canada, and the Social Democratic party. In the Manitoba provincial elections of 1920 the Dominion Labor party nominated Dixon, Ivens, James, and Tipping; the Socialist Party of Canada, Armstrong, Pritchard, Johns, and Russell; and the Social Democratic party, Queen.[91] That these differences affected the Labor church cannot be doubted. Ivens was relieved of the editorship of the *Western Labor News* in August in a policy dispute with the TLC. In the course of 1920 news of the Labor churches began to appear more often in the OBU *Bulletin* than in the former paper. W.A. Pritchard, who in a Calgary election speech declared that he was running against 'the late Mr. Christ,' obviously had fundamental disagreements with Ivens. Yet all these

87 It was a sentence of one year's confinement in the Stony Mountain penitentiary, meted out to him and R.J. Johns, W.A. Pritchard, John Queen, and George Armstrong (McNaught, *A Prophet in Politics*, p. 136). R.B. Russell had earlier been sentenced to two years for seditious conspiracy; Woodsworth suspended with a 'stay of proceedings' which was never terminated; R.E. Bray was given a sentence of six months.
88 *The Searchlight*, 2 April 1920
89 Woodsworth, *The First Story of the Labor Church*, p. 8
90 Woodsworth to Ivens, 24 April 1921, cited in McNaught, *A Prophet in Politics*, p. 144
91 McNaught, *A Prophet in Politics*, p. 140

men, with the possible exception of Queen, manned the pulpit of the Labor church throughout the next year. The experience of the strike prefigured the unity of working class and socialist movements which they all knew to be necessary, but could not accomplish. The Labor church, in preserving the strike experience, was aiming at accomplishing such unity as a permanent fact of Canadian political life.

It was probably in considerable measure due to the existence of such an agency as the Labor church in Winnipeg that the parties were able to co-operate to the degree that they did in the provincial election of the late spring of 1920. However, that Ivens, Queen, and Armstrong were elected to the provincial legislature while serving prison terms was not simply a testimony to the co-operation perpetuated by the Labor church, and probably more than a rebuke to governmental handling of the strike. Labour's electoral victories have been attributed to a leftward swing in Winnipeg due to the educational efforts of the labour leaders and public reaction to the roughshod methods of the government in breaking the strike and in the conduct of the trials of the strike leaders. However, if the labour vote was 42.5 per cent of the total and 80 per cent of Winnipeg voters placed Dixon's name on their proportional ballots,[92] then this suggests that throughout the strike itself there was indeed a considerable body of opinion behind the clergy of the progressive social gospel who deplored the strike but rejected the charges by which the government broke it.[93] An element of unplanned, but effective, co-operation between the radical and progressive social gospel proponents seemed to be in the background of these electoral victories. Woodsworth still had his contacts with the Methodist Department of Evangelism and Social Service, for early in 1920 he wrote at least one of its staff regarding the defence of the strike leaders. A sympathetic reply came back lamenting the 'veil of ignorant prejudice' on the subject in Toronto, but assuring Woodsworth of assistance in 'awakening the people to a sense of responsibility for what is being done in their name ...'[94] A unity of intention, apparently, could still correlate the activity of these two wings of the social gospel, despite the division over tactics, views of the church, and pacifism.

It was that essential unity on the left that was the theme of Ivens' religio-political addresses during the fall of 1919. A new day was dawning in religion, politics, and industry, and 'we must trek whether we will or no ... In religion we are stepping from a night of superstition into the full blaze of a religion for life, and for men instead of a religion for death and angels. The Labor Church must be the beacon

---

92 *Canadian Forum*, Dec. 1920, cited in McNaught, *A Prophet in Politics*, p. 140
93 See below, pp. 109, 111–13, 114–15, 120–31 *passim*
94 18 Feb. 1920, cited in McNaught, *A Prophet in Politics*, p. 133. What, if anything, was actually done is not known.

that flashes the glad message from city to city until the whole earth is aflame.' This emphasis on the needs and expression of the living was part of political and industrial reforms as well. 'Production for use must replace production for profit before we again cast anchor,' wrote Ivens. 'Some may insist on A.F. of L. procedures, while others talk of Whitley schemes, or Plumb Plans or O.B.U. This is more or less incidental to the great forward movement of the hour; it is ours to think clearly; it is ours to have motives worthy of the hour in which we live ... Turn on the light. Turn on the light. Let every worker do his part and the promise of the dawn will not be in vain.' It is notable that this phrasing of the religious basis and essential unity of the task of the forces of the political left was in a message to the OBU paper in Calgary, *The Searchlight*, on the occasion of its inception on 14 November 1919.

It required more than platform rhetoric, however, to weld the Labor church itself into a unity. The eight branches meeting in St James, West Kildonan, Weston, Fort Rouge, Norwood, Elmwood, Morse Place, and Transcona, had busy programmes, directed by their own committees, with oversight by a central representative executive council. Leadership courses existed in religion and economics, young people's study classes were organized, as were women's guilds, and the beginnings of a Sunday School programme.[95] Members of the church came from all Protestant traditions, and from no tradition; from most socialist traditions, and from a variety of 'labourisms.' The problem of combining such a diversity into meaningful structures and activities was formidable. To resolve the frustrations of the Sunday School staff, torn between the Bible and Marx, for instance, Woodsworth had to devise a programme of study ingeniously combining problems in economic relationships with Christian ethics.[96] It was not possible, of course, to satisfy everyone. Some, like the Baptist Sunday School teacher who had left her church because of criticism of the strikers, returned to their folds dismayed by a constant fare of Labor church criticism of the established denominations.[97] And doctrinaire materialists could hardly remain sympathetic with an organization which, by the spring of 1920, had felt it necessary to elaborate a creed declaring its belief in 'a spiritual interpretation of life.'[98]

95 Salem Bland, 'Church Developments,' GGG, 15 Oct. 1919. Ivens' Papers, Ivens' second anniversary message, 1920. By June 1920 there were two more churches, Central and Sargent Ave. WLN, 11 June 1920, p. 8

96 Woodsworth, *The First Story of the Labor Church*, pp. 10–11

97 I am indebted to the Rev. D.V. Coombs, Regina, for this information concerning a relative's involvement in the Winnipeg Labor church.

98 The new declaration of purpose was as follows:
The Labor church believes in
1/A spiritual interpretation of life

During the late winter of 1919 and the early spring of 1920, Ivens was pre-occupied with the legal defence of himself and the other strike leaders. To Woodsworth, free on a stay of proceedings after 7 March 1920, fell the task of maintaining the Labor church, and from his more disciplined mind was to come the fullest and clearest expression of the large purposes of the 'new Social Gospel,' as he sometimes called the religion of labour for which the new church stood. 'Religion,' said Woodsworth, 'is simply the utmost reach of man – his highest thinking about the deepest things in life.' Yet, 'like all ideas and institutions, [it] is closely related to the every day experience of mankind.' Combining the approaches of historical criticism and progressive theology, he noted the emergence of new religious conceptions with the passage of human development through the hunting, pastoral, agricultural, and handwork ages to the machine age. In each transition, 'the expanding forces of a new period burst the narrow confines of the old creed or institution and express[ed] themselves in new forms.' In particular, each age's conception of God reflected the essential aspect of its stage of economic organization – the 'Great Hunter' or the 'Great Architect.' So the modern machine worker, accepting the world 'more or less [as a] vast machine, with each wheel cogging into the other,' at the same time reflects on it in his 'determination to understand and control the machine.' The worker's conception of God, Woodsworth therefore suggested, was 'this great new Life Force that is pulsating in his own veins and through society.' No more can one conceive of the 'worship of an external Deity.' The new worship will be a 'Spiritual Communion' both experienced and expressed in the co-operation of the common life. The Labor church, then, Woodsworth concluded, reached out to the religion of the future, the outlines of which could already be discerned:

The religion of the future will be (1) PROGRESSIVE – dynamic not static. It will lay no claim to finality but rather be 'going on towards perfection.' (2) it will be SCIENTIFIC in its spirit and methods. The universe will be perceived as one and indivisible, each part in relation to the whole. We shall not be afraid of truth, rather welcoming it remembering that the truth only can make us free. (3) It will be PRACTICAL. Our imme-

    2/A continually developing humanity and religion
    3/The establishment on earth of an era of justice, truth and love
The Labor church stands for
    1/Fellowship: We welcome all men and women irrespective of creed, class or race
    2/Education: We seek to know and spread truth
      We believe that knowledge only can make men free
    3/Inspiration: By association we stimulate one another to nobler thoughts, higher aspiration and truer living.
(Woodsworth, *The First Story of the Labor Church*, p. 16)

diate concern is with this present world rather than with some future life. Right relationships with our fellow men are more important than speculative Orthodoxy or ceremonial conventionality. (4) It will be essentially SOCIAL in character. No man liveth unto himself. The highest individual development can be realized only in a social organization. The emphasis is on social salvation. This involves fraternity and democracy. (5) It will be UNIVERSAL. When we evolve a religion that is big enough and broad enough and loving, it will make a universal appeal.[99]

The emerging religion of labour, as Woodsworth expressed it, was more a reflection of the culture of a Canadian intellectual than of the Canadian worker. It was not so much the product of the worker reflecting on the 'vast machine,' as the heir of social and religious conceptions ranging from the apocalypse of St John to Bergson's creative evolution. It combined elements of Joachim of Floris' thirteenth century conception of a final stage of history in which church and state had withered away[100] with the Bundschuh's messianism of the disinherited,[101] filtered, of course, through the positivism of Auguste Comte and the historical materialism of Karl Marx. In Woodsworth's religion of labour, such conceptions were synthesized in support of the restructuring of Canadian society in the interests of all who laboured, but who had been alienated from the fruits of their labour. The nature of his appeal was manifest when, on his departure from Winnipeg to Vancouver later in 1920, a group from the Labor church wrote: 'You know how to do it, Jim. Make their faces shine as you made ours shine with the beauty of that better day; and we have no fear but that in saving the world for others they will have the best kind of a time and in the best possible way save themselves ...'[102] The religion of labour was revolutionary in implication, not in the immediate political sense as conservatives and Royal North-West Mounted Police agents were wont to believe, but in the ultimate significance it vested in the modern labour movement.

From August 1920 to April 1921 the Winnipeg Labor churches were without their primary leadership. There were other able leaders, however, such as S.J.

99 *Ibid.*, p. 15   100 Löwith, *Meaning in History*, chap. VIII

101 Cohn, *The Pursuit of the Millennium*, pp. 123, 250–1. The whole book, of course, is relevant to the point being made. Cohn's work has significance for more than the study of the origins of totalitarianism. As he says, such ideas 'would have had but little emotional significance if the phantasy of a third and most glorious dispensation had not, over the centuries, entered into the common stock of European social mythology' (p. 101).

102 Woodsworth Papers, Correspondence, II; also cited in McNaught, *A Prophet in Politics*, p. 141

Farmer. Ivens continued to be in contact with the churches throughout his imprisonment, and was satisfied with their progress. Little is known of his prison experience, which began on 6 April 1920. On Easter Sunday the Labor church choir visited the prison and sang in the chapel. Ivens spoke briefly and led in prayer. Shortly afterward he was allowed home under guard to see his ill child just before its death on 26 April; for the funeral, conducted by Woodsworth, thousands of workers spontaneously gathered at Ivens' Inkster Avenue home to accompany the mourners.[103] It must have been a difficult time to be away from his grief-stricken wife, but there were many to rally to her support, and Ivens did not allow himself to become embittered by the experience. On the occasion of the second anniversary of the church, he wrote to the congregations with evident satisfaction at their progress:

Pressed though we have been by governmental, financial and religious opposition; circumscribed as have been our efforts by the lack of adequately prepared speakers; cramped as we have been by the persistent refusal of those in power to accord us places in which to meet, yet our movement has deepened and enlarged itself until today we have our Sunday Schools, our Young People's study classes, our Women's Guilds, and until we have some sixteen Churches situated in four provinces of the Dominion.[104]

Ivens' accomplishments in two years had been remarkable. There was much for him to look forward to upon release the following April. So he was able to counsel members of the Labor church: 'Let there be no regrets. It is the price we pay for progress, and we pay it, since we must, without complaint. Our purpose must be to gain, while here, the strength of mind and body and spirit necessary to carry on more effective work for God and the people, in the future.'[105]

103 WLN, 30 April 1920
104 Ivens' Papers, hymn sheet for the second anniversary of the Labor church, cited in
    Pratt, 'William Ivens,' pp. 50–1, and referred to in WLN, 16 July 1920
105 *Ibid.*

6

Progressives on Trial

While the social gospel had pressed its causes forward on all fronts during 1918 and into 1919, the tide of social unrest had risen around it. The radicals had plunged into the midst of the flood and left their mark even at the height of the crest. The unrest of early 1919, the Winnipeg and related strikes, and the development of Labor churches, called for some church response, and from none more than from the progressive social gospel which, hand in hand with the radicals, had led the Protestant churches to their advanced social declarations of recent months. The best measures of their response lie on the pages of the church journals edited, in many instances, by progressives, and in the many church conferences held at the height of the crisis. Although the evidence by no means lies in one direction, it suggests that Woodsworth was mistaken when, in the aftermath of the Winnipeg strike, he declared that the churches had joined the middle class in opposition to the strike.[1]

1 Woodsworth, *The First Story of the Labor Church*, p. 9. No adequate study of the relation of the churches to the events of May and June has been undertaken. D.C. Masters does not concern himself with the question and McNaught's incidental citations implicitly lump church reaction with that of middle class opposition. His evidence – the diary of the Rev. J. MacLean of Winnipeg, the Manitoba Conference location of Ivens, and a brief quotation from a speech of Dr S.D. Chown – does point to that conclusion (McNaught, *A Prophet in Politics*, pp. 107, 111, 117, 118, 119). The evidence, however, is much more varied and subtle than this suggests, and two of his citations are more equivocal than he allows.

The interpretation of the strike as a class struggle, in which the middle class lined up with the authorities against the workers, has serious weaknesses. In the first place, the theory requires a definition of the classes by which to assess the social division during the strike, but any attempt to apply the definition in a city of 200,000 people, half of whom were directly involved in the families of strikers, would clearly encounter formidable obstacles. It would be likely that many who would normally be described as middle class would be among the strike supporters. In the second place,

The Protestant press revealed virtually the full range of possible reaction to the labour unrest of 1919, from bitter hostility to the Winnipeg strikers and their leaders to almost complete sympathy and support. The standpoints taken are a useful gauge of a sector of the public media, but, more to the point, they provide a measure of the influence of the progressive social gospel in the press of the churches, and one gauge of the reaction of the progressives under pressure. Even the conservative editors help set the progressives in perspective.

It was difficult during the winter and spring for progressive social gospellers in the Protestant press to keep the need for social reform in a proper perspective. This difficulty was caused not simply by the rapid growth of conservative reaction inside and outside the churches to the demands of reform and revolution, but by the complex of attitudes in progressive minds to the components of social change, attitudes which were often held in a state of unresolved tension. That the progressives did not sound an entirely uncertain note, come the great strikes of May and June, was perhaps more to be marvelled at than expected.

Many progressives in supporting recent church resolutions on social policy either did not see the conflict of interest involved in 'democratizing' the operation of industry, or believed that the spirit of 'humanizing' relations had converted employers to new ways. For instance, the editor of the *Presbyterian and Westminster*, who commended the Methodist resolutions, believed, despite S.R. Parsons' attacks on

the theory does not do justice to the position of middle class persons who remained in the middle. In the third place, it assumes that all the issues of the strike were 'working class' issues, whereas there was the cluster of problems associated with soldier rehabilitation, and the technical (and for some, semi-mystical) issue of the sympathetic strike. Since there were workers and socialists who had severe reservations about the latter, others were not necessarily motivated by anti-working class attitudes when they opposed this technique. In the fourth place, the device of class itself levels out distinctions which might be quite important, and ignores the significance of religious conviction as a vital qualifying factor on class position. It is odd that McNaught should ignore this last point, because it was such an important factor in Woodsworth's own case. Church reaction at large evinced all possible types of reaction, but most progressive social gospel clergy remained unpanicked by the Winnipeg strike itself, and were skeptical of the charges which formed the basis of government suppression. That there was class struggle involved in the Winnipeg strike none would deny. That that observation may be a beginning but not the end of analysis, the reaction of the progressive social gospel in the churches may in a small way demonstrate.

them, that as Parsons had proposed an industrial council in his plant, he was in substantial agreement with the intention of the resolution.[2] Seeming to validate such positions was the report of Quaker employers in Great Britain, issued early in 1919. Its proposal of a scheme for the gradual but complete development of industrial democracy was enthusiastically reviewed by the Anglican Council of Social Service and secured a prominent place in the social gospel literature of most of the churches.[3] More acute observers like Ernest Thomas wondered how a programme so socialistic could be proposed in the framework of the present system, but, he optimistically added, it was an 'indication of how far appreciation of real values can carry the Christian employer.'[4]

If employers could be expected to fuse business collectivism and democratic ideals, there was little apparent reason in some minds for concern about the differential in the power relations of labour and capital, and hence for the organization of the former. There were several types of industrial council schemes presuming to harmonize the interests of labour and capital. The key factor in the Methodist proposal of the British Whitley scheme was its implicit recognition of organized labour. Other plans, especially those originating in the United States, were intended to by-pass the unions altogether. The importance of the difference seemed lost on the writer of Social Service News and Notes in the *Canadian Churchman*. That a nine-week strike for union recognition at the Dominion Textile Company, Kingston, was defeated in early February seemed a small matter beside the fact that improvements in working conditions and a system of shop committees was promised.[5] Misreading such developments led to the doubtful conclusion that 'humanity [was at last being placed] before economic abstractions' in management practices.[6]

Labour unrest itself was variously interpreted among those with some concern for industrial questions. Conservative churchmen seemed inclined to attribute unrest to the pressure of material needs and the consequent neglect of spiritual values. Church attention to industrial matters was therefore advocated in order that the church might make good this lack.[7] More constructive and more frequently expressed was the view among progressives that, in addition to the pressure of material circumstances, the labour unrest was due to the appropriation by the masses of the message of Christ. Labour was concerning itself, in other words, with the declaration by Christ of the purpose of his coming – to heal the brokenhearted, to preach good news to the poor, deliverance to the captive, recovery of sight to the blind, and to

2 23 Jan. 1919, p. 75

4 CG, 12 March 1919, pp. 7–8

6 *Ibid.*, 10 April 1919, pp. 234–5

3 *Canadian Churchman*, 13 Feb. 1919, p. 103

5 *Canadian Churchman*, 27 Feb. 1919, p. 133

7 *Canadian Baptist*, 12 Sept. 1919, pp. 2–3

set at liberty the oppressed.[8] Thus it could be said, in a sense, that the risen Christ was in the unrest calling the church to her true function.[9]

This interpretation of labour discontent did not constitute an obligation to endorse either labour's diagnoses of particular problems or the means labour used to secure its ends. W.B. Creighton of the *Christian Guardian* argued that the 'day of the club and bludgeon is gone by,' and deprecated the use of forceful means by capital or labour. Although he always stood for the fair treatment of just demands for adequate conditions, he slighted the possibility that these could be secured in the unequal 'warfare' with capital only by means of the threat or use of force.[10] The more cautious editor of the *Presbyterian and Westminster* observed that a 'minority may have to endure its grievances for a long time before the comfortable majority will come to its rescue.' He warned that if growing unemployment were not solved, and a more equitable distribution of wealth and opportunity created, 'another system will be tried,' but added that public authorities were justified in discouraging other means of change than 'argument and the appeal to reason and kindness.'[11] Few labour unions would limit themselves to such means, but progressives of such views, feeling themselves fair-minded and sympathetic to labour's plight, often resented labour criticism of the churches.[12]

It seemed unlikely, then, that many embracing the social gospel could fully face the realistic observation of Professor R.M. McIver of the University of Toronto that the war had neither brought a new order nor destroyed the old one, and that to establish the new it was necessary to tear down the old.[13] McIver's observation may well have sounded like Bolshevism itself to those who were prone to interpret that creed as a desire for tearing down all that is up, and naïvely to contrast it with 'the cry of Jesus, which is up with all that is down.'[14] The growth of such 'Bolshevism' in Canada seemed attested by a mounting and secretive seditious propaganda filtering through the nation in 1918 and 1919. For instance, anonymous circulars

8 Luke 4:18

9 Editorial, 'I Was Hungry,' CG, 27 Nov. 1918, p. 6

10 *Ibid.*, 5 March 1919, p. 5

11 Editorial, 'The Social Conflict,' 16 Jan. 1919, pp. 55–6

12 H.D. Ranns, 'Saskatchewan Letter,' CG, 7 May 1919, p. 18; *Presbyterian and Westminster*, 22 Aug. 1918, p. 167

13 R.M. McIver, 'The New Social Order,' SW, 1 April 1919, McIver was an occasional contributor to SW and the *Presbyterian and Westminster*.

14 Frank Hardy, 'The Coming Rule of Labor,' *Western Methodist Recorder*, 18 March 1918, p. 4

in Toronto in December 1918 exhorted readers to 'arise and seize what is rightfully yours' and proposed a workers' government for Canada.[15] And in March a manifesto of the 'Provisional Council of Soldiers and Workers Deputies of Canada' was distributed in the city, urging the organization of secret councils.[16] In January and February 1919, two doctrinaire radical socialist publications, *The Red Flag* and *The Soviet*, were initiated in Vancouver and Edmonton respectively.[17] Wartime antipathy to aliens and a pathological fear of 'enemy' propaganda had created a public mind ready to exaggerate such phenomena. The social gospel was not immune.[18] The editor of the *Presbyterian and Westminster* observed that such propaganda would seem absurd 'but for the recent overthrow of Count Karolyi's democratic government in Hungary by a dictatorship of Workers', Peasants' and Soldiers' Councils.'[19] Creighton in the *Guardian* was somewhat more alarmist.[20] Nevertheless, as more adequate reports of the Bolshevik revolution became available they were printed in church papers.[21] And writers in the church publications were usually careful to discriminate between Bolshevism on the one hand and most socialist and labour movements on the other.[22] The secret of Bolshevik strength, they claimed, lay in the legitimacy of the cry for reform. Many might not go as far as Ernest Thomas who, in his usually clear way, presented a picture of 'Rival Tendencies in Labor Movements,' and rejected only the course of syndicalism.[23] But just as most writers were not as logical as Thomas, so local church leaders

15 CG, 4 Dec. 1918, p. 3

16 *Presbyterian and Westminster*, 13 March 1919, pp. 143–4

17 Both papers were less concerned with day-to-day labour problems of Canadian workers than with the course of revolution in Russia, the 'Wrongs of Egyptian Peasants,' problems of American socialism, 'Economic and Menshevik Determinism,' etc. Neither survived the year. Microfilm, Department of Labour Publication

18 *Western Methodist Recorder*, 18 Aug. 1918, p. 8; CG, 25 Sept. 1918, p. 3; 22 Oct. 1918, p. 4

19 27 March, 1919, p. 292

20 4 Dec. 1918, p. 3

21 *Presbyterian and Westminster*, 6 Feb. 1919, pp. 125–6, gives an interpretation of the revolution as 'a baptism of fire that will regenerate' a church that had failed her people.

22 CG, 27 Nov. 1918, p. 5; *Presbyterian and Westminster*, 25 July 1918, p. 75; 9 Jan. 1918, p. 35; *Western Methodist Recorder*, March 1918, p. 4

23 CG, 21 May 1919, p. 11. Such prescriptions as this and the foregoing were not very different from the views, for instance, of William Irvine in *Alberta Non-Partisan*, 15 Jan. 1919, p. 6

across the nation may have been still more confused by the cross-currents of social conflict in which they were expected to interpret and apply church social policy for the reconstruction of Canada.

Despite attempts of the progressive social gospel in the churches to keep the need of reform to the forefront, it held in solution attitudes with regard to employers, labour, unions, social unrest, and conflict which it would obviously be difficult to prevent crystallizing into mutually exclusive compounds with the application of the catalysts of social crisis. In this condition, the progressives of the Protestant press across the nation were confronted with the outbreak of sympathetic strikes in May and June 1919.

Given some of their anxious responses to alarmist reports of the previous months, the progressive position held remarkably firm when faced with events which were more than rumour. Of the eight major Protestant publications, only two took up the more extreme interpretation of events in Winnipeg, and these for diametrically opposed reasons. Granted, two others, the *Canadian Baptist* and the *Canadian Congregationalist*, had nothing to say on the subject, but of the six who did two presented strong cases for the strikers, a third combined opposition to the strike with proposals of socialist reform, and a fourth reluctantly subdued its sympathy after the publication of the government's charges.

If this last pattern of reaction characterized the course of response of many sympathizers during the months of May to July, then Professor H. Michel, the author of Social Service News and Notes in the Anglican *Canadian Churchman*, was their prototype. In mid-May he stated that charges of Sovietism were unfounded and unclear. Although he advocated a more extensive system of collective bargaining, he thought the sympathetic strike was bound to collapse in bitterness because it alienated the rest of the community. The state could not permit disputes to reach such a pitch, but he believed the situation retrievable by a wise government pledged to reform.[24] In the issue of 26 June following the arrest of the strike leaders he argued that a charge of sedition was inapplicable and the 'riots' not worthy of the name. However, in July his final but reluctant word was that society had to defend itself against the mistaken methods of the strike leaders and that the constitution could not 'lightly or violently be set aside.'[25]

The strongest reactions in church publications came from Nova Scotia and British Columbia, respectively, areas where radical labour had made its slightest and its greatest penetration. The *Presbyterian Witness* in Halifax accepted from the beginning the interpretation of the Winnipeg Citizens' Committee, and ful-

24 29 May 1919, p. 344   25 10 July 1919, p. 441

minated against Bolshevism and aliens. It urged deportation, and described the strike as 'more than a hint of the smouldering fires of revolution within large organizations in our Dominion.'[26] Some of the *Witness'* alarming information came from an address by Dr G.C. Pidgeon to church representatives on 9 May on the spread of Bolshevism among foreigners. He referred to 'Ukrainian priests and demagogues' assailing 'British Government and institutions,' and to three aliens facing deportation who had been discovered with incriminating letters, revolvers, part of a German officer's uniform, and Bolshevik literature of a virulent kind.'[27] When a year later 15,000 miners stopped work for a day in protest against the conviction of the Winnipeg strike leaders, the *Witness* approved of the language of a Roman Catholic rector in Cape Breton, who described the protest as one 'in honor of a gang of blackguards, who some time ago in the city of Winnipeg resorted to looting, burning and shedding of blood.' The *Witness* added, 'Let us hope that there were few native born Nova Scotians among the striking miners, last Saturday.'[28] Not wanting a Catholic priest to gain all the glory, a correspondent wrote that Protestant ministers also 'raised a voice in no uncertain sound.'[29] This reaction of the *Witness*, however, came from a part of the nation where the social gospel had made virtually no impact whatsoever.

Quite the reverse was the case of the *Western Methodist Recorder* in Victoria, BC. The editor lumped sympathetic strikers and monied interests together, and declared that neither was worrying about improved welfare of the people as a whole so long as class objectives were gained. The strike in Winnipeg was a carefully planned attempt to establish Soviet government in Canada. It was not, he suggested, an expression of trade unionism, but was rather an example of materialistic socialism attempting to exploit labour organization and labour unrest. The editor's sympathies were apparent in his proposal that trade unions would provide a way out of current problems. He advocated utilizing democratic processes to introduce 'as much sane socialism into our national life as we choose, ... without group dictatorship,'[30] and continued to carry articles urging radical social and economic reform. The *Western Methodist Recorder* was clearly speaking out of its own situation, where doctrinaire socialism and the One Big Union had made the greatest impact to date in Canada. Woodsworth himself felt that, in the British Columbia context, the government's argument about the Winnipeg strikers might have been plausible.[31]

26 24 May 1919, p. 1. See also 31 May 1919, p. 1, and 7 June 1919, p. 1

27 *Ibid.*, 10 May 1919, p. 1   28 *Ibid.*, 8 May 1920, p. 1

29 *Ibid.*, 15 May 1920, p. 5   30 June 1919, p. 8

31 *Toronto Daily Star*, 18 June 1919, p. 1

The Presbyterian and Methodist journals published in Toronto exhibited a similar polarity to the foregoing, with the qualification that the *Presbyterian and Westminster* was normally more sympathetic to social and economic reform than the *Witness*, and the *Christian Guardian* was more sympathetic to the strike and more acute in its analysis than the *Recorder*.

The editor of the *Presbyterian and Westminster* immediately attacked the strike, and was ready to seize on all evidence of 'class autocracy.'[32] He accepted without question the Minister of Labour's analysis of the strike as an attempt by the OBU to break the international unions, and probably an effort to overthrow constitutional government. No criticism was voiced in his editorials of the arrests of the leaders or the continued detention of those guilty only of having alien sounding names. He proposed a strike against strikes, and the 'old infallible cure' of 'the application of the principle of brotherhood.'[33] The occasion drove him to ask 'how much farther may the union principle be carried?' – to the entire union? to associated trades? to all workers in a given community in certain contingencies? He did not consider it necessarily in labour's interest to answer 'yes' to all these positions. 'Too great a collectivism means taking decision out of men's hands to some central body thousands of miles away.'[34] In essentials, the editor's views were comparable to those of his forbear of 1872 on the printers' strike of that year.[35]

The editor of *Social Welfare*, Dr J.G. Shearer, was also a Presbyterian, and a better example of the progressive social gospel in that church than his counterpart of the *Presbyterian and Westminster*. Shearer rejected the notion that 'any so-called "Red Five" of the West definitely planned to set up, at the central span of our transcontinental life, a replica of the Russian Soviet.' He pointed to some loose talk that hardly constituted adequate evidence. Although he rejected the sympathetic strike because it nullified the value of contracts which were at the basis of collective bargaining, he reminded readers that 'this is the one city in Canada where employers have ever used an injunction against their own workmen.' He cited Major Andrews' parliamentary defence of the strike leaders as essentially peaceful men desiring a necessary change. Andrews was Unionist member of Parliament for Centre Winnipeg. Shearer also agreed with such examples of press sanity on the subject as the *Vancouver World* and *Le Monde Ouvrier*, which called for understanding and action on the problems behind the strike. Shearer cautiously gave notice that the industrial union may finally be the 'necessary unit to which collective bar-

32 *Presbyterian and Westminster*, 22 May 1919, p. 497; 29 May 1919, pp. 518–19
33 *Ibid.*, 5 June 1919, pp. 549–50; 26 June 1919, pp. 628–9; 24 July 1919, p. 75
34 *Ibid.*, 5 June 1919, pp. 549–50
35 See above, p. 8; *The Industrial Struggle*, pp. 18–19

gaining shall apply,' but it was a condemnation of Canada 'that the workers had had to resort to wrong tactics to secure a correct principle. It was time to recognize that justifiable unrest existed all through Canadian Labor. We had cried "Wolf! Wolf!" only we had said, "o.b.u.! Bolshevist!" The ruse had worked once, it might be tried a second time, but the third time we should be surrendered to attacking forces.'[36]

W.B. Creighton of the *Christian Guardian* followed the strike with more care and insight than any of the editors of other publications. He immediately expressed awareness that the strike was the most significant in Canadian history, and declared that if the 'economic machine' did not remedy a situation in which increase in the cost of living had outstripped wage increases by eight times in four years, the nation would indeed be in peril from those advocating 'absolute control of all industries.'[37] Throughout the crisis he hued to his own declaration of 28 May:

We desire no patched up industrial peace, nor one that does not rest down solidly upon the bedrock of social justice and equality of opportunity. And we can with greater safety run the risk of prolonging the disorder and unrest than of enforcing an unrighteous peace that cannot last.[38]

The editor contrasted the Minister of Labour's statement on the strike with the obvious facts of labour's self-restraint. Whether this was due to prohibition or to the character of William Ivens, the editor observed, it was the 'most orderly law-abiding and respectable type [of Bolshevism] of which we have ever heard.'[39]

Creighton observed and was prepared to come to terms with the new solidarity of industrial unionism.[40] Although the public was being led to associate Bolshevism with this solidarity, the fact was that Canadian labour was scarcely touched with the taint – 'and the idea of federation of unions will not likely die.'[41] Noting the general opposition to the strike in the parliamentary debate on the subject, the editor observed that 'few had any answer but increased production.'[42] He himself felt the sympathetic strike caused needless suffering, and considered it within the government's power to insist that workers refrain from them, 'but if it does so it were well that it exercise its power also upon the half-dozen or so wealthy men who, by their refusal to agree to collective bargaining, have precipitated these strikes.'[43]

Creighton's position remained consistent and trenchant from the arrests through the trials and their aftermath. When the arrests came, he made several pointed ob-

36 sw, 1 Aug. 1919, pp. 266–70

37 cg, 21 May 1919, p. 3

38 *Ibid.*, 28 May 1919, p. 5

39 *Ibid.*, 4 June 1919, p. 4

40 *Ibid.*, p. 5

41 *Ibid.*, 18 June 1919, p. 4

42 *Ibid.*, 11 June 1919, p. 3

43 *Ibid.*, 4 June 1919, p. 5

servations: first, that the Railway Brotherhood Conciliation Committee in reporting failure laid the blame on the employers; second, that although the latter made
an about-face at that point, their assurances did not satisfy the committee; third,
that in the midst of discussions on the subject the government seized the strike
leaders; and fourth, that the *Manitoba Free Press* had denounced this 'strong-arm
policy of breaking the strike.' The editor concluded with a suspicion that the government had little on which to base its charges, and with a hope that an early trial
would bring all the facts to light.[44] When the prosecution, in the trials the next
spring, rested and carried its case on the basis that a sympathetic strike was insur-
rection, Creighton dissented, pointing to its legality in Great Britain and asking
why in any case it was illegal to aid others secure what one has for oneself.[45] When
one of the strike leaders was refused appeal to the Privy Council on the grounds of
full Canadian authority in interpreting her own laws, the *Guardian's* editor commented that this implied a moral obligation upon Canada to set her own house in
order. It did not augur well to Creighton that the Senate refused to pass a government bill repealing the recent amendment to immigration law permitting the
deportation of British citizens without trial.[46]

Creighton represented the progressive social gospel at its best. If the Protestant
press did not unanimously follow his sympathetic approach to the strike, neither
did it take the course of unqualified opposition. Half of the publications refused to
be panicked by the Citizens' Committee or the government. Regional and denominational differences can be seen in the pattern of reactions in the church press, but
in general, understanding of the strike and a sense of its real purposes was strongest
in the areas and denominations where the social gospel had made its greatest impact. The British Columbia publication, the *Western Methodist Recorder*, was the
major exception, possibly because of the long history of extreme radicalism in the
labour movement there. And in this instance criticism was coupled with an affirma-
tion of socialist objectives. For progressive social gospellers in the church press, the
strike seemed primarily to underline the urgency of the social and industrial reforms
they had embraced. Little outward change appeared in their desire for reform, yet
there was, among a few, some evidence of increased reservation toward the labour
movement which, taken together with the new militance of conservative editors in
opposition to radical labour, made a healing of the breach with the radical social
gospel an unlikely prospect. None of the Protestant publications was an official
spokesman of its church, however. Only the periodically assembled courts of the

44 *Ibid.*, 25 June 1919, p. 4
45 *Ibid.*, 17 March 1920, p. 6
46 *Ibid.*, 28 July 1920, pp. 5–6

churches – the conferences, synods, conventions, unions, councils, and assemblies – could deliver the representative mind of the churches on social as on ecclesiastical issues. Of these there were legion in May and June of 1919.

It was in some ways unfortunate that so many church conferences should have been held coincidentally with the Winnipeg strike. Not only the annual meetings of the Congregational Union and the Presbyterian General Assembly (both national gatherings), but perhaps more important, the annual meetings of the conferences of the Methodist church, were scheduled for late May or June. All these bodies were representative of both clergy and laity. All of them had social declarations of unprecedented scope before them. The events which provided their larger social context could hardly have furthered the balance of reason over unreason in their deliberations.

Among the church conferences of June 1919, none was more crucial for the social gospel than the Manitoba Conference of the Methodist church. Like the other Methodist conferences it had to respond to the new social policy declared in the General Conference resolution of the previous fall. But the conference, meeting in Winnipeg, fell on the few days either side of the arrest of the strike leaders, and it was in this context of unproven but ominous government charges that the resolution had to be debated, that Ivens' application for further leave without station for a year would have to be considered, and that the desire of A.E. Smith to be left free to establish a People's church in Brandon would require decision.

The immediate context of church reactions within which the conference met in Winnipeg is difficult to reconstruct with any certainty. How many ministers, like the Rev. Dr David Christie of Westminster Church, protested the use of the church for a meeting to secure recruits for the special strike police?[47] How many staff members of the church colleges, like Professor W.T. Allison, spoke out in sympathy with the strike?[48] How many like the writer of the 'Manitoba Letter' in the *Christian Guardian* supported labour and had no qualms about strikes but balked at the sympathetic strike and believed the strike leaders simply to have been too radical?[49]

Most congregations apparently were split down the middle, and few ministers referred to the issue from the pulpit. 'Can you wonder,' one writer asked, 'that the average pastor, being human, is struck dumb with perplexity?'[50] Conversely, D.N. McLachlan, secretary of the Department of Social Service of the Presbyterian

47 *The Winnipeg General Sympathetic Strike*, p. 20
48 Report of W.R. Plewman to the *Star*, dateline 30 May 1919
49 CG, 28 May 1919, p. 18; 18 June 1919, p. 13; 16 July 1919, p. 17
50 *Ibid.*, 18 June 1919, p. 13

church stated that a note of moderation sounded from nearly every pulpit, and that it could 'not be charged that the Church was stampeded to one side or the other.' He did not think that the sympathetic strike offered a solution to labour's problems, but he considered their demands just and hoped the employers had learned a lesson.[51] A similar position was taken by Canon J.O. Murray of St John's Cathedral, Winnipeg.[52] Even this brief recital of clerical reactions indicates that by no means all of the clergy of Winnipeg shared the view of the Rev. Dr J. MacLean of one of the Methodist city missions that the strike was an attempted revolution perpetrated by radicals, aliens, and Bolsheviks.[53] And obviously many church members were among the half of the city population involved in the families of strikers. Some Winnipeg Presbyterians, for instance, later read with surprise the observations on their recent affairs by the editor of their church paper, the *Presbyterian and Westminster*.[54] One old subscriber wrote rather warmly to the effect that it was obvious that the outside world had been as shut off from Winnipeg as they had been from the outside, and gave the editor and readers quite a different interpretation of events, endorsing the strike and its objectives.[55] The lines in Winnipeg were not drawn between the churches and the strike, but ran through the middle of the churches. That it would be difficult for the churches as organizations to act in such a situation may well have been due not so much to their domination by one class as to their multi-class character.

In such a context of church division, the decisions of the Manitoba Conference regarding Ivens and Smith seem unusually decisive and unprogressive. Ivens was 'located' forthwith, and he was thus prohibited from practicing as a minister of the church. Smith's request for a year without station was refused. Both cases were appealed. In the first case the grounds were that 'location forthwith' was improper procedure and in the second case that the ministerial session of the conference had no power to alter the decision of the stationing committee, which had agreed to grant Smith's request. The Court of Appeal rejected each argument.[56] As a result of these actions the Labor churches were cut adrift from the church and the breach between the radical and progressive social gospel yawned ominously wider. These decisions may suggest that the Manitoba Conference had become 'even more

51 sw, 1 Aug. 1920, p. 303
52 *Toronto Daily Star*, 16 June 1919, p. 5
53 Reid, McNaught, and Crowe, *A Source Book of Canadian History*, p. 400. Also McNaught, *A Prophet in Politics*, p. 117
54 See above, p. 111
55 Arthur W. Smith to the editor, 24 July 1919, p. 91
56 Papers, Court of Appeal, 1919

cautious and conservative than the Methodist church as a whole.'[57] One single fact forces a closer consideration of the cases of Ivens and Smith in order to separate the elements of progressivism and conservatism in the Manitoba Conference of 1919. Salem Bland, himself favourably disposed to both Ivens and Smith, in making an amendment to the Court of Appeal's report on these cases to the General Conference of 1922, made no criticism of the court decision itself or the action of the conference.[58]

In Smith's case, the stationing committee, after hearing Smith and a deputation from his Brandon church, granted by a two-thirds vote his request for a year without station to do what Ivens had done during the previous year. Although this decision was upset by the ministerial session of conference, it was only by a majority of four votes, thirty-six to thirty-two. This vote was on 18 June, the day after the arrests of the strike leaders. It was also three days after Smith had been quoted in the *Western Labor News* as telling a crowd of eight thousand at the Labor church that it was now next to impossible to preach the genuine gospel of Christ in the churches. Rich men, he said, had threatened to leave the church over the General Conference resolution. 'The sympathetic strike,' in contrast, 'was just as religious a movement as a Church revival.'[59] Two months previously he had given proof of this belief by his active participation in a sympathetic strike in Brandon. Confronted with a refusal of his request, Smith did not wait for the committee to prove to him that he could still preach his understanding of the gospel in the church. He resigned immediately as a minister of the Methodist church.[60]

However, despite the hysteria of the time in Winnipeg, the drastic moves of the government, and Smith's association with the strike, he still had almost half the conference with him. One might argue that these men were in a position to know better than to take the government charges seriously. The simple fact was that even Woodsworth on the day of the arrests would say only that if there were a revolutionary design, he did not believe Ivens to be implicated in it.[61] The Smith case was hardly adequate evidence of an unprogressive conference. Under the circum-

57 McNaught, *A Prophet in Politics*, p. 97

58 *Methodist Journal of Proceedings*, 1922, pp. 152, 335

59 WLN, Special Strike Edition #26, 15 June 1919

60 Papers, Court of Appeal, 1919

61 Interview with W.R. Plewman of the *Toronto Daily Star*, 18 June 1919, p. 1. The *Star* itself which had been sympathetic to the workers' cause, but deplored the strike, commented that the arrests could only be explained 'upon the supposition that evidence not known to the public has come into the possession of the authorities.' *Ibid.*, p. 6

stances, the surprising amount of support for Smith might suggest quite the opposite. Was the Ivens' case a clearer indication one way or the other?

The outcome of William Ivens' case was not propitious from the beginning of the stationing committee's proceedings. Having given him a year to work with the Labor church, the committee did not now consider his request for a further term without station to be accompanied by satisfactory reasons. A committee was struck on 11 June to interview him 'regarding his future relation to the Church.'[62] Apparently this interview took place in a haphazard way in the corridors of the conference church. Of the three men in the committee, one was Dr J. MacLean, chairman of the North Winnipeg district.[63] No record of the interview exists, but when the Rev. J.A. Haw, a member of the stationing committee, happened upon the interview, the Rev. M.C. Flatt, representative of North Winnipeg district on the stationing committee and president of conference that year, was pressing Ivens, asking: 'But do you refuse to take a station?' And Ivens persisted in answering: 'You know, Flatt, I can't take a station.' This was reported as a refusal to the stationing committee by Dr MacLean, and he called for 'location forthwith.' However, if Ivens' reply were not construed as a refusal, it would be necessary to serve notice and wait one year to locate him.[64]

Haw drew attention to the distinction between Ivens' reply and MacLean's report, and interpreted Ivens' inability to accept a station as a matter of conscience regarding what Ivens felt to be his call to minister to labour. Haw secured enough support to have the resolution of the committee altered. But a request was also forwarded from two members calling for the location of Ivens. A move by A.E. Smith and G.L. Waite to lay this latter motion on the table failed and Ivens was located by a vote of fifty-three to sixteen.[65] The vote on Ivens, too, occurred on the day following his arrest, 18 June. There can be no doubt that feelings ran high about this 'self-styled dictator,' Ivens 'the terrible,' as *The Citizen* was wont to call him for his part in the strike.[66]

Although J.A. Haw, in taking Ivens' case to the Court of Appeal, hung his case on the technical question of power to 'locate forthwith,' the bulk of his argument concerned the importance of the church leaving men with specialized callings free to pursue them without removing them from the pale of church discipline. It was

62 Copy of the Minutes of Conference, Papers, Court of Appeal, 1919

63 MacLean was probably author of the diary McNaught cites. See above, pp. 104n, 115

64 *Methodist Doctrine and Discipline*, paragraphs 123 and 124

65 For this account, see John Alfred Haw *versus* the Manitoba Conference, Papers, Court of Appeal, 1919. Also, Minutes of the Stationing Committee, *ibid*.

66 *The Citizen*, 19 May 1919, cited in the *Toronto Daily Star*, 20 May 1919, p. 1

a most impressive document he laid before the court in Ivens' defence. However, Haw's argument seemed to allow no place for the church to recall such men. It proposed to keep them within church discipline, but at the same time seemed to free them from the discipline as it existed without providing any other guidelines except the individual conscience of the men concerned. Further, Haw did not argue the question of Ivens' suitability for his self-appointed ministry on other grounds than the strength of Ivens' own feelings and the fact that large numbers had attached themselves to his Labor church. It could very strongly be argued that in so sensitive a ministry, Ivens was a most injudicious person. More important, it could be reasonably asked whether Ivens was performing a specialized ministry for the Methodist church, or whether for him labour had not virtually become the church – the bearer of religious truth to society. Ivens was obviously a problem quite apart from the issues of whether the church should take a progressive or radical stance in social reform. Not to recognize that fact is to distort the significance of his location by the conference. In all probability similar factors would have come into play shortly with A.E. Smith as well. There was, however, a personal injustice, as the *Guardian* observed, in the coincidence of the 'location' of Ivens with his arrest.[67] Knowing the height of feeling toward him, the conference should have postponed the case.

Haw had declared in his defence that 'William Ivens is not on trial. But the Manitoba Conference is on trial; and the whole character of Methodism is on trial ...'[68] In fact, all three were on trial throughout this crisis. Like the Smith case, that of Ivens does not in itself prove that the once progressive Manitoba Conference had become conservative. Undoubtedly it was shaken by the events which swirled about it in June. Never had it passed judgment on, let alone experienced, an event like the Winnipeg strike. It is significant that the conference in no way repudiated the striking workers as such.

When the Manitoba Conference came to declare itself on social issues, it did not sound like an unprogressive body. It stated that the aspirations of labour for justice were sound, and that the principles of collective bargaining must be conceded. It recommended the adoption of the labour programme of the peace conference, which was a progressive manifesto. It approved the formation of national and provincial industrial councils in addition to local shop and works committees. It confined itself to commending the study of the General Conference reports. On the

67 CG, 9 July 1919, pp. 22f. This was the comment of the Manitoba reporter to the
   Guardian.
68 Papers, Court of Appeal, 1919

subject of the strike itself, it took an uninvolved viewpoint, sympathizing with the public regardless of party and regretting that both parties could find 'no better way ... to settle grievances.' It urged constitutional and evolutionary methods upon all desiring reform. And the conference, in an attempt to counter the false implication of aliens in the so-called conspiracy against the government, recorded its appreciation of the presence of 'peace-loving, loyal and industrious non-English citizens,' and deprecated 'any attempt ... to place them in a false position in the public mind.'[69] The Evangelism and Social Service Committee had lost little of its enthusiasm for reform and the optimistic theology underlying it: 'We recognize that the Spirit of God is abroad in the world in the ever-expanding passion for the service of humanity that is manifesting itself in almost every phase of world activity.'[70] This declaration was certainly in the tradition of the General Conference resolution.

That the conference decisions led to the further loss of radical proponents of the social gospel by the Methodist church in the persons of Ivens and Smith was both unfortunate and in its own way tragic, but their departure was not a simple measure of the progressiveness or otherwise of the conference or the church concerned. Many of the social objectives for which these men hoped were in fact being ever more widely espoused in the churches. That the church itself was not an agency for directly carrying out these objectives, none should have known better than they. However ironic it may seem, it may well be that their departure from the church was directly related to growing sensitivity in the church to the claims of the social gospel, rather than to growing conservatism. For persons like Ivens and Smith, deeper involvement in direct action and adoption of a kind of millennial social hope seemed to be their way of resolving the conflicts engendered or heightened in them as the social gospel moved the church further into the field of battle for industrial democracy.

In any case, their separation left the relationship of the radical social gospel to the church in a still more perilous state. They themselves considered their recent fate a further proof of the apostasy of the church. This feeling was echoed by such OBU papers as the Calgary *Searchlight*, which considered that the Methodist resolution 'a program of social and economic reform as good as anything proposed to date ... has vanished. It is numbered among forgotten things,' but Ivens was still 'preaching trumpet-tongued against injustice.'[71]

69 MIR, Reprint of the Report of the Evangelism and Social Service Committee
70 *Ibid.*   71 11 June 1920, p. 4

7

Commitments and Reservations

None of the other church conferences in June 1919 was as delicately situated as that of the Manitoba Methodist Conference. None involved similar confrontations with strike leaders and Labor church organizers who had sprouted in their midst. All, however, were under the pressure of the ominous and confusing events of that month. If the issues were slightly more abstract for many of the conferences, they did not necessarily issue in less dramatic debate. The Presbyterian General Assembly and the Montreal and Toronto Methodist conferences were occasions of intense encounters. When the sound and fury had died and social service leaders in the churches tallied their gains and losses, they were, on the whole, more than satisfied. There were those among the radical social gospel who could be found agreeing with them.

The Congregational Union, just beginning to consider social questions a responsibility, received an unprecedented eight-page report from its Social Service Committee which, along with a consideration of prohibition, immigration, and social welfare provisions, had a moderate statement on the Winnipeg strike. It had no specific recommendations, but expressed the hope that the Royal Commission on Industrial Relations, then sitting, would provide in its report a basis for the solution of industrial problems.[1]

That the severe unrest of 1919 did not inhibit the development of Congregationalist concern for social questions was apparent in a more extensive report a year later which observed that among Congregationalists 'the new thing is the social application of their religious life.' A minister was no longer considered a 'safe man' because he discarded all interest in social matters. The Social Service Committee approved the fact that the entire programme of the Toronto General Ministerial Association had been devoted throughout 1919 and 1920 to the discussion of social issues. Although the union continued to express a rather restricted form of the

1 Congregational Church, Canada, *The Canadian Congregational Year Book*, 1919–20, pp. 25–30

social gospel, its development was, if anything, stimulated rather than inhibited by the social unrest of the time.[2]

The press took scant notice of the Congregational meeting, and little more of the Presbyterian assembly. In the latter case, preoccupation with the national crisis obscured a particularly thoughtful resolution on social unrest. The retiring moderator of the assembly, in his opening sermon, had exhorted Presbyterian clergy to 'preach ... the Lordship of Christ ... Preach the personal Christ' amid the 'muttering undertones' and 'piercing cries ... demanding better conditions, changes and readjustments,'[3] but the social service department did not consider that this exhausted the mandate of the gospel or the content of its message. Not only did it have a progressive social programme to lay before the assembly, but also a notable manifesto on current conditions. Early in the proceedings the secretary of the department, D.N. McLachlan, declared the 'present unrest [to be] a healthy sign that the industrial classes were awakening and trying to find their place in the world.'[4] That not all those on the Board of Home Missions and Social Service agreed with him, however, was implied in a resolution on repatriation, which congratulated 'the great body of our returned soldiers in throwing their influence into the scale in favour of the maintenance of law and order, recently menaced by revolutionary agitators.'[5] When the resolution on social unrest was brought before the assembly, these two approaches to the question were put to the test.

The resolution was an expression of the McLachlan position. It interpreted the current unrest 'a belated protest against injustices that have been tolerated in our social system.' It asserted that industry existed primarily for service, and that this

---

2 *Ibid.*, 1920–1, pp. 22–7. The same could be said of the Society of Friends, which in 1916 broadened the scope of its Temperance Committee to include social reform, and showed increasing interest in social issues until 1924, only withdrawing in the face of the prohibition crisis. No critical debates on social problems marked the yearly meetings of the Society, and sometimes the committee chairman observed that, as a small, largely rural body, it had little scope for action. However, the Friends were aware of their heritage, and under the Rev. Elam Henderson in 1921 and 1924, after the crisis of 1919, the committee spoke unmistakably in social gospel accents for the first time, calling the Society 'to strive to change the retarding environment and to reconstruct the social organism' (*Minutes of Canada Yearly Meeting of the Society of Friends*, 1924, p. 21; see also 1916, p. 5; 1917, p. 9; 1921, p. 5; and 1926, p. 14).

3 *Hamilton Spectator*, 5 June 1919

4 *Ibid.*, 6 June 1919

5 *Presbyterian Acts and Proceedings*, 1919, p. 2659

was a joint obligation of capital and labour. Both this fact and human dignity required a proper share by labour in the control of industry and an equitable reward. In addition, the resolution proposed a broad programme of insurance and improved conditions of labour. It stated its sympathy with labour's efforts, and acknowledged their fundamental right to organize and to bargain through representatives of their own choosing. It reminded organized labour that it was only one part of the world's workers and that the success of their cause depended on winning the sympathy of the people as a whole. On the subject of class and 'group' organization, it stated that while this might be necessary for protection, a factious spirit could be avoided only by placing the common good above their particular aims.[6]

Although some, like Dr W.T. Herridge, wished for a shorter resolution with a greater spiritual emphasis and a stress upon the harmonious interests of capital and labour, the attack from those to the left of the position of the resolution was so strong that Professor Jordon of Queen's University had to defend it from being branded a capitalistic manifesto. The Rev. R.M. Hamilton of Brockville sensed a discrimination against the workers; Dr S. Banks Nelson of Hamilton felt that it treated capital too gently, but that it would at last 'give a tongue to the ministers'; the Rev. J.J.L. Gourlay thought that it reflected the view of some who refused 'to come up close to the case of the poor today'; the Rev. James Savage of Brandon was provoked to what the *Spectator* described as 'a flood of utterances of a highly socialistic nature'; others, like Andrew Roddan of Winnipeg, J.R. Craig of Vancouver, and Dr A.O. McCrae of Calgary, not only were strongly critical of capital, but of past government and church action as well.[7] Apparently this discussion so embarrassed the conservative *Presbyterian Witness* in Halifax that it reported it as

a discussion which, in the interests of the dignity of the Assembly, one must refrain from reporting at length. A long pent up flood of shallow socialism was let loose on the Assembly, which, if it did not startle, at least shamed us for a while.[8]

A committee which was struck to alter the resolution made few changes in it, and after the failure of a motion from more conservative members calling for a new committee and resolution, the original resolution was passed on 11 June.

Since both the Congregational and the Presbyterian meetings took place in Hamilton, the *Hamilton Spectator* was in a good position to observe the mood of

6 *Ibid.*, pp. 2657–9
7 *Hamilton Spectator*, 11 and 12 June 1919; *Presbyterian and Westminster*, 19 June
   1919, pp. 606–7
8 21 June 1919, p. 5

both. 'Nowhere,' it editorialized, 'is this tendency [of reform] of modern times more conspicuous than in the Churches.'[9] However, on the Presbyterian resolution it commented that it was the duty of the church to 'see that its charters are carried out.' Otherwise, the workers would be again left 'to their own devices, to struggle out, unaided, their salvation for themselves,' and the same troubles churchmen deplored would continue to spring up.[10] Such paternalism had not characterized the Presbyterian resolution, but it was true that action was necessary. Here was a fundamental problem of the social gospel. In the strategy of church committees and conferences, it had captured the centres of social action in church structures, only to see its efforts dissipated in the business of local churches. Like Sysiphus, it continually rolled its stone to the summit of church policy, only to have it plummet again and become obscured in the underbrush in the valleys of church life.

The Methodist Board of Evangelism and Social Service, having successfully carried out its summit encounter the year before, was in June 1919 engaged in the second-ary level of that operation. Although some of the Methodist proponents of the social gospel felt in mid-winter that they had lost their Sysiphean stone,[11] a debate in the press over their resolutions marked the approaches to the conferences at which the new statements of social policy would be considered. This debate was largely be-tween S.R. Parsons, past-president of the Canadian Manufacturers' Association, and Salem Bland.[12] In considerable measure it was provoked by papers hungry for controversy. The conservative Toronto *Evening Telegram* cynically observed that 'the Church that frowned upon the commercial and industrial greed favored by Mr S.R. Parsons, would be no more false to its mission than the Church that fawned upon the socialistic and agrarian greed favored by Rev. S.G. Bland.'[13] In contrast, the *Vancouver World* took the part of men like Bland who were, it said, bringing to industrial questions 'a dangerously significant point of view, namely, that of humanizing it, even Christianizing it. That point of view is simply that man is more than meat and human welfare than the manufacture of much raiment.'[14]

9 7 June 1919

10 12 June 1919

11 *Western Methodist Recorder*, March 1919, pp. 4, 5, and 8

12 Also see above, pp. 76, 78–9

13 5 May 1919; see also the *Toronto Daily Star*, 29 April 1919; 15 May 1919. This de-bate also reached the smaller papers of the province. See *The Packet* (Orillia), 8 May 1919

14 10 May 1919, cited in CG, 21 May 1919, p. 2

When Bland later interpreted the Methodist position to the Industrial Relations Commission, both the *Star* and the *Globe* reporters considered it an outstanding presentation.[15] C.H. Huestis, secretary of the Lord's Day Alliance and a man of considerable intellect, wrote a hard hitting attack on Parsons' position[16] – which often seemed to shift from one misunderstanding to another. When Parsons protested that the only alternative to a 'no-profit system of business' was Russian communism, the editor of the *Guardian* sputtered in exasperation that no one 'not even that consummately stupid body the Methodist General Conference' had suggested that a business could be run without profit. But 'we suppose it is useless to try to explain the situation over again.'[17]

By June, as a consequence of this press debate, not only was the public well aware of the Methodist resolution, but the Methodists had been the more stimulated to marshal their thoughts pro and con. Vigorous debate at the conference indicated that the church was not of one mind. The *Hamilton Spectator* commented on the disputation and suggested that the Methodists were 'apologizing for their vision,' and were 'not quite sure, apparently, what they really meant themselves, and are frightened at their hasty zeal' in making radical proposals for social reconstruction a year earlier.[18]

The leadership of the church was aware of what lay ahead in interpreting the General Conference resolution. This resolution had now become well known and in demand from churches of a large number of nations.[19] Chown toured the conferences giving a series of masterful speeches upon present discontents and the role of the church. At some of the conferences, Ernest Thomas was able to fulfil his role as interpreter of the resolution to the church at large. When the evangelism and social service staff tallied the results of their engagements, they did not believe they had met with a single defeat, and Chown observed to the press that all conferences had enthusiastically endorsed the resolution once it was explained to them.[20]

However, if there were no defeats, there were uncertain victories in the records. At the London Conference there was obvious 'need for light on the whole subject,' and the General Conference resolution was not so much commended as passed on

15 *The Globe*, 29 May 1919; *Toronto Daily Star*, 29 May 1919

16 CG, 28 May 1919, pp. 15–16   17 4 June 1919, p. 2

18 7 June 1919

19 Requests had come from a dozen nations, CG, 17 July 1919, p. 7, and by 1922 from almost twenty according to T.A. Moore in the *Western Methodist Recorder*, March 1922, p. 3.

20 Interview with Dr Chown in *The Daily News* (St John's), 2 July 1919

to local churches to be considered.[21] The uncertainty of the New Brunswick Conference was apparent in the request that the ministers interpret 'new viewpoints not yet familiar to us.' The Nova Scotia and Bay of Quinte conferences were more progressive than might have been expected, but stood with the Hamilton Conference one step back from the resolution, endorsing its intent, supporting collective bargaining and joint management, and condemning profiteering and strikes alike. Admittedly these conference decisions were not defeats, but they may be considered victories only in that in most cases they moved the conferences concerned a little closer to the position of the General Conference resolution of 1918.

Only the three western-most conferences registered unqualified support for the resolution at its crucial point – a call for an early actual change in the present economic system.[22] The Alberta Conference called for this reconstruction of the economic order to take place as rapidly as possible, and considered the current unrest to be the birth pangs of the new co-operative order. Of all the reports, that of the Saskatchewan committee was perhaps most thorough and thoughtful. It was optimistic that business and labour meant the same thing in their references to democratizing and humanizing industry, but it called the church to champion the weaker party. It called for a new social order brought in by orderly means, and warned that 'disorderly and unthinking men can turn any good social order into confusion.' It emphasized the fact that the General Conference resolution did not demand the elimination of profit, but of private profit, and declared that benefits to the poorest should be the first charge on production. With regard to collective bargaining it proposed that, however carried out, it should be between co-ordinate units of organization and power. Finally, regarding the right to strike, the committee offered a combination of three points seldom seen in church social literature of the time: first, that when constitutional means should fail to resolve a dispute over a vital matter, both parties were entitled to 'extraconstitutional organization' (a phrase that was not further defined); second, that no party could afford to undermine the authority of clear agreements, yet any worker risking his livelihood for righting injustice to another would commit an act of Christian sacrifice; and third, that none should be robbed of the right to make an effective protest against injustice. The Saskatchewan committee's report was obviously marked by flashes of social radicalism and a deep concern for the requirements of justice.

21 CG, 25 June 1919, p. 25. Also MIR, marked reprints of Conference Evangelism and Social Service Committee reports. Unless otherwise noted the following observations derive from these reprints.

22 The Manitoba Conference is dealt with separately. See above, pp. 118–19

It is perhaps not surprising that the most heated encounters over the General Conference resolution took place in the Montreal and Toronto conferences. Here were concentrated the headquarters of the commercial and industrial systems most threatened by the social objectives of that resolution. In Montreal the press reacted so violently to Ernest Thomas' interpretations of the General Conference statements on social policy that the Hon. E.J. Davies, a member of the Army and Navy Board of the church, indignantly urged T.A. Moore to call a meeting of the board to review Thomas' appointment.[23] Moore wired the conference President to learn more about the content of the press reports and of Thomas' addresses, and at the same time advised Thomas of the influence of the reports 'upon many of our people in Toronto.'[24] Upon consulting with Thomas on his return, Moore was satisfied that the press reports had been seriously garbled and that no reference direct or indirect had been made by Thomas to the strike situation in Toronto or Winnipeg, or to any of the issues in dispute. However, Thomas gave much information about western conditions and described the intellectual and religious standards of labour leaders in a masterly, restrained, and unprovocative way. The Laymen's Association had been most appreciative of his address, describing it as 'certainly a revelation to most of us.'[25] Moore wrote a letter to this effect to Davies, and promised to call a meeting of the board upon Dr Chown's return. But Davies was apparently satisfied that his alarm had been for nought. At the board's executive meeting on 15 July no mention of a review of Thomas' appointment was recorded in the minutes.[26]

It would have been difficult indeed for Davies to have secured the resignation or dismissal of Ernest Thomas. Both Chown and Moore were aware of his 'outstanding ability and social sympathies.'[27] In all probability, his was the finest mind that was to do the social gospel service in Canada. He had come from England after a short period of work with Hugh Price Hughes' London Mission. After studying at McGill and Queen's, he served in Regina and then Vancouver. Both balanced and forceful, he brought to the social gospel a sound training in economics and an ability to restate old truths in new terms, without falling into the perils of the 'New Theology.' At the same time, in his belief that 'the religious man's problem has ever

23 MIR, T. Albert Moore to the Hon. E.J. Davies, 3 June 1919
24 *Ibid.*
25 Whether correct or not, *The Globe*'s report of 30 May 1919 stated that he had felt workers' demands were justified, declared eastern papers misrepresented western labour, and stated that there was no pro-Germanism or Bolshevism among labour leaders. The account does not refer to any remarks specifically on the strikes.
26 UCA, The Methodist Army and Navy Board, minutes of the executive, 15 July 1919
27 Interview with Dr Chown, *The Daily News* (St John's), 2 July 1919

been how to disentangle himself from the mechanics of religion,' he possessed a profound understanding of both the 'churchbound' social gospellers and those whose rebellion against 'Churchianity' was probably part of their reason for immersing themselves in the secular agencies of their social crusade.[28] Before he left Vancouver for a special post with the Army and Navy Board, his sermon on social change and the role of labour in postwar Canada had earned him both praise and a warning from local socialists: praise that he was 'the third minister in Canada who has a real social vision in line with true Christianity,' and a warning that he might also be the third to be scourged for his temerity.[29] That the warning was not followed by the actuality was an indication of the way in which radicals exaggerated a chronic condition in the church, of which the irritation of the Hon. E.J. Davies was a sign.

Despite the efforts of Thomas at Montreal, the conference did not fully endorse the pronouncement of 1918. Criticism centred on certain expressions of both the resolution and the suggestion of particular economic means to achieve the co-operative social order. The conference therefore resolved that it was not the proper function of the church to outline a system of economic life, but to create a spirit of 'love and brotherliness in which social differences have ever found their most ready solution.' It commended the resolution of 1918 to members in their study of how to apply New Testament principles to economic life.[30] Some ministers entered a vigorous protest against business profiteering, and the *Globe* reported a general sympathy for labour, but also a strong feeling that the church should not pronounce support of one class in the community.[31]

The Toronto Conference was probably the most exciting of all, one of the most dramatic in the history of the church to date, and one of a series of critical engagements over the years in that conference between the proponents of a progressive or radical social gospel and their more conservative colleagues. Dr Chown's address to the conference was forceful and progressive, essentially the one he delivered to many if not all the conferences. He counselled the church not to 'be afraid that the Social Gospel is the voice of prophecy in modern life. If we do not do this we compel our people to choose between an unsocial religion, which cannot be Christianity, and an irreligious system of social salvation. Do not, brethren, shrink on account of the hardness of your task. Jesus suffered the loneliness of the social prophet before

28 *Western Methodist Recorder*, May 1918, pp. 3–4, for the factual data and quotations in this account.

29 B.C. *Federationist*, 2 July 1918. Woodsworth and Bland were probably the other two of whom the writer was thinking.

30 CG, 16 July 1919, p. 23   31 4 June 1919, p. 2

us, and is our democratic Chieftain. Like him we must revalue all systems and institutions in terms of human worth.' He rejected the counsel of those who would exclude the church from judgment on economic matters, and asserted that even where no clear answer is seen to problems 'we should cry aloud and spare not to lift up our voice like a trumpet to show the immorality of all oppression and injustice.'

While in British Columbia, just beginning his tour of the conferences, Chown had little to say on the subject of the Winnipeg strike.[32] But when he reached Toronto, the crisis had grown and called for comment. He did not entirely reject the sympathetic strike as a weapon, although he questioned it 'as at present conducted.' In judging such a strike, he said, the purposes of the strikers were not the only factors to be considered. These in many cases were 'actuated by the highest Christian motives.' Yet 'under the camouflage of the beautiful word, sympathy, as far as many of [the strike's] supporters are concerned, there is in reality a purpose to consolidate a force which, as such, is not amenable to conciliation and which does not aim at any constitutional settlement.'[33] Whether Chown's estimate of the proportion of the strikers motivated by these different considerations was right, his statement was substantiated by the balanced reports of Main Johnson to the Toronto *Star*.[34] Johnson, surveying the components of the strike, observed a new gospel of industrial control motivating one group among the strikers, who thought withholding labour power in a general way a means of relatively quickly overturning the industrial system. If Chown exaggerated the numbers of such men among the strikers,[35] that did not nullify his point that their methods were not ones that could, in his eyes, 'be accepted by Christian men.' But in addition to the question of motive was that of the effect upon the community concerned. No person with open eyes could engage in such an action without contemplating among its cumulative results, 'calculated starvation, public disorder and probably death.' It ought to be clear, Chown stated, that this sort of operation was not suggested by the General Conference resolution and was contrary to its spirit. Unlike the extreme radicals, Chown was not prepared to state that the threat of 'autocracy' came entirely from the business community.[36] Indeed, he considered that it was not unrealistic to hope that some of the steps to the new order might be taken by business leaders. But Chown now felt that by the

32 See *Western Methodist Recorder*, June 1919, for a copy of the address there.
33 This is the full quotation McNaught takes out of context when he charges Chown with pronouncing a 'ban' on the strikers, *A Prophet in Politics*, p. 118.
34 See especially his report, 26 May 1919, p. 1
35 This was difficult to ascertain with any assurance. Public statements of leaders of the strike often seemed to cast doubt on the declared terms of settlement. For examples, see above, pp. 88, 91
36 For an interesting analysis by Chown of the reaction of wealthy persons in the church

sympathetic strike labour had prejudiced this development, and had, further, made it more difficult 'for the Church to give [labour] unguarded assistance.'[37]

The social crisis had not forced the Methodist leader out of his progressive stance, but it had forced some reconsideration of commitments. To keep such a position as he was inclining to from becoming anaemic and irrelevant was the call of the hour. But Ernest Thomas, after the encounter in Montreal, was perhaps overcautious at the Toronto Laymen's Association, which he next addressed. After discovering that only five present had read the General Conference resolution, he went on to interpret it in terms not of advocating a change in the existing system but of being confronted with a change. In this situation, the General Conference, he said, had unhesitatingly affirmed the motive of co-operative service as that which should replace the prevailing motive of competition for profits.[38]

Unlike Thomas, the Toronto Conference Evangelism and Social Service Committee did not simply trim its sails to the wind, but took them down altogether. Under the influence of S.R. Parsons and the Hon. E.J. Davies, who had been placed on the committee with eighteen others,[39] it reported its finding on the General Conference resolution by simply observing: 'We have, therefore, come to the conclusion that the report ... is more or less ambiguous and inaccurate as a reflection of the mind of that body.' A storm of protest immediately broke loose.[40] Salem Bland arose to declare that the General Conference statement was the 'irreducible minimum of expression which the Church must give to the world. Christ's ideal,' he said, 'is "In love serve one another"; the world's, "in selfishness fight one another." ' He urged the conference to reject such 'uncertain and wobbly words as the report before us,' and endorse the general conference resolution. Others argued that such division of opinion indicated the ambiguity of that document, and still others that if it were ambiguous, the committee had not proposed any alternative. Parsons entered his plea that without 'competition there is nothing worth having,' and J.O. McCarthy, prominent in the General Board of Evangelism and Social Service and the Brotherhood movement, argued that any competition must be for service and not profits.

to the General Conference resolution of 1918, and of the position of labour in the church, see 'An Introspective View of the Methodist Church,' *Western Methodist Recorder*, Jan. 1920, pp. 4–5

37 For Chown's address, see CG, 25 June 1919, p. 2; also *Toronto Daily Star*, 12 June 1919, pp. 1, 8

38 *The Globe*, 12 June 1918, p. 8

39 *Ibid.*, 14 June 1919, p. 9

40 Unless otherwise indicated, the following account follows the CG, 9 July 1919, pp. 18–19

Some were clearly torn in their respect for persons of such opposed convictions as Bland and Parsons. As the debate raged for its fourth hour in a second session, it looked quite unresolvable. However, when the Rev. John Coburn of the Department of Evangelism and Social Service proposed an amendment, a startled conference saw Mr Parsons rise to second it and ask only for the alteration of a single word. No one was prepared to quibble over a word, and the debate ended with great relief. It was, however, a significant word. Where the amendment proposed that labour should have a larger participation in the 'management of industry,' Parsons wanted 'working of industry.' A third party proposed 'operation,' and this was acceptable.[41]

The Coburn amendment was almost completely a clarification of what had been the intent of the General Conference resolution. It recognized that that resolution could be authoritative only as 'approved by the moral consciousness of the Church'; that there were grave injustices in the economic order that called for remedy; that any lasting solution to these must rest on 'the ethics of Jesus Christ'; that on this basis the church must demand an increasing measure of co-operation in industrial relations, a greater share for labour in the operation of industry, and more adequate conditions of life; that it was not intended in the resolution to commit the church to any 'definite economic theory,' but at the same time it did intend and call for such changes in the structure of economic life as would make it conform to the teachings of Jesus Christ.

The amendment thus maintained the general objectives with both force and clarity, while allowing a considerable plurality of methods in realizing social objectives. That it conformed essentially to the mind of the drafters of the General Conference resolution was evinced by Salem Bland's interpretive articles in the *Guardian* the following month.[42] However, the Toronto Conference victory had been bought at the price of the original resolution's sharp insistence that an adequate change in the social order was not conditional upon changing the individuals in it. This point was left implied in Coburn's amendment, but a clear victory in that regard would have been worth a great deal. Moreover, there was no reference to public ownership of any kind, although any 'believer' might see a mandate for this in the Coburn amendment.

At the end of the round of conferences in 1919, the General Conference resolution of 1918 had been endorsed in the three western-most conferences, substantially ratified in Manitoba, Toronto, and Montreal, conditionally at Hamilton, Bay of

41 *Toronto Daily Star*, 18 June 1919, p. 2
42 16 July 1919, pp. 7–8; 30 July 1919, pp. 10–11

Quinte, and Halifax, and simply considered at London and New Brunswick. The Presbyterian church had passed a resolution on social unrest inclining rather more to labour than to capital. The Congregationalist Union, though less advanced in outlook, was registering gains in progressive social attitudes. Given the state of the public mind in May and June, these were feats of no small significance for the forces of the social gospel to have accomplished. Conference resolutions necessarily strike somewhat of a mean of social outlook. It must be concluded that in the debates of 1919 a considerable force of radicals and progressives of the social gospel existed to the left of that mean and that progressives especially were well entrenched in primary and secondary levels of church leadership at least in the western and central regions.

The conference, assembly, and union debates indicated with regard to the sympathetic strikes of May and June that there was a defensible and rational third position which could be and was held throughout that crisis – a position which sympathized and agreed with the major expressed objectives of labour and which found it difficult to agree with the charges of the Citizens' Committee and the dominion government's representatives. From this point of view, however, the general sympathetic strike was felt to be an unwise and dangerous weapon, likely to do labour more harm than good, especially when there was justifiable reason for thinking that some promoting it were harbouring grand and impracticable designs. The existence of such a progressive body of opinion was of considerable significance in Winnipeg and Canada in the days when the worst of the crisis of 1919 had passed.

The radical social gospel itself, despite the fates of Ivens and Smith, was not of one mind in judging the results of the conferences of June 1919. William Irvine was moved by the performance of the Alberta Conference, under the leadership of Hugh Dobson, to abandon his skepticism of a year earlier regarding the General Conference resolution.[43] On 19 June he declared that the Methodist church was, after all, 'taking the leadership in the great questions of national interest.' At the same time he expressed his appreciation of the position Dr A.O. McCrae of Calgary had taken at the General Assembly of the Presbyterian church.[44] A friend of Irvine's and a sympathizer with the social gospel, Elmo Roper, took a similar stand in his labour paper, the *Edmonton Free Press*.[45] James Simpson in the *Industrial Banner*, Toronto, rejoiced to have such a spate of progressive church statements both in Canada and the United States as grist for his paper's mill throughout the

43 *Alberta Non-Partisan*, 5 June 1919, p. 6. Dobson was the Regina-based western field secretary of the Methodist Department of Evangelism and Social Service.

44 *Ibid.*, 19 June 1919, pp. 5, 6–7   45 12 July 1919, p. 5

following summer.[46] He warned church leaders, however, that although they preferred to fight with ideas and principles, their declarations would arouse 'the
viciousness of modern materialism' to use all weapons at its disposal.[47] Bland, as an
exponent of the radical social gospel, was now, with Ernest Thomas, the chief link
radicals like Ivens and Woodsworth had with the church. Simpson was aware of
their crucial position, and urged labour to give them full support.[48]

The strike brought further tragedy to the relationship between progressives and
radicals, and the tragedy consisted not so much in the fact of greater separation as
in its occurrence when each group, in its own way, was becoming more influential
within its chosen constituency and was under increasingly intense attack. There was
irony as well as tragedy in the heightened alienation, for it was only from the radical
standpoint that the progressives seemed stalemated in 1919 in a cautious church,
just as in considerable measure it was the standpoint of the progressives that made
reform seem in some peril from the course which the radicals now pursued. The
separation was, of course, not complete, and not all progressives and radicals 'read'
each other entirely in these terms – as witness Irvine, Simpson, Bland, and Thomas.
But Simpson had pointed out the potential pitfall of progressives, in the difficulties
that would confront translation of their policies into reality in a world of power.
But at this point even a slight qualification by progressives of their hopes for labour
was immensely significant.

It was ironic, too, that the postwar unrest which was subjected to such hopeful
prognostications by social gospellers should have deepened the rift in the social
gospel ranks. There were to be other occasions when one wing of the movement
would be set against another, but few if any progressives and radicals reflected in
1919 that if the 'world' could so impinge upon their efforts, perhaps a larger question mark hung over the future possibilities of the 'co-operative commonwealth' to
which they were all committed. However, barring the eruption of serious problems
with the labour movement at large, progressives could press on with their programmes, writing off the Winnipeg event as legitimate unrest unfortunately exploited by a minority with syndicalist designs. Just as the church departments of
social service looked forward with high hopes after June 1919 to the victory of their
prospectus for a new Canada, so the leadership of the 'new social gospel' of the
Labor churches saw a future of expanding horizons before them. The élan of both
groups was strong.

46 See issues *Industrial Banner*, 6 June, p. 2; 20 June, p. 1; 27 June, p. 1; 18 July, p. 1;
   1 Aug., p. 2; 5 Sept., p. 1
47 *Ibid.*, 5 June 1919, p. 2   48 *Ibid.*; also 1 Aug. 1919, p. 2

8

Courting the New Businessman

Having won a considerable, if not a total, victory in the recent round of conferences, and having weathered a social crisis of the first magnitude, progressive leadership in the churches turned to the task of winning the church membership more securely to their prospectus for Canadian society.[1] Since early 1918 plans had been in process for an unprecedented interdenominational campaign to equip the churches for a new role in the social era they saw on their thresholds. Before this campaign could reach its climax in early 1920, an event of some moment for progressives was scheduled for September 1919.[2] The mounting industrial crisis of the spring had impelled the government to convene what the churches had been lobbying for for some time – a national industrial conference. Progressives had often argued that one day businessmen might be brought to see the trend toward collective responsibility implicit in their industrial organizations. The Methodists in 1918 had urged the government to mobilize the ingenuity and energy of industrialists for the task of social reconstruction. Perhaps the conference would initiate that development. Perhaps the cup of industrial conflict would be removed from the churches, and the path be cleared to further social accomplishment, not only by them, but by a more united nation.

1 Minutes, Methodist General Board of ESS, Annual Meeting, 26, 27 Aug. 1919. This meeting approved the merging of the work of the Army and Navy Board with its own. The latter had been charged with responsibility for promoting the General Conference report on 'The Church, the War and Patriotism,' in which had been the controversial resolution on 'Church Leadership in the Nation.' The Presbyterian General Assembly had urged the widespread dissemination of its Resolution on Social Unrest, *Acts and Proceedings*, 1919, p. 83. During the summer of 1919 the Methodist bodies prepared literature on various church positions for authorization of publication by the General Board of Evangelism and Social Service meeting 26 and 27 August. At another level of propaganda, see the series of articles through 1919 in the *Toronto Daily Star*, 'Social Questions of Public Interest,' by the Rev. Peter Bryce.

2 MIR, Executive minutes, Methodist Army and Navy Board, 15 July 1919

The National Industrial Conference was the upshot of a Royal Commission on Industrial Relations which had held hearings across the nation from April to June. Under Chief Justice T.G. Mathers of Manitoba, the majority of the commission had issued a report strikingly similar in diagnosis and prognosis to the recent social declarations of the churches. Labour unrest was, in brief, pinned upon the inequalities of wealth, opportunity, and status under which the working man laboured. Appropriate legislation providing social insurance, minimum conditions of labour and remuneration, and greater labour representation in Parliament were called for. The commission urged that industrial conflict should be eradicated at its root, namely, by giving the worker a role in traditional managerial functions. In the latter respect, the commission endorsed the British Whitley scheme of industrial councils which preserved and utilized existing union structures. It was, however, an ominous sign that two of the three business representatives on the commission submitted a thoroughly reactionary minority report, playing down unemployment, attacking unions as unrepresentative of the workers, and condemning social insurance as a threat to the thrift and initiative of labour. If there were to be reorganization of industry, they favoured the Colorado Plan, whereby union and non-union employees elected representatives to a joint works committee to sit with an equal number from management. One hundred Winnipeg employers had proposed such a plan to the commission, but, with other American plans for industrial reorganization, it had been rejected by the commission majority because it had been frequently used to destroy labour unions.[3]

Strangely enough, the churches do not seem to have been among the 486 witnesses to make submissions to the commission. Perhaps they felt earlier communications with the government to be sufficient. However, individuals of social gospel persuasion such as W.A. Douglass, Salem Bland in Toronto, and the Rev. F.E. Mercer in Edmonton, appeared to present their own arguments.[4] In contrast, William Ivens apparently went along with the refusal of the Winnipeg Trades and Labour

3 Royal Commission on Industrial Relations. *Report of the Commission appointed under Order-in-Council (PC 670) to Enquire into Industrial Relations in Canada.* Supplement to the *Labour Gazette,* July 1919. Members of the commission, in addition to Mathers, were Charles R. Harrison, railway conductor, Tom Moore, president of the Trades and Labor Congress, J.W. Bruce, member of the Labour Appeal Board, Carl Riordon, president of the Riordon Pulp and Paper Company, the Hon. Smeaton White, manager of the Montreal Gazette Publishing Company, F. Pauze of a Montreal lumber firm, and Thomas Bengough, secretary. The minority report was submitted by the Hon. Smeaton White and F. Pauze.

4 *Industrial Banner,* 6 June 1919, p. 1; *Edmonton Free Press,* 10 May 1919, p. 2

Council (TLC) to sanction appearance before the commission. Unanimously the council declared that this 'Council understands perfectly the cause of labor unrest as due to production for profit.' Since the government is 'investigating effects of which they are and have always been a party to the cause,' no good can come from any worker appearing 'before the Commission.'[5]

In general, however, the commission found reason for hope in the moderation of most parties making submissions. It noted, significantly, that although both workers and employers agreed on the need for a new basis of industry, the former were the ones who had the most specific ideas and had done the greatest amount of study on the subject.

Most comment in the church press on the commission report was favourable.[6] None went quite so far as Ernest Thomas of the Methodist Department of Evangelism and Social Service who, reading between the lines, saw in it a declaration that the sympathetic strike was the logical outcome of 'unjustifiable opposition of employers' to demands for industrial democracy. It was an obvious pleasure to him that the commission had substantiated the 'Methodist approach to social problems.' But he noted the hostile reaction of 'several employers assemblies' to the commission's generous estimate of the character and ability of organized labour in Canada. And the implications of the minority report he found somewhat alarming. 'Will the National Government dare to act on the report?' he asked.[7]

The first action of the government came in the form of the National Industrial Conference.[8] Representatives of employers, employees, the provincial governments, and a small group representing that indefinable body, the general public, were called to meet in Ottawa, 15–20 September 1919, to consider the recommendations of the commission. The press followed the discussions of the conference with great interest. The progressives of the social gospel looked on with great hope.[9]

The conference failed such hopefuls. Its tenor was not helped by seating in blocs, labour to the right, employers to the left, and the balance in the centre. There were no representatives of radical labour groups present, although when someone claimed on the floor that there were no socialists, one man turned around, grinned, and asked, 'Who said that?' Employers early let it be known that since they had little to

5 WLN, May 1919, p. 1

6 *Presbyterian and Westminster*, 10 July 1919, p. 37; *Canadian Churchman*, 10 July 1919, p. 441

7 CG, 9 July 1919, p. 10

8 Unless otherwise indicated, the basis for the following account derives from two lengthy articles on the conference in SW, 1 Nov. 1919, p. 39, and 1 Dec. 1919, p. 75.

9 CG, 1 Oct. 1919, p. 6

ask, they intended to let the proposals come from labour. However, the employers present met jointly each night, and daily reacted to labour's proposals from an undivided position in speeches that read like directors' reports.

If it could be said that the conference endorsed most of the recommendations of the commission, it was chiefly in terms of suggesting the establishment of committees or boards to investigate the feasibility of the proposals concerned. On the two contentious issues of industrial relations, hours of labour and collective bargaining, no progress at all was made, despite the willingness of labour to drop the question of a closed shop from the discussions. Employers would not retreat from their position that a compulsory eight-hour day would hamper international competition, curtail production, and adversely affect repayment of the national debt. Around the subject of collective bargaining a swarm of questions buzzed, each with a stinger in the form of a potential strike. 'What is the exact form of collective bargaining officially approved by labour? Are sympathetic strikes justifiable? Ought civil servants to strike? Is the principle of collective bargaining compatible with the open shop; and are unionists prepared to allow equal rights to non-unionists?' How are unresolved disputes to be settled? What are the public's rights? None of these questions was answered. Obviously, the many variables between industries made any formula difficult to apply in detail, and by pressing questions of detail the employer group prevented any resolution at all of the crucial question of collective bargaining. With failure on this point, it was of little consequence that some pleaded a great gain made through personal association and confrontation. Was there no personal association and confrontation in the factories across the nation? W.B. Creighton in the *Christian Guardian* gloomily observed that on all points at issue, the employers at Ottawa were as uncompromising in attitude as those in Winnipeg.[10]

What chiefly impressed social gospel observers, however, was the superiority of labour representatives both in knowledge of economic and social questions and in debating skill. They had been trained in another school than directors' meetings. One worker stopped in the middle of his speech and pulled a pocket volume of Ruskin from his jacket to read an extract to the conference. And a young English girl, Helena Gutteridge from the Garment Workers' Union in Vancouver, quite overwhelmed the conference, not only with her quiet passion, but her astonishing grasp of economic matters. But such signs were small compensation for the failure of the conference to do more regarding joint councils than propose a Department of Labour Bureau to gather information and make it available for employers and employees desirous of establishing such councils. To be sure, there was unanimous

10 1 Oct. 1919, p. 6

agreement favouring councils in general, but not any specific plan. It appeared that the Whitley Councils favoured by the commission and the social gospel progressives might rest in peace.

The failure of the conference was in sharp contrast to the apparent success of the Inter-Church campaign which followed, and in the light of some of the campaign's accomplishments, there was evident a greater willingness to be thankful for even the small gains the conference may have made in the field of industrial change.

In 1919 there emerged on the North American scene a church movement with broad vistas and high ambitions for the fulfilling of the social and world responsibilities of the church. To this end it planned to link the energies and programmes of some thirty churches. The first project of this Inter-Church World Movement in the United States was to raise $1,300,000,000 over five years. Prior to embarking on the campaign, and as part of a projected series of social surveys, however, it launched a study of conditions in the United States Steel Corporation. Its three-hundred-page report revealed shocking conditions – twelve-hour days and twenty-four at shift change, for instance – combined with the full complement of union breaking devices. The storm of abuse which United States Steel showered upon Inter-Church only drew further public attention to the movement's case. A hack effort at a counter-study by the company in 1923 was an instant failure, and the twelve-hour day was shortly abolished.[11]

By the time of the publication of the report, however, 28 July 1920, Inter-Church had collapsed as a movement. It was not accurate to conclude, as some did, that the collapse was caused by opposition of wealthy industrialists to Inter-Church's intervention in the economic order. John D. Rockefeller was on the committee under Bishop Francis McConnell which authorized publication, and was one of those who bailed out Inter-Church after its failure.[12] Such facts made both the success and the failure of the movement somewhat equivocal.

The Inter-Church Forward Movement, as it was called in Canada, was born in the winter of 1917–18, and formally established on 6 March 1918 under the guidance of a central Committee of Forty, representing the Methodist, Presbyterian, Anglican, Baptist, and Congregational churches, and the Missionary Educa-

11 Various accounts of this episode exist in Carter, *The Decline and Revival of the Social Gospel, 1920–1940*, pp. 21–2, 66–7; Miller, *American Protestantism and Social Issues, 1919–39*, pp. 36, 210–16; Meyer, *The Protestant Search for Political Realism, 1919–1941*, pp. 58–61; and most recently an article by Ernst, 'The Interchurch World Movement and the Great Steel Strike of 1919–1920.'
12 Meyer, *Protestant Search for Political Realism*, p. 59

tion movement. This was followed by the appointment of a national director, directors of denominational campaigns, provincial executives and organizers, and local community organizations.[13] Late entry by Baptists was soon followed by withdrawal and a separate, but almost simultaneous campaign by them.[14] Through the summer and fall of 1919 the campaign mounted. Inter-Church conventions in every province in October and November were followed by more intensive district conferences, culminating in an every member canvass and a national peace thank offering in February. The campaign was the greatest single example of church co-operation to date and in its scale could be matched by few, if any, other combinations of Canadian voluntary organizations.[15]

In terms of cold cash, the campaign was a success, reaching 125 per cent of the objective, or approximately $15,000,000. Yet finance was not the major feature of the campaign. Allowing for the ever-present temptation of hypocrisy in such matters, church leaders were to be believed when they expressed a paramount concern to equip the church for larger tasks at home and abroad, and to generate as a moral equivalent for war a passion for social service throughout the land.[16] In the multiplicity of notes struck by the variety of speakers and publicity in the campaign, it is not easy to gauge the character of its actual impact. The appeal to the social gospel was constant throughout. Baptists were urged by Dr F.W. Patterson of Winnipeg to recognize their complicity in social guilt, and were driven, according to W.J. MacKay, editor of the *Canadian Baptist,* to better appreciate the possibilities of life, to include in their sphere of interest all the world of God's concern, and to see the vision of the Kingdom of God come on earth.[17] Methodists appointed as national director of their campaign, Charles Stelzle, the dynamic American Presbyterian proponent of the social gospel.[18] Sherwood Eddy from the United States, E.C. Drury, Ontario's new farmer premier, and others whose thought was informed by the social gospel were among convention speakers. The campaign was no small affair to boost church funds, said Ernest Thomas to BC Methodists:

The committee which has formulated our spiritual aims, though so organized as to exclude all who had any part in framing the famous declarations of the General Con-

13 *Canadian Baptist*, 1 May 1919, p. 4; *Presbyterian and Westminster*, 19 June 1919, p. 603; CG, 15 Oct. 1919, p. 22

14 *Canadian Baptist*, 31 July 1919, p. 3

15 *Presbyterian and Westminster*, 25 Dec. 1919, p. 594

16 *Canadian Baptist*, 13 March 1919; *Hamilton Spectator*, 11 June 1919

17 See the issue of 27 March 1919, p. 9, regarding the first major Baptist conference on the subject.

18 CG, 15 Oct. 1919, p. 22

ference, asserts that the whole conception of society as based on enlightened selfishness has broken down. Thus society is left disintegrated with no unifying principle of Action ... The unifying and saving power must be found not in any external bonds but in the renewing of ways of thinking.[19]

The high notes of social concern, reform, and world responsibility, however, were mixed with more conservative and dubious elements. Jingoistic Baptist publicity spoke alarmingly of 'enemies of righteousness' and the withering of 'fair flowers of virtue,'[20] while Methodist publicity more characteristically assaulted social issues like the threat of Bolshevism to labour and capital, and shouted of 'farm and finance embattled,' of a great chasm between alley and avenue, of nation still set against nation, of rising oriental giants, and of principles and practices of government in the crucible.[21] While one speaker called for a League of Churches alongside a League of Nations to establish a spirit of justice and brotherhood in the world,[22] another, Dr James Endicott, virtually warned that without a believing, dynamic Anglo-Saxon race, God would be without workers to transform his world.[23]

This mixture of appeals represented the range of attitudes in the churches much better than any compilation of social gospel discussions and declarations. The alarmism of the appeals coupled with the absence of specific social proposals was clearly calculated to win the support of the largest possible segment of Canadian Protestants. The prominence of the social gospel in the campaign was evident in the issues which the publicity shouted at church members – not the catalogue of sins and personal failings that preoccupied evangelicals of the 1880s, but the social issues of industry, class, nationalism, race. The new revival was a social one, even when organized by the more conservative departments of the churches, like home and foreign missions. Under such auspices the social gospel emerged in its full context, and in that setting took on a more sombre and socially conservative hue.[24]

19 *Western Methodist Recorder*, Oct. 1919, p. 4
20 *Canadian Baptist*, 1 Jan. 1920; 8 Jan. 1920
21 CG, 12 Nov. 1919, pp. 48–9
22 *Presbyterian and Westminster*, 4 Dec. 1919, pp. 512–13
23 *Western Methodist Recorder*, Dec. 1919
24 It should not be assumed that racist and nativist notes were generally vicious. When, for instance, the Ku Klux Klan invaded Saskatchewan in the 1920s, there was a general outcry from the national church publications. See *Presbyterian Witness*, 6 Oct. 1921, p. 6; CG, 10 Jan. 1923, p. 6, 10 Oct. 1923, p. 3, 24 Oct. 1923, p. 3; *Canadian Congregationalist*, 18 Feb. 1925, p. 3; *New Outlook*, 3 Aug. 1927, p. 14, 19 Oct. 1927, p. 24. 'Father' Maloney of the Klan described the United Church as 'Jesuits in disguise,' after a Saskatoon Presbytery attacked his organization (*New Outlook*,

In the aftermath of the campaign, progressives like Chown became more apologetic on behalf of the wealthy in the church. Summing up the social impact of the Inter-Church effort, he observed a great quickening of the spirit of public service by moneyed men whose objective was the 'intensive realization of the golden rule, rather than the rule of gold.' Furthermore, he said, in the course of the campaign laymen had been able to see the 'business efficiency' of ministers, and had been helped to understand why ministers espoused the cause of the poor. A new partnership seemed to have been created between clergy and laity, he said, thus bridging a gulf caused by a 'disparity of circumstances.' Here was a revelation of the anxiety of the church leadership about growing wealth of the laity, an anxiety which had caused apprehension about the fruition of the social gospel. Now it seemed possible as a result of the Inter-Church campaign success to see in a new relationship between a socially conscious clergy and the well-to-do laity, a force, Chown claimed, 'surpassing in influence for human results in business life anything that could be achieved by formal conferences between capital and labor.'[25] Whatever the minor accomplishments of the National Industrial Conference, the Inter-Church campaign had been a resounding success, not simply in raising money, but also, it seemed, in promoting a new social conscience among the business community and a new alliance for social progress in the church.

When C.W. Gordon took up his pen in 1920, under the pseudonym of Ralph Connor, to write a novel, *To Him that Hath*, based on the Winnipeg strike, the result was, among other things, a monument to this new progressive alliance. Jack Maitland, a young returned officer being groomed for the management of his father's wood products plant, serves his time in the works, becomes a union member, and organizes an athletics programme for the men. Under the influence of a young Presbyterian minister by the name of Matheson, he comes to appreciate the economic, social, and Christian imperatives of industrial reform. Circumstances soon propel him into a direct managerial role, and when the city-wide strike comes, he persuades his father to hire his striking workers to build athletics facilities for themselves. At the end of the strike, he and Matheson and an older employer are accepted by all parties as a committee to propose terms of settlement. Maitland and Matheson are instrumental in securing a wage scale geared to the cost of living, a shortening of the work day, and a 'joint committee of reference' for settling disputed

---

9 Nov. 1927, p. 18). However, the general Protestant response in the province was quite ambiguous. For the only complete study of the subject see Calderwood's thesis, 'The Rise and Fall of the Ku Klux Klan in Saskatchewan.'

25 CG, 30 June 1920, pp. 18–19; see also *Western Methodist Recorder*, July 1920, p. 5

matters peculiar to each industry. More than that, a public meeting is called and its approval obtained 'for the creation of a General Board of Industry, under whose guidance the whole question of the industrial life of the community should be submitted to intelligent study and control.'[26] In the denouement of the novel, Maitland wins as his helpmate a girl who, while completing her education in England, imbibed a heavy dose of the latest progressive thought on social issues.

Gordon's piece of fiction was not without its supporting evidence. For at least a few years after the war, amid the high tide of social reconstruction, numerous requests came from businessmen to at least the Methodist social service department for consultations on the relation of Christianity to industrial relations. In response, the department encouraged the organization of classes of employers and employees to study together the New Testament and to discuss the teachings of Jesus with relation to industry. In at least some centres the plan was followed, although how widely and with what response is unknown.[27] Church leaders were undoubtedly impressed when conscientious churchmen like the Masseys provided a cafeteria jointly operated by men and management, established a pension plan, extended the practice of prior options on stock purchasse to regular employees, and developed a system of industrial councils.[28] Early in 1920 a survey of fifty-three representative industries was undertaken by the Social Service Council to determine 'the extent of co-management or welfare work being promoted by employers throughout Canada.'[29] The survey revealed that twenty of the fifty-three plants had some specific provision of recreation facilities, nine conducted educational classes, largely in technical subjects, and eighteen had profit sharing or bonus systems. Although *Social Welfare* described such measures as paternalistic and no solution to basic industrial problems, it conceded that they represented a sense of responsibility not often credited to employers. The survey also found that fourteen plants had well-developed works councils, as distinct from the less elaborate shop committees. These ranged from 'slight adaptations of the representative idea' to comprehensive plans of industrial democracy in Bell Telephone and Gray-Dort Motors of Chatham. *Social Welfare* concluded that 'without strife or rancour, democratic principles are permeating the industries of some of Canada's most successful and really independent men of business.' However, the report also noted that since only fourteen of the plants were significantly organized by labour, the Whitley council system, presupposing thorough labour organization, could not be applied without con-

26 Connor, *To Him that Hath*, p. 279
27 *Western Methodist Recorder*, Oct. 1921, p. 4; Methodist Department of ESS, *Annual Report*, 1922–3, p. 27
28 SW, 1 Sept. 1919, p. 287   29 *Ibid.*, 1 Aug. 1920, pp. 316–17

siderable changes in Canadian industry. That the industrial councils in existence had a tendency to discourage labour organization was apparent in a later report of T.S. Simons and Company Limited, St John, NB, on effects of their efforts to organize a joint council structure.[30]

In the spring of 1921, the movement toward industrial councils seemed likely to gain momentum with belated action by the federal Department of Labour. A conference was called of representatives of the most prominent firms having adopted joint councils of industry.[31] Promotion of the councils was placed in the hands of T.A. Stevenson, a former trade union officer. By June of 1921 he had organized thirty-two councils, one quarter of which were due chiefly to the initiative of managements and workers themselves. Simpson, in the *Industrial Banner*, complained that most of the development was taking place in open shop industries.[32] In June, however, Stevenson was engaged in forming a council of the building trades in Calgary, an industry which was organized.[33] It is clear, however, that the councils were closer in character to the Colorado Plan developed by the Rockefellers than to the British Whitley councils. The government may not have been beyond reproof in introducing even this limited and questionable approach to industrial democracy in 1921. Arthur Meighen, the premier, had been one of the leading figures in the breaking of the Winnipeg strike. His government's star had been in decline for some time. Now, facing an election in late 1921, he had need of what support progressive legislation could bring him. More to the point, the chief Canadian proponent of industrial councils was W.L.M. King through his book, *Industry and Humanity*.[34] King, as the new leader of the Liberal opposition, was the chief contender for Meighen's throne!

King won, but with an uncomfortable number of members of a new party, the Progressives, chiefly from the West, eyeing his every move. One of the first acts of the new government concerned industrial councils. In February 1922 the Minister of Labour called a conference of firms with council structures. All present recommended their extension. In May a further conference with labour and management representatives in the building and construction industries set in motion active organization of councils, still through T.A. Stevenson of the Department of Labour.[35] It was apparent that, in general, those industries which had initiated some

30 1 Aug. 1922, p. 235
31 Canada, Department of Labour, *Report of a Conference on Industrial Relations, Ottawa, Feb. 21 & 22, 1921*
32 6 May 1921, p. 2   33 WLN, 17 June 1921, p. 1
34 King, *Industry and Humanity*, pp. 450–75
35 SW, 1 Aug. 1922, pp. 236–8, 251

kind of council structure were well-established thriving industries like Massey-Harris, International Harvester, Imperial Oil, Swift, Algoma Steel, Gutta Percha, Spanish River Pulp and Paper, and Canadian Consolidated Rubber.[36] These were the Fords, Rockefellers, and Schwabs of Canadian industry. None of them went as far as 'Golden Rule' Nash, William Hapgood, and others in the United States in turning over their industries to full worker ownership and/or management. Yet in the minds of conservatives and progressives of the social gospel they pointed to these ultimate conditions.[37] The *Canadian Churchman* on 5 April 1923 noted the inevitable result – there was 'less talk than there used to be about the incompatibility of Christianity and business.' Thus, despite the Methodist insight of 1918 that the necessary changes in the system as a whole had no relation to the attitude of individual employers, and that the Whitley system requiring worker selforganization was preferable to other council systems, there was a readiness by 1922, if not 1920, to glory in the evidences of the conversion, or socialization of the minds of industrial leaders.

In only one province did there exist something approximating a secondary tier to the local industrial councils. Shortly after the Winnipeg General Sympathetic Strike of 1919, the Norris government created a Council of Industry for Manitoba. This council was not created as part of a general system of industrial councils, but served something of that purpose by being a superior court of conciliation. Significantly, its first chairman was none other than C.W. Gordon. Gordon's experience extended beyond the chairmanship of the committees on industrial relations of the Presbyterian church in Canada and of the Social Service Council of Canada to a number of successful ventures into industrial conciliation in the past. He was one of those who had maintained progressive temper throughout the Winnipeg crisis of 1919.[38] He had not been in the city during the height of those events, being in attendance at the General Assembly of the church in Toronto where, in all probability, he had played a major role in drawing up that body's progressive resolution on social unrest.

The formula on which Gordon operated as chairman of the council was typical of the progressive social gospel. Industry was a co-operative enterprise for the service of the whole community. In its functioning, four factors had to be considered: capital (whoever owned it), labour, management, and the community.

36 *Ibid.*

37 Meyer, *Protestant Search for Political Realism*, pp. 65–75; *Canadian Congregationalist*, 1 Aug. 1923, pp. 3, 4

38 His view of his own position is apparent in the portrait in his novel of the progressive minister with intimate associations in both camps.

Each of these had its rights and responsibilities. The rights were fundamentally simple and the same for all: security, freedom, a fair return, and growth. The responsibility of each was to see that the other was granted his rights. The denial of any part of this formula by any party meant a failure of industrial efficiency in fulfilling its purpose. Gordon believed that insistence on these factors would eliminate industrial strife, and that what was needed was the development of the habit of utilizing the formula.[39]

Gordon's schooling of the parties was apparently quite effective. He brought to the task not only considerable experience but a direct manner and a keen sense of humour. For four years he coped with Manitoba's industrial conflicts, dealing with one hundred and seven cases, all of which he could claim to have settled unanimously. Of these, he estimated that about 55 per cent were in favour of labour. At the end of four years, when the need for his efforts and for the council seemed to have ceased, Gordon resigned as chairman. Industrial strife had dropped to minor proportions and the services of the council were not being called on. Undoubtedly declining recourse to the council was a result of many factors, including depression conditions, but that Gordon, through the Council of Industry, had helped heal the wounds of a badly divided industrial community must be credited.

The Manitoba Council of Industry and the promotion of industrial councils by the Canadian government must have been hopeful signs to the progressive social gospel. They were short steps, but they were better than none, toward social gospel objectives which lay beyond even the Whitley council type of structure. Ernest Thomas, writing for his department after the industrial conference of 1919, described that goal as the complete transcendence of the present separation of capital and labour. This, he said, was 'the only "radical reform."'[40] Sentimentalists might interpret his meaning in terms of a gloss of good will, but to Thomas himself, such a 'transcendence' ultimately entailed a complete revision of property rights in industry. 'All lingering ideas of a man "owning his business" must come to an end, as far as that business is an organization of human lives, energies and services,' Thomas wrote. This did not mean acceptance or rejection of socialism, or any particular economic theory, he said, but it was the 'inevitable outcome of the Christian view of life.'[41]

In October 1923 it even seemed possible that S.R. Parsons, the *bête noir* of the debates of 1918–19, was in process of conversion. An article on 'Industrial Peace

39 Gordon, *Postscript to Adventure*, pp. 374–5
40 Methodist Department of ESS, *Christian Churches and Industrial Conditions*, 1919, p. 4
41 *Youth and Service*, Jan. 1920, pp. 8–9

Through Co-operation,'[42] was interpreted by Ernest Thomas as a 'sincere effort to discuss the issue and put behind the controversy of the past.' Thomas noted both the real similarities in Parsons' proposals to those of the General Conference of 1918, and the continuing issues between them. In particular, he questioned Parsons' claim that 'freer conditions' existed under the council system in his industry. If this referred to lack of unionization, Thomas said, labour was generally freer in proportion to its organized strength.[43] But Parsons rejected the olive branch interpretation of his article, reiterated his view that the General Conference resolution spelled communism, and threatened that 'any attempt to make these declarations effective now, when time has helped to make clear their real meaning, would cause large defections from our membership.'[44] Two replies to Parsons' attack on Thomas bore devastating criticism of competitive capitalism. But the Rev. G.H. Lord of Medora, Manitoba, concluded: 'Ye that are strong must bear the burdens of the weak'; and the Rev. Harvey G. Forster of Welland, Ontario, stated that while the method of industrial reconstruction was not clear, and the present mood unfavourable, once employers were convinced of the new principles their ingenuity would devise methods of expression.[45] Although Thomas himself was obviously quite aware of the uses of the power of labour in forcing industrial reform, progressives like Lord and Forster fell back with most of their brethren on the hope that the real change would come within the centres of capitalist power themselves. For them, Parsons was evidence of perversity, not of a continuing problem of power interest.

The distance of social gospel leaders from business operations would seem to have lent enchantment to the new innovations. Generally, they did not enquire whether plans for industrial councils were applicable in all plants, or in all economic seasons. They could not know that the more 'advanced' schemes in the United States, such as the one at Hapgood's Columbia Conserve Company, would collapse over issues of wage reductions and dismissals early in the depression,[46] but they might have speculated. Some, like the editor of *Social Welfare*, were aware in late 1921 that the British National Industrial Conference, the keystone of the arch of the Whitley scheme, had been dissolved amid labour protests. He observed that 'some cynics (shall we call them, or will it be plain speakers of the truth?) are making assertions ... that remedial labour suggestions are gilt-edged on a rising market, but scrapped in a falling one?'[47] Such observations were crowded from attention by the intriguing spectacle of Roger Babson, prominent American investments counsellor and Con-

42 CG, 24 Oct. 1925, p. 5 43 *Ibid.*, 7 Nov. 1923, pp. 5, 22
44 *Ibid.*, 2 Jan. 1924, p. 13
45 *Ibid.*, 16 Jan. 1924, p. 22; 23 Jan. 1924, p. 17
46 *Ibid.* 47 SW, 1 Nov. 1921

gregational layman, who advised enlightened labour and management policies and reforms which it seemed the privilege of one possessed of the social passion to espouse. Had he been read critically, more heed might have been given to possible corollaries of his claim that 'the religion of the community is really the bulwark of our investments.'[48] But as business appropriated the social service credo and gave expression to it in its particular ways, it became difficult for conservatives and progressives of the social gospel to find an adequate critique of the new businessman.[49]

Even Ernest Thomas, explicating the minimal logic of Methodist industrial policy, inadvertently showed the way to a new business rationalization acceptable to many a socially conscious clergyman:

While denying the validity of private gain as the guiding objective this does not in any way commit the Church to State ownership of factories. It may well be held that private enterprise may be the most effective means by which the community may serve its needs. But the moment this is asserted we have passed from the ground of the abstract right of capital to the social interest of effective service.[50]

What provided Thomas, however, with a basis for further critical inroads on the system gave businessmen an acceptable shibboleth into the new era, and served the more conservative of the social gospel with evidence of a revolution in the making.

It is hardly surprising, then, that the Inter-Church movement in Canada, more successful both in its immediate campaign and in continued existence than its American counterpart, did not attempt to match the American example of an attack upon any specific case of industrial injustice. For progressive social gospellers, the Inter-Church campaign marked a watershed. Even after the Winnipeg strike, the balance of their favour seemed to be with labour. Commentary on the National Industrial Conference seemed to bear this out. It may still have been the case after the campaign, but a reversal of trend in progressive attitudes toward the businessman set in in the wake of Inter-Church. For some months progressives had been observing the emergence of a new ethic of industrial practice in the personnel policies of a number of prominent industries. A new businessman seemed in process of evolution. For that the social gospel could claim some credit. If the unreconstructed industrialists, such as the ironmasters of Winnipeg, or the directors of BESCO in

48 Cited in *ibid.*, p. 74. Babson was not infrequently quoted in the Canadian denominational press.
49 See in addition to the citations above, *Canadian Churchman*, 30 Nov. 1922, pp. 783–4; 22 Feb. 1923, p. 100; 5 April 1923, p. 219; *Canadian Baptist*, 27 Sept. 1928, p. 3; 18 Oct. 1928, p. 14; 14 Feb. 1929, p. 16; 28 March 1929, p. 5
50 *Alberta Labor News*, 4 Sept. 1920, p. 15

Cape Breton held the public stage in terms of the sheer drama of their encounters with labour, progressives could argue that the more unnewsworthy efforts of the new businessman to 'humanize' and 'democratize' his industry had a potentiality worth courting. If the government had not been able to mobilize the nation's industrialists *en masse* for the work of social reconstruction, its modest efforts toward industrial democracy revealed apparent centres of good will in the industrial community. Progressive leaders interpreted this to mean that they were making their own inroads in their own ways in winning businessmen to progressivism. But would their conversion do more than mask the face of power in industry and not compromise the reform of the fundamental system of relationships in the capitalist economy itself? Was William Irvine right when he saw in the Inter-Church campaign for $12,000,000 the hand of the 'big Interests' turning the influence of the pulpit against the 'real forward movement,' the attempt to change the system itself?[51] Here was the perennial dilemma of the progressive reformer, and here, too, was the perennial radical critique.

51 Irvine, 'The Labor Church in Canada,' *The Nation*, 1 May 1920, p. 583

9

The New Christianity

Whether Salem Bland shared Irvine's views of the Inter-Church Forward Movement is not clear. He had, in earlier years, been hopeful that businessmen would recognize the collectivist implications of their own activities of industrial organizaton.[1] If he still held that hope, it was, as in the past, a subdued theme in his thinking. He had committed little energy to the direct fostering of a new mind among businessmen themselves, apart, of course, from the general effect his preaching and teaching might have. His inclination had long been toward the world of farm and labour, and in 1919 and 1920, in the confusion of postwar unrest, when it appeared that some of the advances of the social gospel might be in danger of compromise, his priorities could hardly have seemed in need of change. It was a moment requiring both a large view of the movement of the times, and a sense of the creative centres of impulse and action. These Bland attempted to supply in a book he published in the spring of 1920.[2]

Unlike C.W. Gordon's novel based on the Winnipeg strike, Bland's book hardly sang the praises of the new businessman, but neither could it be described as an attack upon businessmen as such. That it was not marked by any flavour of bitterness in this respect was perhaps surprising, given the circumstances under which the book was written. As the Inter-Church campaign moved into high gear after mid-1919, a confused but determined attack was launched upon Bland by the wealthiest and most prestigious leaders of Broadway Methodist Tabernacle in Toronto, whose pastor he had become the previous February. This attempt to have him removed as pastor was precipitated by Bland's request that he be permitted to spend August in Winnipeg to close his affairs there, and that he be free to accept an invitation to be one of two Canadian representatives at the 'Centenary of Methodism' in Cleveland in the early fall, an invitation that included a request that he undertake a lecture tour in connection with the visit. M.A. Sorsoleil, principal of the Model School, depicted this to the press as a two-month holiday to go on tour for labour.

1 Bland Papers, 'Four Steps and a Vision' [a lecture, 1898]
2 Bland, *The New Christianity, or The Religion of the New Age*

J.T. Baker of the Toronto Hat Company clarified the reasoning behind Sorsoleil's story by charging that Bland made the pulpit a forum of labour problems. 'Mike' Vokes of Vokes Hardware Company, member of the Board of Management for thirty-seven years, and Broadway's largest contributor, feared that Bland's 'disloyal utterances ... might cause a disruption of society,' while his brother, a contractor, bluntly declared that Bland was 'a rank socialist.' None would be more specific or substantial when interviewed by the press, but claimed a general dissatisfaction current in the congregation, 'especially among those who pay.' It seems likely, however, that a majority of the congregation supported Bland from the beginning of the dispute. Chown early made an implicit defence of Bland in publicly announcing that 'a minister of the Methodist Church is not "employed" to preach what his Board of Management asks.' And despite the preferral of further charges by the board and its suspension of Bland's salary for some six months, moderates on the board finally secured a majority and rallied behind Bland.[3]

Although Bland's struggle was rather protracted because of the established position of his detractors, he was able to defeat their efforts decisively and win the confidence and admiration of his congregation. He also had the dubious satisfaction two years later of seeing his chief antagonist, hardware merchant Mike Vokes, publicly humiliated for creating 'front' companies to cover the surreptitious dealings of his firm with the Toronto School Board, of which he was a member at the time.[4] In fighting and winning this encounter, Bland not only won a victory for the freedom of the pulpit and saved Methodist social policy from an implicit defeat, but he also demonstrated that the radical social gospel could win its battles with conservative interests within the church.

That the newly won positions of the social gospel in the church were at stake in this contest was evident in Simpson's instant reaction in the *Industrial Banner*, 1 August: if Broadway officials are 'permitted to persecute Dr Bland because he associates with working men and working women in their organizations, and because he preaches labor sermons, there will be very fertile ground for a Labor Church in Toronto.' Undoubtedly Bland could have established a Labor church more potent than any in existence. He could have argued that entrenched wealth in the church was making his ministry impossible. That he did not take this course was not because he had no sympathy for the Labor churches. On the contrary, he had expected them to spread through the West and, with some effort at propagation, to the major industrial centres of the nation. He welcomed the development as one that would stimulate the older churches to a fuller and more whole-hearted

3 For a fuller account, see Allen, 'Salem Bland,' pp. 179–84
4 *Telegram* (Toronto), 26 Feb. 1921

adoption of 'new sociological ideas and ideals,' which 'in their final and sifted form' he believed the denominations were destined to adopt. Bland was, however, a well-known protagonist of church union and a supporter of the Community church movement in the West. At first glance, therefore, it seems odd that he should have looked so favourably upon the emergence of a class church.

Bland's defence of the Labor church was threefold. It was at once a simple, realistic, and a prophetic defence which may have owed something to the encounter at Broadway. He believed that the established denominations were themselves largely class churches, whether they recognized it or not. It was therefore hypocritical of churchmen to use such a charge to condemn religious fellowship among working people. More important, however, was his belief that church union was not the final stage of church development. Beyond that great possibility lay a greater, 'a Canadian Church ... fashioned to meet Canadian needs and to express Canadian convictions and Canadian ideals.' In this development, Canada would find her soul, but it had to be a development to which all parts of the Canadian community would contribute. None could anticipate its form, but nothing was clearer than that, at the moment, the historic denominations were unable to marshall the religious and social energies of the vital and active part of the working class. It was theirs to make their contribution in their own way, and Bland was prepared to support them.[5] But that he would do in his own way. His third and major defence of the Labor church was its hospitality to the 'new sociological ideas.' At this point, all three developments, the Labor churches, church union, and his envisaged Canadian church, cohered in his thinking. They were all expressions of the thrust of the social gospel in Canadian religious life.

When Bland wrote his first book it could be looked upon as providing a rationalization for the Labor churches. *The New Christianity*, however, was primarily an attempt to bring into historical focus the whole religious movement of which the Labor churches were a part. It was not a scholarly work so much as a tract for the times, but much reading, reflection, and action lay behind it. The book caused no little stir in ecclesiastical circles. It was widely reviewed, and, apparently, quite widely read.[6] *The New Christianity* was an historical work in that it tried to trace the course of movements of democracy and brotherhood through western civilization, and in that it interpreted the various historic forms of the church in terms of their broad cultural contexts. It could hardly be called a pretentious study in these respects, for Bland had other than historical purposes, but it was nevertheless of some significance.

5 Salem Bland, 'Church Developments,' GGG, 15 Oct. 1919
6 *Toronto Daily Star*, 2 June 1920; *Saskatoon Daily Star*, 19 June 1920

Historical criticism of the church's dogma, social teaching, and ethos had not reached any degree of sophistication until the work of Harnack, Troeltsch, and Weber at the turn of the century. Although these works were undoubtedly known in Canada, the latter two were not translated into English until after 1920.[7] Tawney's celebrated lectures were not given until 1922, and not published as *Religion and the Rise of Capitalism* until 1926. However, it was quite natural for a church historian like Bland who had accepted modern critical techniques to apply them to the life of the church itself. Nor might it seem audacious to do so when the historical critics of the Bible in Canadian Methodism had won their struggle a decade earlier.[8]

One of Bland's central points, however, was the intimate interrelation of Protestantism and capitalism. There had been a considerable history of observation on their apparent geographical coincidence. Such observations had been of little concern to the spirit of Protestant individualism, but in the writings of Catholics and Marxists it had been a point of considerable force in the repudiation of Protestantism and religion respectively. To many Protestants, the espousing of such positions by a Protestant must have seemed arch-apostasy. To those progressives and conservatives of the social gospel who had not accepted all the implications of their new attitudes, the threat was probably the greater to their intellectual security inasmuch as they, unlike most of their fathers, shared much of Bland's rejection of capitalism. Did they have then to repudiate much of their Protestant heritage as well? In terms of Bland's analysis they had no alternative but to do so and give themselves to the 'New Christianity.'

It was, therefore, a prophetic work, and it cannot be denied that what history was in its composition was subordinated to that task. It utilized history in the way

7 A. Harnack, *Lehrbuch der Dogmengeschichte* (3 vols.; 1886–9) was translated as *History of Dogma* in 1894–9. More important for the subject at hand was E. Troeltsch, *Die Soziallehren der christlichen Kirchen und Gruppen* (1912), translated as *The Social Teachings of the Christian Churches* in 1931. Interest in the social factors in early Christian development was quite high in Canada by 1923. The bulk of Shirley Jackson Case, *The Social Origins of Christianity*, was based on lectures given recently in connection with the fiftieth anniversary of Wesleyan Theological College, Montreal (see Author's Preface). The more controversial work, M. Weber, *Die protestantische Ethik und der Geist des Kapitalismus* (1904–5) was not translated until 1930 as *The Protestant Ethic and the Spirit of Capitalism*. Its translator, Talcott Parsons, observed that when the translation appeared the work was 'scarcely known outside very limited scholarly circles in the fields of religious and economic history' (Preface to New Edition [New York 1958], p. xiii).

8 Walsh, *The Christian Church in Canada*, pp. 290–2

his first socialist lecture, 'Four Steps and a Vision,' utilized evolutionary science. In *The New Christianity*, Bland sketched the convergence of historical developments in western society and religion which pointed beyond traditional Protestantism. In the first place had been the progressive march of democracy from the twelfth- and thirteenth-century universities, into religion in the sixteenth century, politics in the nineteenth century, and now unmistakably claiming its role in the world of industry. In the second place, the movement toward brotherhood had become 'the great master passion' of the day. The seeds of this had been planted in the early church by Christ, but Paul and John had buried them under the Greek passion for metaphysics. Instead of the true fruit of the vine there had emerged a 'perverse exaltation of dogma and orthodoxy' which had 'withered the heart of the Church.' However, the essential message of Christianity was now being rediscovered by movements both inside and outside the church.

Both the expression of democracy and the 'overflow' of brotherhood stood in sharp antithesis to a competitive and individualistic capitalism. Therefore, Bland argued, the distinctive task of the age was the abolition of capitalism. While it was not entirely clear how this would be done, some initial steps were to be seen in specialization, co-operation, and union of competing industries, but primarily in public ownership. Public ownership, Bland believed, taught men to think socially. Hence to discredit and attack it was to discredit and attack Christianity. That the churches were beginning to see their role in the light of this task, many prewar developments and postwar church statements, especially the Methodist one of 1918, stood in evidence.

In defence of this position, Bland proposed a developmental view of Christianity. He distinguished between unchanging and changing elements of Christianity. The first was a supreme 'devotion to the Lord Jesus Christ.' The second were the elements of institutional and dogmatic expressions of that devotion, which were 'subject to the same influences as fashion the changing social order.' He discerned three phases in the interaction of Christianity and the social order in western civilization, each with its peculiar characteristics. In the feudal period the very insecurity of life led to an emphasis upon structure and order. If the lack of possibilities in this life led to other-worldly tendencies in religion, nevertheless the Roman Catholic church was the 'sublimest achievement of the organizing powers of mankind.' Subsequently the bourgeois or plutocratic capitalist phase was prepared and perpetuated by the emergence of the trading and manufacturing classes, the rise of towns, and the industrial revolution. This phase brought a breakdown of old restrictions sanctioned by the church, and the beginning of a new spirit in church life reflecting 'freedom loving, self-reliant, self-assertive, ambitious burghers.' Thus there was infused into the Protestant movement a primary emphasis upon the economic virtues of industry, thrift, sobriety, honesty, and self-control, and the uneconomic vices of indolence, intemperance, licentiousness, and poverty. Humility and compassion fell to a low ebb. Protestant preoccupation with individual character became so entrenched that wherever the reviving spirit of brotherhood was strongest, for example, in the labour movement, there was least drawing to Protestantism, and this latter fact was but a reflection of the inability of Protestant ideology, except in isolated and unofficial cases, to give sanction and support to the early struggles of labour.

The new power of labour marked the end of the bourgeois phase, according to Bland, and ushered in a new period to be dominated by the values of labour: the duty and right of all to productive labour, to a living wage, and to union or association. To fulfil its role, however, the labour movement would have to broaden itself to include all productive work, and recognize the Christian and religious character of its being. To so interpret labour to itself was the prophetic task of 'this fateful hour.' Labour and Christianity were, in this age, bound up together. 'They [would] come into their kingdom together or not at all.' What he called a 'labor Christianity' was in the making.

Paralleling all the foregoing was a stream of religious-cultural development that Bland loosely called the 'racial impact' on Christianity. Jews, Greeks, Latins, Teutons, all had evolved peculiar forms of Christian life. Another form, which had begun as a branch of the Teutonic, was being added in North America. With the Jewish it would be simple in creed, and would emphasize the ethical. It would not, however, be apocalyptic, but stress 'progressive and aggressive amelioration.' With the Greek it would be inquisitive and speculative, but would reject later Greek orthodoxy. With the Latin it would show a genius for organization and a catholicity of peoples, but would reject episcopacy for lay leadership and democratic polity. With the Teutonic it would be free, unceremonious, and stress personal dignity, but without succumbing to individualism. Bland seemed to think that the author of *La Religion dans la société aux étas unis*[9] had well summed up American Christianity: it was a social religion, with interest in the human and not the supernatural, and an emphasis on morality rather than dogma. It was traditional in that it kept old names and forms even when changing customs. It was evangelical in keeping the figure of Jesus Christ primary, even when it did not recognize his divinity. American Christianity, this writer observed, and Bland concurred, could be called a Christian positivism.

Bland tried to go on and sketch the promise of a 'Great Christianity,' which might emerge in the twentieth century, and into which all the foregoing and

9 The author is not given, but the publication date is listed as 1902.

Russian, African, and Oriental expressions of Christianity might pour their distinctive ways. But at this point he was simply stammering. While the tenor of his work was very optimistic, he was convinced that the civilization of the West was in a state of deep crisis, and that only a full Christianity which drew on the best of its past and related positively to the vital movements of the day could enable men to steer a course through the storm. Bland had always preached that true ethics and true religion were found on the 'firing line,' and he did not now propose an *a priori* system with which to solve the social crisis. Rather he suggested certain approaches to and resources for the struggle. In general, those who would live out the New Christianity must strike 'roots deep in the common earth; treating institutions, even the most venerable, as the mere temporary contrivances that they are; with the faith of Jesus in the human heart and in the ultimate triumph of love, and a willingness, like His, to find a throne in a cross.'

Bland's book was not his first reference to the New Christianity which he discerned in preparation in the forges of history. Some of what he wrote in his tract had been better said in earlier articles.[10] What he did say could have been stated with more qualifications, closer analysis, and more adequate illustration. But he was not writing a treatise for the few, but a tract for the many. He was not composing impartial history for historians, but historical and theological perspectives for present action.

The New Christianity stirred very diverse reactions. Father L. Minehan of Toronto thought its small amount of wisdom had already been given the world by Leo XIII and the pastoral letter of Catholic bishops of the United States in 1919.[11] Like the Rev. Dr Blagrave of St Mark's, Toronto, he had had too much of reconstructions and new christianities.[12] The fundamentalist Baptist minister, the Rev. T.T. Shields, thought the book should be very useful to many, but for the reason that 'the truth is generally to be found in the opposite of what he [Bland] says.'[13] The Rev. A.E. Ribourg, St Alban's Cathedral, was in considerable agreement with many of Bland's arguments,[14] and the editor of the *Presbyterian and Westminster*, while disagreeing with much, felt it a very valuable contribution to the debate on social questions.[15] Methodist reactions were as varied as those of other denominations. Some were cautious, and others linked praise of Bland with criticism of the book.[16] Some saw an unwarranted idealism of labour, but in sermons shortly to be

---

10 For instance, see GGG, 13 Nov. 1918, p. 32; 21 May 1919, p. 40; 13 Aug. 1919, p. 32
11 *Toronto Daily Star*, 2 June 1920   12 *The Globe*, 17 June 1920
13 *Ibid.*   14 *Ibid.*
15 10 June 1920, p. 578   16 *Toronto Daily Star*, 2 June 1920

preached, Bland reiterated what he had said on many occasions, that labour often followed 'narrow and inadequate social theories, a hard materialism, a selfishness to match the selfishness of the employers.'[17]

The book was released at the time of the annual meetings of the conferences of the Methodist church in mid-1920. It did not escape comment. The president of the Toronto Conference Laymen's Association, T.W. Duggan of Brampton, took occasion to score the 'pessimistic prophets.' Identifying Protestantism with Christianity, he asked whether it was the Christian or non-Christian element which had 'made Britain and the u.s.a. the arbiters of the world?' There were problems in the church, to be sure, and Duggan offered his diagnosis and remedy. 'The great machinery installed and worked at great cost [was] not turning out the quantity or quality of product that [might] reasonably be expected.' This failure was due 'to a lamentable lack of intelligent business principles – such as are necessary in mercantile life – being applied to the business of the Church.'[18] Duggan thus offered himself as an unwitting example of Bland's major point. He also illustrated how shallow was the penetration of influential elements among the laity by the social gospel.

However, even official Methodist reaction was unusually cold. T.A. Moore disagreed with Bland's thesis that Protestantism was bourgeois Christianity, and the *Christian Guardian* wrote that the book was 'not a logical and reasoned advocacy of the rights of Labor; the author apparently aims to challenge the attention than to convince ... Few of his readers, probably, will agree with all the author's statements, and probably he does not expect them to ...'[19]

Bland felt that he deserved better of the *Guardian*, and noted with evident disappointment, 'not a good word for it. Compare the other reviews.'[20] What he did not know, and was probably never to know, was that the hand of the Royal North-West Mounted Police had come between him and the church paper. On 12 June 1920 Lt.-Col. C.F. Hamilton of the Mounted Police had written Moore in some perturbation. He was aware of the delicate position he would be in if he were to propose a particular reaction from the church, but he was concerned that

in this country [where] as a rule there is little discussion of principles a book published locally is more likely than not to be given a few eulogistic reviews and then dropped, [does] it not seem advisable ... to subject to a reasonably energetic examination a book which declares that Protestantism "will not survive," and ignores its work in promoting humanitarian endeavour, and which declares that to criticize public ownership is to commit the sin against the Holy Ghost?

17 *Toronto Star Weekly*, 19 June 1920   18 *Toronto Daily Star*, 9 June 1920
19 16 June 1920   20 Bland Papers

Hamilton had other criticisms of the book but his fear was 'that in a very short time it will be acclaimed from every revolutionary platform; and that it will lend to the revolutionary movement an air of religious sanction ...'[21] Moore replied, saying that 'Your reference to Dr Bland's book is much appreciated. Several of us already had taken some steps in that regard and I anticipate that in the near future there will be a public statement made which will cover a good deal of the ground discussed in your letter.'[22] It seems likely that the statement was the lengthy review in the *Guardian* on 15 June.

There is no evidence of the book finding its way onto revolutionary platforms. James Simpson, in the *Industrial Banner*, hoped that working people would take its broad concepts to heart. It was less important to him that it 'start something' in the churches, than that the workers learn to think in such high terms of their mission.[23] In the West the book was more favourably reviewed than in the East. Westerners had their disagreements with Bland, but Professor W.T. Allison, writing in the *Edmonton Journal* on 19 June 1920, felt that at least parts of the book were brilliant. The *Grain Growers' Guide* concurred and sold the book through its book department.[24] The *Saskatoon Daily Star*, noting that *The New Christianity* was being widely read, reflected that 'one reads the book with the feeling that this is just what he has thought all his life, but lacked the powers of expression to put it into words ... [It] is a concentrated form of the message which ministers are sending forth from pulpits today.'[25]

It was of some note that coincidental with these reviews of *The New Christianity*, the Protestant Ministerial Association of Montreal unanimously agreed with the conclusions of a paper by Professor W.A. Gifford, 'Can the Kingdom of God be Realized through the Present Social Order?' The conclusion was negative. The requirements of the kingdom were such that their fulfilment would require changes in the material relations within capitalism. Capital which organized 'other men for private ends [could] only mean lost fellowship, lost equality and love.'[26] Bland could take heart in another evidence of the growth of the New Christianity within the bosom of the established churches.

It is difficult to know who in the Methodist hierarchy were aware of Moore's correspondence with Hamilton. There is evidence of use of Moore's information only

21 MIR, Hamilton to Moore, 12 June 1920
22 MIR, Moore to Hamilton, 29 June 1920
23 Bland Papers, undated cutting   24 8 Sept. 1920
25 19 June 1920   26 CG, 9 June 1920, p. 9

by Creighton and Chown, although in Creighton's case it was probably unwitting.[27] Early in the fall of 1920 articles by Ernest Thomas indicated that if he knew of the correspondence, he rejected its contents and the use made of it by Chown, Moore, and Creighton, both to condemn the Labor churches and Bland's book.

In defence of Bland, Thomas argued that too few people were aware of the influence of economic conditions upon any religious movement. In *The New Christianity* 'indisputable facts' had been presented incisively, but with a maximum amount of challenge and provocation. If Bland had said little of the humanitarian tendencies of some captains of industry, he was writing not of tendencies but of main currents. Some Christian employers, for instance, might make 'splendid, but often futile, efforts ... to make an unChristian system function as a Christian one.' To say that the Methodist or any other church was dominated by one particular class, he explained, did not mean that financiers dictated policy, but that the thoughts, feelings, and interests of one class tended to predominate. He was happy, however, to note proposals for payment of salaries by a central board in order to bypass the power of the employing class in the local church.[28]

Class consciousness was not the preserve of the worker, and not only revolutionary socialists but many employers saw it as inevitably leading to class war. The unclass-conscious worker, Thomas suggested, was often the 'unsocialized' worker, prepared to accept the sacrifice and struggle of others without standing by them in solidarity. To argue complacently that such 'unsocialized' workers were in the church was to miss the whole significance of the labour movement, and was to fail to realize the real danger the church was in vis-à-vis the working class. Class consciousness was not the last word in fraternity, but its contemporary expression in both its industrial and international aspects was not only valuable for future progress in both those fields, but was a vital part of 'God's proclamation of a mighty spiritual fact which has almost faded from Protestant consciousness.'

Were Protestants who rejected the possibility of God speaking through the labour movement prepared to believe that God's creative purposes were revealed only in the church? 'May it not be,' Thomas asked of critics, 'that social evolution itself reveals the creative purpose of God?' If so, then the church was 'under obligation to study the changes which were taking place in the world's life ... and to accept these changes as at least a challenge to the sufficiency of its program and aspirations.'[29] Of course, the churches had in some measure done that already, but it was sometimes suspected that for some in the church bureaucracy, the motivation for

27 See below, pp. 170–3   28 CG, 1 Sept. 1920, pp. 7–8

29 *Alberta Labor News,* 4 Sept. 1920, p. 15

reform was to maintain the church in a position of leadership. But even this interpretation of reforms pointed up the conclusion of Bland and Thomas, that there
was in process a displacement of 'nationalistic and bourgeois Christianity, with its
worship of the strong man in the pew and the safe man in the pulpit, by a Christianity inspired by that sense of solidarity which the labor movement has given to
our world.' Yet, Thomas warned, every conquest by Christianity had resulted in the
infusion of some 'poison' into Christianity. 'Certain tempers' in some industrial
organizations thus needed to be watched even as the inspiration of labour was
accepted. From Thomas' viewpoint, then, the Labor churches could be abused, but
they could also be for some a means of demonstrating 'knowledge of and sympathy
with what they regard as the most vital and significant movement of the age.'[30]

The New Christianity, as presented by Bland and interpreted by Thomas, was
potentially a powerful strategic standpoint at the time. In spite of the opposition it
aroused, perhaps because of it, it pressed the church further in the direction of the
social gospel. Its theoretical disassociation of essential Christianity from its cultural
expression offered a counterpoise to both the partial fact and the charges of domination by the middle and wealthy classes. At the same time as it provided a sanction
for the Labor churches, it established perspectives, and endorsed objectives which
would help make those churches unnecessary. Perhaps it was too much to assume
that progressives in the church could walk that ideological tightrope, but, in the
reactions to the Winnipeg strike, as revealed in the progressive church press and in
the debates of church conferences of June 1919, that expectation did not seem
overly sanguine. Otherwise, Bland would hardly have considered it worthwhile to
put his pen to paper to sketch so confidently 'the religion of the new age.' The other
ground of his confidence was the actual growth of the Labor churches as he was
writing. To understand the true character of these new churches was, for Bland, to
understand better the traditional denominations; hence the urgency of arousing
sympathy among church progressives for the Labor churches. In this respect, the
reaction of Creighton and Moore to *The New Christianity* and the susceptibility of
Moore to the intervention of the forces of internal security were not good omens,
and underlined in their turn the developments of the Inter-Church campaign.

30 CG, 1 Sept. 1920, pp. 7–8

10

Labor Churches

The years 1919 to 1921 were the crucial years of the Labor churches in Canada. They were years of expansion which won them their only recognition as a separate sect in the census. A total of 660 members in six cities was reported in 1921,[1] but that was barely a tenth of the probable attendance in those years at the nineteen churches that had been founded. With the exception of Winnipeg and Edmonton (where perhaps the most controversial of these controversial churches was established), the liveliest churches were founded by A.E. Smith, working from the base of his People's church in Brandon. The moderate success of the Labor church alerted and alarmed elements of both church and state, who found themselves cooperating in a dubious undercover arrangement to keep it in check. While these years of the Labor church, and those of its decline, 1922–7, were a test of the attitude of the churches at large toward an interesting experiment, they were also, and more importantly, a supreme test of what progressive and radical social gospellers had often declared to be the essentially religious spirit of labour.

If the experience of the Winnipeg strike had multiplied the Winnipeg Labor church, the related industrial crises across the nation were the occasion for imitation of the Winnipeg example. Ivens' figure of sixteen churches established suggests that eight churches existed outside Winnipeg by mid-1920. It is difficult to pin these down with exactitude, and to separate actual founding of Labor church congregations from discussion of intention to do so, or rumours of the possibility. There are unconfirmed reports of Labor churches in Cape Breton, Port Arthur, and Drumheller,[2] and of a 'Soldiers and Workers Church' attempted by one Gordon Baker in Montreal.[3] At Fort William a Labor church existed for an undetermined length of

---

1 *Census of Canada*, 1921, I, 756–67, Table 39. The breakdown of this figure was: Toronto, 2; Winnipeg, 547; Calgary, 25; Edmonton, 13; Brandon, 57; St Boniface, 16.

2 Summers, 'The Labour Church,' pp. 383, 390, 491, who relied on the report of Dr D.S. Dix, principal of St Andrew's College, Saskatoon.

3 W.S. Ryder, 'The Labor Church Movement of Canada,' a paper delivered to the

time. On 2 May 1920 Fred E. Moore and A. Henry advocated the formation of a Labor church in addresses at the Trades and Labor Hall in that city. Henry had been an occasional speaker at the Winnipeg churches, and was requested by the Fort William meeting to remain there as head of the Labor church. His conception of the church, however, was barely religious, and his biblical imagery largely rhetorical: 'Pharaoh was swamped by the Red Sea, but autocracy will be swamped by the Reds of Labor.'[4] Labour propaganda was his aim, and the name Labor church a device to get recruits from the orthodox church. 'If it is called a socialist meeting,' he commented, 'there are lots of people who would not come.'[5]

A Labor church was meeting in July 1919 in Saskatoon. A short sympathetic strike there of thirteen unions and 1200 workers had not lasted long owing to differences in the labour movement.[6] A visit by J.S. Woodsworth to the city on 13 July was the occasion for the first meeting of a Labor church. His report suggested that delegates from Saskatoon to the Winnipeg churches had carried back enthusiasm for the idea, and had plans for making Saskatoon the centre for disseminating 'the new social gospel' throughout northern Saskatchewan.[7] An enthusiastic reporter of a second meeting of the church, 'w.m.,' believed that there were good prospects for the future of the Saskatoon Labor church. The programme reported in the *Labor News* seemed a close reflection of the Winnipeg churches, with an address by Dr R.C. Manley on 'Christianity and the Economic Revolution,' and a programme of piano and vocal solos.[8] How long the Saskatoon Labor church continued to meet is not known.

If the foregoing six instances were authentic Labor churches in 1920, then Ivens' figure of sixteen churches was too small, for apart from the eight in Winnipeg, there were such churches in existence in Edmonton, Brandon, Calgary, Vancouver, and Victoria as well, making a total of nineteen. Of these latter churches, all except the Edmonton church were organized by A.E. Smith. Those with the most substantial history were the Edmonton and Brandon churches.

The Edmonton Labor church was the only one of its kind organized with a degree of official involvement of an established denomination. Ironically, it became per-

---

Pacific Coast Theological Conference, Vancouver, 1920, *Western Methodist Recorder*, Sept. 1920, pp. 4, 5

4 MIR, 'Notes on the Labor Churches,' 4 Jan. 1920, reporting Henry's remarks to the Columbia Theatre meeting of the Labor church in Winnipeg.

5 *Ibid.*

6 WLN, Special Strike Edition #19, 7 June 1919

7 *Ibid.*, 18 July 1919   8 *Ibid.*, 25 July 1919, p. 1

haps the most radical of the species. In 1919 the Alberta Conference of the Methodist Church requested G.L. Ritchie to devote his efforts to work among the labour constituency in Edmonton. The precise arrangement is not clear, but apparently Ritchie was given a small circuit of twenty-seven members and was to receive a salary of $750 per year from the conference. The editing of a labour paper seems to have been part of the understanding, and the general purpose to convey 'the comradeship and gospel of Modern Methodism to the unchurched labour of Edmonton.'[9] Some form of Labor church seems to have been in mind.[10]

In any case, the conference was hospitable to the idea. When the Lethbridge district of the church, in the course of the 1919–20 year asked for a declaration of policy regarding the 'People's Church Movement,' the Alberta Conference Evangelism and Social Service Committee recommended 'that the Conference reaffirm the belief and policy of our last General Conference regarding the Christianizing of the economic order and proclaim its willingness to proceed and promote that view of life and policy in any and every group of people who will accept our ministry.'[11]

Ritchie was perhaps not a good choice for this task. He had entered the ministry in 1910, and had since acquired a university education. His experience had been confined to small rural pastorates until 1918 when he requested to be left without station.[12] He seems to have imbibed a modernist theological outlook. That his political sympathies, at least at the outset, were moderately left, seemed indicated by his election in the fall of 1919 to fill out an executive position in the Dominion Labor party.[13] But if he had ability, he did not have the standing or experience that Ivens, let alone A.E. Smith, brought to their efforts.

The first meetings of the church for which information is available revealed a pattern which was to persist throughout its history. Five or six hundred people had gathered on 21 September 1919 at the Allen Theatre. After some introductory remarks about the Labor church, Mr Tom Richardson spoke on 'The New Social Order.' Richardson, a former Labour member of Parliament for Whitehaven, England, described himself as an international socialist, a democrat, and a Christian.[14] He was also a supporter of the Dominion Labor party.[15] At the end of his

9 Summers, 'The Labour Church,' pp. 391–2, citing an item in UCA which it has not been possible to relocate.
10 'Notes on the Labor Churches'
11 *Annual Report*, 1919–20, Methodist Department of ESS, p. 12
12 *Methodist Year Book*, 1915, p. 393; 1916, p. 313; 1917, p. 367; 1918, p. 393
13 *Edmonton Free Press*, 17 Jan. 1920, p. 3
14 'Notes on the Labor Churches'
15 *Edmonton Free Press*, 17 Jan. 1920, pp. 1, 3

address, Carl Berg, a local labour radical, proposed direct action to obtain the ends of socialism, and was sharply contradicted by Richardson.

Attendance dropped to sixty or seventy for the next two meetings, which found Ritchie speaking on 'Banned Literature' and 'Social Religion,' apparently with considerable radicalism, but still in contention with proponents of direct action, the most prominent being Berg. Berg was a frank materialist, who argued that prayer to neither 'the religious or the political God [will] help you in the least.' His apparent enthusiasm for the Labor church was that 'a majority of laboring people do not like the socialist meetings as they are called anarchists, but they can come here and be educated in the right way.'[16]

That Berg's way was not Ritchie's way was clear in the speakers which Ritchie secured during this first year and in their subjects: Principal Tuttle of Alberta College on 'Morals and Economics'; Alderman Rice on 'Social Reconstruction'; Nellie McClung; Professor W.H. Alexander on 'The Suppression of Criticism.' When on 11 January 1920 the church was locked out of the Empress Theatre because of an attack by Ritchie during the previous week upon Judge Metcalfe and A.J. Andrews of the trials of the Winnipeg strike leaders, Mayor Clarke spoke to an open-air gathering of the church and repeated the charges. Such speakers were only moderately leftist and invariably met torrential attacks from partisans of the Socialist Party of Canada.[17] Ritchie's position in the centre of these exchanges was not an enviable one. To tolerate offense to such speakers was to alienate sympathetic backing; to muzzle it would eliminate a part of the constituency he was to attempt to reach. To influence the radicals he had to give them a responsible role in the church, but to do so was to court disaster.

When in the middle of the year 1919–20, the Alberta Conference Committee appointed to supervise Ritchie's work asked about his progress, he could report the existence of a Woman's Auxiliary and several night classes as well as the Sunday meetings.[18] The committee had also asked why he did not preach every Sunday, and enquired as to his membership roll. When Ritchie discussed these queries with the Labor church committee, he informed it that prospects of receiving further support from the Methodist church was unlikely. The committee decided that a bid should be made for the $650 balance owing to Ritchie by having him preach every Sunday. At the same time an effort was to be made to put the church on more solid financial foundations. The committee was suspicious about the request for the membership roll, believing it an attempt to secure the names, dismiss Ritchie, and

16 'Notes on the Labor Churches'   17 *Ibid.*
18 *Edmonton Free Press,* 13 March 1920, p. 1; and enclosed Copy of Report, MIR, Hamilton to Moore, 2 June 1920

draw the members into the Methodist church.[19] By April 1920 a crisis in the relationship with the Methodist conference was reached, and ties were severed with the Labor church. Ritchie, however, was still left without a station at his own request,[20] and was free to continue his work.

During the second year of the Edmonton Labor church a similar condition continued. A division among members appeared on the issue of a minimum statement of belief such as the one used in Winnipeg, with a notable encounter between one P.F. Lawson and Ritchie on the subject on 26 June 1921. When Lawson declared from the floor that anyone who believed in a God helping the workers accomplish their emancipation was a traitor to the working class, Ritchie jumped to his feet, protesting his being called a traitor by Lawson or anyone else. The question of the existence of God was both personal and unprovable, he stated, and 'so long as the workers are so narrow-minded as to bicker and quarrel on such matters, so long will they be divided among themselves.' The speaker of the day, Theophilus Moore, who had spoken on 'The Breach between Churchianity and Socialists, and the Emancipation of Humanity,' joined Ritchie in condemning the unwarranted attack on persons like himself who believed in God.[21]

However, by this date the religious purpose of the church seemed to have dropped from sight. Ritchie had resigned from the Methodist ministry in June 1921,[22] and was opposed to discussing the religious issue in the Labor church at all. 'Religion and God,' he is reported as saying, 'were only an economic issue to him. He saw religion in the solution of economic problems.'[23] With the exclusion of the religious question from the agenda of the Labor church, it ceased to be a church, and became devoted solely to the political and economic aims of labour, in this case interpreted by the more radical wing of the labour and socialist movement in Edmonton. The last report on the Labor church, April 1922, indicated that it was continuing to form a valuable role as a forum for hundreds who regularly packed the theatre on Sunday evenings. G.L. Ritchie and socialists of a religious bent seem to have ceased their association with it.[24]

It was to a person of quite different stature than Ritchie that the other Labor churches in the West outside Winnipeg owed their inception. A.E. Smith, long a

19 *Ibid.*   20 *Methodist Year Book*, 1920, p. 417

21 MIR, Memo on Edmonton Labor church, enclosed in Hamilton to Moore, 29 July 1921

22 *Methodist Year Book*, 1921, p. 389   23 'Notes on the Labor Churches'

24 MIR, Hamilton to Moore, 25 April 1922. Of Ritchie's future course, nothing has been found.

socialist, twice chairman of the Manitoba Methodist Conference, and recent founder of the Brandon People's church, proved to be the missionary of the movement. In March and April of 1920 he undertook a tour of Western Canada to spread the word and found further churches. On his return to Brandon he reported establishing churches in Victoria, Vancouver, and Calgary.[25] Little development seems to have followed in Victoria. In Vancouver, while Smith spoke to well attended meetings, few remained to take part in actual organizational meetings for the church.[26] The small executive, including J. Clarke, Thomas Esart, and C.D. Herbert,[27] received valuable assistance when J.S. Woodsworth returned to Vancouver in August 1920. For some reason he did not use the term Labor church to describe the revitalized organization, but called it the 'People's Sunday Evening.' In addition, however, he organized a Labor Sunday School in which his lessons combined elements of Christianity and socialism.[28] These activities were part of his larger occupation of educational work with the Federated Labor party in Vancouver, a more moderate body than the doctrinaire Socialist Party of Canada which had caused Ritchie such trouble. However, Woodsworth found his work less satisfying and substantial than what he had left in Winnipeg, and when Ivens, out of prison in April 1921, immediately wrote asking him to return to take up the position of secretary to the Labor church there, he was happy to do so.[29] Activity of a kind resembling a Labor church in Vancouver seems not to have survived Woodsworth's departure in late April 1921.

On the way to his new post, however, he found that the Labor church founded by Smith in Calgary the year before had thrived, and stayed for a month giving his service to its advancement.[30] Calgary had had a very successful People's Forum for some time prior to Smith's visit, and Irvine, one of its more prominent supporters, had been active as a speaker and journalist in the city for almost four years. His message paralleled that of Ivens, in that it spoke of the need of a new religious and ethical consciousness to undergird the slowly emerging new social order.[31] It was to the forum that Smith proposed a Labor church, in a radical address, 'The Uprising of the People.'[32] In mid-April, the first service of the church was held in the Bijou

25 'Notes on the Labor Churches'

26 MIR, Enclosed Report, Hamilton to Moore, 21 May 1920

27 Ibid.; Summers, 'The Labour Church,' p. 465

28 MacInnis, J. S. Woodsworth: A Man to Remember, p. 125

29 McNaught, A Prophet in Politics, p. 143

30 Alberta Labor News, 7 May 1921, p. 1

31 Alberta Non-Partisan, 26 April 1918, p. 13; 10 May 1918, p. 13; 24 May 1918, p. 13

32 Edmonton Free Press, 20 March 1920, p. 3

Theatre, with Harry Pryde as chairman.[33] The two hundred persons present heard attacks on the social system and the 'Capitalist Church,' and appeals for brother-hood, since all must bear responsibility for the sickness of the social order.[34] Irvine expressed his enthusiasm for the new church in an article in the *Nation*. Unlike the old churches, he said, the Labor church was a 'new institution capable of containing the new spirit of the eternal Christ incarnate in humanity ... the spirit of every revolt against oppression, injustice and inhumanity.'[35]

Despite a superficial similarity, the characters of the Calgary and Edmonton Labor churches were very different. One measure of this is the fact that despite the controversial character of the latter, the *Edmonton Free Press* (later *Alberta Labor News*) under Elmo Roper almost never mentioned the local church, but followed the Calgary Labor church with some regularity. Whereas in Edmonton it was dominated by direct action advocates and doctrinaire socialists, in Calgary it was in the hands of able socialists who could put a cogent case for gradualism and who could distinguish between 'class struggle as a social phenomenon to be studied and class struggle as the abstract philosophy of radical politicians.'[36]

Of all the churches outside Winnipeg, by far the best organized was A.E. Smith's own People's church in Brandon. Smith had resolved to form such a church when opposition developed to his preaching in the First Methodist Church after a strike of Brandon civic employees, April 1919, in which he had been somewhat involved. On a dramatic evening, 8 June 1919, he told the congregation of his intention. He then left to attend a mass meeting of 2000 in one of Brandon's parks to inform them of his plan, and to urge them to follow him in creating a church which would not turn from the great objective of the brotherhood of man.[37] One hundred and twenty-five of those present signed pledges of support for a church 'where the Gospel of Social Christianity could be fearlessly propounded.'[38]

The church's central committee consisting of twenty-one members, was an able and diverse group. Under the chairmanship of an art teacher and secretaryship of a reporter for the local paper, sat a city alderman, an accountant, a railroad con-

33 *Ibid.* Other members prominent in organizing the church were Mrs A. Corless, W.R. Parkyn, Alderman A.G. Broatch, Miss Coutts, R. Gossett, W. Irvine, Alder-man Fred White, Edith Patterson, A. Nicholson, S. Lunoran. *Ibid.*, 17 April 1920

34 *Ibid.*

35 William Irvine, 'The Labor Church in Canada,' *The Nation*, 1 May 1920, p. 583

36 William Irvine, 'Can the Class Struggle Solve our Social Problem?' *Alberta Labor News*, 25 Sept. 1920, p. 2; report of an address to the Calgary Labor church

37 Smith, *All My Life*, pp. 60–1. Another source suggests it was a meeting of 200 in the Starland Theatre, 'Notes on the Labor Churches'

38 Smith, *All My Life*, pp. 60–1

ductor, a trade unionist, a motor mechanic, a musician, and a trained social worker who took charge of the work among women and children.[39]

Smith was the regular preacher at the People's church, devoting his time to social subjects and religious issues viewed from a modernist perspective. In the place of redemption of sinful man by Christ's sacrifice, he preached a social redemption whereby men's ills would be overcome by fruitful work and equitable distribution. Poverty seemed to be the greatest evil and profiteering the greatest sin. Christ and Paul were interpreted as 'socialists of the first water' whose religion could not be accommodated to the present system. To condense Smith's views so briefly is not to do them full justice, for there was a simplicity and directness in them which had great appeal to the dissatisfied. Furthermore, in the breadth of his church's activities, there was probably a fuller meeting of the spiritual needs of members than in most of the other Labor churches; this despite Smith's failure to grapple with deep personal issues.[40]

The Brandon People's church was more obviously structured as a church than others outside Winnipeg. Morning and evening services included hymns and prayers. It had organized groups for men, women, older and younger girls, and boys. These seemed to be devoted to religious discussions, the propagation of a Christian as against materialistic socialism, and sometimes, as with the men's group, more personal questions, such as problems of marriage and family.[41] What was called a People's Chautauqua was begun on a biweekly basis in the fall of 1921, and combined, in true Chautauqua style, entertainment, education, and religion, but in this case with a left-wing bent.[42] The church had the usual difficulties of keeping above water financially, but in mid-1921 was able to move to permanent quarters. About three hundred were attending at the time, although attendance began to drop in 1922.[43]

Smith was later to be associated with the nascent Communist party, but this association had probably not yet begun. However, local members often came to the church to present their views from the floor.[44] There has been some suggestion that he edited the *Confederate* for the Brandon branch of the Dominion Labor party.[45]

39 *Ibid.*, p. 62
40 See 'Notes on the Labor Churches'; Smith, *All My Life*, pp. 62–3; *The Confederate* (Brandon), published by the Dominion Labor party in Brandon
41 'Notes on the Labor Churches'
42 MIR, 'The People's Chautauqua'
43 MIR, Hamilton to Moore, 25 April 1922
44 Smith, *All My Life*, p. 68
45 Summers, 'The Labour Church,' pp. 379–80

In 1920 he contested and won the Brandon riding for that party in the provincial legislature, joining a Labour-Socialist group consisting of F.J. Dixon, W.D. Bailey, A.E. Moore, Albert Farmer, George Palmer, M.J. Stanbridge, W. Ivens, John Queen, and George Armstrong.[46] These ten with sixteen farmer candidates controlled almost half of the fifty-five seats. Smith's proposal of a cabinet based on group government concepts was rejected, and the Norris administration with twenty-one Liberal supporters and eight Conservatives as a floating vote braved out the subsequent two years. During the election of 1922, Liberals and Conservatives joined forces to defeat candidates such as Smith, and reduced Labor-Socialist representation to six.[47]

Smith's defeat raised the question of his future plans. He was prevailed upon to go to Toronto to organize a People's church there, and generally aid progressive forces.[48] He made the move in August 1923. What happened to the Brandon People's church after Smith left is not known. Smith's efforts to establish a similar church in Toronto was a considerable success for a year, involving the co-operation of various labour and socialist groups. But tensions between these bodies became difficult to overcome as Smith himself moved closer to a Communist position.[49]

Smith's efforts for the Labor church movement ended in mid-1924. He was at another crossroads. Apparently James Simpson, the Rev. Ben Spence, and Dr T.A. Moore, head of the Methodist Department of Evangelism and Social Service, were attempting to form a Sociological Fellowship, and wished Smith to conduct a lecture tour on its behalf among the churches. Old associates were urging a return to the Methodist church. But in January 1925, in a small upstairs room on Gerrard Street, he was accepted as a member of the Communist party. He had embraced revolution as a means of evolution. And although he believed he had given up religious for political means, he seemed but to have joined a new sect for the creation of a new earth in which human alienation and exploitation would be overcome, or as he called it, 'a broad movement which would eventually bring forth the true nature and spirit of man in a classless society of firm, conscious Brotherhood over all the earth.'[50]

46 Smith, *All My Life*, p. 65. Smith is probably including three representatives not usually considered Labour-Socialist, for the figure of seven such is reported elsewhere, eg, *Presbyterian and Westminster*, 15 July 1920
47 Morton, *Manitoba*, p. 379
48 Smith, *All My Life*, pp. 71–2
49 *Ibid.*, pp. 71–5
50 *Ibid.*, pp. 76–7. For more on Smith and a history of the Communist party in Canada in the 1920s, see Rodney, *Soldiers of the International*.

A similar pattern of development was working itself out among the leadership of the Winnipeg Labor churches. In July 1924, when Smith's People's church was faltering in Toronto, the Winnipeg Labor church, celebrating its sixth anniversary, was bravely urging 'all men and women ... to unite with us in the great task of establishing a world-wide co-operative commonwealth [which] the carpenter of Galilee called ... the Kingdom of God.'[51] Ivens and Woodsworth were the speakers. For both men, however, the political task of realizing this great social objective had a high priority on their time, and their Labor churches were in decline. Ivens, once elected to the provincial legislature, had been returned successfully in 1924, and continued to be so until 1936. Woodsworth, after a short period from June to December 1921 as secretary of the Winnipeg Labor churches, had won the federal seat of Centre Winnipeg. In Calgary, likewise, the Labor church had been deprived of Irvine's presence by his election to the federal house. In September of 1920 an attempt had been made to develop relations with other Winnipeg churches.[52] Winnipeg observers noted a more moderate tone in the Labor churches.[53] Upon Ivens' release in April 1921, his concern for the longer term requirements of labour's cause disgusted revolutionary socialists.[54] The Independent Labor party and the more moderate left represented by W.D. Bayley, John Queen, F.J. Dixon, F.G. Tipping, and A.A. Heaps, handled the larger share of lecturing responsibilities.[55] Although some of the more radical elements had begun to leave the fold, others, like John Houston, F. Woodward, and R.B. Russell of the OBU, continued to appear on the church's platforms.[56] While their presence helped maintain the breadth of appeal that was still central to the church's purpose, their very presence seemed to require apology.[57] As in Edmonton there was a running debate on the religious question which sent the more orthodox back to the denominations, despite the fact that Ivens, unlike Ritchie, considered it a vital question for the church. He insisted

51 Ivens' Papers, Hymn Sheet, 1924 Anniversary Service
52 *Presbyterian and Westminster*, 9 Sept. 1920, p. 281. Mr Willcocks, the secretary, sent out 'a very kind and brotherly letter' welcoming an exchange of speakers on Labour Sunday.
53 CG, 4 Aug. 1920, p. 25
54 'Notes on the Labor Churches.' Frank Cassidy of the Socialist Party of Canada, in Calgary, called him 'the oiliest, slimiest, slickest meal-ticket artist that ever placed his teaching before the Labor Party.'
55 OBU *Bulletin*, 7 Sept. 1922; 25 Jan., 1 Feb., 15 March 1923; 12, 18, 25 Sept. 1924
56 *Ibid.*, 27 Aug. 1921; 1 Feb. 1923; 12 Sept. 1924
57 *Manitoba Free Press*, 9 March 1921

that religion was far from an opiate. 'It is not religion that either emancipates or enslaves a people,' he declared, 'but the people, being enslaved or emancipated, evolve a religion that meets the need of their condition.' Religion, he insisted, was a means, not an end, but it was a vital means. For the socialist movement to become divorced from its religious roots was for it to begin to die.[58] In spite of this belief, however, less and less religion was to be found in Labor church programmes. Similarly, the weightier fare of economics and politics began to give way to a wide variety of subjects of general interest. In January 1923, one branch became enthused by a series of health lectures by a Mr Thomas, a natural foods exponent and editor of *Red Blood Magazine*.[59] Illustrated lectures proved popular in 1925,[60] but could not stay the general decline of the church. Five of the eight churches remained active in 1924,[61] but by late 1926 only one branch was still alive.[62] The Independent Labor party attempted, but failed, to keep the church functioning in 1927, and a recently established forum meeting continued the more serious lecturing tradition of the church, while labour and OBU Sunday schools picked up other strands of its labour educational work.[63]

The Labor churches caused considerable anxiety for the leadership of the denominations. Especially significant was the fact that the progressive social gospel of the social service departments seemed to show more concern over the Labor churches than over the sympathetic strikes and the 'Red Scare' of 1919. Methodists were most affected, having lost five ministers in one conference over the issue.[64] But the real problem seemed to be the challenge which the Labor church made to the multiclass nature of church organization and to the large hopes of achieving the righteousness that 'exalteth a nation' by means of church union. There were weighty arguments against the idea of a Labor church, but the real criticism that can be made of church reaction was that there seems never to have been an attempt at consultation on the possibility of this or some similar agency carrying out a special ministry among labouring people. What was more damning still was that, failing such consultation, Methodist denominational leadership was prey to false informa-

58 Ivens Papers, sermon notes   59 OBU *Bulletin*, 25 Jan. 1923
60 *Ibid.*, 29 Jan., 5 Feb. 1925   61 *Ibid.*, 7 Feb., 18 Sept. 1924
62 *Ibid.*, 30 Dec. 1926   63 *Ibid.*, 3 Feb. 1927
64 Address of Dr Chown to the Toronto Conference, CG, 30 June 1920, pp. 7, 8. The names of the five are not given, but they likely included, with Ivens and Smith, R.A. Hoey, who went to work for one of the Manitoba farmers' organizations, and F.C. Middleton, who took up a post with the Manitoba Social Service Council.

tion and exaggerated reports sent them by the Royal Canadian Mounted Police (RCMP). And in false gratitude, one high official voluntarily turned informer on the enterprises of his erstwhile colleagues.

In mid-May 1920 Lt-Col. C.F. Hamilton of the RCMP called on T.A. Moore, head of Evangelism and Social Service for the Methodist church. Hamilton was a man of some accomplishment, a journalist, co-author of a biography of G.M. Grant, a military historian, and war correspondent. During the war he had acted as deputy chief press censor, and had since become assistant comptroller and then intelligence and liaison officer of the RCMP.[65] No doubt the two men discussed the concern of the church over the growth of the Labor churches since the Winnipeg strike.[66] Hamilton apparently explained to Moore that they had been collecting material on the churches since early 1919, and that reports were alarming indeed as to the nature of the movement. Moore agreed that it was at the very least an unsound development, but that it should be allowed to die of its own inadequacy.[67] However, the nature of Hamilton's correspondence with Moore over the next two years made it less likely that the Methodist leadership would come to understand any adequacy the movement might have had. Hamilton promised to send a digest of RCMP information on the Labor churches and Moore said he would 'do something to give publicity to the whole question which will be of value in the direction intimated in our conversation.'[68]

On 2 June Hamilton sent Moore twenty-six pages of 'Notes on the Labor Churches,' condensing reports on speakers, subjects, and numerous extracts from one hundred and forty meetings in Edmonton, Winnipeg, and Brandon. On 17 June a second, shorter report was sent, and subsequently bits and pieces and comments on general developments. It is apparent from the reports that, in at least Edmonton, agents had infiltrated the executive committee of the Labor church. The reports were patently drawn up for RCMP purposes. All the purple passages with revolutionary implications were presented out of context, and little attempt was made to distinguish between the intentions and speeches of the actual leadership of the church and many who spoke their mind from the floor or from the

65 See Berger, *The Sense of Power*, pp. 248, 253; also PAC, Papers of Charles Frederick Hamilton

66 MIR, Moore to Hamilton, 25 May 1920. Copies of Moore's letters are not available in all cases, but general content can be inferred from those of Hamilton. Hamilton's address was Drawer 539, Ottawa. The correspondence continued until 25 April 1922. Sometime in 1920 the Royal North-West Mounted Police incorporated the Dominion Police, and became known as the Royal Canadian Mounted Police.

67 MIR, Moore to Hamilton, 2 Dec. 1920   68 MIR, Moore to Hamilton, 25 May 1920

pulpit but in no real way represented the purposes of Ivens, Woodsworth, Irvine, Smith, or Ritchie.

Late in the correspondence, Hamilton characterized these men as simply engaging in 'humanitarian talk,' as against the blasphemy of the revolutionists, but by then the damage had been done.[69] Some of the reports concerned the International Bible Students whose apocalypticism worried the RCMP as being 'highly mischievous.' Instead of protesting such foolishness, Moore co-operated in finding information about individuals reported.[70] In one case Hamilton had to apologize for the poor quality of a report sent in by 'regular constables' covering Smith in Vancouver. They had reported that he had pronounced the chief sins which had caused the crucifixion of Christ to be 'religious bigamy' and 'mobbed spirit'![71] Most reports, however, seemed reasonably competent, but in relying on them, Moore and his closest colleagues ignored the fact that the Methodist church had other responsibilities in the situation than those of the RCMP.

The notes sent by Hamilton on 2 and 17 June were put to immediate use, which indicated that double checking their authenticity had not been attempted. Moore wrote in thanks, 29 June, that 'you will doubtless have noted that we have had some items in the *Christian Guardian,* and also that Dr Chown has declared the mind of the church in a notable address at Toronto Conference. All this grew out of our conversation and your sending me the notes.' When Hamilton reported that the Rev. Haw of Dauphin, Manitoba, a worker for the Labor party, and the Rev. Ranns, chairman of a Woodsworth meeting in Carievale, Saskatchewan, had been under surveillance, Moore does not seem to have written in their defence.[72]

A few months prior to the organization of the Independent Labor party in March 1921, Moore, on hearing word that Smith had been in conference with labour socialists, reported the fact to Hamilton along with his concern over the new policy that might be being developed. His reporters, he said, 'are not sure whether this may be a policy with regard to organizing on a more stable basis of a so-called labour political party, or whether it shall take some other direct form. We think it worthwhile, however, to mention the matter to you so that your men may have opportunity of investigating the whole situation.'[73] Later, in projecting a trip to Brandon himself, Moore promised to report anything of note that he could uncover.[74]

69 MIR, Hamilton to Moore, 29 July 1921

70 MIR, Hamilton to Moore, 6 July 1920; Moore to Hamilton, 7 July 1920

71 'Notes on the Labor Churches'

72 MIR, Hamilton to Moore, 12 June 1920

73 MIR, Moore to Hamilton, 2 Dec. 1920   74 MIR, Moore to Hamilton, 18 April 1921

Moore seems to have considered, not simply that the Labor churches were mistaken, but that they were an evidence of the moral inadequacy of their leadership. He wrote that they hypocritically preached 'an unselfish gospel ... where the Church businessmen and industry are concerned,' yet developed 'such an abnormal selfishness' as to organize a class church. Hamilton's erroneous information that Ivens had been 'elbowed out of the Winnipeg Labour Church' by Woodsworth, Moore uncritically accepted as proof of his own suspicions as to the moral character of Labor church leadership.[75]

Dr Chown was more charitable in his judgment, but just as firm in his rejection of the Labor churches. He described them as an evidence of Methodist concern for suffering people, expressed by men of keen sympathy – but not so broad in understanding and experience. Christianity could not sanction a class church. It was a catholic religion, he declared, with a world programme, and moved 'slowly toward its predestined heights because it carries all the burdens of mankind.' By contrast,

the history of the labor churches thus far in Canada is a demonstration that the purpose of many who support them is to use the word "Church" as a cloak under which the teachings of revolutionary socialism may be made to reach a larger number of people, and particularly people who are interested to some extent in Christian principles, but are alienated from their former connections by the opinion that the Church is not doing all she might do to solve social problems.[76]

The fairness of this criticism is manifest. It made important qualifications upon the conclusions of Lt-Col. Hamilton.[77] Where Hamilton argued that the very purpose of the Labor church was to cloak revolutionary preaching, Chown simply claimed that many exploited it for that purpose. But Chown's statement left untouched the question as to what the Labor churches and their primary leadership were trying to accomplish. It could well be argued that to regain a church footing with a large section of the working class, it was necessary to risk and even permit such exploita-

75 MIR, Hamilton to Moore, 29 July 1921; Moore to Hamilton, 3 Aug. 1921
76 Address to Toronto Conference, CG, 30 June 1920, pp. 7, 8
77 Hamilton had written as follows: '... the conclusion submitted is that the "Labour Church" is not a religious but an irreligious, or anti-religious device, designed for the teaching of revolutionary socialism under the cloak of religion; that it contains no spark of religion, Christian or otherwise, and that it is a conscious piece of hypocrisy, designed to attract a certain type of person of Christian principles who are interested in social problems and troubled over the attacks made upon the Churches for not solving them' ('Notes on the Labor Churches').

tion by those alienated from both church and state. It is possible that during 1919 and early 1920 there might have been little meeting of minds in any attempted rapprochement between denominational and Labor church leaders. But there was an evident openness in Ivens' mind to a many-sided approach to industrial reform, and the Winnipeg Labor churches at least showed signs of moderation in late 1920. However, if prior to June 1920 there had been any disposition in Methodist leadership to treat the Labor church as a useful experiment, reliance on one-sided RCMP reports from Lt-Col. Hamilton's agents ended any such possibility. Some intelligent observers in the church wished to wait and see what the reaction of labour at large would be to the new movement, but in general there seems to have been a more instant rejection of the radical social gospel over the Labor churches than over any other issue.[78]

The Labor church was probably not a viable institution in Canada. The English Labour churches, of which it was a reflection, had virtually died out in the second decade of the twentieth century. Even the existence of a large, self-conscious working class would not likely have saved the Canadian churches from a like fate. The British Labour churches had been part of a revolution in the social and political attitudes of British nonconformist churches. Since this effect had been transmitted in considerable measure to Canada by the time of the major period of Canadian Labor church development, the role of the Labor church in Canada was much more constricted. It provided a common meeting ground for a badly divided labour movement, but inevitably itself became caught in the divisions it sought to heal. The basis of that attempted unity, the religious significance of labour and of the great strike of 1919, it fostered for a time, but its religious and theological resources were limited, and it was in the logic of its nature that it should either reclothe its social hopes in the more orthodox eschatology of the denominations and take up the more pragmatic politics of social service, or more completely demythologize its own eschatology in terms of a political platform for the disinherited of Canadian society.

The latter course was the one taken by the leaders of the Labor churches. It was notable that as the Labor church went into eclipse, a 'Ginger' group of progressives in the House of Commons crystallized out of the Progressive party to become the political nucleus of the later Co-operative Commonwealth Federation (CCF). Its central figures were the radical social gospellers, J.S. Woodsworth and William Irvine. In Manitoba the leading figures of early CCF history were S.J. Farmer, chairman of the first Labor church meeting, and William Ivens, founder of the churches. For all of them the Labor church was their last formal religious expres-

78 W.S. Ryder, 'The Labor Church Movement of Canada,' *Western Methodist Recorder*, pp. 4, 5

sion.[79] It was the confession of things seen through a glass darkly: that there was a possible world in which the world's work would be done with a sense of brotherly communion; that the self-conscious worker would somehow be able to master the economic machine and direct it toward the filling of human need; that that act was an expression of the divinity immanent in man; that a great struggle lay between the present and that day; that such developments would have profound effects upon all forms of human society, not excepting religion; and that such a world would be a living embodiment of the 'teachings and spirit of Jesus of Nazareth.'[80] This was the essential religious formulation which remained the fundament of the 'new politics' of J.S. Woodsworth, William Ivens, William Irvine – and of A.E. Smith as well.

79 See also McNaught, *A Prophet in Politics*, p. 139
80 See especially Woodsworth, *The First Story of the Labor Church*

11

A Sea of Ambiguities

In 1921 the progressives of the social gospel were faced with an eruption of industrial conflict in the most compromising place possible – the church printing establishments. The situation was symbolic in its complexity. The social gospel movement had won the denominations to progressive social policies and to a new level of sympathy with organized labour, especially in the Methodist church. Among the progressives in that church had also been found the more sane reactions to the Winnipeg strike. Yet the progressive leadership in Methodism had by 1921 totally rejected the sectarian religion of labour of the Labor churches, and had served notice that they could not give unqualified support to radical labour tactics such as the general sympathetic strike. Now, however, not radical but conservative labour unions presented the issue.

On the labour side, in 1921, there was considerable awareness that support for its cause was still high in the churches. Some labor spokesmen knew of the recent formidable attacks by the American social gospel on the primitive conditions at the US Steel Company, and appreciated American church criticism of the open-shop campaign manufacturers had initiated shortly after the war.[1] The situation was, therefore, fraught with embarrassment and pregnant with tragedy when in June 1921 the conservative but highly organized unions of the printing trade called a strike against the employing printers of Toronto. Among them were the church publishers – and the largest of these, the Methodist Book and Publishing Company.

The strike was, in fact, continent-wide. It was the culmination of a two-year effort by the International Typographical Union of America to secure a forty-four hour week. Only eight thousand of the union's seventy thousand members were called out in 1921, but almost all major Canadian cities were affected.[2] The Typo-

1 *Industrial Banner*, 5 Aug. 1921
2 *Ibid.*, 3 June 1921, p. 1. The actual contestants in the Toronto strike were 104 master printers and bookbinders of Toronto Typothetae, and the Toronto Typographical Union #91, the Toronto Mailers' Union #5, the Toronto Pressmen's Union #10, the Toronto Press Assistants' Union #1, and the International Brotherhood of Bookbinders #28. Dennison, *Facts and Figures*, p. 3

graphical Union was a strong, responsible union. Probably most of the Toronto members could not remember when it had last engaged in a strike. It provided generous benefits for its members and conducted training courses which, it proudly asserted, were to compensate for the shoddy training employers gave apprentices.[3] In such a strike as this it laid its strategy carefully, and assessed non-striking members a regular percentage of wages to pay strike benefits to striking members. The early stages of planning for the forty-four hour week had taken place during boom conditions in the industry in 1919. Hopes then had been to secure the new hours with no drop in take-home pay. However, as recession began to affect the trade in 1920 and 1921, locals were told that the wages question would have to be settled on a strictly local basis.[4]

In the Toronto negotiations the union had at first proposed forty-four hours with a weekly wage of forty-four dollars. The employers pointed out that this would be a rather excessive raise. The two-year contract negotiated in 1919 had raised wages from $25.20 to $33.00 per week, and in mid-1920 the employers had, without contractual obligation, introduced another increase to $35.20. However, trade conditions in 1920 had declined, and were still doing so. The best that the employers would offer was forty-eight hours at $35.20, in other words, the same conditions – which, they argued, were really a raise under recession conditions – or forty-four hours at $33.00. The union dropped its wage figure to $38.50 which it said was a basic cost-of-living figure drawn up by independent sources, but it refused to alter its demand for the forty-four hour week. Issues relating to conciliation and arbitration entered the dispute, but the basic contest seemed to be over wages and hours. By the end of May negotiations, clearly deadlocked, broke down, and the strike began on 1 June 1921.[5]

The strike seemed to call for no comment from the progressive social gospel in the churches. Responsible industry-wide collective bargaining had taken place, and only the deplorable fact that negotiations had broken down seemed worthy of protest.[6] Despite social gospel sympathy with general labour objectives, it would have been quite unwise for it to endorse every labour campaign uncritically. Nor

3 Dennison, *Facts and Figures*, p. 19; 'Trade Unions and the Churches,' *Printers World*, nd [ca 1 Aug. 1920]; *Industrial Banner*, 8 July 1921, pp. 1, 4

4 International Typographical Union of America, *Facts About the Forty-four Hour Week*, pp. 30–1

5 For details of the positions of the two parties, see UCA, 1921 *Negotiations Between the Committees Representing the Toronto Typothetae and Toronto Local, No. 91 of the International Typographical Union* (hereafter cited as *1921 Negotiations*)

6 CG, 1 June 1921, p. 8

could it propose that the church adjudicate the technical aspects of an industrial dispute. The dangers in this respect were exactly those from which the social gospel had been trying to rescue the churches. Ernest Thomas put the point succinctly in the first week of the strike, although not in reference to it. 'We dare not seek to emancipate the Church from its thralldom to capitalism by making it the handmaid of some other phase of development which in time will also become an incubus.'[7]

In fact, the strike seemed quite inopportune. As far as the Methodist establishment was concerned, it had, over the previous year, made only 3 per cent on its capital investment, and did not consider it possible to pass on increased costs caused by a higher labour bill to a declining market.[8] The firm itself had not been anti-union. Rather, it had authorized posters urging workers to join and work through the unions. These were some of the points Dr S.W. Fallis, the new head of the Book and Publishing department, made to union leaders in the plant on 30 April 1921. He also warned them that the firm had a large clientele which depended for their programme of Christian education on Methodist publications. If the unions were to strike, he would have to find ways and means of continuing this service.[9]

However, what was to be of more concern to the church than the simple fact of a strike at the Publishing House was the acceptance by Fallis of the chairmanship of the Employers' Defence Committee. His acceptance was probably unwise, but he could hardly foresee the tragic situation in which his position was to place the church, or the extreme embarrassment that it was to cause the social gospel progressives of Methodism. He accepted simply 'upon the principle that I never can refuse to do anything I expect someone else to do if I am otherwise free to do it.'[10] Well aware of the sympathies of many Methodist leaders, James Simpson, editor of the *Industrial Banner*, at first looked on Fallis' position with the hope that he would 'be the means of getting the employing printers out of their present dilemma.'[11] That this would be difficult, he had no doubt:

7 *Ibid.*, 8 June 1921, p. 7

8 This was a figure quoted by Fallis, but it tallies with the financial statement for the Quadriennium 1918–22 in the *Methodist Journal of Proceedings*, 1922, pp. 191–3. Average profit for the Quadriennium was: calculated on invested capital, 5.5 per cent, and calculated on turnover of all departments, 3.8 per cent. Labour publicity seemed usually to use the net profit figure of the firm before the deduction of capital interest charges, which reduced the figure by more than half.

9 MIR, Copy, Address of Dr Fallis at a meeting of the Chairman of Chapels, 30 April 1921

10 MIR, Fallis to D.H. Telfer, 6 Oct. 1921

11 3 June 1921, p. 1

There are some big printing establishments which labor expects to get better treatment from. Included in these plants are those operated by religious denominations. When they enter the commercial world to compete with modern capitalism they must expect to be involved in some rather trying situations, situations which will prove the testing time. They will be called upon to either accept the rules of the competitive capitalist game, which their conferences, synods and assemblies condemn, or project their Christian principles into their business.[12]

The conservative press, noting Methodist prominence in the employers' ranks, chided the church for not living up to its declaration 'in favor of socialism or communism.' The Methodists, having declared against profits, were now arguing their importance, the London *Herald* remarked. The next General Conference, it predicted, could be expected to return to realism in these matters.[13]

The strike was, indeed, to be a testing time. The church was shortly to suffer inter-departmental strife and factional dispute, and have its advanced social policies held up to ridicule by vindictive conservatives and labour alike. But the criteria of the test were not as simple as Simpson, let alone his less understanding colleagues, would have them. And the strike was to mark a stage on the road to social realism, it was true, but the realities it revealed hardly stood as compliments to the idols of the conservative press. Neither were they such as would change the formulation of Methodist social policy. But the complexities and ambiguities of the situation of the church and the social gospel within it were such as to cut a part of the nerve of social action on the one hand, and to fortify it, on the other, with a new sense of realism about the world in which the objectives of social action must be sought. If the new social policies had been won at the cost of alienating a portion of the wealthy and conservative constituency of the church, the new realism was bought at the high price of suspicion of the sincerity of church social policy among even conservative trade unionists – many of them Methodists. Tragedy was compounded in that this decline in trust was due as well to the folly of labour as to the ignorance, self-righteousness, and innocence in the church. Both parties embraced Methodists and workers and both of them the while were enmeshed in and manipulated adroitly by the open-shop drive against unionism itself.

The Methodist firm in Toronto was soon deep in the raw realism of industrial struggle. Early in the strike the employing printers engaged the basement of a building on Richmond Street West for the purpose of recruiting strike-breakers.[14] Al-

12 *Ibid.*   13 MIR, undated editorial cutting
14 *Industrial Banner*, 3 June 1921, p. 1

though government employment bureaus refused to send men to it, Fallis did not hesitate to use its services to replace striking workers. Fallis, of course, was not acting alone. In running the Publishing House, he was responsible to the Central Section of the book committee of General Council in addition to four Western Section representatives, two from the Superannuation Fund Committee and the editors of the various publications of the house.[15]

In May this committee had decided to oppose the demands of the unions, and appointed J.C. Hay, the Rev. T.W. Neal, and Wilfred Kettlewell to consult with Fallis on strike matters.[16] None of the committee members, with the exception of W.B. Creighton, editor of the *Guardian*, had any reputation for a progressive social outlook. However, even he was persuaded of the soundness of the Book Steward's arguments. One step inexorably led to another, and shortly Creighton, who had defended the Winnipeg strikers, argued that the dispute had developed into 'what looks like a conflict with the Union as such and for the open shop.' In our case, he said, church publications had to be brought out, and from the first it was necessary to have the men to do it. Church publications were apparently sacrosanct, while the products of Winnipeg foundries were not! Further arguing Fallis' case, he continued that having incurred an obligation to these men 'who helped us in our extremity,' the firm was forced into an open-shop position to protect them.[17] None seemed aware of a larger context to the local dispute which might affect their judgment of the case.

Nor were Ernest Thomas and the Evangelism and Social Service Department apparently aware at first of this larger context. Thomas defended Fallis at the Bay of Quinte and Hamilton conferences when progressives not close to events attacked the apparent inconsistency of their publishing enterprise with the declared social policy of the church.[18] Thomas had pointed out that Fallis had had signs throughout the Book Room urging employees to attend and work through the union, and that the present dispute was 'whether a particular wage and time schedule is practicable, not as regards the relation of wages to profits, but as regards the continuance of the industry.'[19]

For some reason Thomas' efforts to defend the Book Room were apparently not appreciated. On the day after the Hamilton conference when Thomas attempted to consult Fallis, he was received so rudely that he walked out. On repeating the

15 *The Discipline, 1918,* pp. 181–90, see especially paragraph 275
16 MIR, News item, np, nd
17 CG, 13 July 1921, p. 8
18 MIR, Thomas to Fallis, 26 July 1921
19 MIR, [Ernest Thomas] to the Editor, *The Herald* (London), undated cutting

attempt, he found that Fallis again became personal. Thomas did not repeat the experiment for some time.[20] The pressures of a compromising situation had begun to raise tempers. Creighton, too, gave vent to his frustration in an angry outburst: strikes 'are just as foolish and as stupid as we have always heretofore thought them to be.'[21] Creighton, however, was not as implicated as Fallis, and served in his place as a source of information for Thomas as to the affairs of the Book Room and its steward.[22] By mid-June, not only had Thomas become alarmed at Fallis' mood under pressure of the strike, but the highest levels of the church made their displeasure known to Fallis over the vicious publicity that his Defence Committee had begun to issue.[23]

Employers' advertisements in May had been relatively innocuous, despite their distortions. They referred to the 'better type of printing craftsman' and the 'responsible Union member' as being opposed to the strike.[24] But the unions could point to overwhelming votes over the past two years for the forty-four hour week, for the strike, and for 10 per cent assessments on wages to conduct it.[25]

From 15 June on employer propaganda took on a rabid tone. It complained that the Typographical Union was a totally unconstructive force in the industry, arbitrarily governed, constantly inhibiting initiative and effort, ready to strike on the least provocation.[26] The complaints were formidable, but were replete with calculated distortions, as the unions could easily show.[27] On 23 June the employing printers inserted a large advertisement attempting to prove the tyranny of the International over the local union. The executive of the local unions, it argued, was unable to put to arbitration any of the laws governing it as a local of the International Union! This was the justification of the banner headline of the advertisement: 'It's Against the "Rules" to Arbitrate.' Continuing this masterpiece of deception the advertisement asked:

Would you in your business dealings, approach a man or company for employment and say: "I will from time to time pass laws governing my hours of work and my rate

20 MIR, Thomas to Fallis, 26 July 1921   21 CG, 21 June 1921
22 MIR, Thomas to Fallis, 26 July 1921
23 Thomas to the editor, *Toronto Daily Star*, 25 July 1921, in reply to a public letter of Fallis
24 *Toronto Daily Star*, 4 May 1924; *Mail and Empire*, 28 May 1921
25 Dennison, *Facts and Figures*, p. 6
26 *Toronto Daily Star*, 15 June 1921; *Mail and Empire*, 20 June 1921
27 Dennison, *Facts and Figures*, pp. 8–12

of pay. You will have to concede me such demands. But there are, of course, certain minor points regarding our business relations which we can agree upon after discussion." That is an illogical and impossible position to adopt, yet it is the position existing between the Employing Printers and their former employees.

In point of fact, both parties had been willing to arbitrate, but the scope and points of arbitration differed.[28] The advertisement then announced that, 'finding it impossible to negotiate with the Local Union on the points at variance, we therefore have disbanded our Negotiating Committee and are now operating our plants on the principle of the "Open Shop." ' A special 'box' enclosed the most provocative assertion of all: 'Toronto Printers are forced to take an oath to a foreign controlled union that places their allegiance above matters of society, government and religion. No Canadian should be asked to take this oath!'[29] These advertisements were signed by ninety-eight firms, most of them members of United Typothetae, and the rest members of the Canadian National Newspapers and Periodicals Association. Among the latter were the publications of the Anglican, Baptist, Methodist, and Presbyterian churches. At the same time a circular signed by 112 firms was distributed in the shops urging the merits of the open shop. This circular was soon to be followed by a blank letter which unionists might sign – their resignation from the union.[30]

These latest moves put the strike in quite another light. The Evangelism and Social Service Department, through Thomas, immediately wrote Fallis, describing the advertisements as provocative, making settlement more difficult, and containing charges which were irrelevant, unnecessary, and openly appealing to nationalistic prejudice. Furthermore, according to Thomas, and this was the crucial matter, the advertisements constituted a threat 'to issues of unionism, collective bargaining and working conditions ...' He pointed out that while the rejection of proposals was part of bargaining, scrapping the machinery of negotiation was demanding unconditional surrender, and an example of the dictatorial methods of which the Defence

28 1921 *Negotiations*

29 The oath apparently referred to is Article xii, Section 1 of the constitution of the International Typographical Union of America, in which a member pledges fidelity which may 'in no sense be interfered with by any allegiance that I now or hereafter owe to any other organization, society, political or religious, secret or otherwise,' and goes on: 'shall apply to matters pertaining to the printing industry.' Dennison, *Facts and Figures,* p. 12.

30 *Ibid.,* p. 17

Committee had falsely accused the unions. Giving Fallis the benefit of the doubt, Thomas noted that the action had been taken while Fallis was absent, and was calling it to his attention.[31]

Fallis had been away from the city defending himself at various conferences, and had not sanctioned the specific advertisements in question. That he was already in a position of severe personal conflict can hardly be doubted. His earlier rudeness to Thomas was evidence enough of that. The moves made by the Defence Committee in his absence heightened that conflict by implicating him in a course which now indisputably cut across Methodist policy, although this conflict he never did admit. He later claimed that he would have appreciated a public challenge at the time as an opportunity for dissociating himself from the content of the advertisements in question,[32] but if he had any reservations at the time he gave no expression to them. Furthermore, he had become committed to the open shop itself. Creighton had already explained the reasons. However, when the unions rumoured new hopes for a settlement upon hearing that the Toronto Methodist Ministerial Association was investigating the dispute, Fallis took care to deny such a likelihood. He reassured his new workers that if he was 'compelled by the Church to make such a settlement as will mean displacing the present staff by the strikers, the Book Steward too will go out with those who have stood faithfully with him in undertaking to reorganize and carry on.'[33]

Striking unionists, hardly touched by such 'tenderness' between bosses and scab labour, paraphrased Carrie Jacobs Bond to provide lyrics for this industrial duet:

When you come to the end of a printer's day
And you stand on the curb in thought,
While the "dubs" slink out on their homeward way
To the mess of pottage they've bought;
Can you think what the end of that hell-fired day
Can mean to a bosses heart,
When the sun goes down in a flaming ray,
And the 'dear' friends have to part.[34]

Fallis denied that he was doing more than opposing the unreasonable demands of a branch of the labour movement. But by never publicly criticizing the publicity in question, he remained implicated in the attacks on the character of the union and

31 MIR, copy of letter, Thomas to Fallis, 27 June 1921
32 MIR, Thomas to Moore, 27 July 1921
33 MIR, posters in the Book Room
34 Toronto Typographical Union, *Printers' World*, No 91 (Strike Committee, nd)

committed to the exclusion of the strikers as part of any settlement. The logic of this position was complete non-recognition of the Typographical Union, a position into which he obviously did not want to be put.

Thomas' criticism of this new stage in the dispute was seconded by Simpson in the *Banner*, who struck a heavy blow at Fallis' implication in an anti-union campaign.[35] Simpson raised another issue in the dispute by linking wage policies of the Book Room to the ministerial superannuation fund. It was true that profits from the Book Room were to go to this fund, but the enterprise was not operated to sustain this fund. The profits were calculated after the payment of contracted wages, and Fallis had publicly declared his refusal to give the fund any priority in the concerns of the operation.[36] Nevertheless, the arrangement was not a healthy one and Simpson was correct in gauging the position of the Book Room as nothing less than tragic, 'one from which the church will not recover and will only partly be effaced by a change of name' with church union.[37]

In the meantime at least forty printing firms had settled with the union, with the *Catholic Register* among the first.[38] The *Canadian Congregationalist*, the *Presbyterian Witness*, and *Social Welfare* were all being printed out of town, whether in union shops or others is not clear.[39] Most of the shops, however, were still struck, and the centre of attack began to fall more heavily upon the Methodist Book and Publishing Company. This company was a good target not only because of its declared policies, but also because it was the largest of the firms. Both factors would have made its capitulation a most significant union victory. Early in July a special demonstration by Methodist unionists was being organized by the union to expose the 'supineness' of that church. Thomas managed to persuade Simpson that this demonstration would be ill-advised. On 21 July when he learned that the Trades

35 8 July 1921, p. 4

36 Thomas to the *Industrial Banner*, 5 Aug. 1921. However, it must be pointed out that at the time that Fallis was pleading inability to pay the extra cost of higher wages and shorter hours, the firm did pay out of profits the largest sum in eight years to the superannuation fund, $30,000. *Methodist Journal of Proceedings*, 1922, p. 191

37 *Industrial Banner*, 8 July 1921, p. 4

38 MIR, copy of letter, International Typographical Union, No 91, to Toronto Conference of the Methodist church, 9 June 1921

39 *Canadian Congregationalist*, 29 Sept. 1921, p. 4; *Presbyterian Witness*, 16 June 1921; sw, July–Aug. 1921, cover page. None of these seem to have made any attempt to discuss the issues of the strike.

Council was planning to organize pressure on firms advertising in Methodist and Salvation Army papers, he suggested to Simpson that such tactics 'would only consolidate the enemies of the cause.' Simpson considered this a strong point and agreed to press it at the Trades and Labor Council meeting that night.[40]

With both the character of the strike changed and with the stiffening of tactics against the Methodist establishment, Thomas had been driven to investigate the deeper causes of the dispute. Central to the Typographical Union case had been the insistence that in the negotiations of 1919 it had been led to accept terms it would otherwise have rejected, on the understanding that the forty-four hour week would take effect on 1 May 1921. This promise, however, was not recorded in the minutes of the negotiations. Further, the employers reassembled the negotiating committee of 1919, who in a sworn statement denied that such an understanding was entered into. They did say that the matter had come up in regard to a proposal for a three-year agreement, which as a whole had come to nothing, and that it had further been suggested that if it were general in the United States by 1921, the Toronto printers would follow suit.[41] Andrew Gerrard, president of the International Typographical Union Local 91, however, was prepared to swear before the Toronto Methodist Conference meeting in Orillia that an explicit but verbal promise had in fact been made.[42] The trail of this disagreement led Thomas deep into the complexities of the structure of the printing trade in North America.

As a whole the employing printers had been organized into an association known as United Typothetae of America. More recently this organization had divided into open- and closed-shop sections, of which the former was apparently the larger, including some 5000 of the 5200 printing firms involved. The larger open-shop body in September 1919 repudiated any arrangement which would reduce production, specifically mentioning reduced hours as 'unpatriotic, unwise, ill-timed, and an economic crime.' A year later it pledged member firms not to adopt a shorter work week in May 1921.[43]

However, the closed-shop branch of the trade had been further organized in 1918 or 1919 into an International Joint Conference Council, a body formed cooperatively with the Typographical Union and other unions of the printing trades. In January 1920 it urged that with lower hours there should be no reduction in take-home pay unless the cost of living dropped or economic conditions changed sharply. At the end of the year it passed a resolution 'that this Joint Conference Council considers all members of its constituent bodies are morally bound to adopt

---

40 MIR, Thomas to Moore, 21 July 1921   41 See *1921 Negotiations*
42 *Industrial Banner*, 8 July 1921, p. 4
43 The Master Printers' Association, *Five Facts* (Ottawa nd)

and put into effect the forty-four hour week in May, 1921.'[44] As the clamour of the open-shop campaign had mounted through the fall of 1920, and economic conditions became more severe, it was reasserted that the 'wage scale will remain entirely in the hands of local bodies as it always has.'[45] By April, some employers in the group wanted to break the agreement regarding forty-four hours, but other employing printers and the unions refused.[46]

On the basis of these facts, Thomas was impressed with four salient points. First, the Joint Conference Council was the only effort to create a continent-wide provision for continual peace in the printing industries. Toronto Typothetae was not in it. Why? Second, although only a minority of the trade in North America had agreed to the forty-four hour week, it was a significant enough number to suggest that these terms were not impossible, but were 'resisted by that section of the trade which for some reason stands all of [sic] from the effort to maintain peace by co-operative effort.' Third, although the claim of a binding agreement was correct, the Toronto Typothetae was not party to it and, as Thomas put it, it 'cannot be pleaded against them as contract, but its force as argument is considerable.' And fourth, it was apparent that there was a disposition among some to use this occasion to smash the unions and increase the work week. 'Nor can it be ignored that the signatory of one of these circulars [aiming at eliminating the union] was a party to the binding agreement.'[47]

With these thoughts in mind, Thomas drafted a letter to the *Star* and the *Banner*, with some assistance from Creighton, who had now come to share Thomas' horror over the changed attitude of the employers. The letter to the *Banner* he delivered personally, and as always, he was able to speak frankly with Simpson. In particular, he 'pointed out ... that experience had proved that the Union was keeping its men at a pace which even untrained men can exceed.' Simpson acknowledged the fairness of this criticism, but said that the matter could only be cured by co-operation on both sides.[48] Both the *Banner* and the *Star* printed the full letter without comment.

In the letter Thomas tried to present the best construction that could be put on Fallis' arguments and positions, and urged the unfairness of singling out one firm to

44 International Typographical Union, *Facts About the Forty-Four Hour Week*, pp. 16–19
45 *Ibid.* Also noted in *Five Facts* cited above.
46 *Alberta Labor News*, 7 May 1921, Editorial; *Facts About the Forty-four Hour Week*, pp. 33–6
47 MIR, Thomas, 'Memo on the Alleged Agreement' (Typescript, nd)
48 MIR, Thomas to Moore, 21 July 1921

pillory. With regard to the employers, he argued that a strike was an economic challenge to survive, and the union could hardly complain about employer counter-action, 'even though all that is said about scabs is admitted.' He criticized severely the breaking off of negotiations and the unfair attacks upon a reputable union. He pointed out that those who had said that the fawning on international unions during the OBU crisis of 1919 would be followed by a campaign against the inter-nationals, once that crisis was passed, had not been far wrong. Thomas further criticized the open shoppers' boycott of firms that had come to terms with the union. As for the Methodist church, it had members in all groups. While at first there was a feeling that union demands were untimely, 'there is now a widespread and vocal, a deep misgiving lest in opposition to the known desires of Dr Fallis we are being carried along a road which leads to open conflict, not on this or that particular issue, but against any effective unionization of labor.' Many, he thought, believed that the Methodist firm had inadvertently become linked up with the wrong group, since there was a joint industrial council promoting the best interests of all in the trade. Finally, he pleaded for understanding that the problem of emancipating a publishing house from 'merely commercial traditions' to the social practices en-visaged by the Methodist General Conference of 1918 required time.[49]

A bitter letter was forthcoming in reply from Fallis. Whether written more in haste than anger, it twisted Thomas' statements and abused him unmercifully. Fallis defended the association with Toronto Typothetae and the open-shop group, and referred to certain harassments of 'the wives and families of printers working in our factories,' anonymous letters and notes on collection plates, and picketing methods. With the seamy incidentals of strike conditions weighing so heavily on his mind, it was ironic for him to urge Thomas to view the matters of his (Thomas') letter 'in sporting fashion as incidental and not indicating the real trends.'[50] And he concluded, 'If my friend were as frank about some things as he thinks he is about others, he would be almost as judicial as he imagines himself to be.' Thomas replied briefly that he had not expected an angry response from one whom he 'had de-fended to the limit.' Thomas pointed out that his remarks were not simply his own, and that the hierarchy of the church had communicated the criticism of the De-fence Committee propaganda to Fallis some weeks previously. The lapses in reason Thomas charged to haste, and the personal discourtesy to lapses in Fallis' usual manner.[51]

49 *Toronto Daily Star*, 22 July 1921; *Industrial Banner*, 5 Aug. 1921
50 Fallis to the editor, *Toronto Daily Star*, 23 July 1921
51 *Toronto Daily Star*, 25 July 1921

At the same time Thomas wrote a long, careful letter to Fallis explaining the many sources of his information, and reporting to him that members of the evangelism and social service staff returning from Methodist summer schools invariably reported strong feeling, not over the original dispute, but over the later turn of events in which the Publishing House seemed to be involved in an attack upon unions as such.[52]

On the day following this exchange Fallis had asked to see Thomas, and was most changed in attitude and sympathetic to some of Thomas' suggestions.[53] What had brought about so sudden a change is not clear. Creighton was the one who conveyed the request to Thomas, and may have been instrumental in helping Fallis at least partly back into the 'light.' In any case, Thomas felt that on balance Fallis' strong opposition had served the useful purpose of throwing 'excessive emphasis on our cordiality with organized labor.'[54]

The strife with Fallis seemed to be ended, but the strike continued in earnest. In his recent investigations, Thomas had learned that the strikers were ready to settle for forty-four hours, with arbitration of the wages question. After further discussions with Fallis, and then with union representatives,[55] he sent a confidential letter to Fallis proposing as basis of settlement the following terms:

1 free and open arbitration of wages without limit
2 concessions of the forty-four hour week
3 reinstatement of strikers without discrimination, as soon as vacancies allow.

He advised that he was prepared, if asked, to advance the proposal at a formal level if Fallis felt it justified, but that the third item should be left for adjustment in the course of conversation, it being a difficult point for union leaders to concede in advance.[56] That Thomas included this point was due to no love for scab labour,[57] but to the simple fact that the commitment of Fallis and other employers to their new employees was now part of the tragic situation of which any efforts at reconciliation had to take account.

Acceptance of this slow reinstatement policy by the union would be difficult. But they, too, had made their errors. The promise of forty-four hours seemed a mis-

52 MIR, Thomas to Fallis, 26 July 1921
53 MIR, Thomas to Moore, 27 July 1921
54 *Ibid.*
55 MIR, Thomas to [Moore ?], nd [probably 30 July]
56 MIR, Thomas to Fallis, 30 July 1921
57 Thomas, 'The Forward Looking Church and the Cause of Labor,' *Alberta Labor News*, 4 Sept. 1920, p. 15

understanding.[58] The union had clearly been pressing its luck. In declining economic conditions, many of the employers were probably quite sincere in their estimate of inability to meet the demands.[59] Apparently at least one prominent labour leader in Toronto believed the union had erred in calling the strike.[60] In striking, the union had, Thomas believed, 'played into the hands of men who were less friendly to organized labor than we are.'[61] The conciliation course he proposed at least offered renewed recognition of the union and eventual reinstatement of strikers.

Apparently Fallis was prepared to support such a formula. Thomas went ahead with confidential discussions with union leaders, who assured him that they 'absolutely trusted' him. Thus at the end of July Fallis and Thomas were rather optimistically attempting to work out a solution.[62]

What came of this conciliation effort is not clear, but the strike continued and so did the campaign against the Methodist Publishing House. The unions went ahead with their delayed plan to divert advertising from non-union to union shops as a counter measure to the 'Bosses boycott' of union shops.[63] Methodist members of the Typographical Union drew up a biting leaflet,[64] and circulated it at Methodist church doors on a Sunday late in July. It announced that eighty-four shops had

58 They could have secured those hours at the price of a wage drop from $35.20 to $33.00 per week, but chose to begin with a demand of $44.00 and refused to go lower than $38.50. The latter figure was a basic cost of living figure calculated for the Toronto area (see *1921 Negotiations*). However, in 1919 the wage rate had moved from $25.00 to $32.00 in a two-year contract, but had been raised again in 1920 to $35.20. A 40 per cent raise in two years was good from any point of view. Although a number of firms in the area had settled for forty-four hours by mid-summer 1919, many, like the Toronto Public Library Board, offered only the previous wage of $35.20 per week with a promise of retroactive payment of any difference upon final settlement of the dispute (see *The Mail and Empire*, 23 June 1921).

59 That the union could cite areas like London, Windsor, Regina, or Lethbridge, where forty-four hours was in effect and wages ranged from $39.00 to $47.00 per week, may have been irrelevant to Toronto conditions. There were probably more places that could be cited to put Toronto conditions in a fair light (see *1921 Negotiations*).

60 MIR, Thomas to W. Joyce, 28 July 1921. The leader was probably Simpson.

61 *Ibid.*

62 MIR, Thomas to [Moore?], nd, but enclosed with another letter dated 30 July 1921

63 *Industrial Banner*, 5 Aug. 1921

64 Toronto Typographical Union, No 91, *Promise and Performance*

now conceded forty-four hours (but did not list them or give other terms), and pointed to the vigorous anti-open shop pronouncements of the Methodist Federation for Social Service in the United States. The Canadian church had been looked on as a 'valuable ally' in labour's hopes for a better day of co-operation and confidence between employers and employees. Now the open shop campaign was sweeping away many advances labour had made. Employers were forcing bookbinders and pressmen to submit and sign a renunciation of the union. With such a group, the leaflet suggested, the Methodist church 'in the person of its Book Steward' had aligned.

The reaction to this campaign against the church's Publishing House, and by implication against the sincerity of the church's social statements, revealed something of the social conscience the social gospel had created in the church. The *Banner* reported that in a few instances officials had tried to prevent the circulation of leaflets in the churches, but in most churches it had been freely permitted and some had assisted the distributors. At least one Methodist church resolved that 'no more printing would be done at the Methodist Book Room until it made its peace with the Typographical Union.'[65] Other churches, like Perth Avenue, where the Rev. A. Terryberry was minister, invited Simpson and Gerrard to present the strikers' case. A strong pro-union sermon by the Rev. D.H. Mayor of Goderich was quoted by Superintendent Hopcroft of Donlands Methodist church before a Typographical Union meeting.[66] Troubled letters came to both Thomas and Fallis. One William Joyce, receiving a union pension of eight dollars a week and giving one dollar of that per week to the church, wondered if he was 'justified in using the Union's money to help its enemies.'[67] In far-off Miles, Montana, members of a Methodist Episcopal church working-class congregation confronted their minister with an article attacking Canadian Methodism headlined, 'Profits First, Religion Second. The Methodist Church Has Been Tried and Found Wanting.' 'I don't believe it,' the minister, Thomas Hardie, replied, 'the Methodist Church is in the vanguard for all human betterment.' But he wrote Fallis to make sure.[68] These reactions in the church to the labour campaign, taken together with the uneasiness reported at the Methodist summer schools over the church's course in the strike, indicated that the Methodist church was upon the rack. The conscience which the social gospel had created was torn with problems and doubts.

In the replies of Fallis to such letters as Hardie's in the late summer and fall, it was apparent that despite his reconciliation with Thomas, he had not changed his

65 5 Aug. 1921   66 *Printers' World*, nd [ca 1 Aug. 1921]
67 MIR, W. Joyce to Thomas, 27 July 1921
68 MIR, The Rev. Thomas Hardie to Fallis, 22 July 1921

viewpoint on the strike. Unyielding union attack, of course, would have made this difficult in any case. In mid-summer Fallis replied to his Montana correspondent, stating, 'I would not care to be manager of a strictly non-union shop, because it would mean I was standing for the breakdown of unionism, which, when it has acted sanely and wisely, has undoubtedly brought great advantage to the workers.'[69] When the Rev. D.H. Telfer wrote him in October, expressing the unrest among Winnipeg clergy over the Publishing Company's stand, Fallis reconciled this support of unionism in general with his recent action by replying that Toronto Typothetae were 'an honourable set of men who are honestly striving against what they believe to be a bit of tyranny.' The union, he said, was trying to discredit him so as to 'bring a severance of the Book Room and Typothetae and thereby virtually break the strike in the strikers favor ... That will never occur.' He offered to travel to Winnipeg to defend himself in the terms of the Methodist General Conference statements.[70]

Thus despite the truce with Thomas, Fallis had not accepted Thomas' preference for aligning the Book Room with the Joint Conference Council of the printing industry, nor was he prepared to acknowledge that there may have been ulterior motives in the reorganization of the Toronto Master Printers' Association in 1920 to form Toronto Typothetae, or Toronto 'Teapot,' as the Typographical Union preferred to call it.[71] By-passing the larger context of struggle, he simply held that the Methodist church had declared against the profit motive and for co-operation in industrial service to the community. The unions had prevented the working out of these aims by exorbitant demands which they then tried to impose by means of force.[72] Thus the General Conference resolution was brought into the conflict, not only by strikers as a dubious judgment upon the church as a whole and as a bulwark of their cause, but also by Fallis as a short-sighted rationalization of his action in establishing an open shop, and, by extension, as an unwitting cloak to the operations of the open-shop drive at large to dispossess trade unionism.

That this was in fact the intent of the open-shop campaign in the printing industry was clearer in Winnipeg than in Toronto. There the Employing Printers and Book-binders Association in 1920 did, in stating its willingness to renew the 1919–20

---

69 MIR, Fallis to Hardie, 27 July 1921

70 MIR, Fallis to the Rev. D.H. Telfer, 6 Oct. 1921

71 *Industrial Banner*, 5 Aug. 1921

72 MIR, Fallis to Hardie, 27 July 1921. See also Fallis to the ministers of the church,
    29 Sept. 1921

contract, further agree to introduce the forty-four hour week on 1 May 1921.[73] This agreement went into effect as planned. Just prior to that date, however, organizers from United Typothetae arrived from the United States to organize a branch, 'nominally for the purpose of showing the Winnipeg employing printers how to make more money.'[74] Shortly, however, the question was raised whether to honour the forty-four hour week. After hesitation, the association agreed to do so, but only until the end of the contract year, 30 June, when, if unions did not accept a return to forty-eight hours (which it could safely be wagered they would not do), the firms would lock their shops. This lockout, too, took place, although a few, after initial assent, refused to go along with the manoeuvre.

The new Winnipeg Typothetae branch was served as secretary by a Mr C.B. Gorham, who had come from Atlanta, Georgia, where, according to *Western Labor News* sources, he had a considerable reputation for his anti-union activities.[75] Winnipeg was rid of him in early June, however, when immigration officials deported him for entry to Canada contrary to the alien labour law.[76] But he had accomplished his purpose and organized an open-shop branch of United Typothetae which, according to Knox Magee, would take some $30,000 a year out of Winnipeg in membership fees.[77]

Augmenting the suspicion surrounding the appearance and disappearance of Gorham was the discovery by labour men in Winnipeg of documents over the signature of one J.M. Vollmer outlining efforts to pledge employers to the forty-eight hour week and the open shop.[78] Coincidentally with the appearance of the open-shop phase of the Toronto dispute, one of the Winnipeg printers circulated his customers admitting that the real purpose of the lockout was the establishment of the open shop, and not simply longer hours.[79]

The Winnipeg branch of Typothetae did not survive the attempted lockout. By

73 Resolution of the association, signed by A.W. Puttee, to H.J.W. Powers, secretary of the Winnipeg Typographical Union, No 191, 27 July 1920. WLN, 24 June 1921, p. 1

74 Knox Magee to the editor, WLN, 8 July 1921, pp. 1, 3. Magee was head of the *Saturday Post* printing plant, and should be a reliable source. His story is borne out by more 'conspiratorial' reports, which might otherwise be suspect, appearing in WLN, 6 and 13 May 1921.

75 WLN, 6 May 1921, pp. 1, 2   76 *Ibid.*, 3 June 1921

77 Magee to the editor, *ibid.*, 8 July 1921, p. 3

78 *Ibid.*, 6 May 1921; 13 May 1921

79 Magee to the editor, *ibid.*, 8 July 1921, p. 3

early July at least six of the larger plants and numerous smaller ones had signed agreements with the union. The bad faith of Winnipeg Typothetae was demonstrated when in the first week of July it refused to appear to justify its action before the Manitoba Council of Industry, absurdly claiming that that council could not function in industrial disputes.[80] Typothetae broke up over this issue and a new Employing Printers' Association was formed. By mid-July it was in session with the Provincial Council of Industry chaired by C.W. Gordon.[81] Although in August conciliation sessions were being held daily, some of the more obdurate employers still had strike-bound plants on their hands in mid-September.[82] The council also acted as an arbitration board on wages in those cases where agreement on hours had been reached, and in mid-September a ninety-cent an hour award was given for the term 12 September to 30 June 1922.[83] The possibilities of such a council as Gordon chaired were being demonstrated effectively, despite opposition from extremists of capital and labour.[84]

The evidence for a Toronto campaign similar to that in Winnipeg is admittedly slim, but nevertheless suggestive. In February 1921 the President of United Typothetae was in Toronto counselling master printers to secure a 'normal profit of twenty percent on our sales' and to 'cut out the working man playing one shop against another.'[85] The bulletins of United Typothetae set the tone for Toronto Typothetae propaganda by proposing not only open-shop practices, but elimination of 'all possibility of labor union interference.' Unionism was described as 'the worst industrial plague of all history.'[86] Criticism of the United Typothetae of America for recommending dismissal of all union printers under the cover of the open-shop campaign came from no less a person that the President of the National Association of Manufacturers (USA) on 25 July 1922.[87] There was ample evidence for such a charge by October 1921, when Fallis described Toronto Typothetae as 'honourable men.'

Was there perhaps then also a promise of forty-four hours made to Toronto printing unions? And was the Toronto Typothetae campaign more successful simply because the promise had not been recorded? In September 1921 the Toronto Typographical Union finally turned up evidence which indicated that while no

80 *Ibid.*, 8 July 1921, p. 1 81 *Alberta Labor News,* 9 July 1921, p. 1

82 *Ibid.*, 23 July 1921, p. 1; 10 Sept. 1921, p. 1

83 *Ibid.*, 24 Sept. 1921, p. 1

84 *Presbyterian Witness,* 11 May 1922, p. 11

85 *Toronto Daily Star,* nd, cited in the *Industrial Banner,* 5 Aug. 1921

86 Issues of 25 May, 4 July 1921, cited in Dennison, *Facts and Figures,* pp. 14–16

87 Cited in sw, May 1923, p. 163

very specific promises existed, an understanding may well have been more than 'in the air.' In the June 1919 issue of *Printer and Publisher*, published by the MacLean Publishing Company, there was a report on the negotiations with the union that spring. By a narrow majority the job printers had decided to accept the offer of $32.00 a week. This, the journal said, precluded

the possibility of a strike. The job printers, however, will get the forty-four hour week in 1921 through an agreement made by the Master Printers of America with the International Typographical Union, by which the shorter hours are granted on May 1 of that year ... In view of the fact that the forty-four hour week will come automatically in two years, the printers in favor held that this wage offer should be accepted and no strike vote taken.

It was true that Toronto Typothetae had not under that name been party to the agreement of 1919, but it is worthy of note that the MacLean Publishing Company which recorded this 'understanding' in 1919 was party to the denials of its existence in 1921. Furthermore, it does seem apparent that the 'understanding' had been a part of the negotiating atmosphere in both 1919 and 1921. The employing printers had been living off this understanding for two years! Was it any wonder that as fruitless negotiations with Toronto Typothetae drew to an end in May 1921, union representatives appeared to be being unreasonable and demanding to a relative newcomer in the trade like Fallis?

In the fall of 1921 the annual meeting of the Methodist Board of Evangelism and Social Service deplored the deadlock in the strike, and in a carefully worded resolution blamed the general situation on the 'misunderstanding' by the union and the unfortunate position of the Book Room on 'its affiliation with the United Typothetae of America.'[88] Fallis did not appreciate this latter clause.[89] In contrast, the *Canadian Labor Press* of 19 November 1921 described the resolution in the headline: 'Verbiage Covers Mistake of the Injustice to Printers.'

When the General Assembly of the Presbyterian Church and the General Conference of the Methodist Church met in 1922, the strike was still on. Communications were sent to both bodies by the Typographical Union, Local 91, pleading its case. The General Assembly, under motion of C.W. Gordon, replied that it was in no position to determine whether contracts had been broken, and that 'it is not the function of the churches to provide the machinery for arriving at such decisions.'[90]

88 *Annual Report*, 1920–1, Methodist Department of ESS, pp. 21–2
89 MIR, Fallis to Moore, 11 Nov. 1921
90 *Presbyterian Acts and Proceedings*, 1922, pp. 111–13, 122–3

At the Methodist General Conference the union's letter had been given to the Book and Publishing Committee for action. It reported a resolution regretting 'that there has been a difference of opinion between the Union and the management of the Book Room,' but failing 'to find any charge of unfairness sustained.'[91] This resolution was, in effect, an attempt by the Book Committee to clear its own name. Bland and H.A. Ireland from British Columbia immediately placed an amendment forthrightly invoking the church's declaration for 'the reduction of hours of labor to the lowest practicable point.'[92] They urged the conference to 'fully accept the obligations such principles involve.'[93] There was little doubt that Bland believed that the Publishing House could and should have gone further in meeting the union's position. But his phraseology left open the technical question of what the 'lowest practicable' hours were. A few days before, the conference had defeated an attempt by himself and C.E. Endicott of Saskatoon to secure a presentation of the findings of the Toronto Methodist Ministerial Association on the subject.[94] Despite the efforts of these more radical social gospel exponents, the farthest that they could move the conference was to a position not unlike the Presbyterian disclaimer of competence:

... this Conference declares its fullest sympathy with all just claims of labor, and with the principle of the fewest number of working hours consistent with efficiency and justice to all concerned. We rejoice to know that an offer of arbitration has been made and still stands ... While the statements on the memorial have been carefully considered in Committee, we realize that this Conference, in the time at its disposal, is not in a position to arrive at a decision on the many difficult issues involved, and we believe that these questions can be better dealt with by our Book Committee, which has all necessary authority in the matter.[95]

The dispute continued to torment the Methodist and then the United church until 1944, when a union shop was established in the Publishing House after a sharp debate in general council of that year.[96]

What had begun in 1921 as an apparently uncomplicated dispute over wages and hours had, within a few weeks, become a bitter contest over the survival of a

91 *Methodist Journal of Proceedings*, 1922, p. 119

92 *The Discipline*, 1918, Appendix I, paragraph II

93 *Methodist Journal of Proceedings*, 1922, p. 119

94 *Ibid.*, p. 96

95 *Ibid.*, pp. 129–30. See also CG, 25 Oct. 1922, p. 11

96 United Church of Canada, *Record of Proceedings*, Eleventh General Council, 1944, p. 90

union on the one hand and the church Publishing House on the other. By 1922 the dispute had hardened into an almost impervious state. The issue had placed the church on the rack. Unionists, many of them Methodist, used the church's social policy to belabour the church, and defenders of the Publishing House rationalized its course with the same pronouncements. Neither was using the church's statements in full honesty. The attack on the church served the union as a cover for its nakedness in the face of its own errors, not only in bargaining and the timing of the strike, but in wilfully ignoring the trap that the open-shop campaign had put in its path. Fallis and his committee used the social policy of the church to hide the fact that they had not been as wise as serpents in allowing themselves to be implicated in the open-shop campaign. They tried to explain the campaign charitably, and were led to pronounce unfounded maledictions upon the typographical union. Here was the eternal end of innocence, as the Adam of each accused the other of giving him to eat.

If there is a considerable freedom in the moment of action, there is a not inconsiderable bondage in the result. The union having struck for a good objective had a commitment to its members to return them safely to their jobs, but in striking forced the companies' hands. The Publishing House could hardly have been expected to close down, but in rejecting for sound reasons the union's case and staying open for a worthy purpose, it could not later act effectively to remove itself from the open-shop stigma without ignoring its basic financial argument, its one solid ground in the dispute.

That both parties to the dispute utilized the social pronouncements of the church to defend their causes was a testimony to the impact of social gospel thought, at the same time as it was a measure of its ambiguity. The forthright word which it would have spoken to a world in reconstruction had been turned by the exigencies of that world into a message of equivocation. Or so it seemed. But the formulations of the social gospel in the pronouncements of the church in 1918 and 1919, though conceived in a mood of optimism, had not been intended so much a map of the way as a chart of a part of the land to be reached. That part of the way lay through struggle and conflict did not dismay radicals in the church like Thomas and Bland, who considered that a 'mischievous desire for peace and dislike of trouble' was as 'great a peril to the Church as any idolatry of wealth.'[97] Neither did radicals outside the church, who tended uncritically to take the part of the union, fear conflict.[98] The conservative wing continued to talk vaguely of applying the golden rule to industrial relations, ignoring the degree to which the strike had demonstrated the

97 sw, July–Aug. 1921, pp. 263–4
98 MIR, A.E. Smith to Moore, 13 Dec. 1921

destructiveness that could accompany the selfrighteousness of good men and movements. Progressives like Creighton were more convinced than ever that strikes were simply stupid. The great pronouncements of 1918 and 1919 were referred to less frequently as the times came to be seen in the less hopeful terms of 'strikes and rumours of strikes.'[99] The language of social reform was becoming 'old hat' to some, and a burden to others. With the continuing slump of postwar depression the need of simple social palliations increased its demands on the energies of church social service departments and institutions.

It would be unwise to see this shift in mood and action in terms too sharp and sudden. The General Conference resolution could still rouse a stinging debate;[100] there were still many radical and progressive social gospel articles, chiefly in the *Guardian*; and the social service departments of the church still worked at devising ways of communicating the vision of the social gospel and means of incorporating its insights into the industrial order.[101] But just as the radicals of the social gospel involved in the strikes of 1919, without altering their long-term objectives, turned from an emphasis on industrial to political action, so progressives in the church turned from the complexities and frustrations of industrial conflict to stress other approaches to their social goals. During the industrial crises of 1919 to 1921 other hopeful avenues of expression had been rising to prominence in the fields of progressive politics, evangelism and church union. So complex a movement as the social gospel was a difficult one to defeat over a single issue or group of problems.

99 *Annual Report*, 1922–3, Methodist Department of ESS, p. 24
100 CG, 24 Oct. 1923, p. 5; 7 Nov. 1923, pp. 5, 22; 2 Jan. 1924, p. 22; 23 Jan. 1924, p. 17
101 *Annual Report*, 1922–3, Methodist Department of ESS, pp. 24, 29

12

The Non-Politics of Progressivism

By 1921 endless complexity and power conflicts in the industrial world had seemed to stalemate and pervert much of the social gospel programme, but in the rising political fortunes of the agrarian-based progressive movement social gospel hopes rode high. Not only social gospellers such as Henry Wise Wood, W.R. Wood, E.C. Drury, and W.C. Good in the farm organizations and those in labour political organizations such as Irvine, Woodsworth, Ivens, Smith, and Simpson were optimistic, but also professional persons – social workers, professors, clergy, students – who, if they had not before, at least between 1919 and 1923, looked with increasing favour upon the rise of a progressive political party.

The years 1919 to 1921 were propitious ones for new political movements in Canada. The Union government and conscription issues had shattered old party structures. The Conservative party was least disrupted, and went on to dominate the Union government in the early postwar period. The Liberals were split in several directions – between French- and English-Canadian, between central Canadian and western Canadian. Not only the death of Laurier in early 1919, but the fractured condition of the party, led the Liberals in search of a leader who could restore party fortunes. They found him in mid-1919 in the person of William Lyon Mackenzie King, former deputy minister of labour, consultant of the Rockefellers in industrial relations, and author of the recent book, *Industry and Humanity*.[1] The August convention which chose King as leader also drew up a moderate reform programme which showed the impress of King's thought.

Whether or not King's book was intended as part of the staging of a deliberate drive for a new career in Canadian politics, possibly for leadership of the Liberal party, it was, nevertheless, a serious analysis in its own right of the large questions which hung over industrial society. Apart from an abbreviated version prepared by King for more general consumption, the book was not widely read. Its style was marked by a diffuseness, and its arguments by an ambivalence, that made it possible to quote the book against itself. Perhaps for this reason King's chief biographers have been able to see in it a radicalism of which the Liberal convention of the

1 Published in 1918

summer of 1919 must have been unaware.[2] However, it is very unlikely that either King or the convention were ignorant of the social positions toward which Canadian churches were inclining in the years 1914 to 1919. Certainly King's support of social insurance, of minimum standards, of humane personnel policies, and joint councils in industry, did not move beyond the position formulated by his own church, the Presbyterian church, in 1919. His criticism of the motivation, spirit, and consequences of unfettered capitalism, however strongly expressed, did not exceed that of the Methodist church of 1918, nor did his anticipation of the new degree of collectivism coming to Canadian society. As an associate of Rockefeller, he probably knew of the initiatives leading to the Inter-Church campaign of 1919 and its exposé of the us Steel Corporation. Just as it would be a mistake to exaggerate King's radicalism by viewing his ideas out of the context of such a background, so it would be an error to overdo the unreadiness of the Liberal party convention to accept King's proposals even in their original form. The civic and provincial elections later that year, as well as those of 1920, indicated that the impulse of social reform had not drained out of Canadian society with the great strikes of spring and early summer. The convention itself manifested none of the panic over Bolshevism or socialism that gripped a minority of Winnipeg citizens in May and June. Indeed, some of the planning for the convention suggests that it was to be a rally of Canadian progressivism, with the right to send delegates being extended to the Trades and Labour Congress of Canada, the Railway Brotherhoods, the Council of Agriculture, and the Great War Veterans Association.[3] *Industry and Humanity*, it would seem, was neither too radical for these, nor for the new businessman. As far as the Canadian world of liberal social reform was concerned, the book, like the man, was in the right place at the right time.

Whether the social gospel could claim King as its own would be a matter of some debate. The book was in one major aspect a religious one. It depicted competitive individualism in industry as an instrument of death which, in fear and in disobedience to God's intentions for him, man had brought into the world. It appealed to men to adopt an attitude of faith that an immanent divinity was working out the progress of mankind. Only so, it seemed, could fear be overcome and clarity of vision be attained for mending collective life in general and industrial life in particular. If this was evangelical in appeal, its object was not so much the perfection of the individual as the improvement of society.

2 See Dawson, *William Lyon Mackenzie King*, p. 251; MacGregor, *The Fall and Rise of Mackenzie King*, pp. 230–1; Hutchinson, *The Incredible Canadian*, p. 39
3 Some of the foregoing observations have been made by Ferns and Ostry, *The Age of Mackenzie King: The Rise of the Leader*, chap. x

King was realistic in the significance he attached to the impact of industry upon society, yet any radical effect this might have had was undercut by his belief that the new mind of faith might see possibilities of co-operation between the parties to production which the mere observer of their material relations would discount. Yet this was not so much the necessary conclusion of faith itself[4] as of King's diluted combination of philosophical idealism and Calvinism. His idealism persuaded him that men could rise above material considerations, while his latent Calvinism discounted the possibility that they could do so entirely. Individuals, but not whole societies, might be elected to such grace. Hence, it was unnecessary to require basic alteration in the material relations of production, and unwise to abandon the motivation of material rewards. As a result he compromised the radical standpoint his religious faith provided him with, namely the inadmissability of absolute right of private ownership of capital. His proposal that labour and consumer be co-opted into the decision-making processes of industry along with management and ownership simply finessed the issue posed by the perspective of Christian belief.

The elements mixed in King made him too prudent a man to give full expression to the social gospel, yet he wrote with enthusiasm about the requirements of the social conscience. It has been observed that he ' "reconciled" liberal social science to the requirements of a community wherein the social authority of clerics is great.'[5] Bearing in mind the recent social declarations of the churches, the observation may suggest that King was writing, in his own way, within the categories of the progressive social gospel. In any case, it was surely of no small consequence to King's succession to Liberal leadership that the works of the social gospel lay close at hand in 1919.

In the light of King's writing and his reputation, it would be too much to claim that all social gospel proponents abandoned support of the old parties for the new movements. Some were undeniably impressed with Mackenzie King and the plea and plan for social, industrial, and international peace put forth in his book. The somewhat conservative editor of the *Presbyterian and Westminster* commented that King 'has given long and thorough study to those social and industrial problems

4 As, for instance, Ferns and Ostry conclude, *Age of Mackenzie King*, p. 280. For all the perceptiveness that marks their serious analysis of King's book, their commentary becomes rather precious at times – and nowhere more than where their own commitments lead them to criticize King for 'abandoning ... the rational secular foundations of traditional liberalism,' (*ibid.*) as though that were the major element in the history of Canadian liberalism.

5 *Ibid.*, p. 249. Their point is weakened by their failure to give any content of social thought or policy to such clerical authority at the time.

which are claiming, more and more, the attention of thoughtful men. He is recognized, indeed, as one of the foremost authorities in America.' It was also quite possible that King was in the mind of the progressive editor of *Social Welfare* when he wrote, 'The day is coming, and for not a few politicians now is, when politics is [*sic*] the science of social welfare.'[6] In the realignment of parties that was well under way, the apparent attractiveness of King's application of the social service thesis to industrial relations may well have won considerable support from social gospellers.

However, King was leading a Liberal party largely in the grip of eastern business, and those in the process of rejecting the traditional ethos of the industrial leadership must have had qualms about following King in his new leadership role of 1919. Certainly party traditions sat lightly on evangelical leadership. Political independence had been the theme of addresses by G.M. Grant and the young Bland in the 1880s and 1890s. S.D. Chown always gave his political position as independent.[7] The non-politics of prohibition confirmed such a stance. Such non-partisanism carried over into the politics of social welfare. To speak of such a politics, a politics beyond the strife of partisan contest, was to speak the language of the progressives of the farm and labour movements. Furthermore, the social programmes mapped out by the Social Service Council and the Methodist and Presbyterian churches in 1918 and 1919 were, as noted, distinctly to the left of the Liberal platform and that of the Progressives as well. On the other hand, they were not far to the right of the Canadian Labor party platform of 1921. Which party won their thousands and which their ten thousands among the social gospel at large must remain in doubt.

The notable fact, however, was that part of the driving force behind these political platforms of 1921 was one or another wing of the social gospel. This may have been true of the Liberal platform. Certainly, in the farmers' decision for political action, in the new resolution for labour politics after the Winnipeg strike, in the process of platform formation, and in the campaigning prior to 1921, leading social gospellers played an important, sometimes crucial role. Generally, their efforts were bent to urging a broadly based progressive party – something that, despite the hopes of 1919–23, was to elude their grasp in the 1920s.

The association of the social gospel and the Canadian agrarian movements of the twentieth century has been noted, but never fully explored.[8] However, it is apparent

6 14 Aug. 1919, pp. 148–9; sw, 1 Oct. 1918, p. 14

7 Allen, 'Salem Bland,' pp. 32–6; *Canadian Men and Women of the Time*, 1912

8 See Morton, *The Progressive Party*, pp. 28–9, and Sharp, *Agrarian Revolt in Western Canada*, chap. IV. I have tried to develop the theme somewhat in my thesis, 'Salem Bland,' chap. VI, 'The Social Gospel and the Ideology of Agrarian Revolt.'

that by 1917 all wings of the social gospel seem to have found a place of such prominence in the farmers' organizations that it might well be termed the religion of the agrarian revolt.

The social gospel was not a late attachment to the Grain Growers' movement. E.A. Partridge, who pioneered more ideas and institutions of the western farmer than any other man, was motivated by a practical, ethical Christianity mixed with elements of Ruskinian socialism.[9] The *Guide* lent itself to the propagation of the social gospel, and numerous articles by Grain Growers' leaders testify to the place of the social gospel in their thinking.[10] R.C. Henders, president of the Manitoba Grain Growers' Association for many years and executive member of the Manitoba Social Service Council, was a Presbyterian minister-farmer who rationalized his activities in terms of an emphatic Christian socialism. Henry Wise Wood, president of the United Farmers of Alberta, 1916–31, in promoting UFA Sundays urged ministers to give the farmers the full measure of the social gospel.[11] W.R. Wood, Percival Baker, Norman Smith, R.A. Hoey, W.D. Bayley, G.W. Robertson, and William Irvine stand as but a few more instances of western farm leaders of the time motivated by the social gospel. In 1917 the *Guide* seemed to seal this association by securing the regular services of Salem Bland. In a column entitled 'The Deeper Life,' Bland's social and religious outlook caught and amplified that of the *Guide* and the agrarian leadership.

Even J.W. Dafoe, editor of the *Manitoba Free Press*, was not untouched by the social gospel. Dafoe's progressivism was of a more measured cast than that of the foregoing, but through the most respected daily in the West he reached into countless farm homes. 'The grand problem of the Churches in the twentieth century,' wrote Dafoe, 'is to demonstrate that the mystical elements in human life for which they stand are capable of being translated into practical results in education, in industry, in government, and in social relations.' The future of civilization was 'indissolubly intertwined with the eventual triumph of the ethics of Jesus.'[12] The traditional vehicle of Christianity may have been found wanting, in the mind of Dafoe and in the minds of some among the western agrarian leadership, but the ethical and social gospel was sound. Such were the religious terms in which the western farmers were rallied to the cause.

It may well be doubted whether the social gospel acquired a similar grip on

9 GGG, 14 Aug. 1909, 28 Aug. 1909, 30 Sept. 1919, 6 Oct. 1919

10 See Allen, 'Salem Bland,' pp. 126–51

11 See especially his Circulars Nos 9 and 10 for UFA Sunday, 27 May 1917, Bland Papers

12 28 Oct. 1916

central and eastern Canadian farmers' movements. Not only were they more deeply schooled in traditional evangelicalism, but the eastern rural areas probably received fewer of the recent immigrants who often brought to the West newer currents of social thought in the United States, Britain, and Europe. Furthermore, having a more established way of life, eastern agrarians seem to have reacted with more defensive hostility to industrialism and urbanism as such than did the Grain Growers, who considered that they were building a new society in the West.[13]

Nevertheless, the socal gospel in the church could not ignore the rural social problem in either eastern or western Canada and still believe that 'every form of industry shall be crowned by the Christian ideal of service to humanity.'[14] The countryside seemed to social gospel observers to be plagued by a lack of social life and community ideals, which left the farmer a prey to speculators and a victim of a system which permitted unearned increment in business and commerce. Farmer co-operation as a means of attack upon these economic injustices seemed to require of the church a stimulation of the social spirit of the country dweller and the responsibilities which accompanied 'the new agriculture.'[15] Out of this concern grew institutes, conferences, and summer schools on such rural problems as co-operative methods, community organization, the church and rural life.[16]

Through such channels as these the social gospel was spread into the eastern Canadian countryside and by 1917 had become part of the mentality of many eastern farm leaders. This rural infiltration was the background of the membership of the Dominion Grange and Farmers' Association in the Social Service Council. Early representatives of the association on the council were E.C. Drury, later to become head of Ontario's Farmer-Labour administration of 1919–23; W.C. Good, who was to be secretary of the United Farmers of Ontario and a proponent in the East of the Irvine-Wood theory of 'group government'; and Henry Moyle, secretary

13 Morton, *The Progressive Party*, pp. 72–3. However, just as an important motivation in the Progressive movement in the United States arose from the defensive reactions of declining urban and rural elements within the aggressive industrial order, according to Hofstadter in *The Age of Reform*, so the social gospel would seem to have in its more conservative wing a similar phenomenon. But this is a subject on which firm conclusions must await adequate investigation.

14 MacDougall, *Rural Life in Canada*, p. 126

15 *Ibid.*, pp. 89–90, 116–20, 147

16 Such programmes were carried on in the prairie region as well. For a brief account of one at which J.S. Woodsworth and Henry Wise Wood were speakers, see McNaught, *A Prophet in Politics*, pp. 74, 74n

of the Social Service Committee of the Ontario and Quebec Convention of the Baptist church.[17]

The religious attitude behind the arguments of clergy and lay alike on the issues confronting the farmer (and less directly, labour) was well expressed by A.S. Handicap in articles on 'The Tariff and National Morals' in the *Guide*.[18] He sketched the 'ideal of the Hebrew Commonwealth' interpreted by 'the Great Prophet of the New Judaism.' Only the community was an adequate steward of wealth. Handicap's argument illustrated the prevalent social gospel incorporation of the ancient prophetic tradition. Agrarians easily responded to verses such as those of J.W. Bengough:

> Enough! the lie is ended. God only owns the land;
> No parchment deed hath virtue unsigned by His own hand.
> Out on the bold blasphemers who would eject the Lord,
> And pauperize His children and trample on His Word.[19]

Deep social gospel involvement in the postwar agrarian revolt resulted not only from the fostering of specific agrarian concerns, such as co-operatives, direct legislation, free trade, and the single tax, but also from its prominent role in pressing for a third party based on the Canadian farmer, and in some minds including labour and professional people as well. In Manitoba in 1915, the Revs. R.C. Henders and Thomas Beveridge, supported by the *Guide*, rejected old party ties and ran as independents in Manitoba ridings.[20] The former, as president of the Manitoba Grain Growers, hoped his association in 1916 would develop a greater sense of class consciousness and go after their own interests in the political arena.[21] Under his leadership, and that of the Rev. W.R. Wood, secretary of the association, the Manitoba organization over the next three years moved toward that objective. Although no more pervasive an influence than in Manitoba, the social gospel role in the drive toward political action was more dramatic in Alberta and Saskatchewan.

The task of manœuvring the United Farmers of Alberta into political action fell to the Non-Partisan League, at whose helm were partisans of the social gospel. The Non-Partisan League had been born in North Dakota where, in 1916, it had won

17 *Minutes*, Moral and Social Reform Council, 10 Sept. 1909; Social Service Council of Canada, 5 Sept. 1913
18 GGG, 19 March and 2 April 1919
19 From 'Verses Grave and Gay,' quoted in MacDougall, *Rural Life in Canada*, p. 90
20 GGG, 26 May 1915, pp. 5, 9
21 *Ibid.*, 12 Jan. 1916, pp. 7, 31

an astonishing political victory. It had immediately spread into Saskatchewan,[22] but skilful manœuvring by the grain growers in Saskatchewan, not unsatisfied with provincial government and not prepared yet for direct federal political action, had eliminated the threat of the league in 1917. In the somewhat more diversified and radical population of Alberta and under more able leadership, the league progressed, electing two members to the provincial legislature in June 1917.[23] One of these, Mrs Louise C. McKinney of Claresholm, was provincial president of the WCTU and, like the feminist leader in that province, Nellie McClung, viewed her advocacy of temperance as part of a broad programme of reform.[24] The Alberta Non-Partisan League was aware of its religious dimension. Will Holmes, who frequently wrote on league affairs in the *Alberta Non-Partisan*, observed: "We found our origin among religious people, and were called into being by forces just as sincerely moral as those which launched the movement for prohibition, or those that launched the movement against slavery.[25] Prominent among the evidence for such a contention in the summer of 1918 was the presence of J.S. Woodsworth, working as an organizer in northern Alberta under William Irvine. Irvine's weekly, *The Nutcracker*, had become the *Alberta Non-Partisan*, and Irvine himself one of the most energetic and articulate figures in the league's leadership. The purpose of the league was to complement the farmers' organization with a broad popular party based on the farmer, whose programme would be to establish a non-partisan government and promote a considerable degree of public ownership.

Across the plans of the league for political action by the farmers had fallen the Union government and conscription issues in 1917 and 1918. But despite the support given the government by H.W. Wood and T.A. Crerar, the western vote, although overwhelmingly for Union candidates, was nevertheless half-hearted.[26] When the Union government began conscripting farmers' sons in early 1918, and

22 See Sharp, *Agrarian Revolt in Western Canada*, pp. 77ff.

23 Morton, *The Progressive Party*, pp. 44–8

24 *Alberta Labor News*, 25 Sept. 1920, p. 5. Mrs McKinney was a teacher, born in Ontario, who moved to North Dakota and became state evangelist for the WCTU. She remained active in the WCTU after moving to Calgary, and began a long term as provincial president in 1908. See 'Pen Portraits of Progressive Women,' CG, 16 Feb. 1921, p. 11. For Nellie McClung see Cleverdon, *Women Suffrage Movement in Canada*.

25 12 April 1918, p. 7

26 See Saskatchewan Grain Growers' Association, Board of Directors, minutes, 1, 2 Nov. 1917, p. 16

failed either to conscript wealth or to make any substantial tariff changes, the farmers' estrangement from the old parties became severe. The programme of the Non-Partisan League, which had not ceased activity, again became relevant and urgent. In a few months the issue of political action rose to fever pitch, and in the spring of 1919, in a series of dramatic debates, the UFA was won to political action on the basis of the radical conception of group politics.

The theory of group politics and group government was one of the most radical notions of political reform to gain the following of an important minority in Canada. Significantly, the theories emerged in Canada out of debates in 1919 between two social gospel radicals, W. Irvine and Henry Wise Wood, over the nature of the political action the United Farmers of Alberta should take. For the social gospel it was a matter of consequence, not only for the hope of progressive unity it offered but failed to deliver, but also for the further division of social gospellers in yet another area of social endeavour.

Wood had no political ambitions for himself or the UFA.[27] As an immigrant farmer from Missouri, memories were strong of the disaster for the Farmers' Alliance in the United States when tempted first into Populist political action, then into fusion with the Democrats, and sidetracked by free silver. When Alberta farmers demanded political action in 1919 after two years of prodding by Irvine's Non-Partisan League, Wood overcame his reluctance by insisting that only the first stage of the Populist political action be adhered to. "It is United Farmers of Alberta political action we are going to take,' he had insisted.[28] His original reluctance and this apparent half-measure was a result, however, of more than concern for mere institutional preservation. Wood's leadership of the UFA was conceived in large social, historical, and theological terms. Civilization had been developed, he believed, on the basis of an original 'wrong choice' of autocratic methods inspired by animal selfishness. In the contemporary order, this 'wrong choice' was represented by the industrial organization of the manufacturing interests. The farmers' organizations, in their opposition to the national control exerted by those interests, had evolved a method of voluntary democratic organization. To compromise this development was to jeopardize a great hope of radical civilizational reform. Although Wood seems to have said little about labour and industry as such, he obviously envisaged reorganization in terms of industrial democracy, and an ascending structure of democratic industrial groups co-operating in the solution of national problems – and similarly nations within the world order. These views were clearly in

27 See Rolph, *Henry Wise Wood of Alberta*
28 *Alberta Non-Partisan*, 5 June 1919, pp. 8–13

Wood's mind at least a year before they emerged on the national political scene in October 1919 in the Cochrane by-election.[29] The programme of social reform quite naturally appeared in political garb as 'group politics.'

Since Wood's whole programme was ultimately theological, 'group politics' had a heavy religious cast. Wood was speaking in more than similes when he said that there were those 'who are just as opposed to readjustment along these lines as the Pharisees were to Christ ...'[30] Christ was the teacher and exemplar of the true laws of social development. He represented the original right choice open to human civilization:

Christ promises us that if we follow his word of Life in the service of God, the great Spirit of love, we may establish a world-wide Kingdom over which the great force of love will reign supreme, the nations of the earth will bring their glory into it, the force of evil will cease from troubling, and the people be at rest.[31]

Both experience and reason based on these ultimate premises and purposes dictated Wood's counsel. It was hardly political reasoning: 'the main idea must not be to win elections, but to develop principles.'[32] But once the political decision was made, the UFA, embodying the correct principles of social organization, 'had the right to go on and develop all the political strength [it] could and then for the good of humanity, co-operate with the other units.'[33] Only so did it seem that the new society, the Kingdom of God, could be won without compromising the gains already made. To follow the practice of organizing a broad party and platform to appeal to an electorate permeated by a mixture of principles was out of the question altogether. The only industrial group with which co-operation was immediately considered was labour, and, at least in the short run, such co-operation would primarily be mutual resistance to unjust demands.[34] In the long run, Wood hardly expected to sit in the councils of group government with autocratically organized industry. At least until 1921, he could not have viewed the rising demand of labour and the churches for industrial democracy as less than potent signs of the times.

The political implications of Wood's religious and social ideas were worked out in dialectic with William Irvine, who at first rejected and then adopted Wood's notion to become its most persuasive exponent. Irvine had for some time vigorously

29 GGG, 29 Jan. 1917; 4 Dec. 1918, p. 23; 8 Jan. 1919, p. 47
30 *Ibid.*, 29 Jan. 1917, in an address to the UFA convention
31 *Ibid.*, 4 Dec. 1918, p. 39
32 *Alberta Non-Partisan*, 5 June 1919, p. 8; 19 June 1919, p. 10
33 *Ibid.*
34 See Morton, *The Progressive Party*, pp. 90–3

opposed Wood's concept of industrial political action, warning that it might well result in dictatorship by industrial groups. It was mistaken in its basic premise, he said, that 'the things to be governed were industries, not people.'[35] Wood could counter that industries *were* people, but this was to miss Irvine's point, which was that industry did not constitute the whole life of a people, and that persons within industrial groups might disagree on non-industrial concerns. A separate organization was necessary for the political task of educating, campaigning, and winning power.

Irvine's position seemed to fall in with the traditional rationalization of the party system. However, as a dominant figure in the Non-Partisan League, he was a proponent of rather non-traditional politics. Also, his criticism of Wood was subject to erosion by the political exigencies of winning the UFA to political action, by the theory of politics promoted through the league, and finally, by his theology which was roughly consonant with Wood's. The league opposed partisan politics and government, and offered in their stead 'business government,' which meant, essentially, a cabinet elected by the whole House, with all decisions made on a majority basis. Theoretically, the league had no need of a political platform since it was opposed to partisan government, and was for whatever most of the people decided. Yet the political society the league envisaged required some means of overcoming the polarization of society between 'the people' and 'the interests.' The dominant theme of the league platform, public ownership, would be the first and basic programme of a people's business administration in government.[36] The league seemed to belie its name in promoting a specific platform after the fashion of a traditional party, but its objective was radical political innovation involving the end of party government. Thus in the last analysis Irvine, by implication, agreed with Wood that the democratic political process could be carried out without parties.

It was not surprising, then, that when UFA and league representatives drew up a joint report on 14 May 1919 to present to the UFA political conventions, there was no reference to public ownership. Irvine may have believed that in Wood's concession of outside affiliates with the UFA political department, and the possibility of co-operation with outside organizations in the choice of candidates, he had won a satisfactory modification of Wood's position. He may have believed that Wood had moved toward his formula that 'there is no fundamental democratic principle upon which the farmers or any other unit have a monopoly. If it be a political principle

35 *Alberta Non-Partisan*, 30 Jan. 1919, p. 5; 22 May 1919, p. 5; 5 June 1919, pp. 5–6
36 See *Nutcracker*, 15 Jan. 1917, p. 10; *Alberta Non-Partisan*, 4 Dec. 1918, p. 5; 22 May 1919, p. 5. Woodsworth also adopted this approach in mid-1918 (*Alberta Non-Partisan*, 12 Sept. 1918, p. 11)

it is a people's principle.'[37] But on that basis industrial organization could provide a useful basis of popular representation. Irvine's populism had triumphed over his political sense.[38] That this populist victory rested upon more ultimate considerations, in Irvine's mind, however, was soon apparent.

When Irvine's book, *Farmers in Politics*, appeared in 1920, perhaps its most striking aspect was not so much the exposition of his concept of group government, as the mixture of his political and economic arguments with the religious concepts of the radical social gospel. As with Wood, the progressive drive toward a new social order was vested with religious significance. The 'new religious spirit which is the very soul of the world movement for justice,' he wrote, 'cannot be kept out of politics. Being inseparable from life, it permeates its every department ... The line between the sacred and the secular is being rubbed out. This does not mean that everything is becoming secular; on the contrary, everything is becoming sacred.'[39] Agreement on the theology of radical immanence, the religious concomitant of populism and progessivism, was the ultimate basis of the Irvine-Wood compromise, reinforcing the common features of their social and political views, and making their differences seem less important.

In presenting his book to the public, Irvine sought and secured the services of his former teacher, Salem Bland, as writer of a foreword to the reader. In doing so, he was securing more than the approval of the author of *The New Christianity*, which that same year had been so enthusiastically reviewed in the West. He was securing the backing of a man who had been prominent in rousing the Grain Growers of Saskatchewan to political action one year earlier.

When the directors of the Saskatchewan Grain Growers' Association met in December 1918 to consider the best course before them and to plan for the February convention of a restive membership, intense dissatisfaction with the old parties was on every tongue. Some form of direct political action was endorsed, and it was proposed that Salem Bland should address the coming convention in February 1919.[40]

There can be little doubt that it was to put the challenge of political action as forcefully as possible that Bland was invited to give the major address to the Grain

37 *Ibid.*, 19 June 1919, p. 5
38 W.L. Morton observes that the UFA was substantially won to the Non-Partisan League position (Morton, *The Progressive Party*, p. 88), but it seems clear that the UFA only adopted the parts of the programme it was already in agreement with.
39 See p. 53
40 Saskatchewan Grain Growers' Association, Board of Directors, minutes, 12 Dec. 1918, p. 37

Growers of Saskatchewan. In 1913 Bland had excited the annual convention of that year with an impassioned appeal for a new party of the people. The leadership had sidetracked the notion then,[41] but Bland's appeal had not been forgotten, as his introduction to the convention revealed. Bland had been prominently associated with almost every progressive endeavour in the West, as the *Guide* reminded its readers. He had been on the executive of the Free Trade League in Winnipeg in 1910, had been honorary chairman of the Single Tax and Direct Legislation Association at least from 1916 to 1919,[42] and had had an informal tie with the Non-Partisan League. Still unstationed after his dismissal from Wesley College, he had joined Henry Wise Wood on the platforms of the Chautauqua organization in the summer of 1918, its second successful summer on the Canadian prairie.[43] Furthermore, Bland had just played a leading role in winning his church to a pronounced progressive stand on reconstruction, and while in the East had furthered his association with Canadian labour by attending the Trades and Labour Congress in Quebec. This last point was of some moment, since Bland was close to some persons in the Saskatchewan association who were actively promoting a closer relationship between the labour movement and the Grain Growers. On the day following the directors' meeting, George Broadley of the Regina local, and author of a column in the *Regina Daily Post*, wrote Bland telling him of various moves designed to encourage labour-Grain Grower co-operation and asking for his comments.[44] The selection of Bland to address the convention may well have been intended to influence the delegates in the direction of a broad rather than a narrow agrarian party concept.

Bland did not disappoint the association leaders. Speaking on 'Canada's Challenge to the Grain Growers,' he presented the urgency of the state of the nation, so crisscrossed with lines of cleavage that it had 'little hope of permanency' unless a party born of and among the plain people of Canada rallied the moral energy of the nation. To this task he summoned his listeners. Farmers would be the 'bond of union' in a party comprising workers, veterans, professionals, and small businessmen as well. The words fell on ready ears, and 'echoes of Dr. Bland's prophetic speech' reverberated in the corridors throughout the rest of the convention.[45]

41 GGG, 26 Feb. 1913, pp. 7, 10; see also Spafford, 'Independent Politics in Saskatchewan Before the Non-Partisan League,' pp. 1–9

42 *The Single Taxer and Direct Legislation Bulletin* (Winnipeg), 1916 through 1919

43 GGG, 7 Aug. 1918, p. 32. See also 21 Aug. 1918, pp. 9, 31–2 for the *Guide*'s enthusiastic view of Chautauqua.

44 Bland Papers, Broadley to Bland, 13 Dec. 1918

45 *The Leader* (Regina), 19 and 21 Feb. 1919

The Saskatchewan association did not directly adopt the creation of a third party as Bland proposed, but it did plan to lead a 'People's Movement' in federal politics. At the request of one-quarter of the locals of any district, the board was to call conventions of supporters of the New National Policy, so 'that they may best secure the election to Parliament of suitable representatives.'[46] James Somerville, president of the Saskatchewan Labor party 'in embryo,' had addressed the convention. Although he stated that the Farmers' Platform did not go far enough to receive the support of labour, he was listened to quite cordially.[47] Apparently both groups were reluctant to cement an alliance, but the Saskatchewan decision nevertheless was to move in the direction of a broadly based rather than an agrarian political party.[48]

Although the directors tried to slow the pace of developments in June, by the end of the summer conventions had been held in all Saskatchewan constituencies.[49] A similar process was under way in Alberta and Manitoba as well. In early July the *Guide* had supplied its readers with a special 'Political Campaign Number.' Among articles on the planks of the Farmers' Political Platform was one by Bland on 'The Patronage Evil.'[50] By that time, however, he had moved to Toronto, and but for his column in the *Guide*, which continued until October, he had no further direct involvement in prairie developments. A party of the people which he had long advocated seemed about to emerge, proposing reforms which he had long supported, and baptized with the social gospel he had so persuasively preached.

The association of the social gospel and the agrarian movements quite naturally carried through the organizational period following 1919 and the provincial and federal victories of 1919 to 1921. In the West the followers of Irvine and Wood rode to political victory in Alberta in 1921. At the Saskatchewan Grain Growers' convention in 1920 another level of social gospel involvement was evident in the presence of young ministers like A.C. Burley, Harold Wilding, and J. Griffith.[51] Many others were members, often on executives of local associations, a practice encouraged by the Methodist Department of Evangelism and Social Service. No less a person than its Western field secretary, Hugh Dobson, was a member of the inner policy group of the Regina constituency organization of the Progressive party.[52] And in Manitoba, W.R. Wood, secretary of the Manitoba association,

46 *Ibid.*   47 GGG, 26 Feb. 1919

48 Saskatchewan Grain Growers' Association, Board of Directors, minutes, 22 Feb.
    1919, p. 49

49 *Ibid.*, 5 June 1919, p. 55. This was in order to ensure representation of 'all classes
    of supporters of the Platform.'

50 GGG, 2 July 1919   51 CG, 17 March 1920, p. 25

52 *Ibid.*, 15 Dec. 1920, p. 14. UCA (BC Section), Dobson Papers, Correspondence
    1921–3, File w, R. Wood to Hugh Dobson, 12 July, 26 Sept. 1921

addressed special letters to the rural clergy of the province, urging them to follow the example of others in joining and furthering this broad 'social and community organization' for 'the promotion of better citizenship and of economic and political justice.' In all its work, he said,

we believe we are practically seeking to inaugurate the Kingdom of God and its righteousness, and we confidently appeal to all who are moving in that direction, for sympathy and help. Practically all our leaders are active members of the Church. Many of them owe most of their training to the Church. There is much common ground between us, and the goals we seek are one.[53]

The actual response to this letter is not known, but the relationship it declared was noted two years later by Normal Lambert, secretary of the Canadian Council of Agriculture. The aim of the Progressive party, he said, was 'to give "politics" a new meaning in Canada,' and 'hand in hand with the organized farmers movement on the prairies' in this task 'has gone religion and social work.'[54]

The relationship between the farmers' movement and the clergy was a more restrained one in central Canada than in the West.[55] However, when the United Farmers of Ontario (UFO) won their striking victory in October 1919, they found a responsive chord in the editors of the *Guardian, Presbyterian and Westminster*, and *Social Welfare*, all representative in varying degrees of the social gospel.

The *Presbyterian and Westminster*, most restrained of the three, hailed the election as an indication of 'an independence of thought and action which was badly needed in Canadian politics.'[56] The editor was most impressed with Drury, leader of the UFO forces, a 'student of economic questions' with a 'BSA from Guelph,' a Methodist, and a local preacher.[57] Creighton in the *Guardian* had expressed support of the UFO entry into politics in early September, but had erred in expecting twenty to thirty seats as against the forty-five actually won.[58] He was critical of the idea of class government and urged the broad conception of a people's government on the UFO. However, he was not fearful on this count, for the UFO and labour, which had won eleven seats, were not in politics for favours but, as he said, for justice. This farmer-labour alignment was not simply a new partisan movement. The 'old political traditions are outgrown,' he commented, 'but the two great parties as yet seem unaware of it.'[59] Shearer in *Social Welfare* followed Creighton's

53 Bland Papers, letter, 17 April 1919, enclosed in Wood to Bland, 18 April 1919
54 *Presbyterian Witness*, 23 June 1921, pp. 10–11
55 CG, 15 Dec. 1920, p. 14
56 23 Oct. 1919, p. 372
57 *Ibid.*, 6 Nov. 1919, p. 414
58 10 Sept. 1919, p. 6
59 *Ibid.*, 19 Nov. 1919, p. 7

more progressive approach. The 'Farm and Workshop' were on the throne, he wrote, in a 'revolt of the people' against 'the game of party politics,' in which 'privilege was continuing to have its innings regardless of whether Grits or Tories were in power.[60]

Creighton and Shearer represented the prophetic passion of the social gospel much more than the editor of the *Presbyterian and Westminster*. The latter insisted on the sober observation that, despite Drury's opposition to class government and legislation, the government as constituted *was* a class government. With wider support it might become 'a real People's Party which may be of great service to the country.'[61] The simple addition of Labor party support would probably not have satisfied the editor, who had never looked with great sympathy on labour's political activities. Creighton had cautiously proposed some form of group government to the UFO,[62] but was in any case happy with such evidences of Drury's broad position as the passage of the superannuation bill against the declared UFO platform position. Drury had secured UFO convention support for his stand in December 1920, and despite failure to adopt the name 'People's Party,' the facts, as Creighton saw them, read that way anyway.[63]

More specific in his support of the entry of the farmers into politics was Ernest Thomas, and more radical, as usual, having taken up the defence of group politics. His defence was notable as the only extensive commentary upon the theory by an official representative of the social gospel in the church departments. Whether Thomas, writing as Edward Trelawney in the *Guardian*, had read Irvine's *Farmers in Politics* is not clear, but he had been much impressed with M.P. Follet's *The New State*, sometimes speculated to be the source of Wood's ideas.[64] There were four aspects to Thomas' defence of some form of group government: first, he observed that the British Parliament had grown through the accession of class groups; second, he argued that Canadian society was becoming more, not less, class conscious; third, he noted a growing cynicism about government due, he said, to a lack of 'inwardness' or to a 'non-relation to actual units of the people' – the present system had become a mechanical affair, based on the 'fiction of isolated individual voters,' an aggregation detached from reality and dissolved the day after voting; and fourth, he saw group politics as a vital reflection of the living truth that 'no one thinks alone, no one decides alone, and no one creates policies alone.' Men were the products of group fellowship.

In these latter ideas, Thomas was following the lead of Bernard Bosanquet,

60 1 Dec. 1919, pp. 60–1
62 CG, 22 Oct. 1919, p. 6
64 Rolph, *Henry Wise Wood*, p. 64

61 25 Dec. 1919, pp. 590–1
63 *Ibid.*, 29 Dec. 1920, p. 4

whom he described as the 'chief spiritual interpreter of the state for a generation,' and who had given his blessing to Follett's ideas.[65] The group, as Thomas described it, was a reflection of Follett and not unlike Wood's fundamental concept. It was what arose out of the intimate and open-minded reaction of persons on one another, creating a social product, 'social mindedness.' Thomas allowed a variety of groups – family, religious associations, professional and occupational organizations, each sovereign in its own sphere. It was in industry, Thomas believed, that a sense of group fellowship had failed to develop, but was growing. Most of the business of society, Thomas clearly felt, would be settled in terms of group self-government. The problems of group relations, he optimistically felt, would be at a minimum since, 'as the absolute necessity of interdependence comes to be recognized, the community will insist on the right of untrammelled freedom of speech and assembly as a prime condition of its own existence,' and none would dominate the others. To complete such a system, Thomas believed it was necessary to recover the group character of Parliament. He was not clear as to how this was to be accomplished, whether by the representation of all the groups he had discerned, or only of the major occupational groups. Either approach would have to overcome formidable difficulties. One way or another, however, it was necessary to introduce co-operative principles into the Canadian Parliament and eradicate the system of debate and government based on the opposition of groups and the ascendancy of one over another.[66]

As the election of 1921 approached, it was apparent that the social gospel in the student world – that is, among the leadership of the nascent Student Christian Movement (SCM) – was fully in accord with the developing progressive alliance in politics. Frequent contributors to the SCM publication, the *Canadian Student*, such as J. Davidson Ketchum and Sidney Hooke, were often to be found on the pages of the recently established progressive journal, the *Canadian Forum*.[67] The editor of the *Canadian Student* declaimed against 'a competitive system which crowds the

65 Follett, *The New State: Group Organization the Solution of Popular Government*
66 'Group or Party Government,' CG, 2 Feb. 1921, p. 6; 'Group Thinking the Salvation of Democracy,' *ibid.*, 9 March 1921, p. 7. See also *Industrial Banner*, 9 April 1920, p. 1. There is a clear connection between Thomas' espousal of group politics and the prominent role he adopted in promoting fellowship groups in 1928 after the first thrust of progressive politics had gone into decline. See below, pp. 293–4
67 See for example, *Canadian Student*, Nov. 1918, pp. 18ff; Jan. 1919, pp. 1–2; Nov. 1921, pp. 1–2; Feb. 1924, p. 131; and *Canadian Forum*, Sept. 1922, pp. 749–53; Dec. 1922, pp. 76–8; April 1923, pp. 204–6; Aug. 1923, pp. 335–6. See below, pp. 307–8. Ketchum was a frequent editorialist in the former publication, while C.B. Sissons, a cousin of Woodsworth, was editor of the latter.

market with commodities in periods of spending and then enforces idleness consequent to overstimulated production.'[68] Hooke argued that workers were correct in their circumstances to turn to socialism and to criticize the church for alliance with vested interests.[69] Two articles in 1921 urged students to view their concerns and outlook as identical with those of the Progressive party. M.H. Staples, director of education for the UFO, author of *The Challenge of Agriculture*,[70] and a member of the graduate group of the SCM, depicted the essential similarity of the two movements. Both, he said, had encroached on territory held by other organizations; both were reform-minded and democratic in spirit and structure; and both believed in the essential goodness of human nature.[71] Ernest Thomas, in a subsequent article, thoughtfully analysed and rejected propaganda condemning 'class' and 'group' political action. There was no need to fear the 'new, inarticulate energy' of the agrarian movement, he said, but it was important for enlightened citizens to co-operate with it to avert its becoming a narrow class movement.[72] There is no way of measuring how many students in or out of the SCM took up the challenge of these articles, but such writing reflected the temper of the SCM as revealed in the minutes of its general committee, the reports of its conferences, not to mention the *Canadian Student* itself, during these early years of the movement's life.[73]

By 1921, then, it was quite evident that, from the inspirational work of Bland and the educational work of Irvine to the leadership of Wood, Henders, and Drury, from the participation of local prairie preachers to the sympathies of the editors of and contributors to the Protestant press and the SCM, the social gospel had invested heavily in the creation of an agrarian-based political party to give expression to the concerns of progressive Canadians.

The social gospel was not confined in political influence simply to the primarily agrarian wing of progressive politics. In keeping with their concern for a People's party, a number were at work promoting labour political groups, despite the rude jolt the strikes of 1919 had given hopes of farmer-labour co-operation, especially in Manitoba. Unfortunately, in the socialist and labour wing of this movement of progressive politics there was as much dissension between constituent groups as there was difficulty over the question of farmer-labour relations at large.

68 Nov. 1921, pp. 1–2   69 *Ibid.*, Nov. 1918, pp. 18ff.

70 Published in Toronto in 1921

71 *Canadian Student*, March 1921, pp. 20–2

72 *Ibid.*, Oct. 1921, pp. 13ff.

73 SCM Archives, Toronto, minutes of the general committee, Student Christian Movement of Canada; Student Christian Movement, *Building the City of God*, p. 490

From 1918 to 1920 the Dominion Labor party (DLP) in the prairie region, the Federated Labor party in British Columbia, and the Independent Labor party in central Canada were the chief vehicles of social gospellers of a labour political orientation.[74] With the OBU-TLC split in 1919, however, a conservative reaction in the latter spread into the DLP to such a degree that in early 1921 the original leaders in the Winnipeg group felt the need of a fuller political expression of their socialist views. In March 1921, consequently, an Independent Labour party was formed in Winnipeg[75] comprising leaders F.J. Dixon (MLA), S.J. Farmer, W.D. Bayley (MLA), and William Ivens (MLA). The latter three, and possibly Dixon as well, were leaders in the Labor church and exponents of the social gospel.[76] The *Manitoba Free Press* observed that their departure tightened up the relationship of the DLP with the trade union movement, and described the new organization as a 'group of non-descripts.'[77] When Woodsworth returned to Winnipeg in June 1921, he joined this group. Not everywhere, apparently, was abandonment of the DLP deemed necessary by socialists. In Calgary, Irvine continued to be a leading figure within it, and in April 1921 a proposal of co-operation in the coming election from the UFA was readily accepted.[78]

When in August during the Winnipeg convention of the TLC an attempt was made to federate the various labour-political groups into one Canadian Labor party (CLP), the radical social gospel was prominent. James Simpson, who had done much to bring the conference together, was provisional secretary. Woodsworth was spokesman for the Federated Labor party of British Columbia. A.E. Smith, together with most of the Manitobans just mentioned, were present. An executive was elected, representing all provinces. Each provincial representative was to call a provincial convention as soon as possible. The TLC had given the party its tacit support and in September the Dominion Labor party united with the new party. Although the Winnipeg ILP group soon withdrew, labour's political stance in the fall

During these years, the SCM was the only national student movement in Canadian universities. See below, pp. 220–3

74 See above, pp. 51–2, 81, 90. For the fullest account of labour politics in the period 1890–1930 see Robin, *Radical Politics and Canadian Labour*.

75 McNaught, *A Prophet in Politics*, pp. 147–8, not to be confused with the ILP in Ontario which was participating in Drury's government there.

76 See above, chap. 5

77 21 Oct. 1921, cited in McNaught, *A Prophet in Politics*, p. 148. In later years these 'non-descripts' were to be seen as the main line in the development of a political party for labour in Canada.

78 *Alberta Labor News*, 23 April 1921, p. 2

of 1921 seemed more formidable than it had ever been.[79]

Simpson, as secretary-treasurer, had been instructed by the conference to seek a working agreement with the Progressive party leadership. When in September Staples and Good (both social gospellers) of the United Farmers of Ontario were named to the CLP executive, the most delicate part of a progressive political alliance seemed to be in the making.[80] The significance of the alliance, some social gospel proponents argued, was that the stability of the farmer mated with the economic understanding and determination of labour would provide the most fruitful basis of desired change.[81] In such a combination, extremist tendencies in labour would be subordinated. Ironically, however, just as some formal arrangements were being concluded to bring a working alliance into being, other trends were eroding the ground on which the alliance was to be built.

By 1921 difficulties too numerous for any formal or lasting arrangement to comprehend prevented even the degree of federal co-operation between farmer and labour forces that had existed in provincial elections in 1919 and 1920. Then only the more militant farmers were committed to political action and were more open than were their colleagues to alliances with labour. This contrast was to become clearer in comparisons of the 1920 and 1922 campaigns in Manitoba, for instance, and those in Ontario in 1919 and 1923.[82] As farmers campaigned, the more radical elements of their platform were increasingly ignored.[83] And although social gospel proponents commonly cited the natural bent of the farmer toward co-operation, the striking independency of Progressive party constituency organization not only mitilitated against formal arrangements with other bodies,[84] but ran counter to the more disciplined politics which labourites advocated. In actual fact, of course, the farmers were far superior in organization. Representative conventions could easily be summoned. Labour and progressive elements in the cities could not reproduce this situation in order to complement the farmers' movement in a broadly based Progressive party.[85]

79 *Ibid.*, p. 148; Smith, *All My Life*, pp. 69–70; *Industrial Banner*, 8 July 1921, 9 Sept. 1921

80 CAR, 1921, pp. 507–8. For other evidence of co-operation see *Industrial Banner*, 14 Oct. 1921

81 Bland Papers, Salem Bland, 'The Call of Canada to the Farmers,' *The Farmers' Sun*, [ca Oct. 1921]; *ibid.*, vol. 59, no 71, Labour Day Address, Owen Sound (undated cutting from *Owen Sound Advertiser*)

82 Morton, *The Progressive Party*, pp. 226–7, 212–15

83 *Ibid.*, p. 118   84 *Ibid.*, pp. 118–19

85 *Ibid.*, pp. 214–15. The confusion of the ILP and the CLP in Ontario is a good instance of this (*Industrial Banner*, 8 July 1921, p. 1; 24 Feb. 1922, p. 1). The fact that

Finally, differences between provinces and regions held problems for the creation of the kind of progressive political alliance most social gospellers advocated. The UFA with a cohesive organization and a coherent political philosophy, a strong position vis-à-vis the cities, and the most lucid exponent of its 'group politics' prominent in the Labor party, found no great difficulty in co-operative electoral arrangements. In Manitoba, however, there existed a deep conflict between the powerful urban interests in Winnipeg and the countryside. This conflict was exacerbated by mutual hostility between labour and all but the more militant farmers over the Winnipeg strike on the one hand and the 'farmers' juries' on the other which had convicted its leaders. In Ontario, growing strife over the issue of broadening out, rural defensiveness, and attacks on labour campaigns for the eight-hour day kept joint farmer and labour activity at a minimum. In the light of such a complex of problems, any co-operation at all was a minor miracle.

Given this tangled state of farmer-labour relations, the radical proposal of 'group politics' and 'group government' made much sense, at least as a tactic if not as a final governmental arrangement, for it proposed further consolidation of occupational organizations for political purposes. William Irvine's book, *Farmers in Politics*, published in 1920, expounding this theory was, therefore, a response to a very pressing problem of political action.[86] Salem Bland, writing in the foreword, expressed general agreement with Irvine, but he was never a clear exponent of 'group politics.' In numerous addresses in the course of the campaign of 1921, speaking now to a UFO picnic, or a Labour Day gathering, then on behalf of a farmer or labour candidate, sometimes to a women's rally, occasionally with a returned soldier, he urged a 'democratic entente of farmers, labor, soldiers and women.'[87] His concept of the 'entente' was a loose one, involving a farmers' party, a labour party, and a returned soldiers' party, around which he expected nearly all the lower middle class, some of the upper class, and three-quarters of the ministers to rally in an 'irresistible political and ethical force.'[88] As at the Grain Growers' convention of

in Sept. 1921 the UFO appointed W.C. Good and M.H. Staples to the executive of the CLP could hardly alter this condition, and only slightly obscured the problems in farmer-labour relations.

86 The emergence of this theory and its significance will be discussed below.

87 Labour Day Address, Owen Sound. See also the *Star Weekly* (Toronto), 19 June 1920; Bland Papers, Stratford, MS, 'The Reign of the Common People,' Labour Day Address, 6 Sept. 1920; *Toronto Daily Star*, 15 June 1921; *The Orillia Times*, 16 June 1921; *Owen Sound Advertiser*, 15 July 1921; *The Globe*, 30 Nov. 1921; *The Spotlight* (Smith's Falls), cited in the *Toronto Daily Star*, 30 Nov. 1921

88 Bland Papers, 'The Call of Canada to the Farmers,' *The Farmers' Sun*, [ca Oct. 1921]

1919 in Saskatchewan, Bland was less interested in final political arrangements than in spurring on the association of the groups in which he saw the most hope for the regeneration of the nation.

Despite evidence that might have been cited to confound the political activists of the social gospel, such an alliance seemed well in the making in the latter half of 1921. The compromises of the Wood and Crerar factions of the farmers' movement in January 1920 had cleared the way for federal political action by the agrarian groups. In August of 1921 the Canadian Labor party had brought together all the significant labour political groups, a surprising number of them led by active social gospel proponents of labour politics. A link had been forged with the farmers' Progressive party in September. To be sure, in the December election, labour efforts were hardly successful, only Woodsworth and Irvine winning seats in the federal House.[89] That fact, however, seemed to realign Woodsworth and his Winnipeg supporters with the Progressive movement at large, for the exciting news of the election was that the Progressives had elected the second largest group of representatives to the House of Commons, and Woodsworth and Irvine quite naturally joined the Progressive party caucus.

The Progressive triumph was, among other things, then, a triumph of the social gospel. Not only were leading figures of the social gospel prominent in every stage of progressive political development, but their ideas, from their theology through to their various tactical proposals, had made a deep impression upon the movement. Their sense of the immanence of God in his creation, moving men to co-operation in the establishment of a kingdom of justice and goodwill, provided a sense of ultimate significance which made even difficult problems matters of secondary importance. The progressive movements – and now their political victories – were a sign that real religion, full of prophetic passion, true brotherhood, and an urgent sense of justice was possessing the people. The spirit of Jesus and the spread of democracy were triumphing together in the modern world. This 'non-politics of hope' of the social gospel was one of the secrets of Progressive party power in 1921,[90] but in the practice of real politics in the subsequent five years that strength might also prove to be its weakness.

89 Woodsworth in Central Winnipeg and Irvine in Calgary East. Irvine's victory was hailed by Elmo Roper in the *Alberta Labor News* as 'the best of the good news' of the election (10 Dec. 1921. See also issues of 3 Sept. 1921, p. 89; 29 Oct. 1921, p. 8; 12 Nov. 1921, p. 1)

90 The phrase 'non-politics of hope' is borrowed from Meyer, *The Protestant Search for Political Realism*, chap. VI, 'The Non-Politics of Hope,' pp. 118–29

13

The New Evangelism

Despite the Progressive victory – perhaps in some measure because of it – there was constant need of the renewal of the social passion. For radical social gospellers the ambiguous stance of the churches in the printers' strike and the reaction of the social service progressives to the Labor churches was evidence enough of the need. The progressives themselves had been discomfited by the strike and may well have had an uneasy conscience over their response to the New Christianity and to Labor church leadership. Conservatives in the church, and probably most church leaders, had long been anxious over the declining fortunes of traditional evangelism. Methodists in particular were concerned over the waning of prayer meetings. Thus, from various standpoints, the time was ripe for the formulation and promotion of a new evangelism. It was important for the fortunes of the social gospel that response to this need came from within its ranks and in a form that could carry its social vision once more into the heartland of Canadian Protestantism.

The new evangelism was the application within the church of studies of the records of the life of Jesus evolved in the years 1916–21 in yet another movement on the fringe of the church, the nascent Student Christian Movement. Ernest Thomas was to achieve such success in transplanting these studies in church soil that it was believed for a time that a substitute for the long declining prayer-meeting had been found. That these studies, apparently unrelated to social gospel concerns, in fact were another vehicle of it, was suggested by the response of the Calgary district of the Methodist church, known for its social radicalism. Its enthusiastic endorsation noted that the studies 'cut the tap-root of much of the pernicious theological and political propaganda of today without even mentioning them.'[1] This appeared to be a subtle tool indeed.

The new evangelism was a phase of a century and one-half old quest of the historical Jesus. That quest had been brought to a climax and a new beginning by Albert Schweitzer in 1902. His now famous book, *Quest of the Historical Jesus*, had reviewed the quest and presented his own analysis and solution of the problem.

1 *Annual Report*, 1921–2, Methodist Department of ESS, p. 101

But in Schweitzer, as in other landmarks of the discussion, there had been a combination of disciplined science and a desire to discover a new, present relevance of Jesus, obscured by the accretions of the needs of other men in other times. Schweitzer considered the key to the historical Jesus to lie in Jesus' expectation of an imminent arrival of the Kingdom of God, but in this, he said, Jesus was mistaken. He might have left his conclusion there in all propriety, but he was driven to make his own testimony to the meaning of Jesus. Schweitzer's expression of his experience of the person of Jesus was a *non sequitur* to his scientific conclusion, but it was as influential as his analysis:

He comes to us as One unknown, without a name, as of old, by the lakeside, He came to those men who knew him not. He speaks to us the same word: Follow thou me! and sets us to the tasks which He has to fulfil for our time. He commands. And to those who obey Him, whether they be wise or simple, He will reveal Himself in the toils, the conflicts, the sufferings which they shall pass through in His fellowship, and, as an ineffable mystery, they shall learn in their own experience who He is.[2]

If Jesus' expectation had been mistaken, there might have been an end of it. Or one might have concluded that the rest of the message, with the eschatology excized, was valid. Or again that the eschatology had a meaning apart from its historical realization. Or that Jesus had simply been mistaken as to the time of the realization of the kingdom.

It was obviously of some consequence to the social gospel which of these conclusions was accepted. The first precluded any social gospel. The second might have contented moralists. The second and the third in various interpretations might satisfy some conservatives and progressives of the social gospel. The last was the hope of the more ardent progressives and the most radical exponents of the movement. In the studies of the new evangelism, there were several options open to participants; but since the studies were being undertaken in a context where the social gospel had made a large impact, it was clear that 'the tasks which Jesus had to fulfil for that time' would include those of the social gospel. As in Schweitzer's work the conclusions may have existed in a certain tension with the method, but that may have had the advantage of promoting continuous study.

In the second half of the second decade of the century, the Bible studies of the student movements in Canada shifted from works by the popular liberal preacher and author, Harry Emerson Fosdick to a programme developed by an appealing

2 Schweitzer, *Quest of the Historical Jesus,* p. 401

professor, Dr H.B. Sharman.[3] His method was simplicity itself. He assembled, in more accessible form, the records of the life of Jesus and asked only, who is this man? And what is he saying? The conclusions he left to his students. His non-directive leadership allowed him only to ask occasional piercing questions. Our task, he said, is not to make disciples of Jesus, but to show them Jesus. 'He must work for himself.' However, the study was not academic in purpose. Nor was the end the acquisition of a code of morals, but 'a principle for my relation to my fellow man, – valid, workable, possible, always easy to apply, marked by the highest idealism, yet practicable. A principle for my relation to God, – all-comprehensive, even though all-exacting.'[4] Canadian students had first encountered Sharman at conferences with the American student YMCA and YWCA at Northfield and Brome Lake. In 1918 he moved to Toronto and became a prime mover in the organization of the Student Christian Movement of Canada, and subsequently one of its chief mentors.[5]

The 'Sharman method' quickly spread, involving large numbers of students at regional and national conferences, in the intramural programme of the student YS, and later in the Student Christian Movement. At Toronto, for instance, in 1918 there had been at least twenty-five courses directed by Sharman and possibly another twenty led by students familiar with the method. Enthusiastic students exclaimed, 'A whole new world is being opened up to us.'[6] Sharman dominated the Bible study of the SCM throughout the 1920s, surviving a shift in student mood in 1925–6. Through the creation in 1928 of a six-week summer seminar training leadership for 'the method,' he bid fair to dominate the 1930s as well.[7] In various parts of the nation leading practitioners of Sharman's method emerged, such as Dr Bronson at Acadia University.

Sharman, himself, was not noted for his advocacy of social gospel concerns, but he could not have been uninterested, else he would hardly have accepted the chair-

3 See Student Christian Movement of Canada, *This One Thing*, for a sketch and commentary on Sharman's career.

4 H.B. Sharman, 'The Value of Bible Study,' [an address to the Brome Lake Conference] *Canadian Student*, Oct. 1918, pp. 12–15

5 See SCM Archives, minutes of the General Council of the Student Christian Movement, 1–3 Jan. 1921. Sharman was chairman of the Interim Committee and of the General Committee.

6 *Canadian Student*, Oct. 1918, p. 22

7 SCM Archives, minutes, General Committee of the SCM, 23–5 Sept. 1927; 3 and 4 Jan. 1928; 21–3 Sept. 1928; 7–11 Sept. 1929

manship of a Joint Board of Employers and Employees in the Toronto clothing trades, an example of a single unit of the Whitley-type industrial council system.[8] The social gospel, in any case, had heavily impregnated the student movement he came to serve in Canada, and it supplemented Sharman's studies with groups on social problems and the social teachings of Jesus.[9] Student YMCA leaders, like L.S. Albright in the Maritimes, urged the replacement of the lingering church prayer meeting with 'solid studies.' Can prayer meetings, he asked, 'give us an intelligent grasp of the whole world problem of Christianity? Can they beget in us the social passion to deny self in order to set up the kingdom?'[10] He accused the old methods of being responsible for making Christians 'individual saints and corporate sinners, personal Christians and social and industrial pagans.'[11] The new evangelism, in his mind, had to combine both the 'evangelization and Christianization' of life.[12]

At the Central Area conference, September 1921, the peculiar combination of interests which was to characterize the SCM for many years was manifest. The search for the Jesus of history under Sharman was combined with lectures by S.H. Hooke interpreting the faith of Jesus as being 'in "up to the neck," ' and one's faith in Jesus involving the completion of that venture in one's own life. The private secretary of Arthur Henderson, British Labour MP, was with the conference the whole time, interpreting the programme and principles of labour, while Mr Staples of the UFO undertook a similar task for the farmers' movement. At the conference, 75 per cent of the students enrolled in groups on social and industrial problems as against such areas as education and missions. Even the character of the latter was evincing a new stress on reform of social and economic conditions abroad.[13] It was not surprising that one of the hallowed moments of such conferences was J. Davidson Ketchum's playing of William Blake's 'Jerusalem.'[14] The 628 delegated students and professors who gathered at the first national conference of the SCM, 28 December 1922–2 January 1923, considered a broad range of social and national questions

8 Thomas, 'The Forward Looking Church and the Advance of Labor,' *Alberta Labor News*, 4 Sept. 1920, p. 15

9 *Canadian Student*, Nov. 1920, p. 27; Oct. 1925, p. 181

10 CG, 14 Jan. 1920, p. 12

11 *Ibid.*, 14 April 1920, pp. 10–11

12 *Ibid.*, 4 Feb. 1920, p. 9

13 *Ibid.*, 26 Oct. 1921, p. 13. The next year (and perhaps in 1921) an employer representative was invited to speak, but did not show up, *Canadian Churchman*, 12 Oct. 1922, pp. 655, 72

14 See SCM Archives, typescript report of the First National Conference

intended to equip them for 'Building the City of God' in Canada's 'green and pleasant land.'[15]

The parent YS, especially the YMCA, had not been happy at the loss of their student movements. In fact, the decision to separate completely had taken them somewhat by surprise.[16] But the decision, partly engineered by student leaders such as E.H. Clarke, was a clear reflection of a gulf which had deepened between the student movements and the parent organizations.[17] The editor of the *Guardian* quoted one advocate of the SCM as describing the YMCA as 'a creature of the business men and used by them. It was definitely allied with their view of life, inclinations and interests.'[18] This was a somewhat harsh judgment, but to a considerable extent the separation of the student movements into the SCM, formally accomplished at the Guelph national conference in December 1920, was a condition of the full emergence of a social gospel in the SCM and of the free discovery by students of the tasks Jesus laid on them for their time.

From the first year of the new movement, both Salem Bland and Ernest Thomas were associated with it. Both were Bible study resource leaders for the SCM at the University of Toronto,[19] both addressed SCM meetings on the campuses and at conferences,[20] and both wrote articles at one time or another for the SCM publication, the *Canadian Student*.[21] Among the preachers of Toronto, Bland was probably the favourite, with large numbers of students attending his services at Broad-

15 The figures do not include 67 international student observers and over 400 less formally accredited student participants (Student Christian Movement of Canada, *Building the City of God*). During the year prior to the conference, students across the country had studied a booklet of seven studies on country life, the concern of the community in industry, society, and industrial discord, new Canadians, missions, internationalism and war, internationalism and co-operation (SCM of Canada, *Some Canadian Questions*). This was the first conference of Canadian undergraduate students (*Canadian Forum*, Jan. 1923, Editorial).

16 *Canadian Student*, Jan. 1921, p. 25

17 Ross, *The YMCA in Canada*, pp. 226–32

18 CG, 19 July 1922, p. 6

19 Interview with E. Harold Toye; *Annual Report*, 1922–3, Methodist Department of ESS, pp. 37–9

20 CG, 26 Oct. 1921, p. 13; 11 Oct. 1922, p. 21

21 *Canadian Student*, March 1919, pp. 10–14; Nov. 1919, pp. 3ff; Oct. 1921, pp. 13–16

way Tabernacle. Of the two, however, Thomas was more intimately involved in the programmes of the SCM. The movement, in the first year, specifically requested the Methodist Department of Evangelism and Social Service to authorize the devotion of part of his time to leading SCM studies. This was granted. He prepared the programme of study for the national conference of 1922–3,[22] which was then expanded as a text for the Brotherhoods and the Religious Education Council of Canada. In his travels he led studies and gave addresses to SCM groups across the nation.[23] Throughout the 1920s, at least, his devotion of time to the work of the SCM was never questioned by the Methodist Board or its United Church successor.

It was in the SCM that the new intensive evangelism of the early 1920s in the Methodist church had its birth. In presenting an encouraging report of the results of the first year of its application in the church, 1921–2, Thomas described it as an attempt to carry over into the church the force that such studies had demonstrated in the SCM.[24] Furthermore, their applicability in the church had been discovered when group studies presented by Thomas to SCM units in various centres attracted church workers in considerable numbers.[25] Moore outlined the rationale of the study of the 'experience of Jesus' by saying that 'too often the influence of Jesus is weakened by some speculative theological interpretation of the story.' The new method endeavoured 'to present the compelling personality of Jesus to men so that it will elicit its own response, leaving the new experience free to voice itself in language most appropriate to itself.'[26] The words could well have been Sharman's.

Strategically, the first task of the new evangelism was training the leadership of the church in conducting studies of the life of Jesus. Throughout 1922–3 this effort took Thomas from one coast to the other. In Alberta he had tutored half the ministers of the province. In one city civic leaders attended, and as many as one hundred and fifty persons attended evening sessions. At Mount Allison University a class of forty followed the studies. Most of the programmes were jointly sponsored by the Presbyterian church, and the newly formed Religious Education Council of Canada had all its staff undergo the experience.[27] The report of the department in 1923–4 noted that summer schools such as those of the Hamilton conference and the Canadian Chautauqua in Muskoka (otherwise known as the Muskoka As-

22 *Annual Report*, 1921–2, Methodist Department of ESS, pp. 23, 39; 1922–3, pp. 37–9
23 UCA, Methodist Department of ESS, *Intensive Evangelism*, and covering letter to ministers
24 *Annual Report*, 1921–2, Methodist Department of ESS, pp. 23, 39
25 *Intensive Evangelism*, and covering letter to ministers, 18 Sept. 1922
26 *Annual Report*, 1921–2, Methodist Department of ESS, p. 23
27 *Ibid.*, pp. 37–9

sembly) had featured the new intensive evangelism. In the *Guardian* of 2 January 1924, a resolution from one of the three Toronto districts commended Thomas' scholarship and avoidance of dogmatism in his week-long study with them. The occasion was taken to report that he had also just completed similar visits to St Thomas, Welland, Orillia, St Mary's, and the Toronto West district. In 1924, however, the amount of time of the department being consumed by the church union and prohibition causes was beginning to tell on other programmes, and another shift was in process. It was not so much an abandonment of the new evangelism as a pragmatic shift in priorities. The General Board of the department observed three groups, different in character and requiring different methods: those who knew not, as the board put it, that the Victorian age was supposed to have passed away; those who were frank unbelievers; and those with a nominal belief. To cover such a range the board decided to employ 'special preachers of various types' using both older mass methods and the 'new evangelism' which Thomas had transferred from the SCM to the churches.[28]

In 1923, when Bland had completed his term at Broadway Tabernacle and was unable to secure another circuit in Toronto, he had requested that he be left without station and was free to become a free-wheeling practitioner of the new evangelism. For some years lectures and sermons on the 'Pre-eminence of Christ' had had a central place in his teaching and preaching. He had also led two-week missions on social evangelism, which had had a remarkable impact in prairie cities.[29] In the former he had attacked 'the religious standards set by the professionally religious and by people of certain temperaments, too long regarded as the specifically religious temperaments.' He asserted in their place 'the simple and human and catholic standards of Jesus.'[30] In his social evangelism, Bland had, in a 'plain, unvarnished' way, dealt with social questions as religious issues involving the 'incarnation of God in human institutions and relations.'[31] These emphases upon Jesus and social issues were combined in the fortnightly series he delivered in numerous centres, 1922–5, under the title 'The Real Jesus and His Message.'

Bland was a powerful preacher, and a remarkably approachable one.[32] The reports that came back to the Department of Evangelism and Social Service were

28 CG, 3 Dec. 1924, pp. 17–18   29 *Ibid.*, 8 Jan. 1918, p. 2
30 GGG, 16 Jan. 1918, p. 34
31 As reported by H.G. Cairns, CG, 8 Jan. 1918, p. 2
32 So discerning an observer as C.B. Sissons remarked that upon return from England, where he had heard what were reputed to be the greatest preachers of the day, he had then heard Bland again, and was convinced that he outshone them all (conversation with the author).

enthusiastic about his persuasive pulpit manner and his engaging ways in discussion. Ministers from the Lakehead where he spent all of April 1924 praised his rare combination of 'reverence and frankness, patience, tact and incisiveness.'[33] Vancouver, Moose Jaw, Toronto, Stratford, and Montreal were among the other cities where people responded in like manner.[34] As usual, however, his preaching was not unattended by hostility. In fact, he would have been alarmed had it not been.

Bland once observed that when a principle achieved universal assent it lost its ability to inspire and its relevance. And on another occasion he noted that the traditional preaching of the gospel awakened no hostility, whereas for a minister to attempt to relate it to social, political, and economc issues was to request a dismissal. In traditional evangelism the church was 'in the air.' She was 'preaching beautiful principles' but 'not touching anything or anybody.' She was 'like the propeller of a steamer that is racing out of water doing nothing.'[35] His fortnightly series ended with the consideration of three subjects, 'Jesus Teaching About Wealth,' 'Jesus Teaching About Competition' and 'What To Do.'[36] It was a sign of the changing times that it was not these social subjects, but the theological aspects of the New Christianity and the new evangelism that now aroused deepest hostility.

One of the more notable attacks on the new evangelism followed a preaching mission of Bland's in Montreal. The Montreal *Gazette* headline, 'Bland Denies Divinity of Our Lord,' had initiated a controversy in the paper until a letter from Bland gave full notes of relevant passages of his addresses, putting newspaper comments in context.[37] On Bland's return to Toronto, the *Telegram*, which seemed to be a rallying point of fundamentalists as the *Star* was of liberals and modernists, tried to box him in on the subject.[38] But he was never easy to corner. If the incarnation had not involved limitation, how could we know God at all in Christ, he asked in reply? Jesus' humanity was a necessary condition of his revelation of the meaning of the eternal and infinite God for man. From the humanness of Jesus to the coming of the kingdom, the debate hinged on the value placed on human nature. There

33 CG, 28 May 1924, p. 14
34 *Ibid.*, 5 Dec. 1923, p. 8; 7 Jan. 1925, p. 13; 22 April 1925, pp. 15, 16; Bland Papers, 'Socialism and Christianity,' delivered to an economics class, University of British Columbia, 23 Feb. 1924
35 *The Globe*, 18 Oct. 1920, speaking at Charlton Avenue Methodist Church, Hamilton, Ontario
36 Bland Papers, newspaper clipping, nd
37 CG, 22 April 1925, p. 16
38 20 April 1925

seemed to be an implicit rejection of one's own humanity, Bland said, in the frantic defense of the divinity of Jesus and in the apocalypticism of pre-millennial views of the kingdom and the second coming. As such it was a rejection of responsible discipleship and a reliance upon mechanical means of salvation. 'The tragedy of Christianity,' Bland observed, 'was the people who believed that trust in Jesus would save them from Hell, when it did not save them from pride, selfishness and prejudice which make Hell here and hereafter.' A like tragedy were those who believed in a cheap and spectacular apocalypse which would not make one soul know God better. 'Jesus began the conquest of the world by a cross. As he began so He would finish. The Kingdom of God can only come through the spirit of Christ.'[39]

The attacks of fundamentalists on the 'heresies' of liberalism and modernism in theology had been mounting in the United States since the publication in 1910–12 of *The Fundamentals: A Testimony to the Truth.* Although few of the Canadian churches were as seriously divided on the question as were many in the United States, the issue was a pressing one. The Baptists were increasingly disturbed through the 1920s by T.T. Shields of Jarvis Street Baptist Church, Toronto, until in 1927 the Ontario and Quebec convention repudiated him and his followers.[40] In 1922 the Toronto General Ministerial Association was almost evenly divided in a debate on pre-millennialism which verged on real hostilities.[41] Correspondence in the *Christian Guardian* ran rather heavily through the middle 1920s on matters related to the fundamentalist-modernist issue, with the editor occasionally taking the lists against the former.[42] And in the Presbyterian church, fundamentalist anti-unionists identified advocacy of church union with modernism, and then attacked both with the same weapons. However, whatever the degrees of coincidence may have been, there were prominent liberal spokesmen, such as Principal Fraser, on the anti-union side.[43] In most of the churches it was apparent that fundamentalism was causing a considerable stir.

Although the issue did not technically involve the social gospel, the same root attitudes to the Bible, theology, the church, and society were usually held by liberal theologians and social gospellers alike. Except on the more conservative social service wing, it would be difficult to dissociate the one from the other. The acri-

---

39 *Ibid.*

40 *Canadian Baptist*, 20 Oct. 1927, p. 1

41 *Toronto Daily Star*, 7 Feb. 1922

42 For example, 15 March 1922, p. 6, and letters in the same issue, pp. 16, 17

43 UCA, Pidgeon Papers on Church Union, *Official Organ of Methodists Denies the Atonement*, nd; A Group of Presbyterians, *The Need of the Presbyterian Church*, nd; and 'Copies of Letters in the Press,' typescript, nd

monious debate in the Baptist church has been held responsible for the departure of a potential progressive leadership in social questions to the United States, and for an overly cautious attitude in the rest of the church lest the wrath of fundamentalists be stirred unduly.[44] It also impeded the effectiveness of such new and more radical exponents of the social gospel in the Baptist church such as Dr M.F. Mc-Cutcheon of Montreal.[45] The Methodist Department of Evangelism and Social Service was forced to devote time to the preparation of literature for combatting fundamentalist extremism. As a result, in 1922–3, a series of pamphlets on the *Christian Hope* were circulated by Moore's department.[46] In the Anglican church the slowly emerging social gospel was contested sharply on conservative theological grounds by Canon Dyson Hague of Toronto. In repudiating an article by Canon Vernon of the Council for Social Service on the 'Coming of the Kingdom,' December 1922, he argued for a personal second coming, regardless of whether this was pre- or post-millennial, but added that

the revival of post-millennialism, especially in the Methodist Church, has done much in the last half century to substitute the conception of a better world for the return of the Saviour [to which the Anglican Church must hold] though Rome may displace, Unitarianism may falsify, Arianism may transpose, rationalism may deride ... in these terminal days.[47]

Hague was probably a more formidable opponent than most, but in all the churches a mounting pressure from persons of his views was in evidence.

It was significant that the first notable fundamentalist attack on Bland came in 1921 after the failure of conservatives to defeat him or the church social policies for which he stood. Bland had addressed the Western Association of Congregational Churches in Hamilton, 5 April 1921, on 'Evangelism and Industry,' in which some of the theses of the *New Christianity* had been delivered. The Rev. T.D. Rayner, in inviting the association to meet next at Watford, put the condition that none holding the views of Bland should speak. It was a significant incident, not because Rayner represented any powerful economic interest threatened by Bland, but because he did not. He was one of many small-town ministers and many humble lay-

44 G.P. Albaugh, 'Themes for Research in Canadian Baptist History,' *Foundations*, VI, Jan. 1963, pp. 52–3. D.R. Sharpe to the author, 22 July 1963

45 *Canadian Baptist*, 17 May 1923, p. 1

46 Methodist Department of ESS, *Christian Hope*

47 *Canadian Churchmen*, 21 Dec. 1922, p. 835. See the same page for quite contrary view by the Rev. H.T. Archbold of Victoria, BC. For Vernon's article, *ibid.*, 30 Nov. 1922, p. 776

men who had been made restive by the rise of liberal theology and the social gospel. They were people who in some cases felt a deep need to find a place away from industrial problems and social tensions where they might refresh their spirits. In other cases, however, they were apparently persons who had found a false security in rigidly held beliefs, and who could thunder that the 'voice was the voice of theology but the hand was the hand of destruction.' However, that there was a parallelism of interest and outlook between such a mass of people and those represented by S.R. Parsons would be difficult to deny. Although the substance of the belief of one might not be reducible to that of the other, the diversion of the social gospel from the task of application by conservatives and fundamentalists in theology suited the frontal opposition to social gospel remedies by many businessmen in the churches. Both groups normally shared traditional Protestant preoccupation with the individual.[48]

The Rayner incident was also significant of a 'know-nothing' character, in which it represented the bulk of fundamentalism, in contrast to Canon Hague. When telephoned by the *Star*, Rayner said that he did not disagree with Bland's labour views, but those on theology. The interview continued:

What peculiar views do you object to?
I will not speak as to that.
What is your criticism of those peculiar theological views?
I won't say what it is!
Have you ever heard Bland speak?
No.[49]

Rayner had absented himself during Bland's address. The upshot for the Congregational association was that Bland was defended to the hilt at the association, and Rayner's views repudiated.[50]

Bland's victory was, however, only of penultimate significance. The offensive which the Rayner incident represented failed to carry the policies of any of the major Protestant churches. In most of the Protestant press there were no supporters of William Jennings Bryan, but rather many trenchant critics of him over the Scopes trial at mid-decade.[51] Nevertheless, the fundamentalists had their reward, for they were a part of the influence which forced liberal theology onto the defen-

48 S.R. Parsons to the editor, cg, 30 March 1921, p. 11
49 *Toronto Daily Star*, 7 April 1921
50 *The Globe*, 6 April 1921; 7 April 1921
51 *Canadian Churchman*, 30 July 1925, p. 485; 6 Aug. 1925, pp. 503, 507 (the latter quoting Bland); cg, 8 April 1925, p. 3

sive, and elbowed the social gospel from a position of social attack to that of theological disputation. Thus, between 1922 and 1929, the tide of literature on the
application of the social gospel ebbed in Canada, and the defence and propagation
of the social gospel required a more extensive confrontation with specifically theological and religious issues than perhaps it had intended.[52] It could be argued that
in both its religious and its social tasks the resources of the social gospel were notably
increased with the founding of such periodicals as the *Canadian Student* in 1918,
the *Canadian Forum* in 1920, the merger of the Congregationalist, Presbyterian,
and Methodist publications in 1925 under the editorship of W.B. Creighton, and
above all, by the *Toronto Daily Star* securing at mid-decade the regular services of
Salem Bland.

Nevertheless, just as recourse to the new evangelism reflected an underlying ap-
prehensiveness in social gospel ranks following ambiguities of their experiences in
industrial reconstruction, so the fortunes of the new evangelism were subtle indications of a growing crisis for the social gospel. It was in the problems of the Brotherhoods and the Social Service Council, in the success of church union, and in the
decline of prohibition, in the rise of the new social work, in the shifting outlook of
the student movement, and the resurgence of pacifism that the proportions of the
crisis became clear for all to see. And in the continuing crisis, the religious question
only became the more insistent.

52 The titles of Canadian religious writings in general became more theological after
    1922 and remained so for the rest of the decade. Some examples are: *The Son of
    Man Coming in His Kingdom* by Alfred Gandier, principal of Knox College, To-
    ronto, and liberal guide to those perplexed by pre-millennialist and post-millennialist
    disputation; John Line, *Inspiration and Modern Criticism* and *The Doctrine of
    Christ in History*; Richard Roberts, *The Christian God*

14

The Demise of
the Brotherhoods

On the eve of the first world war a 'brotherhood mystique' had been waxing in British nonconformity. This development was fostered by a Brotherhood movement which believed it represented a return to the mind of primitive Christianity, and that brotherhood was the goal of the evolutionary process in society. The Brotherhoods proclaimed 'a new socialism of Christian inspiration and purpose,' and were in the midst of a campaign to win the British and European labour movements to their views when the war broke out.[1]

In Canada, the movement at this time may not have been quite as radical or as ambitious, but in 1912 Woodsworth noted the frequency, at least, with which social questions appeared on the programmes of church brotherhoods.[2] In the years immediately following the war, both the Canadian and the international movements extended their activities, and in the encounter of the Canadian with the British movement, the former took on still more of the latter's character.

This growing radicalism was not true of the Brotherhood of St Andrew of the Anglican church. A determined effort was made to foster this organization after the war. Occasionally it had conventions with its American counterpart on such themes as 'The Challenge of the New Day,'[3] but church leaders kept it hedged closely with intrachurch activities. Canadian leadership wondered why 'men from the Old land' had a strong feeling against the organization. It is difficult to judge whether this attitude was due to difficulty in adjusting to the more voluntary character of North American Anglicanism, or whether they found the organization too restrictive.[4] Although the *Canadian Churchman* could become quite eloquent about brotherhood,[5] it felt that the Brotherhood movement at large had no solid foundation, and that it was preaching its message, like the prewar pacifists, where it was least

1 See Leete, *Christian Brotherhoods*, pp. 272–3, 281, 315–17
2 Woodsworth, *Organized Helpfulness*
3 *Canadian Churchman*, 11 Sept. 1919, p. 591
4 *Ibid.*, 5 Dec. 1918, p. 784
5 *Ibid.*, 9 Dec. 1920, p. 798

needed.[6] However, despite the absence of a progressive note in the Brotherhood of St Andrew, Anglicans were involved in the establishment of federated Brotherhood units as these spread in Canada during 1918–19.[7]

The Canadian Baptist churches were not as caught up in the movement as the neighbouring Northern Baptist Convention of the United States. Their publication did, however, carry news of the activities of the Brotherhoods. Undoubtedly this was because of the attention given it by the Northern Baptist Convention and because Dr Clifford, a prominent English Baptist, was a leading figure in the international movement.[8] There seem to have been Baptist Brotherhoods which this news served, and which participated in local federations.[9] A reporter from Montreal for the *Canadian Baptist* was obviously speaking from an inside position when he observed about the Montreal Federated Brotherhood that 'this brotherhood is an aggressive and progressive organization and is destined to make its influence felt in the administration of civic affairs of the city at no distant date.'[10]

All that can be reported regarding Congregationalist participation is that one of its ministers most outspoken on social problems, the Rev. George Adam of Montreal, was on the general council, and that a Congregationalist, T.B. Macaulay, president of the Sun Life Assurance Company and founder of the movement in Canada,[11] was the honorary president.[12]

The General Council of the Brotherhood consisted of not more than fifty members, divided approximately evenly between clergy and laity, and representing some two dozen cities of the dominion. Prominent in the council were leading figures in the social service departments of the churches, the Rev. John MacNeill (Baptist), Dr C.W. Gordon (Presbyterian), the Very Reverend L.N. Tucker (Anglican), and the Rev. John Coburn (Methodist). Among them were many who had taken outspoken progressive positions in the debates on church social policy in 1919. Professor W.T. Allison who had given words of encouragement to the Winnipeg strikers was a council member, as was W.B. Creighton of the *Guardian*, the Hon. Charles Dunning of Saskatchewan and H.H. Stevens, an MP from Vancouver. The president of the Canadian Federation in 1920 was T.A. Moore, head of the Methodist Department of Evangelism and Social Service, while the past-president was J.G. Shearer, head of the Social Service Council of Canada. Chairman of the Board

6 *Ibid.*, 3 June 1920, p. 360   7 CG, 26 Nov. 1919, p. 39
8 *Canadian Baptist*, 23 Sept. 1920, p. 5
9 CG, 26 Nov. 1919, p. 39; *Canadian Baptist*, 31 Jan. 1918, p. 12
10 31 Jan. 1918   11 See above, pp. 7, 11
12 MIR, *Constitution of the Canadian Brotherhood Federation* nd [ca 1920], and a list of current officers

of Directors and general treasurer was J.O. McCarthy, former controller of the City of Toronto and a long-standing member of the Methodist Board of Evangelism and Social Service. Probably the only individual in a more strategic position than Mc-Carthy in the movement was Thomas Howell, the general secretary.[13] The movement's close ties with the progressive social gospel in the churches were manifest.

The postwar influence of the British Brotherhood movement began in the spring of 1919 with a cross-country tour by William Ward and William Heal, two of its front rank leadership.[14] One of their purposes was to promote the first postwar International Brotherhood Congress, to be held in London during the coming September. The Canadian delegation was the second largest in a total of sixty-five delegates from twenty countries.[15] The address which was given most publicity on the return of the delegation was that of Arthur Henderson, veteran British socialist and Labour member of Parliament, on 'Brotherhood and the World's Unrest.' Political unrest, he had told the congress, was due to a dying system of class rule, industrial unrest to the demand for economic organization to overcome the 'anarchistic individualism of the profiteering capitalist system,' and moral unrest to the Christian development of the consciousness of the responsibility and dignity of the individual. It remained true, he claimed, that 'the soul of all improvement was the improvement of the soul' and that one 'can't get out of a reorganized society more than you put into it, in the way of personal character, moral idealism and the spirit of brotherhood ...' But it had become apparent, he said, that the key words of Christianity had a social as well as a personal significance. To hunger and thirst after righteousness was to feel the compulsion of a new divine society in which there would be neither exploiter nor exploited. Just as Christianity was a movement among people oppressed by Roman imperialism, to-day, in the midst of the downfall of capitalist imperialism, forces of brotherhood were gathering which it was the task of the Brotherhood movement to interpret and develop into the new society.[16] This was the kind of message which men who had just committed their churches to forward-looking social policies were pleased to hear.

There were those in the labour movement who scorned the development of the Brotherhoods. Elmo Roper considered such observers short-sighted, and in the *Edmonton Free Press* pointed out the role the Brotherhoods had played in relation to the British labour movement.[17] In March, he and other labour leaders addressed and led discussions in various Edmonton Brotherhoods on socialism, Christianity,

13 *Ibid.*
15 sw, Nov. 1919, p. 33
17 *Edmonton Free Press*, 24 Jan. 1920, p. 8

14 cg, 28 May 1919, p. 19; 25 June 1919, p. 18
16 *Ibid.*, pp. 29–31

and labour party ideals.[18] In the same month, the Methodist Department of Evangelism and Social Service was asked to co-operate with the Inter-Church World Movement in the United States to produce a study course on social questions for use in the Brotherhoods.[19] The task was turned over to Ernest Thomas, who seems to have become the author of most such studies produced by the department.[20]

A second world congress held in Washington in early October 1920 had 'overflow' sessions in Toronto a few days later. Both gatherings were well announced and publicized in the Baptist, Methodist, and Presbyterian publications.[21] The Toronto sessions involved British and European delegates in city pulpits, 17 October, with four mass meetings in city theatres and a final banquet for eight hundred addressed by E.C. Drury, premier of the UFO government of Ontario.[22]

At the Washington conference there had been a division of opinion or emphasis, with Americans interpreting the Brotherhoods from a church-centred point of view and the British from a more free-wheeling position, concerned to appeal, as the churches could not, to the 'growing constituency of noble manhood just beyond its pale' who found the 'Church inadequate to express their high aspirations, but who are not yet hostile to the Church.' These the British Brotherhood would approach on the basis of 'the passionate humanism of Jesus.'[23] The British movement treasured its position of freedom from ecclesiastical control, and maintained that the churches should accept this condition in an agency which was complementary to it in working for the redemption of a divided world. That there were Canadian church leaders unprepared to credit this view was not long to remain hidden.

The one hundred and fifty Canadian representatives were impressed, not only with the British delegates' views of the nature of the organization, but with their social radicalism with respect to industrial questions. They accepted the British view that 'to stand pat is to take sides on behalf of a system which is impeached by the best thought of the age,' and that the working-class movement had to be interpreted

18 *Ibid.*, 6 March 1920, p. 1; 20 March 1920, p. 4

19 *Minutes,* Executive of the Methodist Board of ESS, 9 March 1920

20 *Annual Report,* 1919–20, Methodist Department of ESS, p. 34

21 CG, 22 Sept. 1920, p. 18; 27 Oct. 1920, p. 11; *Canadian Baptist,* 23 Sept. 1920, p. 5; *Presbyterian Witness,* 7 Aug. 1920, p. 1; *Presbyterian and Westminster,* 16 Sept. 1920, p. 290; 14 Oct. 1920, p. 423

22 CG, 10 Nov. 1920, p. 13

23 Edward Trelawney, 'Advancing World Brotherhood,' CG, 10 Nov. 1920, p. 13. Edward Trelawney was the pseudonym Ernest Thomas used to prevent his overexposure in the church press (Marjorie MacDonald, former staff member of the *Guardian*).

as a 'spiritual passion for self-realization and brotherhood.' They would welcome, but did not specify, social and economic changes necessary to provide industry with a means for the practice of brotherhood.[24] These were the general points of view carried back to local Brotherhoods by delegates and to other audiences by Harry Whitehorne, a British journalist who lectured across the country following the congress.[25]

The congress elected the Canadian general secretary, Thomas Howell, as world commissioner. The Northern Baptist Convention agreed to release Dr S. Willcocks to head up work in Canada and the United States. And T.A. Moore was elected a vice-president of the international movement.[26] He was one of the few Canadian delegates to attend the third world congress in Prague, August 1921, whose purpose apparently was to rally European interest.[27]

Both the independence of the Canadian Brotherhood Federation and the spirit which it was imbibing caused some alarm at the annual meeting of the Methodist General Board of Evangelism and Social Service in November 1920. Only after a sharp debate did the board decide that the movement had a place at 'the hem of the Church's garment,' that it should not be hampered by 'rigid ecclesiastical control,' but that it was of the greatest importance that it develop 'in closest co-operation with the Churches.'[28] In 1921 it was reported to the annual meeting of the board that the Brotherhoods had progressed well during the year, and that more and more congregations were awakening to the role Brotherhoods could play in relation to the church on the one hand and civic and social problems of the community on the other.[29]

The department continued until 1923 to foster the movement, but two shifts in emphasis became apparent in its thinking and action on the subject. From 1921 on, executive and board minutes show a declining emphasis upon aims of social action and a corresponding emphasis on the activities of the groups as a means to comradeship in the Brotherhood. Here was one sign that the frustrations of social reform in the years 1919 to 1921 were taking their toll of middle-class social gospel en-

24 *Ibid.*

25 *Ibid.*, 5 Jan. 1921, p. 20; *Canadian Baptist*, 6 Jan. 1921, p. 5

26 CG, 10 Nov. 1920, p. 13

27 Minutes, Executive of the Methodist Board of ESS, 2 Aug. 1921; *Western Methodist Recorder*, March 1922, p. 3

28 Minutes, General Board, 2–4 Nov. 1920; CG, 17 Nov. 1920, p. 16

29 Minutes, Annual Meeting of the General Board, 8–10 Nov. 1921; *Annual Report*, 1921–2, Methodist Department of ESS, pp. 13–14. Figures giving numbers of Brotherhoods or membership are given in none of the reports.

thusiasm. The other development grew out of the decision of the General Conference of 1922 to authorize official organization of congregational Brotherhoods, a move which resulted in a mounting degree of programming for the Brotherhoods by the Methodists. While acknowledging the movement's need for freedom from ecclesiastical control, their interest was at the same time enveloping it as a church men's organization.[30] This change did not mean that the church was taking over the Canadian Brotherhood Federation itself, but that it was tying the units related to its own congregations so completely to a denominational programme that the programme of the national federation could be of little effect.

For reasons which are not clear, the affairs of the Canadian Brotherhood Federation between 1921 and 1923 fell into a state of disorder. Perhaps this confusion was due to such factors as an inadequate replacement of Thomas Howell as general secretary, depression conditions, waning of social reform enthusiasm, or the effect of a consolidation movement in the churches' relationships to social service agencies[31] – or all of these together. In any case, in March 1923 William Ward of the World Brotherhood Federation was in Canada to effect an immediate reorganization, which Methodists hoped would clear the way for an extension in the organization of local Brotherhoods.[32] Future progress did not occur, and in 1923 the future of the Brotherhood Federation as a force in Canadian affairs was sealed.

In 1920, as an outgrowth of the great Inter-Church campaign, there had been created an Inter-Church Advisory Council, one of whose purposes was to co-ordinate social or religious activities of an interchurch character.[33] From the beginning the Brotherhood movement was one of its concerns – and it is more than likely that the creation of the council caused some apprehension in Brotherhood ranks. Such fears would have been heightened had officials read the Presbyterian statement of one particular purpose of the Inter-Church council – 'to simplify and co-ordinate the efforts of the various organizations which claim to represent all the Churches, and draw their revenue from the Churches ("Y.M.C.A., Y.W.C.A., Federation of Men's Brotherhoods, Social Service Councils, etc.") yet are not controlled or even guided by any of the Churches.'[34] In the meeting of the board in 1922, increasing

30 *Annual Report*, 1921–2, Methodist Department of ESS, pp. 13–15; 1922–3, p. 43.
   Minutes, Executive, 12 March 1923; General Board, 4–5 Sept. 1923, p. 13
31 See below, pp. 243–8, 260
32 Minutes, Executive, Methodist Board of ESS, 12 March, 1923
33 *Canadian Baptist*, 27 May 1920, p. 4; *Presbyterian and Westminster*, 20 May 1920, pp. 503, 512–13
34 Minutes, Annual Meeting, Presbyterian Board of Home Missions and Social Service, 17–27 March 1920, pp. 35–6

antipathy was represented by the terse statement in the minutes of the annual meeting that 'it was agreed not to appoint representatives to the Board of the Men's Brotherhood Federation.'[35]

No doubt the Canadian Brotherhood Federation could see the writing on the wall. When, with the progress of church union, the inevitable question of a men's organization for the new church arose, the federation seized the opportunity to present itself as the means of filling this need. A committee was appointed by the Inter-Church council to consider this possibility, and both J.O. McCarthy and William Ward, international president, presented the case forcefully to the council itself.[36] However, although the federation appeared to be prepared to co-operate fully with the uniting churches as a projected men's organization, it does not seem to have been prepared to sacrifice its identity or its peculiar ethos.[37] Presbyterian representatives on the Inter-Church council seemed unwilling to settle for less than complete church control. They first noted that the Brotherhood had only 'a slender hold on the Presbyterian Church,' that the 'form of any men's organization would have to be considered *"de novo,"* ' but that all possible lessons should be learned from existing organizations.[38] When Brotherhood representatives argued the urgent need of action lest opportunities be missed, Dr Edmison, chief Presbyterian spokesman, said frankly that 'a Movement half outside and half inside the Church would not serve.'[39]

The Methodists, through W.B. Creighton, tried to keep the Brotherhood as a live option, but were not prepared to sacrifice relations with the Presbyterians on the altar of the Canadian Brotherhood Federation.[40] Furthermore, the subject may have been a delicate one for Methodists to defend, since the Presbyterian church in the United States had withdrawn support from the Brotherhood movement because 'one man and one denomination' had come to dominate it.[41] The search for a United church men's organization went on, but with the rejection of the Brotherhood, that movement's days were numbered in Canada.[42]

35 *Ibid.*, 22–9 March, 1922, p. 45

36 UCA, minutes, Inter-Church Advisory Council, annual meeting, 17 Nov. 1921; 30 Nov. 1922. Minutes of a conference between a committee of the Inter-Church Advisory Council and the Board of Directors of the Canadian Brotherhood Federation, 21 Feb. 1923

37 *Ibid.*   38 *Ibid.*   39 *Ibid.*   40 *Ibid.*

41 *Canadian Churchman*, 3 June 1920, p. 360. The man and the denomination are not named, but the denomination was probably Methodist.

42 It remained represented on the Executive Committee of the Social Service Council of Canada at least as late as 1924. Its representative was Mr J. Allister Stewart, BA.

The rejection of the Brotherhood was hardly justified by any alternative that the United church was to bring forth for a generation, if then. The church-centred service club with a special concern for the 'boy problem' seemed characteristic of most discussions of the practical working alternatives during the rest of the decade.[43]

Many local Brotherhoods had acquired deep roots, and undoubtedly much of their basic outlook was perpetuated in succeeding organizations. Some of these had perhaps never moved far from church-centred activities, but in the days of the vigorous debates on church social policy, even many of these seem to have been caught up in the more radical aspects of the Brotherhood vision.[44] Whether, in any case, the Brotherhood Federation itself would have survived or maintained the character that it seemed to be developing between 1919 and 1922 is questionable. It would seem to have been predominantly middle class in character and highly optimistic in mood. Lacking any deep personal stake in the reforms which it advocated, and having no vigorous Canadian equivalent to the British labour movement to inspire or exercise it, its enthusiasm might well soon have been dissipated. Perhaps the parable of its future was that in 1928 the founder of the first Canadian Pleasant Sunday Afternoon Brotherhood, T.B. Macaulay, reported eight straight years of increased profits to the policy holders of Sun Life Assurance Company of which he was president. He remarked on that occasion that: 'It is indeed a happy thought that all that growth in size and all that growth in prosperity mean increased service to humanity, and service at steadily lowering cost to our policy holders.'[45]

Had the Brotherhood movement simply been a rationalisation for a further elaboration of the capitalist system? For Macaulay the movement's message was not inconsistent with the attitudes of welfare capitalism.

Macaulay did not represent the whole mood or purpose of the Brotherhoods, nor their programme of 1919 to 1922. But with the withdrawal of church support from the Canadian federation, any further contribution to the cause of Canadian progressivism by the Brotherhood movement was drastically curtailed if not ended in 1923. The ecclesiasticism of a new church had taken its toll before it had been born, and the social gospel could, at another point of its existence, temper its message in the conflicting currents and intractability of the world to which it was bringing its good news.

43 *Western Methodist Recorder*, April 1923, pp. 4–5; *Canadian Churchman*, 2 Aug. 1923, p. 491; CG, 11 March 1925, p. 18; UCA, minutes, Conference Concerning Evangelistic Methods, 28 Dec. 1925; *New Outlook*, 30 March 1927, pp. 12, 22
44 *Western Methodist Recorder*, Oct. 1919, p. 10
45 Advertisement, *Canadian Churchman*, 1 March 1928, p. 144

15

The Dilemma of the Social Service Council

As the drive of the social gospel slowed in 1922–3, some confessed that they had hoped for too much. Others, believing that their objectives had been both socially sound and practicable, plodded ahead expecting a turn of the tide. The editor of *Social Welfare*, J.G. Shearer, owned to this attitude and encouraged tired social service workers with Arthur Hugh Clough's 'Courage':

> For while the tired waves, vainly breaking
> Seem here no painful inch to gain,
> Far back, through creeks and inlets making,
> Comes silent, flooding in, the main.[1]

The Social Service Council also felt the hand of disillusion, but lived in hope.

In the council, Shearer had built an organization of no small significance. It had the ready ear of governments and civil service departments.[2] If labour and farm representation ceased to be active after the war,[3] progressive groups considered the Social Service Council of Canada an ally in their cause. The *Canadian Forum*, reviewing the work of the council in 1923, paid it the honour of critical admiration:

No one can question the very excellent work which the Council has done to elevate the moral tone of the press, to preserve a degree of decency in moving pictures, and to drag into the clear light of day conditions of living and of employment that could survive only in darkness. From questions such as these the Council has recently gone on to give attention to matters mainly economic, such as safeguards for workers, unemployment and a minimum wage. In their discussion of such subjects there is a natural tendency to stress the moral aspect and make light of the financial. We deplore the tendency toward centralization of industry and the loss of rural population; yet every new demand upon the employer makes it more difficult for the small man to carry on, and places additional burdens on the back of the primary producer. Two queries emerge –

1 sw, Aug. 1923, p. 215   2 *Ibid.*, Feb.–March 1926, pp. 119–20
3 *Ibid.*, 1 Feb. 1919, p. 105

do we want to squeeze out the small employer, and how much can the primary producer stand? These are questions the s.s.c. cannot ignore.[4]

The *Forum*'s criticism of the council was just, but it was as much a revelation of itself as a reflection on the council. It appears that the council was less in reaction to the fundamental forces of industrialism than the *Forum*, less enamoured of the conservative concept of the sturdy yeoman and the small businessman. Right or wrong, it was true that the council was at the time much more concerned about urban social problems and the plight of the unemployed worker than with the farm or small businessman. But in its tendencies to moralism, the strong evangelical heritage of such leaders as its presidents in 1923–4, Dr George Pidgeon and the Rev. R.J. Wilson, represented a 'progressive conservatism' of another variety. Before the decade was out this moralism was to create tensions with the new forces of scientific social work, while neither this common heritage nor that of the social gospel was able to prevent tensions of another sort with the church social service departments. The Social Service Council felt closely allied to both areas of work and believed strongly in the need of interrelation. But hindered by its past, plagued by financial problems, undermined by church union, and compromised by emerging tensions between the churches and secular social work, the Social Service Council went into decline in the second half of the decade.

Having created a substantial nation-wide structure, the Social Service Council, between 1918 and 1924, developed a programme of research, publicity, and pressure for legislation whose breadth was apparent in its standing committees on industrial life, Indian affairs, political purity and the franchise, social hygiene, criminology, the family, child welfare, immigration, and legslation.[5] Its publication, *Social Welfare*, was the only Canadian one in its field. Annual conventions attracted considerable attention, and in the course of those years representation in the council came to total twenty-one national affiliates.[6]

In the years immediately following the war the Social Service Council of Canada took hope in mounting evidence of legislative accomplishment, 'the benefit of the

---

4 Feb. 1923, pp. 132–3   5 sw, March 1924, pp. 110ff

6 This figure does not include provincial units. In addition to those listed for 1918 on p. 64, there were by 1924 also the Canadian Prisoners Welfare Association, the Canadian Association of Trained Nurses, the Canadian Conference of Public Welfare, the National Council of Women, the Federation of Women's Institutes, the Victorian Order of Nurses, the Dominion Council of the Royal Templars of Temperance (compiled from lists of members on the inside covers of sw).

years of dogged agitation and unencouraged educational efforts of the Churches and their departmental organizations, the Women's organizations [and] similar private, and local bodies in the same work ...'[7] Periodically it compiled lists of the legislative trophies of the social welfare lobby. Such lists were not unimpressive, and the council could take a large share of the credit for welfare legislation protecting the more vulnerable and bringing social support to the less fortunate. Its larger plans for industrial reforms, and its more sweeping social and unemployment insurance proposals, with the exception of old age pensions, did not reach the statute books of that generation, and a more just society which treasured the dignity of its members remained in the distance. There was no very clear path to that society, but for the Social Service Council it remained the goal to be sought.

Although the federal council of the organization was only rivalled in its progressiveness by the Manitoba Social Service Council, all the provincial units were engaged to some degree in attempting to promote the spectrum of concerns of the national organization. The strategy of provincial work of the social service councils, however, was to specialize on a limited number of appropriate objectives. The history of many of the units slighted these intentions somewhat. Since many had been created by a merger with, or grown out of, provincial temperance organizations, this heritage tended to dictate the predominant concern. This relationship with temperance was nowhere more true than in the Maritime provinces. In Nova Scotia, for instance, where industrial problems were to be a critical issue during the decade, the secretary, H.R. Grant, in articles in the *Presbyterian Witness*, dwelt on nothing but temperance questions. At its annual meeting in 1920 it considered problems of child welfare, mental deficiency, prison reform, and housing as well as prohibition, but the large campaign for which it was larding its treasury was the coming referendum on the Temperance Act the next year.[8]

The Nova Scotia council had, however, a model structure in the County of Pictou. Local councils in centres such as New Glasgow, Stellarton, Westville, and Pictou, representing churches and community agencies, formulated policy and programmes to deal with community problems and projects. In New Glasgow, for example, the council financed all philanthropic endeavours, secured supervised recreational facilities, Victorian Order of Nurses and other social workers, and dealt with temperance and moral reforms. Local delegates sat on the county council to consider questions common to the area and to participate in finance campaigns. Such a structure throughout the nation, *Social Welfare* observed, would make the Social Service Council one of the most powerful organizations in Canada, being

7 sw, May 1921, pp. 211ff   8 *Presbyterian Witness*, 20 March 1920, p. 1

practically 'irresistible to repress evil and constructively to promote all that is worth-while.'[9]

Although the Ontario Social Service Council was one of the most substantial, it had never developed any local council structure. At its annual meeting for 1920 in Peterborough, it was able to report legislative accomplishments that gave it great hope. Mothers' allowances had come into effect during the year, a minimum wage law for women workers had been passed, juvenile courts had been extended, and a bill passed removing the stigma of illegitimacy from the child and compelling fathers' support. The passage of this last item was an indication of the closeness that existed between the Social Service Council and the United Farmers of Ontario government. Drury had requested such a bill from the Social Service Council, and had passed it almost as drafted. Drury himself was one of the major speakers at the meeting, which decided to emphasize housing problems, rural problems, and to seek changes in the family desertion law during 1921.[10] As long as the Ontario Temperance Act remained unchallenged, the Social Service Council in that province continued to press its efforts along such lines as these.

Social service councils were, in general, best organized and had the longest history in western Canada. In the three prairie provinces, each council had two or three paid staff workers by 1918. In British Columbia a council was formed in 1911, but its programme is not clear apart from a *Social Welfare* comment on 'excellent work in moral and political reform.'[11] In Alberta the council began as the Alberta Social Service League, and was under the direction of a general secretary, the Rev. A.W. Coone, a field secretary, the Rev. A.P. Archibald, and a child welfare secretary, the Rev. E. Bishop. The history of the Saskatchewan council, under the Revs. W.P. Reekie and W.J. Stewart in 1918, went back to 1907, as did that of Manitoba.[12] Although child welfare, public health, and care of defectives seem to have been of special concern to most of these, all of them, between 1919 and 1923, prostrated themselves financially in the vain struggle to defend the temperance acts secured in each province in the previous decade.

Manitoba seemed to have by far the best articulated provincial council in the Social Service Council of Canada.[13] Under the chairmanship of Dr C.W. Gordon for many years, it had waged an unremitting campaign for a temperance act, which

9 1 May 1921, p. 220 10 *Canadian Baptist*, 19 May 1920, p. 7
11 sw, 11 Oct. 1918, p. 4 12 *Ibid*.
13 This was probably not unrelated to the fact that in 1921 a Manitoba Public Welfare Commission tabled what, according to sw, 1 June 1921, pp. 252–3, was probably the most complete and valuable study of social service possibilities and responsibilities of any community ever carried through in Canada. The long period of ferment

it won in 1916.[14] In 1918, the council was a body representing thirty province-wide agencies, including Catholics and Lutherans. A staff of three directed its affairs: the Revs. D.B. Harkness and McNair were general and financial secretaries respectively, and the Rev. F.C. Middleton was in charge of a new Department of Community Organization.[15] The purpose of this programme seemed to be to provide voluntary community organizations with a central body for co-ordination and co-operative social development, not unlike the Pictou County model but somewhat more progressive in temper. In some respects it appeared midway between a civic administration and a community church, and undoubtedly much of the ethos of the latter western development undergirded this Manitoba plan. The annual meeting of the Manitoba Social Service Council in 1920 voted to continue the community programme,[16] and in 1921 a meeting of representatives of community clubs decided unanimously to remain under the aegis of the Social Service Council of Manitoba.[17] Two years later, the Manitoba council, in financial distress, had to be taken over by the federal council of the Social Service Council of Canada. Whether these ambitious programmes survived the 1923 temperance battle and the financial drought, or whether they disintegrated or continued on separate footings, is not clear.

Five other councils in 1923 went into 'receivership' with the federal council: Prince Edward Island, New Brunswick, Quebec, Alberta, and British Columbia. Although most of these were kept operating, the reports of the provincial units to the annual meeting of the Social Service Council of Canada in 1926 tell the story of a much enfeebled organization, with only British Columbia and New Brunswick showing real vigour.[18] The provincial organizations had been badly battered on the rocks of temperance defeats and depression, and the end was not in sight. The reversals of liquor and finance had struck the nation together in 1920. The depression lifted briefly in 1923, but the battles for temperance were to intensify until 1926. Yet had it not been for other problems besetting the national organization, the stream of its support might have risen higher and prevented the degree of damage that occurred in the provinces.

In 1918 the Social Service Council of Canada felt secure in its relation to the social service departments of the churches. It seemed understood that the church departments would engage in institutional work, intensive education, and publicity in

of the social gospel in Winnipeg undoubtedly contributed to the outlook of such a commission as well as to the strength of the Social Service Council.

14 See Allen, 'Salem Bland,' pp. 88–94

15 sw, 1 Dec. 1919, pp. 65–6   16 *Ibid.*, 1 March 1920

17 cg, 30 March 1921, p. 10   18 sw, Feb.–March 1926, pp. 120ff

their own constituencies, and stimulate an interest in social service work among their own people. The Social Service Council would complement this work by research, general education, legislative lobbying, and 'other work that from its nature can only be done with the maximum efficiency on an interdenominational basis.'[19] In addition, a slightly different temper prevailed in the national council, apparent in the smaller amount of attention given to matters of moral reform than in either the church departments or the provincial units. However, the basic identity of programme became a vulnerable point in the Social Service Council of Canada with the organization of the Inter-Church Advisory Council of 1920, one of whose tasks was to co-ordinate the social service programme of the churches. With the revival of the church union movement in 1921, a question mark hung still more ominously over the future of J.G. Shearer's organization.

Prior to the emergence of these issues there arose a simple question of the multiplicity of financial appeals emanating from the expansion of social service programmes, both of the Social Service Council of Canada and of the churches. Financial co-operation had been achieved in the Inter-Church campaign. It was in the early stages of the planning of this campaign that the Methodist Department of Evangelism and Social Service in March 1919 formed a committee to consider the relation between the department and the provincial social service councils.[20] This investigation seemed to imply no judgment on the Social Service Council of Canada, for at the annual meeting of that year, the Methodist contribution was raised from $700 to $1000.[21] At the same time it was suggested to Methodist conferences that they permit only one appeal for all evangelism and social service purposes. It was notable that where this was undertaken and followed through in its implications for the Social Service Council, the results were beneficial. In Saskatchewan, where the method was applied and the general board and the Saskatchewan Conference shared in support of the Social Service Council budget, that provincial council was the only western one to survive the financial crisis of 1923.[22] It appeared that the national council stood only to gain from the Methodist proposal.

Little reaction was elicited from the Social Service Council of Canada, however, until the Inter-Church Advisory Council, concerned about overlapping jurisdiction, took up the question in 1921 and proposed a full-scale reorganization of the national council.[23] The latter's executive seemed eager to co-operate in working out

19 Minutes, Annual Meeting, 1918, Social Service Council of Canada, p. 9
20 Minutes, Executive, Methodist Department of ESS, 12 March 1919
21 *Ibid.*, Annual Meeting   22 *Ibid.*, Executive, 29 March 1921
23 Minutes, Executive, Inter-Church Advisory Council, 28 Jan. 1921, 6 May 1921;
     Annual Meeting, 17 Nov. 1921

the vexed problem. It immediately circulated its units to discover their mind on the subject of greater uniformity and economy in the work, and specifically on the advisability of financing national and provincial work through one fund. All the churches, units, and bodies in the council were in basic agreement with the exception of the two strongest units, Ontario and Manitoba.[24] The executive, therefore, prepared for the annual meeting in January 1922 a proposal for central financing and budgeting, with federal and local councils as part of one structure whose responsibilities at each level would be well defined and whose staff would be specialists in different fields and available for service in any of the provinces.[25] The annual meeting, however, failed to recommend more than annual reporting by provincial units to the federal council of the Social Service Council of Canada.[26] It seems likely that Manitoba and Ontario were responsible for blocking the executive's plan. Baptists reporting on continuing efforts at reorganization in 1923 noted Ontario's steadfast opposition to surrendering 'its more highly organized work ... to the larger body.'[27] The national organization was in a dilemma of the first order between church pressure and the survival instincts of its most powerful units.

That there were some in the Methodist department prepared to use financial pressure was evident in the proposal adopted by its executive in December 1921 that future grants be conditional on effective reorganization.[28] From this date on grants were considered on an *ad hoc* basis, which added considerable anguish to the Social Service Council of Canada. Furthermore, it was apparent that the Methodist board was proposing a tough line with respect to the Ontario Social Service Council. It pressed the Ontario unit to act simply as a clearing house, and not to initiate new activities or seek associate and sustaining memberships. These activities, the Methodist board believed, gave the impression that the Social Service Council was responsible for all necessary social service work. When the council made no reply to these urgings of the board, the executive moved that a response be again solicited.[29] No response is recorded, and in May 1922 the Methodist executive put a ceiling of $1000 on all future grants to the Social Service Council of Canada.[30]

This hard line was in apparent contrast to that of the Presbyterians. They were as pressed for finances as were the Methodists, perhaps more acutely so. Deficits in the social service department were tided over in 1920 and 1921 by Inter-Church campaign funds. Falling income forced a drastic curtailment of their expansion programme.[31] However, while a party to the Inter-Church pressure for reorganiza-

24 sw, 1 March 1922   25 *Ibid.*   26 *Ibid.*
27 *Year Book*, Ontario and Quebec Convention of Baptist churches, 1924, p. 247
28 Minutes, Executive, Methodist Department of ESS, 7 Dec. 1921
29 *Ibid.*, 20 Feb. 1922   30 *Ibid.*, 29 May 1922
31 *Presbyterian Acts and Proceedings*, 1922, Appendix, p. 3

tion, there was never any question raised about applying Presbyterian grants as a means of pressure. In fact, in its last three years as a church it raised its sum to $1500.[32] Shearer tried to use this fact to secure raises from the Anglicans and Methodists, but neither took the bait.[33]

In the course of 1923, reorganization became more feasible. The counter-attack upon provincial temperance achievements and the impact of the depression upon resources led several units to seek support for their own staff from the national body.[34] Thus, when the churches urged reorganization on the Social Service Council of Canada again in 1923, the council was able to reply that it had taken over full responsibility for six units. However, the churches had also asked that a reduction in budget be made in 1924, with a substantial one in future years. To achieve this, they proposed that the national council reorganize so as to become a clearing house for its units,[35] a proposal which would have drained the organization of much of its impact.

Shearer, however, was not prepared to preside over the dissolution of an effective instrument of the churches and the social gospel, and replied that the new responsibilities for provincial units required additional staff. Hence, although the budget had been reduced to $14,250 in 1923, he proposed that it be raised to $18,750 in 1924 to provide for an assistant secretary. The national council's commission on reorganization urged the executive of the Methodist Board of Evangelism and Social Service to declare its support of the Social Service Council of Canada in terms of its original mandate to co-ordinate church units in regard to legislation, conferences, and congresses for educational purposes, research, and co-operative endeavour, without competing with the church units or interfering with their financing. The commission promised to continue its work until these objectives were met.[36]

Immediate church reaction to this proposal is not clear, but it could hardly have been favourable. The Social Service Council of Canada went ahead with the appointment of an assistant secretary, the Rev. J. Phillips Jones, MA, BD, a very able man, originally from Wales, and with long experience in Winnipeg, the heart of the social gospel in Canada.[37] But at this crucial moment in the fortunes of the

32 *Annual Report*, Presbyterian Board of Home Missions and Social Service, *ibid.*,
   1922–5
33 Minutes, Executive, Methodist Department of ESS, 12 March 1923, 10 April 1923
34 SW, March 1924, p. 118
35 Minutes, Executive, Methodist Board of ESS, 19 Dec. 1923, 27 Feb. 1924
36 *Ibid.*   37 SW, May 1924, p. 145

Social Service Council of Canada, one of its greatest assets was cut off in the death of J.G. Shearer. He was the widely acknowledged dean of social service work.[38] With his removal from the scene in March 1925 there was less hesitancy in dealing unkindly with the future of the Social Service Council.

T.A. Moore was almost immediately in touch with Canon Vernon of the Anglican Council of Social Service, sounding him out on drastic reductions of grants. Vernon replied that if the Methodist board did likewise, he would suggest to his executive that they give only a nominal $50 or $100, as against the usual $750. The executive of the Methodist board took no immediate action,[39] but when in June, with funds low, Jones made an urgent appeal for contributions, promising 'to go on deputation work as soon as possible,' the executive sent $500 and decided to confer with the Presbyterian board as to future grants to the Social Service Council of Canada.[40] The annual meeting of the general board, 29 September to 3 October 1925, referred the usual request for $1000 for the council to the executive with power to act.[41] What immediate action was taken is difficult to learn, but in 1929 at the end of a period of prosperity the United church was giving $1000 to the Social Service Council of Canada annual budget, less than two-fifths of the amount the three churches separately had given. Nor was there help forthcoming from the continuing Presbyterian church, which kept its membership in abeyance.

Jones stayed with the organization through difficult years until 1934.[42] *Social Welfare* continued publication, providing still a valuable medium for those engaged in social service work. The council also undertook useful research on the causes and effects of unemployment, a central theme of efforts in 1925. It had for some time propagandized for adequate unemployment insurance, and for public works programmes planned in advance.[43] It pointed to the disastrous results of such unpreparedness when the Ontario Department of Lands and Forests sent over one hundred men to do construction work in Northern Ontario, making almost no provision for them, forcing most of them to trek back to Toronto as best they could.[44] Its researches in 1925 pointed up the fallacy of the generalization that none need be idle who were able and willing to work, and showed that unemployment was primarily a cause, not an effect of idle habits. In this, as in the past, it continued its service in breaking down the conceptions of Protestant individualism. But

38 See articles on his death in sw, April 1925
39 Minutes, Executive, Methodist Board of ess, 15 May 1925
40 *Ibid.*, 22 June 1925
41 *Ibid.*, Annual Meeting, 29 Sept.–3 Oct. 1925
42 *Year Book*, Baptist Convention of Ontario and Quebec, 1935, pp. 203–6
43 sw, Feb.–March 1926, pp. 126–30   44 *Ibid.*

except for a few years in the 1930s under C.E. Silcox, the Social Service Council seems never to have regained the vigour it had displayed between 1914 and 1924.

Like the Brotherhoods, the Social Service Council of Canada was essentially a victim of consolidation of church social service forces. Evidence is somewhat slight for a close examination of motives. However, in establishing the Inter-Church Advisory Council in 1920 to co-ordinate, among other things, the social service work of the churches, there must have been awareness of encroachment upon the role of the Social Service Council of Canada. The advisory council was, perhaps, a project of greater grandeur in its conception. Nonetheless, as the church union cause progressed it became apparent that in most respects the two-thirds of the Protestant population who supported at least three-quarters of Protestant social service work would be under the umbrella of a single church. This fact seems to have eliminated the Inter-Church Council.[45] It also reduced the apparent necessity for the Social Service Council, and placed the unit church representation still lower in the parallelogram of forces in the council. For the Social Service Council it was obvious that its fulfilment would lie either in a complete church union, or a complete Inter-Church movement, with either of which it could merge. What developed was neither, and the Social Service Council of Canada was finally faced with the choice of permitting domination by the churches and cutting back its programme, or maintaining its independence and losing much church support, and thereby much of its *raison d'être*.

Furthermore, it was obvious that the social service mystique had worn thin in the church departments. After the heady talk of radical changes and complete social reconstructions, it was impossible to return with the old enthusiasm to the now traditional social service programmes. It was not incorrect to observe a new orthodoxy of social service and business efficiency in the churches.[46] The church social service programmes were substantial pieces of work, and now needed not only inspiration, education, and consultation with the Social Service Council of Canada, but also – perhaps especially – the cash to make them operate. As for the resurrected issue of temperance, the council with its interdenominational and secular associates showed little overt concern for it, preferring social issues of housing, unemployment, and child welfare. It seemed, also, from the church point of view that there was needed a new injection of 'good news,' 'a changed heart and a recognition of things not seen,' 'a "new evangelism"' that [would] deal adequately with Christian truth mak-

45 The minutes of the council end with the appointment of a committee, 18 Dec. 1924, to consider future policy and report at the annual meeting in May 1925. There seems to be no minutes or record of that meeting having been held.

46 Davidson Ketchum, 'The Saving of God,' *Canadian Forum*, April 1923

ing God real to men and at the same time doing justice to the needs of the present hour.'[47] This evangelistic task was the responsibility of the churches, not of an organization dominated by interdenominational and secular agencies. In terms, then, of the pressing needs sensed by the church departments, there seemed very few grounds on which they could justify the existence of a strong, expanding Social Service Council.

The council, however, was not prepared to resolve its dilemma. When it took stock of its situation in 1925, it still felt that there was an urgent need for an inter-denominational organization to serve as a mouthpiece of the churches and organizations of kindred aims. To secede from the 'honoured place' it had earned in the confidence of the country would be to 'injure the best interests of Canada.' There-fore, the executive proposed to the annual meeting in 1926 that it carry on along lines of past work, uniting the social forces of the country and 'through investiga-tion, education, legislation to suppress traffics, prevent social problems and generally to promote all forms of economic, moral, political, national and religious welfare.'[48] But whether ideally or not the Social Service Council of Canada still had a legiti-mate role to fulfil, to insist on the *status quo ante bellum* was to fail to recognize reality. The price of that failure was a lingering death, or at least a half-life, measured by the activities let alone the promise of earlier years.

47 *Presbyterian Acts and Proceedings,* 1924, Appendix, pp. 6–7
48 sw, Feb.–March 1926, pp. 119–20

16

The Social Gospel and Church Union

Despite the fate of the Brotherhoods and the Social Service Council, it was, at least in the short run, the good fortune of the social gospel that church union negotiations, on-again, off-again since 1902, between Congregationalists, Methodists, and Presbyterians, were revived in 1921 with high prospects of success. The social gospel was then entering its period of postwar crisis, and this coincidence eased the tribulations experienced in promoting the social gospel prospectus for the new industrial Canada. At the same time it heartened those who watched with dismay the first successful breaches of the legislative ramparts of temperance. Both could visualize an endless chain of social accomplishments awaiting this new consolidation of the forces of righteousness. It was easier to build a new church than to build a new world, but the former task could serve the latter. Thus it also seemed the good fortune of church union to have social gospel energies poured into its realization, but the fact that it was a social gospel in crisis that aided the cause was not a good omen for the new church.

Church union and the social gospel were, in fact, complementary causes. If the mission of the church was simply to pluck brands from the burning, said Salem Bland, then one might rest content with small denominations. But 'when we think of the enthronement of Christ in the commercial and industrial and political life of Canada, not in some indefinite, far-off time, but in our generation, we can only think in terms of the United Church, or of that still grander union of Churches which this union will make at once more easy and more imperative.'[1] Such language was the common currency of church union and social gospel partisans in the decade preceding actual union in 1925.

The church union movement was a product of many causes, and had preceded the period of social gospel influence. Church union was a hope that had been discussed both before the Presbyterian union of 1875 and after that of Canadian Methodism in 1884.[2] By the 1880s the established Scottish church affinities of

1 CG, 31 Oct. 1923, p. 5
2 *Presbyterian Witness,* 6 March 1924, pp. 5–6

George Munro Grant and the evangelicalism of Morley Punshon were combined with an intoxicating sense of the possibility of a vast new nation devoted to the ways of righteousness.[3] Such liquors (and only such!) were drunk by future leaders of the social gospel, Bland and Thomas, at Queen's University where Grant presided.[4] But the social gospel was still in its early stages when in 1902 Presbyterians carried their invitation to the Methodist General Conference in Winnipeg, and made of this nationalistic and evangelical dream a matter of practical church politics.

The social gospel in its rise was able largely to identify with the traditions underlying the union movement. Its world hope was not contrary to liberal nationalism, and its immediate social hopes were, naturally, to be articulated for such communities as were then in existence. There was no contradiction between the nationalism of Bland's exhortation that to discover her soul Canada would have to emerge religiously from the colonial stage it had left politically,[5] and the universalism of Chown's question: 'But if a divided Church could not speak with moral influence to a *divided* [prewar] world, how can a divided Church speak with good effect to a future *united* world?'[6] The new church would not be established or narrowly national, said George Pidgeon, but it would express the 'distinctive religious type' that was appearing in Canada. One of the marks of that type, he suggested – and he was president of the Social Service Council of Canada at the time – was that 'the Churches of Canada have succeeded in working out the moral and social problems of the country along Christian lines in a rare degree ...'[7]

Pidgeon was basking in the more conservative forms of legislative reform, but he would not have disagreed with the Congregationalist minister J.W. Pedley that the outstanding business of the church was still the Christianization of Canada. While earlier doctrinal and denominational rigidity had impeded the service of the kingdom of God, Pedley said, concepts of modernism and social salvation were impelling a broad social advance under the cry, 'Canada for Jesus Christ and His Kingdom.'[8] At the same time, another commentator observed, 'probably no country in the world today offers such a favorable and promising field for a full-orbed and clear-cut proclamation and application of the Social Gospel as this Canada of ours.' The new church was appropriately emerging in the early years of Canadian na-

3 *Ibid.*; *Walsh*, pp. 216, 290–2   4 Allen, 'Salem Bland,' pp. 28–32

5 GGG, 15 May 1918, p. 4

6 UCA, Pidgeon Papers on Church Union, S.D. Chown, address on 'Church Union,' 1922

7 *Presbyterian Witness*, 1 March 1923, pp. 6–7

8 *Ibid.*, 22 Jan. 1925, pp. 5–6

tional consciousness, and in the broad categories of Christian humanism must be open to 'every type and every experience' in order to 'nurture national deals and public life.'[9] Chown probably gave the most concise formulation to this liberal, evangelical, and nationalist social Christianity of the church union movement. It was the 'duty of Christian patriots,' he said, 'to use the bonds of religious unity to promote the national oneness of the Dominion that we may attain to a clarified consciousness and conscience concerning the supreme mission of our country in the life of the world.'[10]

In the same way that the social gospel absorbed the nationalistic roots of church union, it had little difficulty in relating to the interests of evangelicalism. The close relation of the social gospel to its evangelical background has been noted. Even more radical members of the social gospel often put opponents in confusion by their unsuspected conservatisms. Thomas, for instance, did not say much on the subject, but he, with the most conservative Methodists of his day, was opposed to the waltz.[11] There was a broadening interest in life, in entertainment and the arts, which marked the social gospel, but almost to a man its proponents were supporters of the major planks of moral reform which had preoccupied evangelicalism at large. They had simply incorporated them in a grander social outlook.

That the social gospel did not become a major issue in the union controversy which split Presbyterianism was probably not due so much to any status it held in the dissident camp as to the broad coincidence of the unionist polemics of those persuaded by the social gospel with those of unionists in whom the older *mélange* of evangelicalism and nationalism was still the primary force. Those who attacked the former were easily countered by the latter.[12] Nevertheless, there were attempts to raise the issue. Ephraim Scott, the editor of the *Presbyterian Record*, which paid almost no attention to social questions between 1918 and 1929, was alarmed by a pastoral of Chown in which the latter warned his people that the battle for the religious control of the nation would be lost in the next few years without church union. Chown was not very specific in what he meant. He did state that he was not referring to the school question alone, again in an agitated state, but 'to the whole movement in Canada in the religio-political realm.'[13] The reference was probably

9 *New Outlook*, 11 Nov. 1925, p. 5. The writer was Robert Milliken, Methodist ESS staff member.
10 Pidgeon Papers, S.D. Chown, 'A New Year's Message,' 1 Jan. 1924. See Magney, 'The Methodist Church and the National Gospel,' for an extended discussion of the evolution of this position.
11 CG, 30 March 1921, p. 18
12 *Presbyterian Witness*, 26 Feb. 1925, p. 2
13 Pidgeon Papers, Chown, 'Church Union'

also to the counterattack on temperance legislation and the complex of causes of the social gospel. To Scott it revealed a Methodist intention to create of a united church a 'religio-political machine.'[14] He did not carry the argument far, however, but W.D. Tait, professor of psychology at McGill University, picked up the issue and tried to drive it home.

'Their chief claim,' Tait said of social gospel proponents of church union, 'is that church organization will solve social problems.' Some did indeed seem to argue so, but only if the larger framework of their apologetics was ignored. But even on this inadequate foundation Tait had to rely on *non sequiturs* to build a case. The contributions of great individuals in history testified for individualism and against organization, he suggested. Organization was the curse of the modern world. The people who required social aid were usually the victims of organization, he said, and to add yet another organization was only to add fuel to the fire. There may have been a strong argument against church union as rationalized by the social gospel, but the anti-unionists failed to marshal it. Tait was undoubtedly correct when he said that 'spiritual unity is not a necessary consequence of social or ecclesiastical organization,' but this did not meet Chown's argument that Christian love and spiritual unity had to seek expression or remain sentimental.[15]

Anti-unionists had more success attaching the label of modernism to the union forces, a charge which normally implicated progressives and radicals of the social gospel. In late 1924 pamphlets and leaflets of the Presbyterian Church Association (anti-unionist) broadcast evidence of Methodist captivity to modernism, its denial of vital doctrines of the church. Methodism, it appeared, no longer had any 'message for a sin-burdened world.'[16] Certainly the social gospel often lay wide open to this attack. In its orientation to the future, and its emphasis on life rather than form, it looked upon creeds and institutions as temporary habitations. Nevertheless, the church was an essential part of their gospel. It was an expression of the vital fact that Christianity was a social religion.[17] The attack on denominationalism was an attack on confessional rigidity, and the social gospel, with unionists at large, rejected both.

14 *Presbyterian Witness*, 10 Aug. 1922, pp. 21–2
15 Tait, 'Church Union and Social Service,' *The Need of the Presbyterian Church*, p. 8; Pidgeon Papers, Chown, 'A New Year's Message'
16 Presbyterian Church Association, *An Open Letter to the Members and Adherents of the Presbyterian Church*; A Group of Presbyterians, *The Need of the Presbyterian Church*; Kew Beach Presbyterian Church Association, *Official Organ of Methodists Denies the Atonement*; all in Pidgeon Papers
17 For example, Salem Bland, 'Creeds and their Value,' GGG, 13 Feb. 1918; also 'Thoughts About the Church,' *ibid.*, 5 March 1919

Neither attack was necessarily modernist. Baptists had noted in surprise in 1921 not simply the absence of discussion of the theological implications of union, but actual argument from partisans of union that theological differences were not so great as to constitute a difficulty.[18] However, a doctrinal basis of union had been published in 1915 and accepted – even lauded – by some anti-unionists who now attacked it.[19] Furthermore, the line of modernism apparently cut across unionist-anti-unionist lines, for Principal Fraser, himself president of the Presbyterian Church Association, had condemned the basis of union as too orthodox for 'those brought up in the atmosphere of evolutionary thought.'[20]

Differences in interpretation of basic doctrine were part of the historic life of a living church. Fundamentalists absolutized specific interpretations of such doctrines as the atonement, and pronounced the doctrine decayed when their interpretation was not endorsed. But the series of studies on the basis of union published by the new church in 1926 demonstrated that doctrinal decay could not be charged against the union movement.[21] There were theological issues of consequence which could be pressed against social gospel proponents of church union, but the complexity of the lines of division deflected them, and fundamentalist anti-unionists were hardly the ones to carry the attack.

In yet another contentious and perhaps finally the most crucial development in the history of church union, the social gospel was a fundamental factor. That development was the Community church movement which originated in the West, and spread into Ontario.[22] The material problems of the western churches were real. Inevitably, there had grown up in the West small towns with 'four shabby little conventicles, four woefully underpaid ministers, four little Sunday Schools, four little choirs and four little deficits.'[23] Religion can put up with such things if it has a mind to. It seems likely, however, that not simply physical necessity or prospects of church union in the early successful negotiations, but the contemporary rise of the social gospel in the West motivated the churchmen to cope with these problems by means of the Community church.

18 *Canadian Baptist*, 16 June 1921, p. 8
19 Pidgeon Papers, R.E. Welsh to [the press], 5 Jan. 1924
20 *Presbyterian Witness*, 27 Nov. 1924, p. 6; Pidgeon Papers, J. Russell Harris to [the press], nd
21 *The Message of the Basis of Union*
22 See Buck's thesis 'The "Community Church" and Church Union.' Study of the Community church movement is limited, and pays almost no attention to its ideological dimension.
23 Pidgeon Papers, W.M. Birks, 'The Scandal of Schreiber'

When the *Grain Growers' Guide* in 1916 invited discussion on the role of the rural church in the West, it utilized an article by Washington Gladden, prominent in the social gospel in the United States. Gladden cited studies which suggested that the overall church population in a rural area varied inversely with the number of churches. But quite apart from such facts, he said, the prime business of the church was to diffuse the spirit of co-operation in the community.[24] In encouraging letters on the subject, the *Guide* asked not for dissertations on doctrine but 'practical ways and means by which the rural church can help mankind to live up to the ideals taught by Christ.'[25] All letters on the subject scored church divisiveness, and urged co-operation in community service as a Christian ideal. Some wanted to be fired with an enthusiasm for a redeemed humanity, rather than soothed to contentment with 'the trivial round, the common task.'[26] Woodsworth in his writing and speaking between 1913 and 1917 for the Canadian Welfare League and the Bureau of Social Research widely promoted the role of the church as a community centre. The church of the future, to his mind, would operate on the premise that 'to really save one man you must transform the community in which he lives.'[27] The whole bent of Salem Bland's thought pressed in this direction, and when the Community church movement arose he gave it his full support. For him, it pointed to a Canadian church in which Canada would find her soul, and to the New Christianity of which he was the prophet.[28] The social gospel, in short, was expressed in the West not only in the great agrarian organizations, but also in the creation of Community churches.

The Community church was the one hard fact that church union negotiations, renewed in 1921, could not ignore. In particular, it was a problem for Presbyterians. By 1923 George Pidgeon, assessing the church union situation, observed that the Community church had made progress in Northern Ontario. As a result, only nine Presbyterian churches were in existence between Orillia and Winnipeg, outside Port Arthur and Fort William.[29] Methodists, fully united on the question of union, were in no jeopardy from the new movement, but Presbyterians with an adamant anti-union component stood to lose whichever way they turned.

However, this 'hard fact' was more than just a neutral item in the catalogue of pros and cons of at least some prominent Presbyterian unionists. It was an indication for them of the vital new social spirit abroad in the church and the nation.

24 'Country Church Failures,' GGG, 17 June 1916, pp. 7, 29
25 *Ibid.*, 20 Dec. 1916, p. 8
26 *Ibid.*, 18 April 1917, pp. 24–6; 11 July 1917, p. 25; 14 Nov. 1917
27 J.S. Woodsworth, 'Sermons for the Unsatisfied,' *ibid.*, 30 June 1915
28 Bland, 'Church Developments,' *ibid.*, 15 Oct. 1919
29 *Presbyterian Witness*, 8 Feb. 1923, pp. 8–9

George Pidgeon, shortly to become the first moderator of the United Church of Canada, declared that 'A new community consciousness has awakened. The spirit of unity and a desire for efficiency in community service are making themselves felt, and the Church is expected to lead in the realization of these aspirations.'[30]

The Community church was not the only evidence of this 'new community consciousness.' It is notable that when union negotiations were shelved in 1916, the Social Service Council made immense strides in organization, which only ran into serious difficulties when the church union drive was renewed and in sight of success. The 'community spirit' seemed to be taking its own channels as opportunity arose! Although not its most progressive leader, Pidgeon had been deeply involved in the Social Service Council. He not only had his finger on the religious pulse, he was part of the pulse itself. A more radical person, Bland, agreed with Pidgeon. A growing 'community spirit' was at work, he said, and, through a united church, would achieve 'a nobler and fairer human life than ever was inspired by denominational loyalty.'[31] It was not simply as an institutional reality, then, that the Community church movement impelled church union, but as an expression of the religious force of the social gospel.

Such a brief sketch suggests that the social gospel, in several of its phases, was a primary force in church union. Its presence was apparent in the character of the justifications for union, in the prophetic expressions of religious and social hopes which accompanied the unionist campaign, and in the Community church phenomenon which preceded union. Because it was subtly mixed with other and older traditions of evangelicalism and nationalism, and since the lines of division over union were complex, however, the social gospel rationalization of church union did not come under prolonged direct fire in the controversy.

Church union, then, was, among other things, a triumph of the social gospel. After the high drama of the last assembly of the Presbyterian church in June 1925, its Presbyterian reporter to the *New Outlook* could contrast the one-time exotic character of social service sessions with the all-pervasive influence of social questions in 1925. 'The Kingdom of God ... this very world of factories and homes and governments – as the subject of redemption – these were the stuff of the assembly's thinking.'[32] It was not inappropriate to describe the social gospel as the new orthodoxy.

But if in some respects the social gospel had become the orthodoxy of the uniting churches, it was as a considerably weakened complex of ideas and programmes. Tensions with radicals, frustrations in democratizing industry, new hope in the

30 *Ibid.*   31 CG, 31 Oct. 1923, p. 5   32 8 July 1925, pp. 30–1

socialized businessman, dangers of sectarianism of Labour churches and Brother-hoods all had a telling effect, and as mid-decade approached, the more established forms of social and moral reform began more completely to dominate the stage. Furthermore, the turn of the economic tide in 1920 coincided with a turn in the liquor tide, and by 1924 the Methodist Evangelism and Social Service staff were reporting a high proportion of their time spent in battle with the Moderation and Liberty leagues.[33] By 1923 a shift in mood was evident in most of the centres of the social gospel in Canada. This shift is best illustrated in the most radical component of church union, the Methodist church.

The last General Conference of the Methodist church in 1922 occurred just prior to the change in mood, and still largely reflected the postwar crest of the social gospel. The annual conferences, however, provide the better barometer of the trend of the social gospel in the church. The Cape Breton problem kept industrial con-cerns in the eye of the Committee of Evangelism and Social Service in the Nova Scotia Conference until 1924 when the central interest shifted to peace.[34] From a fairly optimistic treatment of grave economic problems in 1921, the New Bruns-wick and Prince Edward Island Committee reverted by 1923 to encouragement of thrift, and the virile independence 'which made our fathers strong.'[35] The Bay of Quinte Committee stressed personal moral issues in 1922 and 1923, but showed a revival of 1921 progressive social concern in 1924.[36] The London Conference, always more conservative among central Canadian conferences of the church, had an especially brief Evangelism and Social Service report in 1922, and in a small shift in 1923 showed a new concern for international questions.[37] Industrial ques-tions concerned the Montreal and Hamilton Conference committees until 1923, with the former expressing itself in more radical terms. In 1924 both stressed temperance and evangelism.[38] The Toronto Conference Committee showed a more restricted agenda in 1921, and in 1922 a strong emphasis on evangelism in traditional terms. By 1924, however, perhaps due to the 'new evangelism' emphases of Thomas, the committee presented a definition of evangelism which included 'the application of Gospel principles to social industrial and political affairs, and the establishment of

33 *Minutes*, 1924, Annual Meeting, Methodist Board of ESS, 13–14 Nov. 1924. See below, chap. 17

34 *Annual Report*, Methodist Department of ESS, 1920, pp. 57–9; 1921, pp. 70–2; 1922, p. 85; 1923, pp. 71–3; 1924, pp. 66–8

35 *Ibid.*, 1921, p. 73; 1923, pp. 73–6

36 *Ibid.*, 1921, pp. 63–6; 1922, pp. 76–8; 1923, pp. 61–5; 1924, pp. 61–3

37 *Ibid.*, 1922, pp. 70–2; 1923, pp. 54–7

38 *Ibid.*, 1921, pp. 61–3, 68–70; 1922, pp. 74–6, 78–84; 1924, pp. 64–8

the Kingdom of God among men.'[39] Although the western conferences were most given to social and theological radicalism in the church, they reflected the nation-wide trend. The change, however, was more in mood than content. The Manitoba and Saskatchewan conferences of 1923, for instance, were reported as 'sober,' with normally controversial issues rousing little enthusiasm.[40] The Alberta Conference showed little change, but with the others in 1924 moved its centre of interest to peace issues.[41] At the same time a revived interest in evangelism in the West was clearly of the Bland-Thomas variety. By and large, the prairie pattern held true for the British Columbia Conference as well. Across the front of Methodism there was a resurgence not simply of old ways, but of more traditional preoccupations marked by years of filtering through a social gospel screen.

The United church inherited, of course, a large agenda of social reforms which few had expected to be accomplished overnight. Church union as a tactic of social gospel hopes was accomplished. To the extent that the union campaign sublimated social gospel frustrations, the success of 1925 again exposed its hopes to the en-counter with the principalities and powers of the world.

One of the worldly powers was the church itself. This was not often as apparent to progressives established in the church bureaucracy as to those like Bland, Thomas, or Ketchum in the SCM, in whose view the spirit of Christ had to win a daily resurrection over the mechanics of religion.[42] However, before the new church could be brought into play in pursuit of social objectives, a mammoth job of re-organization had to take place. This task was as large in respect to the Departments of Evangelism and Social Service as to any other part of the church, and for the social gospel more crucial. The new structures of social service in the church were worked out in a three-way dialectic between the existing departments, the Com-mission on Permanent Organization, and the church at large represented by the General Council.

There seems to have been a struggle for place and preference in the background of reorganization, in which a test of the strength of evangelism and social service forces in the uniting churches was involved. This department of the Methodist church had represented the main trend of recent Methodism,[43] but there had al-

39 Ibid., 1921, pp. 56–8; 1922, pp. 68–70; 1924, pp. 51–4

40 CG, 4 July 1923, pp. 9, 12–13

41 Annual Report, Methodist Department of ESS, 1923, pp. 82–5; 1924, pp. 74–8; pp. 8off

42 Canadian Student, Dec. 1924, p. 69; Western Methodist Recorder, May 1918, pp. 3–4

43 New Outlook, 21 Oct. 1925, p. 16

ways been a sizeable minority who had opposed the association of evangelism with social service, two endeavours which the social gospel viewed as but different sides of the same coin. In the Presbyterian church, financial pressures had led to the subordination of evangelism and social service within the more conservative Board of Home Missions and Social Service in 1915.[44] The Commission on Permanent Organization split the difference by continuing the Methodist practice of a separate board and department, but reducing it in size to one general secretary and three field secretaries. This was smaller than the previous Methodist staff, and only half the size of the current combined departments. Furthermore, the executive of the board was to exclude the field secretaries from influence as *ex officio* representatives. This reduced position brought an immediate protest from departmental officers.[45] The test of strength on these issues at the General Council of June 1926, however, was won without difficulty by the Department of Evangelism and Social Service.[46]

Further additions to the prestige of the department were in store. The proposed elevation of T.A. Moore to the secretaryship of General Council was at first protested by the department's executive,[47] but his move to that position still further enhanced the status of that department in the church. D.N. McLachlan of the Presbyterian department stepped into the place vacated by Moore. As had been the pattern in recent years in both of the two larger churches, the symbolic head of the church, the moderatorship, went to a person whose major interests had lain in social service, George Pidgeon. Chown, who might have brought a more forceful expression of the social gospel to that post, in an act of high statesmanship withdrew from a contest with the Presbyterian leader. When the continuing Methodist and Presbyterian departments received orders to cease all official functioning on 30 September 1926,[48] a position of unassailable strength was held by the new Department of Evangelism and Social Service in the new church.

This position of strength, however, was not put to the service of bold new plans or initiatives in any field of social endeavour in the years from 1925 through 1928. In terms of social welfare and social change the more strategically located settlements and all-people's missions had been given to the Department of Home Missions, while the administration of the redemptive homes and child welfare institutions, totalling eleven institutions, was left with the Department of Evangelism

44 Presbyterian Board of Home Missions, *Annual Report*, 1915–16, p. 8
45 UCA, Minutes, Executive, United Church Board of ESS (Methodist), 17 March 1926
46 *New Outlook*, 30 June 1926, p. 14
47 Minutes, Executive, United Church Department of ESS (Methodist), 22 June, 19 Aug. 1925
48 Minutes, Executive, United Church Board of ESS, 3 Sept. 1926

and Social Service.[49] Apart from a small amount of expansion in some directions, there was no change in any of these programmes.[50] The board was still puzzled over the problem of replacing the Brotherhoods with some adequate men's organization.[51] It continued its relationships with numerous bodies, among them the Social Service Council of Canada whose grant amounted to $2000, two-thirds of the grant to the Prohibition Federation of Canada and $600 less than the combined churches had given.[52] The figure was to drop to $1000 by 1929. Hugh Dobson, field secretary for the western conferences, was perhaps most actively related to the social service councils of any of the staff, aiding efforts in the fields of child welfare, 'community building,' and race relations.[53] Thomas' special role of assistance to the SCM was reaffirmed,[54] and he was given particular responsibility for research. He was still the department's most exciting leader of studies and conferences,[55] although he was soon to become the centre of a smouldering conflict within the department.[56] The reports of the rest of the staff, and those of the conferences as well as the National Board all reflect sober preoccupation with established causes.

A few new notes marked the continuing force of a few radical centres in the church. The first conference of the United church in British Columbia provided an issue in 1926 for the General Council, an issue which was to become a more agitated question in the early years of depression: a proposed equalization system for ministers' salaries 'consistent with the spirit and example of the early Christians and the declared deals of the United Church.'[57] The second General Council in 1926 established a minimum salary scale with recourse to maintenance and extension funds for needful congregations, but the scheme was not mandatory, and hardly met the demands of the British Columbia Conference. The issue was a vital one for the social gospel in the church. The effectiveness of the social efforts of the

49 *Ibid.*, 17 March 1926. This seems a conservative division, with the socially strategic institutions going to home missions, and the institutions of palliation going to evangelism and social service.

50 Minutes, Annual Meeting, United Church Board of ESS (Methodist), 29 Sept.–1 Oct. 1925

51 *Annual Report*, 1925–6, United Church Board of ESS, pp. 9–10

52 *Ibid.*, 1926–7, p. 11

53 *Ibid.*, pp. 29–30

54 *Ibid.*, 1925–6, p. 10

55 *New Outlook*, 6 Jan. 1926, p. 24; *Annual Report*, 1926–7, United Church Board of ESS, pp. 33–4. See also *Canadian Student*, October 1925, p. 24

56 See below, pp. 281–2, 294

57 *New Outlook*, 20 Jan. 1926, p. 25

church depended on a 'will to justice' within the organization, as well as on the creation of a new and larger structure. But this problem, not solved in prosperity, was left to become a more difficult and bitter issue in the depressed conditions of the 1930s.[58]

An obvious dissatisfaction with attempts at industrial reform aroused the first General Council to request the department for a new study and report on the subject,[59] but the report presented to and adopted by the second General Council represented no advance from the dilemmas of the church in this field. Since the statement was in no way modified by General Council, its shortcomings were not due to compromises in conference, but to compromise in the committee of fifteen established to draw up the report to council in the first place. The antinomies of the report reflected a committee polarized between S.R. Parsons on the one hand and James Simpson and Ernest Thomas on the other.[60]

To be sure, the statement insisted on the observation of conditions and ideals which could be radical in application, and which, at the least, could not let the conscientious rest in peace with the present system. But at every turn it cut the nerve of reform of the system as such. It seemed to impel men of Christian motivation to transform present organization, but told them that before deplorable evils could be removed 'all must repent and get the new mind which the Kingdom of God demands.' In judging all acts by motive alone it failed to do justice to the significance of means and consequences, the dimensions of morality by which systems as against persons are most adequately judged. The statement stressed the social gospel concept of corporate guilt. It was true that there was none righteous, but the very demand for industrial democracy by the church indicated that at present actual responsibility lay more in certain quarters than others. In a sense, the statement recognized this by addressing its major proposals to 'those to whom God had committed the direction of industrial affairs.' But if all had sinned, even while under church tutelage, how could hope be placed in the gentle persuasion of industrialists? The answer seemed to lie in the social gospel myth that the social principles of Jesus had been only recently rediscovered and explicated. Thus, industrial leaders who had willingly listened and absorbed the economic virtues of Protestant individualism could be presumed to be as amenable to the influence of the new economic virtues

58 See Barker's thesis 'The United Church and the Social Question: A Study of the Social and Theological Outlook of the United Church of Canada after Thirty-five Years,' pp. 353–65

59 *Annual Report*, 1924–5, United Church Department of ESS (Methodist), p. 10

60 *Ibid*. Other Methodist members were T.H. Everson, and the Revs. John Garbutt and W.B. Smith.

of Christian socialism. That the power interests of industrialists might lead them to see certain virtues as vices was as absent from the statement as any suggestion that to change their will might necessitate the mobilization and use of a formidable counter will. Labour, consequently, was told that 'no change in methods of control of industry will right any grievance apart from a holier purpose and finer motive than those which are being supplanted.' Thus a document which was shot through with social gospel concerns was fundamentally an evangelical appeal.

It seemed at points in the statement that something, however, had been learned from the industrial crises of a few years before: 'We recognize that in this complex life, with its roots so deep in the past, the fuller application is never easy.' But with that bow to experience, the balance of the document gave no support to a reform of the system as against the reform of motives. Was it simply for this that a new church had been created? Yet, part of the social gospel rationalization of the reason for the new church was the growing power of the 'community spirit.' Who was to say industrialists were immune? Both the hope and confusion of the social gospel were written in this statement on 'The Christianization of Industry.' And it was abundantly clear in the personnel of the drafting committee that a repetition of the radical statement of 1918 was precluded. The 'strategy of the committee' seemed to be declining in significance as a weapon of the social gospel in Canada.

A notable minority at the General Council of 1926 was able to impress upon the Department of Evangelism and Social Service the need for something more adequate than the uncertain trumpet they had sounded. Nothing, however, was forthcoming before the depression underlined the inadequacies of the system itself once more.

There were several possible excuses for failure of notable advance upon social objectives shortly after the union of 1925. The moderating role of Presbyterians has been adduced as a factor.[61] The years 1925 and 1926 were largely years of reorganization, of establishing new patterns of working together, and undoubtedly, to a degree, of rest from the years of strife. Furthermore, the church was preoccupied with the growing crisis over prohibition. All these factors were important, but their role was to hinder progress with the more fundamental reason for failure to pursue social issues in new terms and with new vigour, namely, the failure of the social gospel to absorb the meaning of the crises which it had experienced.

One year after union the mounting prohibition crisis broke upon the new church. It was at precisely this point that the editor of *Saturday Night* was alarmed. 'The New United Church is sure to be a sinister influence in the political life of the

61 Silcox, *Church Union in Canada*, pp. 457–8

country,' he wrote in July 1925.[62] The next year would indicate whether his fear was well founded or not. By 1926 most of the time of the Department of Evangelism and Social Service was given over to the now critical struggle for the defence of the last major legislative outpost of prohibition, Ontario. The social *cause célèbre* of evangelicalism, but fully endorsed by most social gospel partisans, was at stake. Not only the morale of conservatives but of progressives and many radicals was involved in the outcome. For social gospel conservatives this was the one social issue in which defeat would produce a sense of crisis. Those disappointed and puzzled by the problems met by other thrusts of the social gospel in industry and politics were in danger of having their confusion compounded. A temperance act in the hand was worth two industrial reforms in the bush. Victory was essential. But the critical question recognized by few was whether such a victory would refurnish the arsenal of the social gospel any more adequately than defeat. The failure of the United church to take any new initiatives in the first three years of its existence, despite its excuses, suggested that union may have simply placed more power behind relatively ineffectual weaponry and more minds behind ineffective strategic concepts.

62 Cited in the *New Outlook*, 15 July 1925, p. 3

17

The Prohibition Crisis

It would be difficult to exaggerate the significance of the prohibition movement for the social gospel. Most social gospel leaders had been schooled in temperance campaigns. Although prohibitive legislative proposals were negative, they were in service of a positive view of the full and free life. F.S. Spence, for instance, Canada's most prominent prohibitionist in the early years of this century, described prohibition as part of 'the great gospel of liberty.' He himself was a Liberal of some consequence, and a proponent of public ownership of public utilities and extensive social insurance.[1] If some came to view prohibition as a great good in itself, others, like the editor of the *Western Methodist Recorder*, recognized that prohibition was not an ideal condition. Voluntary abstinence was preferable, but 'human nature in many things has not yet reached that moral elevation, and so, evil things which endanger the public welfare, have to be kept down by law, that is by prohibition.'[2] It was the prototype of that group of social reforms whose accomplishment might free progressive forces for the constructive tasks of the social gospel.[3]

What these more constructive tasks were varied from left to right across the spectrum of the social gospel. Partisans on the left like Bland and Woodsworth had by the second decade given priority to other social causes. Both saw the gross inequities of the economic and social system as a more basic cause of human suffering than the liquor traffic.[4] In 1913 Bland, as a single taxer, had declared real estate speculation to be as great an evil as ever liquor had been,[5] and when in 1920 he summoned the church to a struggle for a new co-operative social order, it was in

1 sscc, p. 309; Ruth Spence, *Prohibition in Canada*, pp. 3–15; Denison, *The People's Power*, pp. 29–41; Plewman, *Adam Beck and Ontario Hydro*, pp. 30ff

2 *Western Methodist Recorder*, July 1920, p. 8

3 *Presbyterian and Westminster*, 10 June 1920, pp. 582–4.For further indications of this, see the first group of documents in Allen, 'The Triumph and Decline of Prohibition,' in Bumsted, ed., *Documentary Problems in Canadian History*, II; also the *Report of the Twenty-first Convention of the Canadian* w.c.t.u., 1920, p. 46

4 McNaught, *A Prophet in Politics*, chap. IV   5 Editorial, ggg, 26 Feb. 1913

terms of an almost century-old temperance campaign that he cast its scale.[6]

Shearer and partisans of the centre were more prone to emphasize piece-meal social welfare legislation, while on the right, advocacy of reforms applying the prohibition principle were the favoured means of giving one's social service and removing standing temptations to sin. But one and all heard ringing in their ears the slogan of the Israelites of temperance as they struck their tents to make for the promised land, 'Let us go up and possess the land, for we are able ...'[7]

Between 1918 and 1922 that objective was near success. In 1918 one of the great problems obstructing the success of such acts, inter-provincial trade in liquor products, was cleared away, at least temporarily, by a federal government order-in-council prohibiting not only such trade but the manufacture and importation of liquor until one year after peace was declared.[8] Quebec city had gone dry in late 1917 and the Quebec government had announced in 1918 that the following year it, too, would enact a comprehensive temperance act, thus completing the roster of provinces with such legislation.[9]

The temperance and prohibition acts defined 'intoxicating beverages' in terms of an alcohol content that permitted the public sale of low per cent beers under the careful scrutiny of the law. Prohibitionists tempted their luck by changing their slogan 'banish the bar' to 'banish the beer.'[10] The federal order-in-council represented the full objective of the churches. T.A. Moore crowed, 'Ever since [1839] we have been saying, "we want it! we'll have it!!" and now, thank God, we've got it!'[11] The Presbyterian Board of Home Missions and Social Service announced: 'The liquor traffic is gone forever. It can never come back,' and reviewed the many blessings of even partial prohibition.[12] The *Western Methodist Recorder* believed that 'nothing on earth will induce [Canada] to return to the old state of things at any later day.'[13] And the Anglican Council for Social Service continued a strong and reasoned support for prohibition into the peace years.[14]

6 Bland, *The New Christianity*, p. 47

7 Bland Papers. This slogan was frequently on the publicity of the temperance organizations of the 1880s and 1890s.

8 'Report of the Board of Home Missions and Social Service,' *Presbyterian Acts and Proceedings*, 1918, Appendix, p. 12

9 *Ibid.*, CG, 10 Oct. 1917, Editorial

10 *Presbyterian and Westminster*, 1 May 1919, p. 421

11 *Hamilton Spectator*, 8 Oct. 1918

12 'Report of the Board of Home Missions and Social Service,' *Presbyterian Acts and Proceedings*, 1918, Appendix, pp. 12, 29–33

13 Jan. 1918, p. 9   14 *Bulletin of the Council*, Sept. 1919

As early as 21 November 1918, however, the *Churchman* observed the makings of a hard struggle. Only two days after the armistice 'the enemy opened fire' with cards distributed in Toronto and other cities calling for the reopening of the bar-room 'for the health of the people.'[15] The federal order-in-council had only been for a specific short-term period, but apparently the liquor interests were afraid that the measure might become permanent. Distillers' representatives met in early February to lay before the government an alternative to prohibition.[16] In June their fears were lessened when the Senate, in amending a bill to enact the order-in-council concerned as statute law, struck out the provision 'and for twelve months thereafter.'[17] Nonconformist wrath waxed hot over this step. The Senate, that 'Prussian oligarchy,' was accumulating a record of opposition to progressive reforms that elicited numerous demands in the church press for its reform or abolition.[18]

Despite these signs of opposition, the structures of temperance remained intact through 1919. Church leaders were confident that with one more great effort, full success would be theirs, as it recently had been for their kindred in the United States. As the prohibition movement kept up its pressure, Chown succinctly phrased the temper of the conflict with the liquor interests: 'The measure of their hatred is the measure of their fear, but we have no other programme but to make them hate us more.'[19]

Despite the defeat of temperance forces in a referendum for a government-controlled liquor sales system in British Columbia in 1920, the cause continued, on balance, to make progress until 1922. In late October, two weeks after the British Columbia defeat, the three prairie provinces and Nova Scotia took advantage of a recent federal law prohibiting liquor export to any province whose population wished such protection. All contests were won, with Ontario following suit the next April.[20] A similar victory had been scored in New Brunswick in mid-1920.[21] Thus in 1921 liquor sales in at least seven provinces were confined to those permitted under temperance acts, and in two provinces a broader range of sales was controlled through government outlet systems. The Presbyterian board happily declared:

15 21 Nov. 1918, p. 743

16 *Presbyterian Witness*, 15 Feb. 1919, p. 1

17 *Ibid.*, 28 June 1919, p. 1

18 *Ibid.*, 28 June 1919, p. 1 and 5 July 1923, p. 1 lists several instances.

19 CG, 19 Nov. 1919, p. 9

20 'Report of the Board of Home Missions and Social Service,' *Presbyterian Acts and Proceedings*, 1921, Appendix, p. 8

21 *Presbyterian and Westminster*, 15 July 1920, p. 56

The Social Service branch of our work has entered on a new phase. The struggle against the liquor traffic and other giant evils is nearing success; one more effort and the question will be settled for all time. Vigilance will continue to be the price of safety ... [but] our energies are turning more and more to the positive side of our work.[22]

There was probably still little reason for anxiety when the international convention of the World League against Alcoholism met in Toronto, November 1922. The General Secretary of the league set the efforts of Canadian prohibitionists in the perspective of the larger social task the Presbyterian board was referring to:

Prohibition in America in fact has been the direct outcome of the recognition, in part at least, of the insistent injunction of the Man of Galilee himself to the effect that the social order was his great objective and that the changing of that order through the establishment upon earth of a kingdom of righteousness and peace was the mission whereunto he was sent. The effect of such a movement as that of prohibition of the beverage liquor traffic on the establishment of that kingdom of righteousness among men cannot be adequately measured or even estimated.[23]

This assembly of 'good men from every land ... battling only against evil,' as the *Witness* described it, heartened its hosts in their struggle to maintain and extend their influence as part of the 'new world war' against the scourge of alcohol.[24]

Encouragement also came from labour's growing support of the prohibition cause. As late as 1917, apparently, trades and labour councils were largely arrayed against it, believing it to be advocated by large employers for such class purposes as increased production. With prohibition in effect, however, workers seemed to be giving union affairs and labour problems greater attention, trades councils and labour papers began to switch their arguments, and the restoration of open sale became denounced as a new weapon of class oppression.[25] If aspects of this line of argument sounded like prohibitionist propaganda, they were, but they nevertheless did reflect increased support from labour. In its 10 October issue, 1919, the *Industrial Banner* in Toronto published a page of testimonials from labour figures and organizations supporting prohibition. In the campaign the next year against the proposal of government control in British Columbia, Thomas found that labour leaders Pettipiece, Kavanagh, and McVety, once opposed, now stood with others like Tom Richardson and W.R. Trotter for prohibition. 'Labor gains,' he was sure, 'will make

22 Cited from reports to the General Assembly, 1920, *ibid.*, 10 June 1920, pp. 582–4
23 sw, Jan. 1923, pp. 71–4   24 *Presbyterian Witness*, 7 Dec. 1922, p. 4
25 *Youth and Service*, Aug. 1919, pp. 114–15

up for the weak and defectives of the Vancouver Club and the Union Club and the big employers.'[26]

There were further instances of support from labour across the nation. J.W. Findlay, Trades and Labor Congress representative on the Mathers Commission of 1919, favoured prohibition of everything over 2 per cent.[27] John Queen of Winnipeg strike fame told a large workers' meeting in Cobalt, Ontario, that 'Booze was no friend of the Worker,' and that without prohibition the strike would not have been an orderly one.[28] Sympathy with prohibition was obviously present in the Women's Labour League which grew out of the strike.[29] The editor of the *Alberta Labor News*, E.E. Roper, described liquor as 'a finished product that is of less value than the raw material from which it is manufactured,'[30] and urged labour support in the October referendum in 1920. During the strike at Glace Bay, Nova Scotia, in 1922, miners under the mayor organized a special constabulary to prevent any infringement of the Liquor Act. All vehicles entering the area were searched, secret distilleries sought out and destroyed. No violence accompanied the strike, *Social Welfare* triumphantly announced.[31] In the Manitoba referendum campaign of mid-1923, labour leaders William Ivens and W.D. Bayley gave extensive service under William R. Wood, who resigned as secretary of the United Farmers of Manitoba to head up the prohibition forces.[32] Agrarians had been partisans of the cause for some time, and it seemed a further reason for hope that the leadership of the labour movement was now inclining in the same direction.

In observing labour's shifting attitude, prohibitionists were apt not to enquire after what was cause and what effect. Thomas observed that British Columbia lumber camps, once difficult to organize, had since prohibition delivered 19,000 paid up members to union rolls.[33] However, this period also coincided with one of revived militance in labour attitudes. It was probable that prohibition gained from this fact as much as it gave. Stephen Leacock, an arch-opponent, accepted the prohibition thesis as a means of attack. Employer support of such measures had been shortsighted, he argued, for although higher production was an immediate consequence, the drinkless worker, deprived of simple comforts of life, would angrily

26 *Western Methodist Recorder*, Oct. 1920, p. 3; Hugh Dobson to T. Jackson Wray, 4 Dec. 1920, Dobson Papers, General Correspondence

27 *Edmonton Free Press*, 10 May 1919, p. 1. See also WLN, 14 March 1919, p. 4 for the Winnipeg TLC reaction to anti-prohibition propaganda.

28 CG, 30 July 1919, p. 2

29 *Alberta Labor News*, 25 Sept. 1920, p. 5

30 *Ibid.*, 23 Oct. 1920, p. 8   31 Nov. 1922, pp. 29–30

32 CG, 11 July 1923, pp. 4–5   33 SW, 1 Dec. 1920, pp. 25–6

demand luxuries, harbour envy, and attack social inequalities. 'See to it that he does not turn into a Bolshevik,' he warned. This was the 'Capitalist view,' according to the *Industrial Banner*, and it countered with the 'workers' view' that alcohol lames and stupefies the working class, depriving them of an understanding of the injustices of which they were victims.[34]

Whatever the reciprocal relationship of prohibition and labour militance, as the first years of the 1920s passed the Canadian temperance forces had need of such allies. A consistent and nation-wide propaganda battle was well under way, having proved itself in the British Columbia campaign of 1920. Alarmed at the nature of this campaign, the Methodist church sent a confidential letter to its ministers on 22 November 1920 to acquaint them with the fact that 'reactionary forces are working with ceaseless vigilance and great subtlety ... [in a] concerted effort to discredit Prohibition Acts and create a state of mind in which even Prohibitionists will welcome an appeal for Government Control and sale of liquor.' The letter observed seven main features of the opposition propaganda: 1) that lawlessness had followed in the wake of prohibition, and further 2) that it was inherent in its character to make criminals of men; 3) that the law was un-British, and different from other laws; 4) that an increase in the use of drugs was a consequence; 5) that liquor had medicinal values; 6) that there was no difficulty obtaining liquor anyway; and 7) that real temperance was the objective – 'the bar must never return.'[35] The letter called on ministers to activate circuit leadership and initiate a counter-campaign to that being promoted by Moderation leagues in the West and Liberty leagues in the East.

The features itemized in the Methodist letter dominated the campaign against prohibition over the following six years. It was a struggle passionately conducted and notoriously difficult to analyse. As a subject for a full length study it would be difficult to match, and its neglect may be due to the depth of emotion the subject generated and the latent feelings of conflict which still arise over it. It is only possible here to make a few observations on the main features of this great debate, if it can be given so dignified a title.

The issue which dominated and pervaded every other was that of the relation of prohibition to crime. There were two interrelated but not mutually dependent aspects to this issue. In the first place was the question as to whether such laws as prohibitionists had secured, and even more, those they still wished, did not enter a

---

34 *Industrial Banner*, 10 Oct. 1919, p. 4. The *Banner* regularly carried advertisements
   of the Ontario Referendum Committee of the prohibition forces.

35 Bland Papers

field beyond the competence of law. In the second place was the problem as to whether in actual fact prohibition was a breeder of criminal activity. Both were difficult questions, but the latter, seemingly more accessible, and certainly more sensational, harvested the overwhelming portion of attention. Furthermore, most arguments on both sides tended to assume that the answer to the latter determined the answer to the former, that social utility was the final criterion of law. This, of course, was one of the master convictions of the social gospel. It would take either extensive social resistance to its application or a major ideological shift, or both, to dislodge that criterion. The prohibition struggle was a test of that conviction.

A cursory (and therefore hazardous) survey of the debate as seen, chiefly, through the church press suggests that prohibitionists had the better case in the second instance. Oppositionists spoke of a crime wave following prohibition, but like Stephen Leacock, whose lectures were widely circulated, seldom quoted figures, declaring the fact to be obvious.[36] If a crime wave were in existence, commented Creighton in the *Guardian*, it would be no surprise after the repressions and disciplines of wartime and problems of readjustment.[37] However, when prohibitionists marshalled their statistics, whatever else they proved, they hardly indicated a crime wave. Whatever the reason, almost invariably they showed a decline, not only in crimes relating to drinking, but in all criminal offenses when measured against the immediate prewar, pre-Temperance Act period.[38] This, despite a larger population, seemed irrefutable proof to prohibitionists of the efficacy of their legislative accomplishments.

Oppositionists argued that there was as much drinking going on as before, only now it was covert. Obviously this was a difficult charge to substantiate or to refute. The best estimates and observations suggest otherwise, however. The number of breweries seems to have declined. In Alberta, for instance, five in 1920 as against seven in 1915 were operating, producing a lower per cent product. Actual sales in the province, including bootleg activity, were estimated by the Attorney General at about $5,000,000 in 1920 as against $14,000,000 in 1915.[39] If consumption were equal, an equivalent amount of social disturbance might have been expected. Covert drinking might not produce as many open crimes to raise statistics, but it might have other measurable expressions. Surveys of industrialists, school inspectors, magistrates, clergymen, social workers, the opinions of chiefs of police and

36 CG, 13 April 1921, p. 8   37 *Ibid.*

38 For instance, *Presbyterian Witness*, 17 March 1921, p. 6; 7 Dec. 1922, p. 16; CG, 4 Oct. 1922, p. 27; 28 Nov. 1923, p. 4; 20 Feb. 1924, p. 4. See also Ontario Alliance, *Ontario Six Years Dry, 1916–1922*

39 *Presbyterian Witness*, 9 Aug. 1923, p. 10

those of labour leaders all seemed to coincide in affirming the beneficial results of the temperance acts in Canada and of prohibition in the United States in the first half of the 1920s.[40] It would have taken both an immense amount of bootlegging and police corruption to make the drinks go around.

On balance, prohibitionists argued, Canada under the temperance acts was experiencing no general upsurge in crime but rather a notable decline in some forms of criminality and an indirect but incalculable number of social benefits. But despite the existence of a good case for the social utility of prohibition, the unexciting figures and surveys paled before the dramatic stories of rumrunning and banditry on the border.

That there was bootlegging and its ancillary activities, prohibitionists were quite aware. They knew that Canadian fishing schooners were lured to run liquor into eastern American ports,[41] that export liquor houses existed just north of the prairie border as depots where armed convoys of American autos loaded themselves with the contraband goods for bootleg sale in the United States.[42] The conclusions prohibitionists drew from such activities, however, were quite different from those inferred by their opposition. The latter seemed to argue that the law created the crime, and because it did not end liquor traffic, it was not only faulty but begged disrespect of the law in general. However, it was pointed out in return that there were few laws which eliminated offenses in the area of life they were meant to control. Illegal activities under the temperance acts were matters of choice on the part of offenders, prohibitionists argued, not simply a mechanical consequence of the law's existence.[43]

The opposition tried to show that bootleggers preferred the temperance acts to

40 Surveys and reports cited during this period were: a Report of the Federal Prohibition Commissions of the USA, CG, 8 Feb. 1922, p. 6; independent investigations of two large newspapers in the USA, *ibid.*, p. 11; *Manufacturers' Record* (USA) survey, *Presbyterian Witness*, 4 June 1922, p. 3; *Literary Digest* poll, *ibid.*, 10 Aug. 1922, p. 3; Board of License Commissioners (USA) to manufacturers, school inspectors, and clergy, CG, 27 June 1923, p. 3; report of W.A. Raney, attorney general of Ontario, *ibid.*, 20 Feb. 1924, p. 4; a report of the Kingston Chief of Police, *ibid.*, 7 Feb. 1923, p. 2; letter of Professor George M. Wrong to *The New Statesman*, SW, May 1922, pp. 177–8

41 CG, 26 March 1924, p. 8

42 *Presbyterian Witness*, 3 March 1921, p. 11; CG, 10 Jan. 1923, pp. 5, 24. For accounts of such activity, see the annual reports of the RCMP during this period, *Commons Sessional Papers*

43 *Presbyterian Witness*, 14 Aug. 1924, pp. 2–3

alternative means of control because their opportunities were enhanced thereby, but their bluff was called when prohibitionists cited the referendum returns at the acknowledged rum port of LaSalle, Ontario. Only 2 of 266 persons voted for the Temperance Act and against a government-controlled outlet system.[44] Furthermore, bootlegging had been an active pursuit before the Temperance Act era[45] and, under government-control systems in British Columbia and Quebec, could be shown to be still a flagrant abuse. The *Ladies' Home Journal* carried extensive reports on both provincial situations in the best muckraking tradition.[46] If temperance and prohibition acts did increase the level of some illegal activities, this was to be measured against the crime and social distress prevented. It was also to be measured against the will to enforce the law. Prohibitionists were pleased when the governments of the prairie provinces joined with their neighbouirng states and the government of the United States to find ways and means of controlling traffic across the border.[47] But they were furious at the federal government's refusal for years (until 1930) to deny clearance to liquor shipments into the United States despite its government's protests.[48] The amount of bootlegging, border running, and related criminal activity was clearly not an absolute in itself.

The problem of outlaw activity under the temperance acts, prohibitionists laid largely at the feet of the liquor interests themselves. They did score lack of enforcement and acknowledged a problem of social adjustment to the new laws,[49] but conniving subterfuge and open offence by distilling and brewing companies they read in the reports of increased smuggling and bootlegging.[50] Prohibitionists did not, during this time, have at hand a careful study to confirm this belief, but there were impressive pieces of indirect evidence. Attorney General Manson in British Columbia rendered a harsh verdict for himself and his predecessor when in 1925 he charged:

There has never been a day when the brewers have not spent every minute of it doing their utmost to contravene the will of the people and to defy the Government of British

---

44 *Ibid.*, 13 Nov. 1924, p. 3

45 *Ibid.*, 9 Aug. 1923, p. 10, cited 751 convictions in 1915 in Alberta alone.

46 Reviewed in *ibid.*, 13 Dec. 1923, pp. 3–4; *ibid.*, 26 June 1924, pp. 2–3; CG, 11 June 1924, p. 4

47 Minutes, Annual Meeting, Methodist Board of ESS, 8–10 Nov. 1921

48 *New Outlook*, 23 Jan. 1929, pp. 93, 111; 19 Feb. 1930, p. 174. See also Knotman, 'Volstead Violated: Prohibition as a factor in Canadian-American Relations'

49 CG, 4 Oct. 1922, p. 27

50 For example, 'Report of the Board of Home Missions and Social Service,' *Presbyterian Acts and Proceedings*, 1923, Appendix, pp. 127–8

Columbia, and to tear down the law of the land. If the Legislature says confiscate them then I am prepared to confiscate them.[51]

Prohibitionists had access to the files of attorneys general. In at least Alberta and Saskatchewan men like the Revs. E. Bishop and J.L. Nichol were selected for government offices relating to education and law enforcement in this field.[52] The particulars of a judgment like Manson's were undoubtedly known to them. They suspected that Moderation and Liberty League funds had a similar source in the coffers of distillers and brewers. Some support for the anti-prohibition campaign, apparently, even came from abroad. French interests reported in *Exportateur Francais*: Our action assumed the most diverse forms: drawing up of tracts and pamphlets ... and their distribution through Canada, press publication and controversies, furnishing of funds at the right moment.[53]

The professed interest of these organizations in temperance, prohibitionists did not believe for a moment. Their insincerity seemed patent when, after their mid-decade victories, they continued to campaign for expansion and variety of outlets. Their early hostility to the bar turned to proposals for outlets that sounded suspiciously like that venerable institution.[54] Prohibitionists believed, in short, that the very interests that were behind the campaigns for government control were also those responsible for the illegal practices the campaigns fed upon. It was not until 1928 that the *Interim Reports* of a federal Royal Commission on Customs and Excise revealed how accurate such suspicions were.

Surely here were sensational charges to match those of the Moderation and Liberty leagues. But even in combination with barrages of statistics, they did not persuade the people. In hard-fought referendums on the subject of government control in Manitoba, Alberta, Saskatchewan, and Ontario in 1923 and 1924, only Ontario held fast. The tide had turned. Five provinces had decisively rejected not simply prohibition but the less prohibitive Temperance Act structure. The watchword of the prohibition movement suddenly became not 'possess the land' but 'hold the line.' The line did not hold. In 1926 the Ontario Temperance Act yielded to 'government control' after a desperate fight. For the bulk of the Canadian population it made little difference that prohibition forces seemed secure in the Maritime provinces. What little comfort was derived from that apparent security faded as the

51 Quoted in CG, 7 Jan. 1925, p. 3

52 *Annual Report*, 1920–21, Methodist Department of ESS, p. 89; Minutes, Executive of the Department, May 29, 1922, UCA

53 Cited by *Presbyterian Witness*, 2 Oct. 1924, p. 1. *Exportateur Français* was the publication of the French Wines Exportation Commission.

54 CG, 24 June 1924, p. 4

New Brunswick government in 1927 proposed and secured a system of 'government control.'

It was possible to react to these defeats by reference to a 'crusade of whisper and insinuation moving from province to province.'[55] Disappointed prohibitionists could cynically refer to the appeal of a full treasury through government liquor revenues, and wonder who was likely to control whom.[56] The *Guardian* offered as a reason for the victory of 'government control' the observation that people easily forgot that dealing with the liquor problem in any way was always tremendously difficult and perplexing.[57] In itself, this was neither a condemnation of 'government control' nor a confirmation of the temperance acts. That the *Guardian* used the argument at all in late 1923 represented a shift in attitudes that had not yet generated a reappraisal of policies.[58]

Several features of the experience of the years 1920 to 1926 served to break up for some the monolithic interpretation of the liquor evil which generations of campaigning had built up. In the first place, a large part of the community had remained unpersuaded. These were not represented simply by 'Eye Opener Bob' of the *Calgary Eye-Opener*, who campaigned in season and out for beer as the solution to the ravages of whiskey.[59] More significantly, a large part of the Anglican constituency remained unconvinced by prohibition arguments, and the erosion of early *Canadian Churchman* support was obvious as early as 1921 when it saw much merit in 'government control.'[60] One of its columnists considered the Manitoba referendum a model of deliberation and judgment – despite the large foreign population, he patronizingly added.[61] In the preliminaries to the second contest over the Ontario Temperance Act, the publication supported Canon Cody, who had taken a strong position for 'government control' after an investigation of the operation of the new systems in effect in the prairie provinces.[62] Prohibitionists charged that Cody had only seen the 'right' people,[63] but the stubborn political fact remained that he spoke for many people who were unpersuaded by the prohibitionist case.

In the second place, just as the monolithic interpretation had made of honest dissenters dupes of the liquor interests, so the temperance laws tended to make

55 *Presbyterian Witness*, 27 Dec. 1923, pp. 2–3
56 CG, 14 Nov. 1923, p. 6   57 *Ibid.*
58 *Ibid.*; *Presbyterian Witness*, 31 July 1924, p. 1
59 5 April 1919   60 *Canadian Churchman*, 31 March 1921, p. 201
61 *Ibid.*, 19 July 1923, p. 457
62 *Ibid.*, 12 March 1925, p. 163; 4 Nov. 1926, p. 720
63 *New Outlook*, 17 Nov. 1926, p. 6

criminals out of those who had been regarded as victims of the traffic. Clergymen who became involved in law enforcement, though they might spend most of their time dealing with organized sources of the traffic, could hardly fail to consider the consumer as an accomplice. What, after all, was the real source of the illegal traffic in liquor? Ringing charges might be made about the 'interests,' but they were only the flagrant organized instances of what social gospel prohibitionists called 'the un-socialized man.' Once simply under the judgment of the moral law, the 'unsocialized man' was now, with respect to liquor consumption, largely under the condemnation of criminal law.

This change in status was probably less apparent to prohibitionists than to those honestly opposed to them or to those in the grip of alcohol. For both of the latter, this outcast status undoubtedly heightened opposition to prohibitionist policies. The prohibitionists themselves, used to sitting in judgment on this subject, found in the new role little change. Partly for this reason, it is, in fact, difficult to document any clear alteration in their attitudes to the victim-cum-criminal. Both relationships were founded less on gospel than on law, and both were surrounded by elaborate rationalization.

The rationalization was apparent in the arguments with which prohibitionists met charges of infringement of personal liberty. Liberty, it was rightly observed, extended no further than the rights of others. The family of the drinker had a right to the promises of wedlock and adequate nourishment; the merchant a right to payment of bills; the community a right to a safe and peaceful life.[64] But prohibition legislation was not necessarily the only means of protecting these rights to the extent that they were threatened by 'drink.' With the proposal of 'government control' another way was opened, and the issue was no longer simply the right of the drinker versus the rights of others, nor whether the state should or should not interfere. That much was a signal advance for which the pressure of prohibitionists was largely responsible, but they found it difficult to enter the new situation of rational discussion of alternative means, having long been the single opponents of the giant evil.

Social gospel prohibitionists had argued that only the 'socialized man' was the free man. Since the 'socialized man' was sensitive to the rights of others the law was of no account. He was free of its burden.[65] But this argument evaded the real problem of political liberty. Not the 'free man' but the 'unfree man' was its subject. It was at this point that Moderation and Liberty leagues, whatever their backing, had a telling argument which could capitalize on what appeared to be widespread

64 *Presbyterian Witness*, 9 Oct. 1924, p. 3
65 Ernest Thomas, 'Prohibition and Personal Liberty,' *Youth and Service*, Aug. 1919,
   pp. 117–18

reservations about the temperance acts and the further proposals of prohibitionists.[66]

The unity of the prohibition movement was still further disrupted at key points in its alliance with progressive forces in the failure of the methods of direct legislation to yield the desired political solution. From the dominion-wide plebiscite in 1898 favouring prohibition to the successful provincial referendums of the 1910s, the people had registered support of the true way. But from 1920 to 1926 the same methods had largely registered a negative verdict. Some blamed the foreign vote in the cities, for it was apparent that the Ontario countryside had largely held firm in 1924.[67] Who were these, the *Witness* asked, that their opinion should be weighed with that of doctors, teachers, and judges?[68]

The possibility of trust in the 'people' had clearly been a result of the creation of a rather broad consensus during the latter nineteenth century. However, this consensus was breaking up in the 1920s partly under the impact of the great wave of immigration since the turn of the century. But the problem was deeper than that, for even allies in the cause were backing away from earlier support. In Alberta, despite the United Farmers' platform of prohibition, the UFA government declined to give aid or comfort to the prohibitionists in the campaign of 1923.[69] In Saskatchewan where the Grain Growers' Association was the power behind the government, association support of prohibition failed to keep the government and the province in line.[70] Even progressive governments were unprepared to stake their lives to prohibition policies which they had hitherto accepted.

This reluctance should not have surprised prohibitionists, but their surprise and disappointment were a consequence of their own political tactics. Prohibition had not been the only reform that they had desired of governments, but they had made it one of overriding significance. The referendum had been a useful way of avoiding partisanism in the politics of prohibition. But the referendum had also been a means by which progressives proposed to overcome the old party system. The Progressive party based on the farmers' movements had been considered by social gospel progressives to be a different breed, a rally of the forces of righteousness, a non-partisan party. It was not expected to behave as its forerunners. But the facts of political responsibility made the liquor problem one among many for them as for other

66 The argument, however, seems seldom to have been developed in an impressive fashion. Certainly the lectures of Professor Leacock and those of Dr Michael Clark left much to be desired on this point. For these and other anti-prohibitionist literature, see Dobson Papers, B 3, 10 ('Moderation League literature').

67 *Presbyterian Witness*, 6 Nov. 1924, p. 1

68 *Ibid.*

69 CG, 5 Dec. 1923, p. 14

70 *Ibid.*, 21 Feb. 1923, p. 11

governments. In the mood created by the temperance battle of the 1920s, progressive governments were as loath as any others to stake their lives on a single issue. At this point prohibitionists were the authors of their own disappointment. Non-partisan politics had backfired.

Although there were to be later uses of the plebiscite on this subject in Canada, the effective end of the referendum road came in Ontario in 1926 when Premier Ferguson announced that he intended to place his government's life on electoral support of a system of government control. Sensing this pending decision, the United church social service departments decided in December 1925 to begin campaigning 'before the issue becomes officially political.'[71] In January they placed their concern over the politicizing of the issue before representatives of the government. The latter frankly replied that the prohibitionists had helped bring the matter into the political arena by criticism of the government. Government spokesmen further charged, somewhat irrelevantly, that the prohibition forces had not assisted in the enforcement of the Ontario Temperance Act.[72] As the campaign developed later in the year, prohibitionists were fighting with their backs to the wall. The *New Outlook* charged that Ferguson was 'openly throwing in his lot with the liquor interests with which he has all along been in closest touch and sympathy,' and described him as 'cleverness without character.'[73] The *Canadian Churchman*, by contrast, referred to the 'high plane' of his campaigning.[74] Ferguson quite naturally tried to keep the temperature of the temperance issue at as low a level as possible, and to present it as part of a larger platform. But the *New Outlook* scored him for making it a political issue and 'the one supreme issue of the forthcoming election.' Moreover, the editor felt, 'We are faced by the most serious moral crisis in the history of our young nation.'[75] Nothing less than such a conviction, Creighton declared, 'would ever have led this paper into participation in a political campaign the way it has been led into this one ...'[76]

In New Brunswick the government followed Ferguson's example and assumed

71 Letter to members of the sub-executive of the Presbyterian Board of Home Missions and Social Service and the executive of the Methodist Department of ESS (minutes, Executive, Methodist Department of ESS, 14 Dec. 1925

72 Notes on an interview with government officials, 26 Jan. 1926, in *ibid.*

73 27 Oct. 1926, p. 12

74 9 Dec. 1926, p. 813. Both the Anglican Primate and Archbishop Williams had approved government control.

75 10 Nov. 1926, p. 12. See also Coburn's views, pp. 18–19

76 *Ibid.*, 1 Dec. 1926, p. 12

responsibility for a government sale bill in 1927, but without an electoral contest. The issue had at last been restored to responsible politics. The question was whether the churches would follow. The *Telegram* saw the defeat in 1926 as just retribution upon the United church for 'interference in politics.'[77] A layman declared, 'A month of Sundays devoted to political sermons decided me to vote the other way,'[78] but the *Star* was happy to have been leagued with 'so great a company of preachers.'[79] The *Churchman* was not opposed to parsons participating in politics, but considered certain ground rules necessary. Normally politics should be excluded from sermons, it said, and in all cases should be informed, charitable, non-abusive, and high-principled.[80]

Prohibitionists were not easily deterred, and undoubtedly felt that their cause came within the *Churchman*'s rules. Creighton applied salve to the wounds of the embattled movement:

> Truth crushed to earth shall rise again;
> The eternal years of God are hers;
> But error, wounded, writhes in pain
> And dies among her worshippers.

He persisted in seeing signs of the overthrow of the system of government control which defied 'every consideration of humanity.'[81] Although the United church in 1928 eschewed partisan activity, it steadfastly declared:

When, however, a great moral issue such as the liquor question is thrust into the political arena, it is the right and duty of the Church to instruct its members as to the merits of the issue in the light of the sacredness of personality and the bearing of the issue involved upon life interests, and to persuade them to exercise their citizenship in a manner worthy of the gospel.[82]

The morale of the prohibitionists, however, was so low by that date that extensive campaigning of any kind was extremely difficult. The overwhelming proportion of time of most of the staff of the Department of Evangelism and Social Service from 1926–9 was deployed in trying to restore the broken spirit of the prohibition movement, and to fight local battles over minor phases of the main issue.[83] Some of

---

77 *The Telegram* (Toronto), cited by the *Canadian Churchman*, 16 Dec. 1926, p. 829
78 *Ibid.*
79 Cited in *ibid.*
80 *Ibid.*, 23 Dec. 1926, p. 846
81 *New Outlook*, 8 Dec. 1926, pp. 12, 13
82 *Annual Report*, 1928, Board of ESS, pp. 12–13
83 *Annual Report*, 1926–7, United Church Board of ESS, pp. 32, 35; 1927, pp. 27–9; 1928, pp. 23–5

these they won; others they lost. Both in spirit and organization the prohibition forces were in disarray. In 1927 the efforts of Dobson, Coburn, and Millison revived the Saskatchewan Prohibition League,[84] and in 1928 a fairly enthusiastic convention was held.[85] But reports of the convention in January 1930 indicated that the province had 'not yet recovered from the shock of the wet victory of July, 1924.' 'Not much' it was felt, 'can be done just now in the way of a provincial effort.'[86]

John Coburn reported a similar condition in Ontario: 'Division in the ranks and the actions of some persons once prominent in [Ontario Prohibition Union] councils have made the work of the Union exceedingly difficult.'[87] Tensions existing between those who were searching for a new approach to the question broke into the open with the severance of the Rev. Ben Spence from the union to form the Canadian Prohibition Bureau.[88] Spence was a fiery proponent of absolute prohibition and an ardent socialist who now proposed seeking the desired goal by means of a campaign for an amendment to the British North America Act giving the federal government jurisdiction over the matters relating to manufacture and trade in alcoholic beverages. Only a minority of the prohibition forces, however, followed him in this move. The stress in temperance activity, rather, was placed on education and the old course of securing pledges of total abstinence in order that the signer might 'serve God and humanity' with all his powers.[89] This campaign was pressed in the churches, and governments and secular institutions of education were urged to promote temperance instruction.[90] With such a programme it was hoped that 'There will be a new record of progress in another generation.'[91]

The dismay of temperance advocates was the greater during the confused period after 1926 in that most still felt they had a good case for the social utility of their proposals. Furthermore, they firmly believed that the government control systems were not working out well. Higher consumption of alcohol accompanied a growing number and diversity of outlets, and crime rates seemed to move in direct correlation. It was an angry, almost unbelieving, and grim recital of events and conditions to which Sarah Rowell Wright, in her presidential addresses in 1925 and 1927, treated her followers in the Women's Christian Temperance Union. 'If ever we

84 *Ibid.*, 1927, pp. 24–5   85 *New Outlook*, 22 Feb. 1928, p. 22

86 *Ibid.*, 8 Jan. 1930, p. 46

87 *Annual Report*, 1927, United Church Board of ESS, pp. 27–9

88 *New Outlook*, 21 March 1928, p. 2

89 *Annual Report*, 1928, Board of ESS, p. 49

90 *Ibid.*, pp. 13, 51–2; 1929, pp. 13–15; *New Outlook*, 30 May 1928, pp. 12, 13; 23 Jan. 1929, p. 100

91 *Ibid.*, 8 Jan. 1930, p. 46

needed a prayer-hearing, covenant-keeping God, it is now,' she lamented, 'when our hopes for Canada are for the *Present moment* immersed in the sea of a great and almost universal defeat.'[92] Yet when Ferguson in Ontario asked to be judged in 1929 on his record, Ontario electors resoundingly rejected the United church's urgings that 'the "wet" hand be removed.'[93] The *New Outlook* reflected that this victory did not mean an endorsation of Ferguson's liquor policies, but if there had been any doubt about the need to rethink the whole issue and come to firm decisions, its editor was now convinced of the urgency of that course. Specifically, he counselled, the movement must now either move fully into politics, or declare the field of moral suasion and education to be its sphere of action.[94]

Ernest Thomas, just prior to the defeats of 1926, had noted that something more than facts was needed to enlighten the apparent blind spots in the thinking of the population. The church, he said, must give new emphasis to the spiritual and human aspects of the liquor question. He proposed a shift from concern for legislation to education to create a new sense of values and a more scientifically based understanding of the nature of the problem created by any alcoholic consumption.[95] He prepared a short study, *Alcohol and Life*, for the church, and lectured widely presenting a 'fresh examination and restatement of the ethical and religious aspects' of the problem, which was commended for its absence of propaganda and politics.[96] By early 1930 Thomas had worked his way through to a new position which, while endorsing the same long-run objectives, was marked by a new sense of social realism that demolished attitudes central to the prohibitionist campaign. That the leadership of the temperance organizations, despite a basic agreement on the current priority of the tactics of education, was unready to absorb this new understanding of their role was immediately made manifest.

Temperance legislation, Thomas said, was not an end in itself, yet prohibitionists had allowed their passionate indignation against the drink traffic to lead them into the use of any weapon to hit the trade. The 'cause of temperance' might be aided thereby, 'but not so the rule of Jesus in the life of men.' The fundamental role of the church, Thomas suggested, was to make men rich in insight, not in dogmatic

92 *Report of the Twenty-fourth Convention of the Canadian* w.c.t.u., 1927, p. 96; see also 1925, pp. 55–68; and *New Outlook*, 13 Jan. 1926, pp. 9, 27; 3 Feb. 1926, p. 17; 7 Dec. 1927, p. 24; 27 Feb. 1929, p. 237; 1 May 1929, pp. 458, 475; 29 May 1929, p. 562; 19 June 1929, p. 631

93 *Ibid.*, 23 Oct. 1929, p. 1065   94 *Ibid.*, 6 Nov. 1929, p. 1112

95 *Ibid.*, 24 Nov. 1926, p. 4

96 *Annual Report*, 1926–7, Board of ESS, p. 34; *New Outlook*, 26 Feb. 1930, p. 195

judgments as to the right conduct of others. The desire for a society of social righteousness was a great moral goal, but it did not follow that the selection of the next step towards it was a clear moral issue. That was a matter of political wisdom, which was not necessarily inherent in 'goodwill or love for the Lord Jesus.' Since the defeated laws were declared inadequate not only by lawbreakers but by thousands of law abiding citizens, one must seriously consider whether the political wisdom of those laws was not, in fact, debatable.

The condition of legislative effectiveness, Thomas argued, lay in a consensus of public opinion. Hence the failure of the temperance acts could in no wise be explained by the 'perverseness of some provincial politician.' The task of the church was 'to create a community in which the legislative regulations [would] embody social custom.' In making the particular case for abstinence, Thomas proposed only the use of the most accurate, restrained educative methods, and was prepared to wait until social usage crystallized into law.[97] These views were but an elaboration of Thomas' observation following the defeat of 1926. Old Ontario had died, he said, and the church 'must refrain from insisting that her standards be imposed by the State on that larger body of people which constitutes the State.' This position did not mean, he had added, that the struggle for the ideal social order should cease; but it did mean that Protestants should be chary of demanding legislation in advance of a broad social consensus.[98]

A.J. Irwin, general secretary of the Ontario Temperance Union, reacted immediately to Thomas' article. Irwin was Bland's old colleague of Wesley College days, and in 1939–40 was to lead the last prohibition thrust in Canada in a march on Ottawa for wartime prohibition. He gave short shrift to Thomas' suggestion of the competence of politicians on the subject, endorsed the church's right to 'declare her judgments' in a political contest, cited the proven social utility of the restrictive laws, and used Thomas' own judgment on the campaign of 1920 in British Columbia, 'the infiltration of rumour,' as a valid explanation of the train of defeats. But Irwin's most significant reaction was to Thomas' observation about the niceties involved in the political decision as to the next step to the goal. It was true, Irwin said, that there might be doubt as to the moral value of next steps when both were toward the goal, but this was not the case when one was toward and the other away.[99] Thomas' new social realism was lost on Irwin, and no doubt on many of his fellows.

Thomas' stance not only created tensions with the prohibition organizations but disrupted relations with his departmental colleagues and seriously affected his rela-

97 *Ibid.*, 8 Jan. 1930, pp. 31, 44   98 *Ibid.*, 22 Dec. 1926, p. 5
99 *Ibid.*, 12 Feb. 1930, p. 153

tionship with a considerable segment of the United church at large. Hugh Dobson, in particular, felt the thrusts of Thomas' articles keenly. Still the department's western field secretary, but now based in Vancouver and a veteran of every western prohibition campaign since 1913, he resented Thomas' charges of unscrupulous propaganda, and felt that Thomas' special function in the field of investigation led him too easily to assume that no one else did research worthy of the name. Whether Thomas left himself open to this may be questioned, but warm were the letters that passed between the two men, between Dobson and their mutual superior, Dr McLachlan, and between Dobson and others on the subject of Thomas' provocative new views, not only on prohibition but on still more fundamental questions.[100] This problem in relationships seems not to have worked itself out as late as 1936,[101] and in the meantime D.N. McLachlan confessed: 'It is becoming difficult to provide work for our friend Dr Thomas on Sundays. While a few groups are arranging to have him speak to them, the response to our attempt to introduce him into this kind of work has not been very successful.'[102]

If there were personal reasons for the new difficulties centring on Thomas, it was equally clear that there were personal and institutional costs entailed in the search for new policies, even among those who agreed on the long-range goals. Perhaps it was well that McLachlan, as the new department head succeeding Moore, was a past Presbyterian in whose church there had always been more dissent on the liquor question than among Methodists. For his part, in contrast to Irwin and Dobson, he could credit 'government control' with some gains over pre-temperance act systems of liquor control, and acknowledge that reform was halted for the time being at least. A new, less ambitious policy had been formulated by the church, stressing education and personal abstinence, with a long-term goal of complete elimination of trade in beverage alcohol. This has remained basic church policy since, but in no respect has it made measurable advance. The reforms which the new church envisaged had indeed been halted. Old Ontario had vanished. Old Canada, too, was rapidly disappearing, and the agenda of reforms dating from the old evangelicalism became irrelevant in method if not in content.

The crisis in the prohibition movement had taken a heavy toll of social gospel energy and morale. The new United church had been forced into heavy activity in defence of the conservative wing of the social gospel, and had lost on all counts. The

100 Dobson Papers, General Correspondence 1926–8, File M, Moore and Thomas Correspondence; Hugh Dobson to W.L. Armstrong, 14 May 1928, *ibid.*, File A
101 Hugh Dobson to W.E. McNiven, 5 and 9 Sept. 1936, *ibid.*, 1933–6, File MC
102 D.N. McLachlan to Hugh Dobson, 18 Sept. 1931, *ibid.*, 1928–33, File McLachlan

2B

links between the heritage of evangelicalism and progressivism, which comprised the bonds of the conservative social gospel especially, were badly eroded. The optimism of social reform, based on both those traditions, was largely dissipated under the counter-attacks which occurred between 1920 and 1926. It had been impossible to 'possess the land' in the name of the conservative social gospel, as it had proved impossible in the name of progressives and radicals earlier in the decade. By 1927 the nerve of the social gospel would seem to have been cut. However, all wings of the movement had left a deposit of advance in social organization, although not necessarily in the form or to the extent they had hoped. Even though frustrated, some retained high hopes, especially on the conservative wing. Here was where the weight of Canadian Protestant tradition lay. But that sense of hope was deceptive, for a new secular society was arising in Canada not, ironically, unabetted by the more progressive and radical wings of the social gospel.

18

The Disenchantment of Social Service

'We are filling out a decade of disenchantment, and of our disenchantment many men have made a book. But very soon disenchantment will have become our normal mind, and we shall hardly know that things were ever different.' The words were those of a social gospel partisan living in Montreal.[1] Although they were written in another connection, they could not have been more apt had they been intended for the social service movement, whether with respect to its social work hopes or to its industrial prophecies. In spite of its trophies in both areas, the developments of the decade had overtaken not simply the organizational structures of social service, but the very categories in which its devotees had viewed their work.

When the Social Service Council of Canada in 1926 concluded its appraisal of its situation in the post-church union period, it had decided to continue along the lines of its past work. However, not only had the church structure of social service altered, but the whole field of social work was undergoing increasing specialization, secularization, and organizational consolidation. The mystique of social service had always held the direct impetus of religious motivation to be essential to the effective practice of social work, and, rightly or wrongly, churchmen had interpreted this as requiring the prominence, if not dominance, of religious institutions. Both the church social service departments and the Social Service Council of Canada had based their work on this belief. At the time of church union T.A. Moore observed that in the United States

the movement for social service has become almost wholly divorced from organized religion. This makes for the loss of the religious incentive in redemption, and the loss of ethical outlook for the Church. It has been the ceaseless effort of the uniting churches to avert this cleavage in Canada, and constant adjustment will be required if the Church is to render its full aid to social redemption and to find its own life enriched by streams of human sympathy.[2]

1 Gifford, *The Christian and Peace*, pp. 23–4
2 *New Outlook*, 10 June 1925, p. 23. See also the remarks of F.N. Stapleford on the

The churches and the council were not averse to many of the new developments in social work, but that those developments should be fully secular was quite outside the standpoint of the progressive social gospel. Hence the process of secularization constituted a threat both to the mystique and institutional expressions of social service in the churches and produced a further disorientation of the social strategies of both the new church and the Social Service Council.

Deeply involved in the crisis over prohibition, the churches gave less time to developments in social work at mid-decade than did the Social Service Council of Canada. If for a short time this fact potentially enhanced the position of the council, it did not rescue it from its dilemma.

Co-operation in social welfare activities was not entirely new after 1914. Associated Charities organizations had existed in Canadian cities from the 1880s, attempting both to rationalize the securing and dispensing of charitable funds and to help the needy help themselves. Not only the growth of the social problem, but also the dawning sense that the problem was a social one spurred the development of new methods, movements, and organizations. In the course of the second decade of the new century, new impulses to co-operation brought local groups in the larger cities together in such organizations as the Neighborhood Workers' Association in Toronto and the Social Welfare Association in Winnipeg. By 1918 each association boasted a general secretary and civic support. The Neighborhood Workers' secretary was F.N. Stapleford, a Methodist minister of social gospel persuasion who had trained in sociology at Chicago and lectured in the subject at the University of Toronto. In 1918 and 1919 he was also the organizational centre of a new, enlarged system of welfare campaigning through a Federation for Community Service.[3] The secretary of the Winnipeg association, J.H.T. Falk, a social worker of English background and no formal training and a man of more secular inclinations, was similarly engaged in 1919, conducting a vigorous investigation of Montreal social services. As a result a Council of Social Agencies was established, but both Falk's report and the reaction to its proposal of a co-operative system based on three councils, Roman Catholic, Protestant, and Jewish, revealed the besetting problems and rivalries in the field at large. Overlapping work, competition for funds, 'money-attracting' criteria in choice of board members, condescending attitudes to paid

aggressive social attitudes of the Canadian churches and the religious motivation of Canadian social workers in his report of the Canadian Conference of Charities and Corrections (CG, 3 Oct. 1917, pp. 3–4).

3 For most of the foregoing see *After Twenty Years*, Stapleford's account of the Neighborhood Workers' Association. See also articles by him, CG, 21 Feb. 1923, p. 5; SW, 1 July 1920, pp. 290–1 and July 1926, pp. 189–90

social workers, overdependence on a single dedicated individual, inadequate records, ugly institutions: the problems in Montreal simply exaggerated those elsewhere. When Montreal religious bodies murmured against the council proposal 'as lacking in Christian principles in its constitution and plan of operation,' *Social Welfare* criticized such discontent by observing that 'Montreal has long been the center of individualistic activity and policy in social work.' Many members of the new council apparently had not looked kindly upon the Social Service Council of Canada, but the editor of *Social Welfare* wished them permanent success in their courageous experiment.[4]

Even while consolidation was taking place, however, new ventures were assuming independence. In 1920, for instance, the child welfare activities of the Social Service Council blossomed into the Child Welfare Council under Charlotte Whitton. And with the increasing scope of welfare activities came soaring costs. Between 1918 and 1930 the welfare budget of the City of Toronto rose from some $18,000 to over $300,000.[5] All the indices pointed to continuing expansion, escalating costs, and further consolidation as a new profession was being born out of the concerns of a new social age.

Despite developments prior to 1920, there was by that date no broad national organization in the social work field apart from the Social Service Council. As early as 1913 there had been an attempt, in the Canadian Welfare League, to consolidate social service workers and groups nationally outside the churches and the Social Service Council of Canada. J.S. Woodsworth had been the prime mover. The effort merged in 1916 with the Bureau of Social Research created by the prairie governments. The bureau was also placed under Woodsworth, and an advisory council included some of the executive members of the earlier league. This course of development came to an end when Woodsworth was dismissed in early 1917 over his opposition to the government registration programme, and a bid by the national Social Service Council to take over the bureau's work was not accepted. In the course of the same decade a Canadian Conference of Charities and Corrections had been initiated, and at its 1917 meeting had altered its name to the Canadian Conference on Public Welfare. The new name, suggested Stapleford, betokened a new view of 'crime and poverty as pathological conditions which may be largely removed by a readjustment of social forces.'[6] The new view and the new name, however, did not bring the organization into effective national existence. In 1920,

4 See 1 Jan. 1920, pp. 95–8 for the full account. For a sketch of J.H.T. Falk's career see Jackson's article in *Canadian Welfare*.
5 Cited in Stapleford, *After Twenty Years*
6 CG, 3 Oct. 1917, p. 8

in the first months of the postwar depression, the Council of the Conference met jointly with the Social Service Council. Later in the year, the two organizations experimented further by running their annual meetings concurrently.[7] For whatever reason, the experiment was not repeated and both organizations, along with the rest of the country, entered a belt of economic storms. The besetting problems, however, were not simply financial. Still faced with internal dissensions, the social work battalions, in the view of Creighton in the *Guardian*, also confronted at the war's end a jaded constituency, weary with well-doing, and more taken with grand plans of social and economic reconstruction.[8] For a brief period, trading on leftover war patriotism was successful. When, however, depression conditions struck home the immediacy of need, and the more radical designs of the social gospel began to pale, a new enthusiasm arose in the ranks of social workers, as in the church settlements and city missions. New proposals began to appear for Canada-wide secular organization of social workers and agencies.

The occasion for a new drive to this end was the fifty-first annual meeting of the National Conference of Social Work (of the USA) in Toronto, 25 June–2 July 1924. As in several fields of nascent social endeavour, the meetings of an American body had been one of the few means of association of Canadians of like purpose. At the meetings a Canadian Association of Social Workers was projected, and was successfully constituted in 1926.[9] The Canadian section of the national conference further established a committee of representatives of thirteen organizations to plan a 'common medium of concerted action' and a 'Canadian Conference.'[10] The chairman of this committee was Dr Carl A. Dawson of the McGill School of Social Work. Although the committee was to report at the next National Conference of

7 SW, 1 July 1920, pp. 290–1   8 See 21 Feb. 1923, p. 5

9 Professor Dale, director of the Toronto School of Social Work, was to head the organizational committee, but upon his illness the task reverted to George B. Clarke of the Family Welfare Association. 'Through the Years in CASW,' *The Social Worker*, XXVII, 4 (Oct. 1959)

10 SW, July 1924, pp. 187ff. The organizations and their representatives were: Public Health Association, Dr C.J. Hastings; Child Welfare Council, Mr A.P. Paget; Mental Hygiene Committee, Dr C.M. Hincks; Social Hygiene Council, Dr Gordon Bates; Tuberculosis Association, Dr Wodehouse; Red Cross Society, Mrs H.P. Plumptre; Canadian Association of Child Protection Officers, Judge Ethel MacLachlan; Public Welfare Commission, Judge D.B. Harkness; Canadian Association of Social Workers, Dr J.A. Dale; Canadian Association of University Education, Miss Ethel Jones; Victorian Order of Nurses, Miss Smellie; Social Service Council of Canada, Dr J.G. Shearer; Inter-Church Advisory Council, Dr E. Thomas.

Social Work,[11] it was not until 1928 that it was finally possible to hold the proposed all-Canadian conference.

The Social Service Council of Canada was happy about these developments, despite their apparent implications for the council's future. It had been pleased to provide the Canadian Association of Social Workers with regular space in *Social Welfare*, an arrangement which continued until the publication of *The Social Worker* in 1932. The Social Service Council considered that the organization of the Canadian conference more than justified the faith of those who some thought over-optimistic in 'preaching the gospel of the Development of a National Consciousness in Canadian Social Work.' The editor's sense of identification was clear: it was an event, he said, which 'spurs us on to future achievement.'[12] It was conceivable that an enlargement of secular social work organization and church social service pro-grammes might mean a larger role for the Social Service Council in the ground between them. It was a hope of low probability.

This progression of events coming on the heels of church union pressed the Social Service Council still further from the centre of a field which it had recently domin-ated. This was evident in that in 1924 the seventeenth annual meeting of the coun-cil in St John, New Brunswick, had attracted one hundred persons in addition to representatives of the provincial units and those from over thirty organizations of national scope.[13] But in 1928, when the annual meeting was held following the All-Canadian Conference of Social Work, 23–25 April, only thirty-two persons were present as delegates.[14] By contrast, 710 registered for the larger meeting, 424 of them as voting delegates. Furthermore, between 1924 and 1926 the Social Service Council had lost five affiliated national organizations, all, significantly, from the group of secular bodies in the council.[15] There were, of course, still weaknesses in the structure of the new Canadian conference. In 1928 only two delegates were present from British Columbia, fifteen from the prairie region, and twenty from the Maritime provinces.[16] Similarly, the Canadian Association of Social Workers prior to 1938 had no branches east of Montreal and none between Winnipeg and Van-

11 *Ibid.*   12 May 1928, p. 171

13 *Canadian Baptist*, 6 March 1924, p. 11

14 sw, May 1928, p. 178

15 *Ibid.*, Oct. 1924, p. 258, inside cover list ceased to include the Dominion Grange and Farmer and the National Council of Women of Canada; Feb. 1925, p. 82, dropped the Canadian Council of Agriculture; Aug. 1926, p. 214, dropped the Canadian Council of Public Welfare; and Oct. 1926, dropped the Canadian Asso-ciation of Trained Nurses.

16 *Ibid.*, p. 178

couver.[17] But despite these weaknesses there was a greater breadth and potency in the new organizations. This contrast was the more sharp given the churches' attitude to the Social Service Council of Canada. Apparently one of the criticisms of the council by the churches had been the number of secular affiliates it contained.[18] Such a criticism seems counter to Moore's concern to preserve a religious dimension to social work. It may, however, have come from other than social centres in the church or it may have been a perverse expression of Moore's intent. However, the loss of several secular affiliates seems not to have increased church interest in the council.

Such secular organizational developments were in part a result of the rise of the social gospel, and contributed to its crisis in the later 1920s. The new organizations were permeated by individuals of social gospel inspiration. In the sermon to the national conference in 1924, W.A. Cameron of Bloor Street Baptist Church, Toronto, spoke of the kingdom that comes personally but also 'comes to society with a new social order which reshapes men and women who live under it.'[19] Woodsworth, noting the new spirit and methods of social work, suggested that one day the conference might meet in the name of a 'new politics.'[20] Carl Dawson, the chairman of the committee to organize a Canadian Conference of Social Work, spoke in the accents of the social gospel when he addressed a Montreal alumni conference on the subjects, 'The Church and Social Reality,' 'The Modern Mind and the Kingdom,' 'The Call for a Prophetic Ministry,' and 'The Relation of Jesus to the Christian Religion.'[21] It was not only the role of the church to redeem men, he told an Anglican Synod on another occasion, 'but to redeem the forces that will help men to realize the best ends of life.'[22] The social gospel, apparently, was a not inconsiderable force in the new organizations.

Nor was the gulf between those represented by the Canadian Conference of Social Work and the social service centres in the churches one respecting scientific techniques. The Social Service Council had separated itself from its past in 1913 as the Moral and Social Reform Council by its wholehearted acceptance of survey and social research methods as a basis for proposed legislation and social action. Its secretary, J.G. Shearer, had been proud of this fact.[23] It was still the requisite of

17 Maines, 'Through the Years in CASW,' p. 11
18 Silcox, *Church Union in Canada*, p. 92
19 *Proceedings of the National Conference of Social Work*, pp. 44–7
20 *Ibid.*, p. 92
21 *Presbyterian Witness*, 12 Oct. 1922, p. 2
22 *Ibid.*, 26 Oct. 1922, p. 2   23 SW, 1 July 1922, p. 211

effective social work. Facts were the basis for making social ideals come true, said Carl Dawson. 'Utopias have generally gone to pieces because too much based on idealization and too little on a knowledge of human behaviour.'[24] Such a gulf as existed was more at the level of sophistication, subject matter, and objectives. But still more important was the difference in ethos that surrounded each endeavour.

The new social work was, in this respect, represented by J. Davidson Ketchum and F.N. Stapleford. The latter, for instance, described social work as marking not only the passage from an individualistic era that forgot the individual to one of 'socialized individualism,' but also from environmentalism to an exploration of the real possibilities of the individual. Social work was concerned to move on from legislation to relate it to individual needs and develop the emotional resources of life. The preconceptions of 'social service' had made it judgmental in its approach to individuals, but to the new social work this was a cardinal sin. Judgment cut the social worker off from the lump he was leavening. 'Judge and Be Judged' warned Davidson Ketchum – this was not the way of Jesus.[25] A morally neutral language was in process of emergence, in which actions were described as 'unwise' or 'deleterious,' but not 'wrong' or 'reprehensible.' The new social work was less certain than 'social service' of the kind of person it wanted to emerge, and at the same time more optimistic about the course of self-realization an individual would find when aided from a standpoint of 'moral indifference' as Ketchum put it, or of 'judgment based on fact' in Stapleford's terms.[26] Institutions were viewed not simply as restraining or ordering social life, but in terms of their capacity to elicit and develop the resources of the individual. Such institutional change was to be the work of Woodsworth's 'new politics,' and social work was to it as evangelism had been to social service. The marks of a new faith were about the new social work when Stapleford in 1926 saw in it 'a new note of hope, a recrudescence of the human spirit.'[27] This, in the realm of social work, was the expression of the immanent theology of radical reform.[28]

There seems to have been no explicit criticism of the new social work from the Social Service Council. This was not because the Rev. J. Phillips Jones shared its outlook. Rather, he spoke in terms of the 1914–18 formative period of the Social Service Council of Canada. Preaching the gospel created the social problem, he declared, echoing Charles Stelzle of the epic 1914 Social Service Congress. 'The moment we speak of a New Way of Life we are in the thick of social reconstruction.'[29] If there was still truth in this declaration, it was a way of thinking becoming

24 *Ibid.*, Feb. 1923, pp. 93–5
26 *Ibid.*; sw, June-July 1926, pp. 189–90
28 See below, pp. 302–6
25 *Canadian Student*, Nov. 1925
27 *Ibid.*
29 *Canadian Baptist*, 22 April 1926, p. 2

less and less congenial to the new social worker. If such a preaching of the word impelled some students into social work, it did not sustain them, Ketchum said, in the face of studies which made church social service work seem quite inadequate, Christian theology bankrupt, and Christian ethical judgments the mere reflection of culture and class. Ketchum, himself, was evidence of the beginnings of this development. Few wrestled with the problem as he did, and if the Student Christian Movement held many such, they often developed, despite their sense of inspiration from the person of Jesus, a sense of alienation from the churches.

If Jones did not voice reactions to aspects of the new social work, D.N. Mac-Lachlan, general secretary of the United Church Department of Evangelism and Social Service, did. In his reports from 1926 to 1929 he warned of the danger of a social work that had lost its sense of God, that was fundamentally an expression of faith in man's ability to realize the good. His criticisms were put in the terms of passionate involvement of the social gospel:

As a corporate experience the individual must recognize himself bound up with all others, so that the wrong in the life of every other individual is acknowledged to be his. Exponents of the Social Gospel have persuaded us of this. It is unquestionably the feeling that we and all others have not acted as our brother's keeper. When this comes with its searching implications, we are driven to identify ourselves with the efforts of Holiness to remedy that which is wrong.[30]

His picture of a social worker was thus set in terms of 'a self-identification with sunken, broken, harrassed lives, whereby the Divine power within the worker flows into the life of the person under consideration.'[31] MacLachlan was hardly a conservative in theology: 'Our forefathers had a doctrine of original sin,' he said, but 'the social worker in the Church or out of it, does not require any of those theories.'[32] But his picture of the social worker was not that being purveyed in the schools of social work. It hardly represented a standpoint of 'moral indifference,' or 'judgment based on fact.' It was, in fact, not the portrait of a social worker at all, but of the Christian saint. There was, of course, a sense in which it was proper to speak of the social worker, regardless of his religious profession, being a vehicle of the healing grace of God. And it was always possible for the social worker to be a saint. But sainthood was not a career, it was a life, and social work in Canada was in the 1920s becoming a career dominated by secular co-ordinates.

With the delineation of the lines of struggle in the modern world between religion and secularism by the influential International Missionary Conference in Jerusalem

30 *Annual Report*, 1926–7, United Church Department of ESS, p. 25
31 SW, May 1928, pp. 182–4   32 *Ibid.*

in 1928, it appeared likely that the reaction of the church would continue to fall in the lines of T.A. Moore, J. Phillips Jones, D.N. MacLachlan, and their comrades of the progressive social gospel. Such a delineation, however, reflected a crisis not only in the structures but also in the theology of the social gospel. Developing within a mixture of liberal and evangelical theological categories which stressed the continuity of the human and the divine, the social gospel had bestowed varying degrees of sacrosanctity to certain secular movements and envisaged social service as a way of regenerating national life. Radicals often seemed to consider that such work and the agencies promoting it had an inherent meaning – almost a character of holiness. Some had viewed farmer and labour movements in this way. It was not surprising that Woodsworth was a central figure in both areas of development. In this sphere, as in the other, the pressures of social reality were again splitting those inclined to a radical optimism about the inherent meaning of secular movements from those for whom such meaning (and hence real social advance) was inseparable from right thinking, or the spiritual transformation of men, and hence inseparable in the last analysis from the church. Woodsworth was joined by Stapleford and Ketchum in representing the former radical secularizing trend. T.A. Moore held to an institutional interpretation of the latter position, and it was only a slightly more flexible version of that stand that D.N. MacLachlan presented to the 1928 Conference of Social Work.[33]

Almost a decade earlier, Ernest Thomas had virtually announced the breakup of the marriage of liberalism and evangelicalism that had given birth to 'social service.' In the social service movement, he said, the evangelical idea of Christian perfection in the completely loving life was carried away by a tide of crude liberalism which saw 'no inner unity to life, but only external relations which were to be ameliorated as opportunity would allow.' Thus, he said,

we came to that miserable makeshift we have sometimes called "Social Service" ... but which as thus interpreted did not express that deep spiritual transformation of our ways of thinking which will enable us to verify for ourselves the will of God ... Given that spiritual socialization, the social service will be "our spiritual liturgy" ...[34]

It is consonant with Thomas' view to observe that evangelicalism passed on to this conservative wing of the social gospel as well as to some progressives and radicals a tendency to view sin as particular sins, to estimate a particular type of character, shorn of certain vices and endowed with certain specific virtues, as its ideal. Its acceptance of a 'crude liberalism,' was, in social service circles, combined with a

33 sw, May 1928, pp. 182–4
34 *Canadian Student*, March 1919, pp. 10–14

type of environmentalism or reform Darwinism adapted to the removal of said sins, and hence to aid in the production of said character. If the social service legislative programme was designed to remove the hindrances to 'perfect people in a perfect society,' evangelism was its counterpart in creating socialized persons for a new community. The social service programme to this end was broader than evangelicalism itself had allowed and the Social Service Council had moved beyond the narrow, negative programme of moral reform, but there lurked throughout it older evangelical preconceptions. Thomas pointed out how mechanical the social service enterprise could all become.

He suggested what seemed a more excellent way, more vitalistic in character, in which respect he shared much with the new generation of social workers and students, but which safeguarded something of the concern of Moore and MacLachlan. 'Sacraments,' he said, 'are keynotes to remind us that all human relations are phases of the Divine.' In human institutions God was expressing 'His own thought in fact.' On this basis, Thomas advocated the independence of such movements as the new social work as 'organs of the sacred community' with their own tasks. However, for him the church was necessary to perform its task of interpreting community life in terms of its spiritual wholeness and its origin in a God of love. The church was one organ of society among many, and its first role was to be the church.[35] Social work (like labour) could not play the role of a new church. It was free to do its work, but its best understanding of that work, Thomas believed, was impossible without the presence of the church in society.

As the crisis of the social gospel was running its course after mid-decade, the time had come to return to this theme. Thomas' reflections on the prohibition defeats had stressed the need for the church promoting richness of insight rather than formulated judgments and social exhortations. The coincidental development of small fellowship groups in the church was an evidence of the need. That these groups were often inspired by the new Oxford movement of Frank Buchman was of some concern to Thomas' department, and when it decided to foster the trend in its own way, Thomas was asked to write a series of studies to serve the groups. The *Fellowship Studies* of 1928 were the result.[36] They were substantial little studies, borrowing somewhat from Alfred North Whitehead. Their purpose, Thomas wrote, was to promote 'a deeper and richer experience of the presence of God ... intimate fellowship ... meditation and prayer.' For him, neither the studies nor the groups necessarily represented abandonment of social action. Rather, both were signs of

35 *Ibid.*

36 United Church of Canada, Joint Committee of the Board of ESS and Religious Education, *Fellowship Studies*

the breakup of the marriage of evangelicalism and liberalism that had been but one, and for him an inadequate, way of linking religion and social reform. 'Can we rest in a merely practical attitude to Jesus,' he asked, without at the same time embracing 'the worship of Jesus as the embodiment in terms of human life of the eternal creative energy of the universe'?[37] An older radical, like Salem Bland, was doubtful, and scribbled in the margin as he read, 'The worship of Jesus has often been the substitute for obedience to the teaching of Jesus – the deadly enemy of the religion of Jesus is the religion about Jesus.'[38]

Thomas was occasionally rather mischievous or downright provocative in his demolition of the social service marriage, and may sometimes have earned a portion of his colleagues' consternation. An address to the Dominion Social Service Council in 1928 was described by Dobson as one of the cleverest of Thomas' career, but Dobson believed it was 'calculated to give a wrong lead,' and Dean L.N. Tucker described it in private as 'buffoonery.' When Thomas later in conversation over the dinner table dropped the remark, 'I always hold that religion has nothing to do with morality,' Dobson made a note of it and wrote to McLachlan in both concern and disagreement: if this were so, how could one justify the uniting of evangelism and social service in one church department?[39] Thomas was not proposing the department's dissolution, but he was in effect turning the question back, 'How indeed?'

However that question were answered, the uneasiness of Bland and Dobson with Thomas' probing of social gospel foundations was a testimony to the degree to which a religious mystique had gathered around the social and moral dimensions of the gospel, and perhaps, as well, to a dawning awareness that the time was approaching for breaking camp and striking out for new ground. Certainly, six years later, in a sermon before General Council, Bland felt compelled to give voice to what he now questioned.[40] For the moment, however, there was sufficient evidence to make the watchful church progressive or radical wary. The new secular organization of social work, as well as its ethos, implied a drift from the religious structures and thought which had done much to give shape and substance to the development of social work in Canada. Ironically, the moorings that had tied the enterprise to Christian concepts and resources were weakened, in part, by the radically immanent

37 *Ibid.*, Study IV
38 The copies of *Fellowship Studies* in the United Church Archives are from Bland's library.
39 14 May 1928, Dobson Papers, General Correspondence, 1926–8, File A, Hugh Dobson to W.L. Armstrong
40 Allen, 'Salem Bland,' pp. 200–1

theology of one wing of the social gospel. Simply to trust the movement of the Spirit in men and institutions was to abet the progress of the very secularism that the influential International Missionary Council of 1928 in Jerusalem was describing as the chief foe of religion in the modern age.[41] Someone like Thomas could find reason for hope in the new situation. But however one responded, it was evident that, in taking flight, the new social work was bursting the chrysallis of social service and forcing the church departments and the Social Service Council into a search for a new relationship to yet another area of the secular world.

The fostering of social work and of industrial reform had been two of the major preoccupations of the social service movement. If it now found itself overtaken in the former field, it was, perhaps, with respect to its industrial gospel that the message rang most clearly that the enchanted world of the Social Service congresses of 1914–18 had vanished. In 1924, *Social Welfare* had prefaced its Labour Day issue with a quote to the effect that while the church's ministry dealt with personal factors and not mechanics, it should be able to offer a diagnosis of every social maladjustment, and its treatment should extend to individuals and social structures alike.[42] Until the end of Shearer's leadership, the publication persisted in celebrating the religious significance of labour. Between 1926 and 1929, however, its Labour Day issues became more preoccupied with industrial questions in general. In 1927 it appeared to be strongly influenced by the concept of the new businessman that appeared with Inter-Church in 1921.[43] In 1928, for the first time, no invocation of social gospel passion appeared on the lead page. In its place were editorials on vocational guidance and employment bureaus.[44] Finally, in 1929, Labour Day was duty noted as a community festival, on which occasion the church takes note of 'the personal aspects of industry,' but the actual embodiment of Christian ideals in industrial life was to be left to industrialists.[45] It seemed only to be in riders to such comments that it was suggested that the church should be on the watch for unfair labour practices of employers.

That the industrial gospel of social service had shifted from prophecy to pragmatic acceptance of the basic structures of the system was evident in the common weakness of church, Inter-Church, and Social Service Council responses to the persistent and bitter disputes in the coal fields and steel mills of Cape Breton. Here

41 *The Christian Life and Message in Relation to Non-Christian Systems*, Report of the Jerusalem Meeting of the International Missionary Council; see Rufus M. Jones, 'Secular Civilization and The Christian Task,' I, 284–338

42 sw, Aug. 1924, p. 215

43 *Ibid.*, Aug. 1927, p. 483

44 *Ibid.*, Aug. 1928

45 *Ibid.*, Aug. 1929, p. 242

were industrialists who showed no sign of possessing the new mind of the socialized businessman, and invited the social gospel's word of prophetic judgment.

Cape Breton steel and coal industry was dominated by the British Empire Steel and Coal Company (BESCO). Here conditions were as appalling as Inter-Church (USA) found them to be in United States Steel. Approximately 75 per cent of the men worked an average of twelve hours per day, and to earn one Sunday off every two weeks between shift changes had to work a straight twenty-four hours. In the coal company, labour was fully organized, but in steel, craft organization persisted, covering between 50 and 80 per cent of the men. No concessions were made to collective bargaining.[46] After thirty years of large-scale operations, Glace Bay, the centre of operations, could still be described as lacking 'the beginnings of civilized organized life':

... there are no streets in any accepted sense of the word. There are simply chunks of road, with rows and rows of wooden huts on either side. There are no sidewalks to mark off the ditches. There are no street lamps to light up the darkness. No trees can grow in that soil, and a bit of green is a rarity. The scene then is always the dark, uneven, lumpy road, the rows of boxlike huts, the mine tressel in the distance, smoke stacks, smoky skies, crude fencings, and rugged, stern, bare sea cliffs. In the early spring it rains a good deal, and the atmosphere is clammy, foggy, drizzly, with raw, bitterly cold, ice-drift winds.[47]

The Cape Breton towns were company owned and policed by company police. All the abuses of the arrangement came into play with the strike for recognition of the union and collective bargaining beginning in February 1922, followed by unrest and strikes for the following three years of depression, short work, and attempted wage reductions. Returning prosperity and a new management later in the 1920s brought a temporary truce, but fundamental economic and social conditions remained unchanged when the great depression of the 1930s bore down upon Cape Breton.

The Inter-Church Advisory Council, established on 7 May 1920 following the success of the Inter-Church campaign, undertook no such attack upon industrial conditions as had Inter-Church upon the steel company in the United States. On several occasions it put off calling a congress of churches on industrial affairs, finally justifying this on the basis that similar ventures in the United States had not met with marked success.[48] Such a conference was entirely within the frame of reference

46 SW, Jan. 1920, p. 93   47 *Ibid.*, Aug.-Sept. 1925, p. 221
48 Minutes, Executive, Methodist Board of ESS, 31 March 1920; Minutes, Inter-
   Church Advisory Council, 28 Jan. 1921, 6 May 1921, 18 May 1923

of the council, which included co-ordination in such fields as surveys, simultaneous campaigns for special objects, preparation of common literature, and action for religious and missionary education and community betterment.[49] Five boards of five churches were involved in the structure. Although Methodist Evangelism and Social Service representatives, Chown, Creighton, and J.O. McCarthy, were of a progressive temper, the rest of the council lay to their right. The institutionalism of the Inter-Church Advisory Council was soon apparent in the rejection of the Brotherhood movement, but was obscured by the passionate belief in the incalculable social consequences that would accompany the unification of church efforts.[50] That sin was not permanently in this world was a cardinal belief of evangelicalism and the social gospel. The potent combination of these two dictated a strategy of a massive and disciplined encounter with those forces which withstood the Kingdom of God. This was the strategy which underlay the Inter-Church movement in Canada, and obviously required attack upon employers such as BESCO. It chose as its first task, however, the consolidation of the social, educational, and missionary agencies of the church rather than, as Inter-Church (USA), a frontal assault upon industrial injustice.

If there was some merit in this longer-term outlook, it gave little comfort to workers in distress in Cape Breton or elsewhere. The single joint act of Inter-Church on behalf of these afflicted men, women, and children came in 1925 after appeals for help from the churches in the area. In May 1925 the five churches protested their inability to adjudicate the dispute, but issued appeals for gifts on behalf of the strikers.[51] This was not, however, the only joint or unilateral church effort to aid in solving the problems of the strife-torn community. Presbyterians approached Methodists in May 1920, proposing use of $100,000 of the recent campaign funds to establish a Community or Institutional church there.[52] But this was hardly an adequate approach to so gigantic a problem, and the staff, in perplexity, soon reported inability to do more than touch 'the fringe of our extensive jungle,' let alone 'penetrate, or control or revolutionize' the communities. Therefore, the church had fallen back on an emphasis on education for the children of the area. There did, however, seem to be one answer proposed to the overall problem. The district superintendent of the Maritime Synod of the Presbyterian church pointed to the contrast of the steel and coal towns with that of Imperoyal, the Maritime model

49 Minutes, Executive, Methodist Board of ESS, 23 April 1920; *Canadian Baptist*, 27 May 1920, p. 4

50 *Presbyterian Witness*, 7 June 1919, p. 4. See above, pp. 138, 250–2

51 *Ibid.*, 21 May 1925, p. 1

52 Minutes, Executive, Methodist Board of ESS, 17 March 1920

company town of the Imperial Oil Company.[53] Again the evidence of the new socialized employer masked the real face of power in industrial life.

The Presbyterian, Methodist, and Social Service Council presses gave rather more support and publicity to the workers in their dreadful predicament than did the Inter-Church Advisory Council. The Presbyterian editors declared sympathy with the workers' aims but had difficulty in refraining from lecturing them for not behaving as though the new age were already here.[54] Presbyterian ministers such as A.M. MacLeod and J.H. Hamilton in the area occasionally had to write correcting the editor's repetition of press inaccuracies and company propaganda.[55] These men scored undue attention to a small 'red' element, which, if it complicated the situation a little, did not affect basic issues. The combined ministerial association of Glace Bay and Sydney had protested wage cuts,[56] and the Presbytery of Sydney in 1924 declared BESCO had shown insufficient respect for 'the human element in industry' for the successful undertaking of an industrial enterprise. Its proposal, however, was an industrial council to jointly determine the matters at issue, and the co-operation of corporation and governments to provide adequate housing and sanitation.[57] But despite the Presbytery's hopes, the plain facts were that neither the corporation nor the governments in Halifax or Ottawa had much intention of taking any effective action. The federal government was sharply goaded on the subject by Woodsworth and his associates in Parliament. Ottawa, however, only sent troops on request, and appointed a Royal Commission. The troops seem to have been quite unneeded, and the company had had to scour the countryside for a county judge who would sign the requisition.[58] The commission apparently made no investigation of the financial ability of the company despite widespread belief of stock watering and actual ability to pay higher wages.[59] After receiving the report, the King government declared the matter *ultra vires* the federal government.[60] The company's attitude was evinced by the curious delay of over three months in bringing the steel plant into operation to fill orders placed by the CNR in the midst of a period of six months unemployment which had reduced families to wearing sack clothing and living off mushrooms picked in the woods.[61]

53 *Acts and Proceedings of the Forty-Seventh General Assembly,* 1921, Appendix, pp. 22–4

54 *Presbyterian Witness,* 30 March 1922, p. 12; 31 Aug. 1922, p. 3; 19 July 1923, p. 1; 26 March 1925, p. 1

55 *Ibid.,* 28 Sept. 1922, pp. 18–19; 5 Jan. 1922, pp. 9–11

56 *Ibid.*   57 *Ibid.,* 29 May 1924, pp. 7–8   58 CG, 20 Sept. 1922, pp. 10–11

59 *Ibid.,* 12 April 1922, p. 23; 6 Feb. 1924, p. 8; 5 March 1924, p. 7

60 *Ibid.,* 4 March 1925, p. 3

61 *Ibid.,* 11 March 1925, p. 10; 25 March 1925

The *Christian Guardian* aired these conditions and called for government action, as did William Irvine and J.S. Woodsworth in the House.[62] But, observing pressures for the Social Service Council to make an authoritative pronouncement for the churches, the *Guardian* excused it from doing so by saying that 'the Churches are face to face with the fact that a pronouncement in such a case might easily offend both the Labor forces and the Capitalists.'[63] This was a curious piece of reasoning in a publication that was taking a strong stand on the dispute and in a church that had not hesitated to incur the wrath of the liquor industry. When had it become its policy not to offend with difficult but true sayings? For a possible answer it is instructive to look back at Creighton's first reaction to the Inter-Church report on US Steel. 'Evidently,' he said, 'the heads of the Steel Company are misinformed of the facts of their own business.'[64] The implication seemed to be that a man, especially a Methodist like Judge Gary, head of US Steel, would not knowingly tolerate inhuman conditions if they could be changed. Experience had proved otherwise. In 1925 Creighton was asking how many Christian businessmen in Toronto neglected their Christian duty when paying their workers.[65] Apparently Chown's optimism about the social effects of the Inter-Church campaign in associating influential laymen and a socially conscious pastorate had not proved entirely accurate, not simply because no significant communication had continued, but, Creighton suggested, because powerful leaders of industry lived far from the pastors of the people affected by their power. Creighton's problem seemed not to be that church statements would alienate labour or capital, but that he no longer knew what word the church could speak to either. However, if his urge *was* to preserve influence, he was gaining it at the loss of relevance and the atrophy of the word of judgment.

Whether accepting Creighton's reasoning or not, the Social Service Council did not, in the 1920s, make any pronouncements on the Cape Breton tragedy, despite pressure upon it to do so. It did, however, give space in its publication to trenchant analyses of the Cape Breton situation in 1923 and 1925.[66] An article in the latter year interpreted the workers' condition as 'a brilliant reflection of a system of production and distribution of the world's goods, which allows a group of men to trade on the vital needs of their brethren.' This was direct enough, but how was the situation to be overcome? Archaic party politics were rejected as an answer. 'We must leave old schools and seek new,' counselled the writer, a research worker for the Canadian Brotherhood of Railroad Employees. What constituted the 'new' was

62 *Ibid.*, 4 March 1925, p. 3. See also SW, Aug.-Sept. 1925, pp. 217–18
63 CG, 25 March 1925
64 *Ibid.*, 1 Sept. 1920, p. 4
65 Editorial, CG, 25 April 1925
66 SW, Aug. 1923, pp. 230–2; Aug.-Sept. 1925, pp. 219–24

rather vague beyond an unhesitating probe of the validity of all institutions in terms of 'social ill or well-being.' Thus, in the last analysis, even the trade union researcher remained academic and unengaged.

The Inter-Church council had offered aid to suffering workers, but neither analysis nor proposals of reform. Creighton in the *Guardian* seemed to have lost the voice of prophecy in the situation, and his church, in its statement of 1926, 'Christianiza-tion of Industry,' did not make good that lack.[67] The Social Service Council after 1925 reverted to pragmatic discussions of industrial problems. This transition from prophecy to pragmatism for industry was perhaps sharper than the shift in mood from social service to the new social work, but in both areas it seemed that by 1927 an enchanted world had disappeared and there stood in its place one where actual accomplishment did not realize hopes, nor failure totally end them. Creighton, him-self, in defending the social gospel from critics, gave unwitting expression to the new mood in January 1927:

Social Service is past its first youth and some people are prone to say in these days that the movement for social betterment along Christian lines has failed. In this country they see only the slipping back from prohibition. South of the border they see the diminishing of many a hope for social reform.[68]

What did Creighton see in 1927? In 1910, he observed, the social service depart-ments had no assets, and only 'a dream and a passion,' but in 1926 the institutional means of social service tallied over $90,000 in assets.[69] What, however, had become of the passion – the core of the thrust of the social gospel – he did not say. What was said and unsaid suggested that the crises of the progressive social gospel left the churches in the hands of a combination of business efficiency whose prowess was abetted by the prosperity of the later 1920s and an orthodoxy of social service whose magic had largely fled and whose strategy had been overturned. The proponents of the theology of radical reform in the Student Christian Movement certainly thought so,[70] although they were hardly prepared to argue that half a loaf was not better than none.

It would be easy to simplify the condition of the progressive social gospel in the later 1920s, and to misinterpret the evidences of a new religious mood concerned more with the traditions of religion, the inwardness of the religious life, and the

67 See above, pp. 261–2   68 *New Outlook*, 12 Jan. 1927, p. 19
69 This would not include the institutions once under social service but now under the Board of Home Missions.
70 Davidson Ketchum, 'The Saving of God,' *Canadian Forum*, III, 31 (April 1923), 204–6

concreteness of personal experience. The evidence was there, but it was not un-mixed. The pages of the *Canadian Baptist* suggest that Ontario and Quebec Bap-tists, for instance, with the purging of T.T. Shields and his arch-fundamentalists in 1927, began to show a more unreserved interest in social questions. In 1924 an Alberta School of Religion, organized by progressive preachers associated with H.M. Horricks, began a long series of yearly programmes serving as many as two hundred people each summer with lectures in a liberal religious vein and on social issues of a progressive character.[71] When Woodsworth addressed the school in 1927, some felt his views on the church incorrect, but there was general agreement with his social and political views.[72] No less a person than Principal D.L. Ritchie, of United Theological College, Montreal, could write in 1926 a vigorous defence of the social gospel.[73] And when in 1927 a new interest in church architecture, reli-gious symbolism, and ritual appeared on the pages of the *New Outlook*, the social passion was there to counter it. R.J. Irwin, a young minister whose name was to be better known among the radical Christians of the 1930s, wrote with indignation:

Let us with high resolve declare for the Christianizing of Industry and the cleansing of political and social life ... Let us present Jesus Christ's way of life to men, and beholding him they will need no outward forms and symbols. The man on the street ... will not be won by the mechanics of a church service. He will be won by the appeal of reality only, in this age of shams.[74]

But what communicated reality and what sham, a respondent wondered as he looked out over the variety of 'crazy and grotesque structures' on the religious land-scape.[75] Such a response might well have come from Ernest Thomas, who would have been quick to add that the social concern had not lapsed, but was finding renewal at a deeper level. The representatives of social service had difficulty credit-ing such an assertion, from Thomas at least, and younger radicals like Irwin and older ones like Bland were too suspicious of the new religious mood to accept Thomas' assurances. However, even among the critics of the church progressives from the social gospel strongholds in the SCM, a deeper religious experience was being promoted – radical and uncompromising, to be sure, but, nevertheless with a conscious social reference, and like its counterpart in the churches, born of mid-decade disillusionment.

71 Archives of Saskatchewan, Papers on the Alberta School of Religion, interviews with
the Revs. Stanley Hunt and Arthur Rowe, secretaries of the School; *New Outlook*,
29 Sept. 1926, p. 18

72 *New Outlook*, 21 Sept. 1927, p. 24   73 *Ibid.*, 24 Feb. 1926, p. 6
74 *Ibid.*, 6 July 1927, p. 26   75 *Ibid.*, 10 Aug. 1927, p. 18

19

The Theology of Radical Reform

In 1920 progressive intellectuals in Toronto founded a publication, *The Canadian Forum*, intended to give expression to creative ferment in the arts, literature, and politics. Both older leaders of the social gospel and younger radicals of the SCM contributed to its pages in its early years. This is not to suggest that the association ceased thereafter. There were probably not a few on its subscription list for whom the social gospel was, and continued to be, a primary motivation of progressive activity.

Salem Bland, Henry Wise Wood, Ernest Thomas, and J.S. Woodsworth wrote early articles or reviews on socialism, group politics, reform movements in the church, and progressive opinion in Canada.[1] But the writers who set the religious-philosophical tone of the publication in its first three years were young intellectuals like Margaret Fairley, Mary K. Ingram, Irene Moore, A.J. Duff, H.J. Davis, H.M. Thomas, and especially J. Davidson Ketchum and S. H. Hooke. Although most of their contributions were confined to the first three years, and the incidence of items of a religious character fell off sharply thereafter, whenever such items did appear later in the 1920s they exhibited the same orientation and temper as these 'pioneers.' They may then be said legitimately to represent the theology of radical reform as it lived in the minds of a significant part of the *Forum* constituency.

Several of these writers were associated with the SCM. Ketchum and Hooke were prominent among its leadership and wrote frequently for the *Canadian Student*. That their *Forum* articles dropped in frequency after late 1923 may have been due to professional preoccupations, or to a decision by the editors that the publication had had enough of a good thing. It seems more likely, however, that the priority of pragmatic political and social questions on the one hand, and a crisis in religious belief on the other, were the forces at work in the separation.[2]

The theology of radical reform was a modernist compound of Christianity, Berg-

---

1 *Canadian Forum*, Nov. 1922, pp. 54–6; Dec. 1922, p. 72; Feb. 1923, pp. 140–2; Nov. 1924, pp. 40–2

2 The number of articles and editorials on religious subjects between 1920 and late 1923 was fourteen as against ten for the rest of the decade.

son's creative evolution, and a touch of prometheanism which seemed to derive from Nietzsche. It was a theology which obviously contributed much to the birth of the secularism which attended the decline of social service. Margaret Fairley spoke of a new notion of religion, an attitude, not a creed, one which took account of biology and psychology as well as of the masters, and was always discarding old forms. Its goal was the most energetic personal life, which would revolutionize the human race.[3] Mary Ingram described a 'New Humanism' whose sign and seal was the resurrection of Christ, a position which Irene Moore seemed to accept.[4] Ketchum argued that a new theology needed to take account of the incompleteness of creation as indicated by such signs of further change as the occurrence of genius (an omen of the human future), growing lack of sympathy with the social heritage, and the discovery of evolution itself. It was now possible, he wrote, for one to be conscious of the 'Evolution-impulse,' which was the moral law within, ordering and restraining the voices of hunger and love. However, this 'true Voice of Nature' was not simply negative. Positive form had been given to it by 'the great Pioneer of the Evolutionary Stage.'[5] Hooke, in a mystical and monistic article, 'That One Face,' elaborated Ketchum's point, taking as his twin starting points the discussion of the historical Jesus and the mood of modern science. Relativity theory seemed to place man in an open universe, between 'the natural world and the world of new possibilities.' Jesus was the signpost, pioneer, and demonstrator of this new way. The apocalyptic expectation of Jesus' time was, he said, of a 'new, different and better order of society.' Thus it might be said that 'eschatologists and science meet at the point where Jesus is the pioneer of the realm of the new laws of life.' This new region was open to scientific exploration and its laws interpenetrated those of the physical world.[6]

Ketchum noted that Hooke had ignored the question of God as such, and that it was the 'Saving of God' that was at issue in a world which, under the tutelage of science, was able progressively to replace a capricious supernatural being in every sphere of life.[7] Hooke, in 'A Modern Lay Apologia,' in effect endorsed this replacement of ultimate authority, stating that the appeal to the Bible, councils, even to Jesus was no longer possible, in the traditional sense, because all were the result of historical and natural causes, political intrigues and interpretations. Experience was the only authority for any person. Although he suggested that there was both an historical and a timeless quality to experience, which should have allowed for an accumulation and communication of authoritative experience, Hooke seemed to

3 *Ibid.*, Jan. 1922, pp. 493–5

4 *Ibid.*, May 1922, pp. 621–3; June 1923, pp. 271–2

5 *Ibid.*, Sept. 1922, pp. 749–53

6 *Ibid.*, Dec. 1922, pp. 76–8   7 *Ibid.*, April 1923, pp. 204–6

seal off this possibility by arguing that since the ideas which clothed experience were transitory, experience could not be said to validate the ideas. Perhaps he was taking pains to avoid the pitfalls of idealism, but if there was no timeless way of expressing timeless experience, how could it be known as timeless? Somewhat paradoxically he concluded that, from the standpoint of his apologia, the great figures of religious history become one's fellow travellers.[8] But what of God? 'The true Mass, the body of God, is the universe of knowledge, beauty, order, love.'[9]

Such a person as Hooke found himself in close agreement with Julian Huxley, who argued that the idea of God, that is the idea of the whole of the reality with which man is in contact, would continue to have an important biological function.[10] It was not difficult for Hooke to say, therefore, that Christianity came closest to the requirements for a universal religion set up by Huxley.[11] For religious radicals on the political left it was true, as H.M. Thomas observed, that the historic symbols of the race were in eclipse.[12] They blamed this on the irrationality of contemporary industry and political society, on the self-centredness of modern art, on the smooth combination in the churches of social service and business efficiency. But while their criticism was not entirely incorrect at these points they were not aware of the degree of their own subscription to irrationality in 'evolutionism' in the name of science. In their trinity, they seemed to cast the totality of experience as God, the 'evolution-impulse' as the Holy Spirit, and they wished to see Jesus as the Christ who revealed the evolutionary way to them. They were genuinely grieved that 'the Church ... can have no Christ but the Christ of the theologians; irrespective apparently of whether this is the Christ to heal a troubled world, and raise mankind nearer the Divine ...'[13]

There were some among subscribers who criticized these writers for calling falsely in the name of science for an impossible worship of an impersonal life force. Science, they pointed out, had nothing to do with the 'tender things' with which it was being so generously associated.[14] But when such articles did not appear in 1923–4, there were those who missed the 'amiable disputations.'[15]

However, the discussions were not so much disputations as variations on a theme.

8 *Ibid.*, Aug. 1923, pp. 335–6   9 *Ibid.*, March 1923, pp. 168–70
10 *Ibid.*, Dec. 1924, p. 81   11 *Ibid.*, Jan. 1925, pp. 110–12
12 *Ibid.*, July 1923, pp. 302–4
13 J. Duff, 'The Saving of Religion,' *ibid.*, Oct. 1923, pp. 13–14. See also W. Harvie-Jellie, 'Difficulties in the Way of a Young Man's Faith,' *Presbyterian Witness*, 22 Feb. 1923, p. 5
14 F.H. Brewin, Donald D. McKay, and F.J. Moore to the editor, *Canadian Forum*, May 1923. At least two of these were Anglican and Moore was general secretary of the scm at Toronto.
15 E. Wyly Grier to the editor, *ibid.*, Feb. 1924

They were unanimous in their rejection of the old gods and the old generation, and almost at one in their description of the new theology. It represented more than youthful reaction, and even more (or less?) than the search for a fuller religious expression.[16] It was a way to a new social order.

It was one consequence of this social evolutionary theology that the SCM quite self-consciously looked upon itself as a 'movement' and not as an institution. It interpreted its being in terms not unlike those of the *Forum* writers. After all, many of them were among its leaders. It was concerned with 'reality,' not 'form'; its international character represented new world possibilities. It had, as its leaders declared, been part of one of the few international organizations to survive the war.[17] It had a part in initiating the World Student Relief programme[18]; it was in touch with the thinking of students around the world, especially in Britain, the United States, Poland, and China.[19] Surely the movement was a thing of great promise. In the words of one of its leaders, 'nothing short of a new world order [was] involved in its ultimate expression.'[20]

This view of the movement meshed the study of Jesus and the theology of radical reform. The SCM followed one who turned 'from the blandishments of a "career," ' to attempt 'to remake, single-handed, the world according to his own ideas.' He was put out of the way by the 'interests' along with a couple of rogues, 'but the s.c.m. believes that Young Man was right and the "interests" were wrong; it believes, too, that avowal of his principles is scarce less deadly now than then ...'[21]

16 Ernest Thomas, 'Insurgent Movements in the Church,' *ibid.*, Feb. 1923, pp. 140–2

17 *Canadian Student*, Oct. 1922, special international issue. The SCM inherited this publication from the Council of Canadian Student organizations. It was kept going through the 1920s with considerable difficulty. It was edited by E.H. Clarke, national general secretary from 1921–5. In 1923 an editorial board was set up. Although Clarke was editor, others, especially Davidson Ketchum, contributed editorials during this period. From 1925–7, H.N.C. Avison edited the magazine from Montreal. Isobel Thomas, later secretary to the League for Social Reconstruction, was appointed to follow Avison. She remained on the board when F.J. Moore took up the post in late 1928. The magazine was considered a forum of discussion and news and not an official mouthpiece of the movement.

18 *Ibid.*

19 *Ibid.*, Dec. 1922, pp. 8–9

20 R. DeWitt Scott, 'The Student Christian Movement in Canada,' *Presbyterian Witness*, 7 Sept. 1922, pp. 10–12. Scott was SCM secretary at McGill University.

21 Editorial, *Canadian Student*, Oct. 1921, pp. 5–6. See Edward Trelawney [Ernest Thomas], 'The Christian Students are Moving,' CG, 26 Oct. 1921, p. 13

There was more than a slight promethean spirit in the movement's approach to the problems of setting the world right. God, as most Christians understood him, was not so much use to them as Mr Wells' 'Captain of the World Republic' who, 'amidst the darkness and confusions, the nightmare stupidities, and the hideous cruelties of the great war, fought his way to Empire.'[22] It sometimes seemed that still more preferable was the God to whom thanks could be given for leaving his world incomplete, so that man could undertake its completion. There seemed to be a mandate rather than a condemnation in Jesus' words that, since John, 'The Kingdom of Heaven is taken forcibly and the violent drag it toward them.'[23] Despite recent catastrophe, history was not the endless rolling of a Sisyphean stone, and it was not the part of men of faith to surrender to pessimism, but to 'set themselves into the current of events and find fresh opportunities for dragging in the Kingdom.'[24]

Although some castigated the old world in its ease for believing in the evolutionary coming of the kingdom, the most vocal students and leaders of the movement utilized the same concept in a more activist cast, and interpreted the kingdom in terms of 'the evolution of humanity ... towards the higher and universal type of society where the energies now dissipated in enmity (and sin in all its forms) will be conserved in a correspondingly higher quality of insight, achievement and experience ...'[25]

Both the mood and theology of the SCM[26] alarmed many in the churches.[27] However, the leadership of the social gospel in Canada found nothing to condemn in it. Salem Bland, Ernest Thomas, W.B. Creighton, and Richard Roberts[28] may have brought more profundity and subtlety in their counsels to the movement, but they endorsed the new adventure in terms remarkably like those above. Bland, for

22 Editorial, *Canadian Student*, March 1919, pp. 1ff
23 *Ibid.*, Feb. 1921, pp. 9–12. The source of this wording is not given.
24 *Ibid.*   25 *Ibid.*, March 1921, pp. 11–14
26 It must be pointed out that the *Canadian Student* was a forum for debate, not for the expression of official views of the SCM. However, the editorial board was in the hands of responsible officers of the movement. Care has been taken not to use student articles if they did not substantially reflect either the views held by those in leadership positions or prevalent opinion in the SCM publication.
27 *Canadian Churchman*, 21 Dec. 1922, pp. 836–7; 3 Jan. 1924, p. 5. CG, 30 Aug. 1922, p. 4
28 *Ibid.*, 19 July 1922, p. 6; *Canadian Student*, Dec. 1922, pp. 6–8; Oct. 1923, pp. 7–9. Roberts, in 1922, was the new Welsh pacifist minister of American Presbyterian Church, Montreal.

instance, argued, with a significant twist in his reasoning, that just as ancient science had been used to express the religious insight of the Hebrews, so might modern science offer insights to serve religion.[29] Roberts' numerous addresses to SCM units utilized the categories of evolutionary science to 'interpret' biblical theology and the biblical hope for society.[30] When Sherwood Eddy, idol of student movements around the world, addressed the students of Toronto, he presented a 'carefully thought out analysis of the world's need for a new and spiritualized society, in which each individual might forget himself, his desires, yes, and his own soul also, and simply give himself to the spirit of life as one unit of the one great fellowship.'[31] Well might Edis Fairbain, himself a radical and pacifist Methodist, write asking whether there was, in fact, a *student* movement!

The outlook of the SCM progressives and radicals clearly dovetailed with the social, political, and economic aims of those associated in the *Canadian Forum*. Rejection of traditional authorities in church and society led Hooke to sympathize with workers who turned to socialism and criticized the church for alliance with the vested interests. 'The frank confession of those in the Church who really care is that he is right.'[32] The editor of the *Canadian Student* interpreted 'reconstruction' in Canada as requiring a good deal of pulling down.[33] In 1921, the pulling down and reconstruction not having taken place, he foresaw only a future of economic 'boom and bust.'[34] With an election in the offing, articles in 1921, one of them by Ernest Thomas, urged students to view their interests and outlook as identical with those of the Progressive party.[35] When the Fellowship for a Christian Social Order was formed in the United States in 1923 under the chairmanship of Sherwood Eddy, the editors of the *Canadian Student* were eager to call to the attention of readers the founding of an organization dedicated to

the creation of a social order, the Kingdom of God on Earth, wherein the maximum

29 *Canadian Churchman*, 30 July 1925, p. 485

30 SCM Archives, Minutes, General Committee of the SCM, 2–3 Jan. 1924; CG, 11 Oct. 1922, p. 21. *Canadian Student*, Nov. 1924, p. 51. Later in the decade Roberts put this together in a book, *The New Man and the Divine Society*. A reviewer in the *Canadian Student*, in speaking of Roberts' work, said, in 'four swinging strides [he] carries the reader from the amoeba to the Kingdom of God' (*Canadian Student*, Jan. 1927, p. 123). This reminds one of Bland's title to his first lecture on socialism, 1897, 'Four Steps and a Vision.'

31 *Canadian Student*, Nov. 1923, pp. 54–5

32 *Ibid.*, Nov. 1918, pp. 18ff

33 *Ibid.*, Jan. 1919, pp. 1–2

34 *Ibid.*, Nov. 1921, pp. 1–2

35 See above, p. 214

opportunity shall be afforded for the development and enrichment of every human personality, in which the supreme motive shall be love; wherein men shall co-operate in service for the common good; and brotherhood shall be a reality in all the daily relationships of life.

To this end the fellowship would attack luxury, concentration of power and privilege, autocratic control of industry, production for individual profit and power, all race, class and national antagonism, and war.[36] It was in line with criticism of the Canadian social and economic order and in sympathy with the newly founded fellowship that the editor of the *Canadian Student*, observing the new Labour government in England, announced a close relationship between 'real thinking and radicalism.'[37]

Almost coincidentally with the sharp decline in religious articles in the *Forum*, the religious thought of the scm leadership entered a period of crisis. For some it was a slow process, for others, a sudden rending of the veil. A period of introspection began, which was quite general by 1926.[38] An attempted rejuvenation in the winter of 1926–7 failed, and with a dogged persistence the leadership cultivated its garden, reassessed the nature of the movement, and prepared for the day when once again 'an angel would trouble the waters.'

The immediate cause of disillusionment was the Indianapolis Convention of the Student Volunteer movement of North America in the winter of 1923–4. The Student Volunteer movement was an interdenominational organization for the promotion of missionary service by students. Its conventions were large and enthusiastic. For many delegates, apparently, the Indianapolis experience had created a sense of higher purpose and greater determination. But the editor of the *Canadian Student* briefly told of another reaction:

There were, however, some who, oversanguine as to what might have been happening 'underground' since 1919, were led to dream of things taking place at Indianapolis which it is now clear could not in cold reason have been expected.[39]

The scm round of summer conferences in 1924 seemed to leaders to confirm the fact that a new student generation that knew not the passion of the New Jerusalem but would be at ease in Zion had succeeded to the universities. Both the leadership

36 *Ibid.*, March 1923, p. 26   37 Feb. 1924, p. 131
38 scm Archives, Minutes, Quebec and Ontario Presidents' Conference, 21–2 Nov.
   1925
39 *Canadian Student*, Feb. 1924, pp. 156–7

and 'friends' of the movement felt it their right to ask that students 'be inwardly eager to answer life's deepest question.' For the SCM to yield to the temptation of American civilization to gloss over the hard and puzzling facts of life, it was suggested, would be to cease to be a true student movement.[40] But even these had to admit that it was unreasonable to expect of this student generation what others had failed to accomplish. The new generation was averse to both the activism of reform and missions and to the heady brews of Hooke, Ketchum, and company.[41] 'It is well for eager reformers to recognize,' the latter wrote, 'that they will not dance to our frenzied piping.'[42]

The prophet of this new period in the life of the SCM, however, was the same Davidson Ketchum. At first, in resignation, he wrote of the inevitable rhythm of life, a wave of conservatism, a breathing space. But in a series of articles and replies to critics throughout 1924–5, he worked out the beginnings of a new standpoint for himself and the SCM. Neither his thought nor his anguish easily reached students at large in the movement, and even some of the leaders were perplexed. Wanting a copy of one of his talks to a University of Toronto group, the editor of the *Canadian Student* light-heartedly reported that seventy-four of the seventy-five present could not recall what the subject was, the seventy-fifth had been unable to hear, and Ketchum had forgotten!

He began his reconstructive articles with a short but difficult piece on 'A God-Forsaken World.'[43] Ketchum seemed obviously God-forsaken in his disillusionment. He was aware of, and rejected, reassurance by pat theories which saw the experience as a testimony to free will, or a test of patience. The one comfort was that Jesus, too, had experienced God-forsakenness:

On the same dark foundation of despair on which we stood, and on no other, he had built, through faith and love of men, a divine, immortal fabric ... Where God had failed a man had conquered.[44]

Critics replied that he was making too much of the idea. They asked whether Jesus was deluded prior to his last minute experience of God-forsakenness. The general secretary of the national movement, E.H. Clarke, wrote that no records tell of a Jesus whose experience would bear out Ketchum's article. And one comforter explained that Ketchum was trying to say that we are forsaken by the God of our inadequate ideas, but never by the real God.[45]

Ketchum in turn replied that he was indeed referring to 'the traditional God,'

40 *Ibid.*, Oct. 1924, p. 5
42 *Ibid.*, Dec. 1924, p. 68
44 *Ibid.*, Feb. 1924, pp. 148–9

41 *Ibid.*, March 1920, p. 168
43 *Ibid.*, Feb. 1924, pp. 148–9
45 *Ibid.*, March 1924, pp. 166–72, 191–2

and in particular to two attributes: that God is a person who can do what he wants; and that God can be counted on to 'look after' those who trust in him in a real physical way. Bertrand Russell's already famous phrase, Ketchum said, described the experience of that God getting up and leaving. That Ketchum's experience was real, his critics and his comforter seemed to ignore. In the crisis, he was not sure of even 'the real God,' or of Jesus' teaching about God. But he was captivated by Jesus' life of 'utter faith and self-giving': 'tho' all else fall, that will stand firm.'[46]

Ketchum and Hooke seemed to do their thinking together. In March 1925 Hooke wrote an article on the liberty of the Christian life, basing it on Ketchum's recent writing. This in turn opened the way for Ketchum to relate his experience to the SCM. The purpose of the movement, he concluded, was to contribute directly to the gradual metamorphosis of 'our present "pagan" society' into that 'realm of free souls' which Hooke described:

This radical development is not hastened merely by the production of engineers who disbelieve in the virgin birth [nor] enthusiasts who have tried out Christian Ethics in Business and discovered that 'it's a fact, man, profits actually *increase* ...' A million such ... will still lie powerless to do more than look on in perpetual distress while the world is controlled by greater and ever more sinister forces of tyranny and greed. Humanity will not believe in what it cannot see; faith in the possibility of a new order will never be evoked except by the joy and suffering of those who are visibly living in it here and now ... The power to live thus is not cheaply won ...[47]

Could the SCM become such a new community? By 1926 there was a resurgence of interest in the personal aspects of religion in the movement, but often this meant 'enjoying the quiet, thoughtful study of the life of Jesus' and wondering whether 'anything with such an individualistic aim [should be called] by such a collective term' as 'movement.'[48] Not for such was Ketchum's sober vision.

Ketchum and Hooke probably represented a minority in the SCM. But when the General Committee met in January 1926, it was equally clear that they also marked a general tendency in the movement. The most important decision of the meeting was to schedule a national conference for the next winter in order to 'think out the practicability of the ideals of Jesus and the implications of the Christian way of life for group living with particular reference to the National life of Canada.'[49]

46 *Ibid.*, March 1924, pp. 166–72

47 *Ibid.*, March 1925, p. 163

48 *Ibid.*, March 1926, p. 168. See also Nov. 1924, p. 51 for a report on Richard Roberts' presentation of personal religion to a camp of the BC unit.

49 SCM Archives, Minutes, General Committee of the SCM of Canada, 2–3 Jan. 1926

In March, Helen R.H. Nichol, national educational secretary, honed the purpose to a sharper edge by asking a series of searching questions around the central query, 'Can a Group follow Jesus?' Is there a group anywhere, she asked, that has ever adopted and stood behind 'a recognizably "Christian" attitude to a social or political problem in Canada or in any country?'

It is not, 'Will Jesus' demonstration of life work?'; it is 'Has it *ever* worked? Does it work?' 'Is it practicable for group living in the relations of human experience?' ... For five years we have studied Jesus ... I should like to see a small conference of students who have done enough study and following of Jesus to understand him, consider together whether Jesus' life is any answer to this problem.[50]

Such questions went straight to the root of the justification of a social gospel. Discussion of the conference was still more pointed at the September meeting of the General Committee. Proposed questions for the conference were 'How may an individual express in our present systems the truth that he finds in Jesus?' 'Is the disharmony which many individuals feel between themselves and these systems contrary to the teaching of Jesus, or to the impracticability of that teaching, or to something in the individuals themselves.'[51]

Here was no echo of the great call to build the city of God that had summoned the national conference of 1922–3, but rather a manifestation of perplexity and basic reconsiderations. A question mark was clearly being etched in 1926 above the synthesis of the studies of the life of Jesus and the social gospel. Significantly, the conference of 1927–8 was not to be open, but inclusive of members only. The title of the conference study book, *Man at Odds with His Society*,[52] suggests the Niebuhrian phrases of neo-orthodoxy, such as 'Moral Man and Immoral Society,' that were shortly to mark the break-up of the continuities of the old social gospel in America, and herald the emergence of a new, more radical and realistic social Christianity. That end was not in sight in 1926 and 1927, and several possible courses lay open. Part of the SCM constituency was shortly to find a more congenial home in the Inter-Varsity Christian Fellowship, a more conservative organization that moved onto Canadian campuses from the United States in 1928. This represented a development on the other extreme from the position of Ketchum and Hooke, yet the implications of both were very similar – a vital renewal of the relationship of religion and social reform would have to be mediated by a new sectarian community, a deepened religious experience, and a more profound social under-

50 *Canadian Student*, March 1926, pp. 165–6
51 SCM Archives, Minutes of the General Committee, 24–26 Sept. 1926
52 SCM of Canada, *Man at Odds with His Society*

standing. These were the issues that moved to the centre of SCM concern as a sense of crisis in its concepts broke into full awareness in 1926.

That the expression of postwar disillusionment was more extreme in the leadership of the SCM than in other movements of the social gospel was probably due to two major factors. First, the immediate postwar student generation was one that had had first-hand experience with war, and sometimes seemed consumed with the belief that they were the bringers of a new order. How many times had they been told this? On what basis could they justify their terrible deeds in war? However, student generations change more quickly than any. The leaders who emerged in the first postwar years found themselves facing an entirely different student body by 1923–4. The potential for disillusionment was combined with a situation geared to its maximum impact. The likelihood of a deeper confrontation with the problem of meaning may have been built more into the circumstances of the SCM leadership than those of the leaders of any other of the movements of the social gospel.

There were probably other reasons as well. The social outlook of the other movements was based largely on older and other traditions. The conservative social gospel in the church could always fall back on its evangelical background of moral reform. The progressive wing was heavily influenced by the environmentalism of reform Darwinism. The older radicals had both of these in their bones, but added an element of revisionist Marxism. These were established ways of thinking. They had been appropriated by the social gospel as part of its apologia, and substantial communities of endeavour lay behind them. This was not so true of Bergson's creative evolution or Nietzsche's heroic alienation, which seemed to characterize the Forum writers. On these counts such persons were in a more exposed position. Their disillusionment being more radical, they were perhaps in a position to engage in a more creative reconsideration of the social gospel. Whether they would or not remained to be seen.

The immediate effect of this crisis in the SCM, however, was to bring a degree of disengagement of religious thought from the reform forces associated in the Canadian Forum. This reflected in another way what had occurred to the Labour churches, to the New Christianity and the New Evangelism, and to the gospel of social service. In the experience of most, if not all, phases of the social gospel in Canada, social and religious exigencies were forcing asunder what the social gospel in God's name had put together. Just as the social crisis posed the question of the nature of the world of social, economic, and political life, so the crises of the 'religion of the new age' questioned the very nature of religion and its relation to social existence.

20

The Resurgence of Pacifism

The resurgence of pacifism and peace movements in Canada after 1922 was in part a reassertion of the social gospel concern for the international order, once more showing signs of crisis, and at the same time a sublimation of the crisis in the social gospel's prospectus for Canadian society. The major thrusts of the peace issue, beginning in 1923–4, and again after 1926, coincided with the low points of disillusionment in the ranks of the social gospel. Consequently, its contribution to the creation of an adequate Christian peace programme and to the formulation of a viable Christian ethic in international relations was an equivocal one. In diverting a large part of the social gospel from absorbing the meaning of the crisis experiences, the peace movement served neither itself nor the social gospel. However, as in the wake of the prohibition defeats there was, in the person of Ernest Thomas, an engagement of a social gospel mind with the issues of peace and war which pointed to the birth of a new, more realistic social gospel.

It must have been a shock to J.S. Woodsworth to read a cover message from the editor in the 20 February 1924 issue of the *Christian Guardian* announcing that 'for the future many of us are ready to say that, if God will grant us grace to live up to our present determination and ideal, never again, under any condition, will war have our sanction and blessing.' The editor, W.B. Creighton, had been author of the editorial on pacifist ministers in May 1918 that Woodsworth had felt read him out of the church.[1] Now Creighton was announcing his conversion to the cause. Woodsworth and others who had suffered for their beliefs during the war might have been pardoned if they felt a twinge of skepticism. Douglas Hemmeon, a pacifist in Wolfville, Nova Scotia, who had paid a price for his pacifism in 1914, wrote asking for a reasoned statement of how the editor had reached this position.[2]

The question was a valid one, for neither Creighton in his editorials nor contributors to his publication had shown any recent evidence of agonizing thought over international questions. In this the *Guardian* was not untypical of the Protestant press in

1 See above, p. 49   2 CG, 2 April 1924, p. 12

Canada. In the first three years of peace it had carried very little discussion of international questions. Understandably, most of what little appeared was on such subjects as the attitude of the allies to the defeated powers, the League, and the International Disarmament Conference in Washington, 1921. Presbyterian publications were the most optimistic and forgiving in temper. With regard to a defeated Germany, only the *Presbyterian and Westminster* suggested that the allies might adopt a vengeful attitude that would need restraining.[3] Forgiveness could be given too lightly, they all counselled, and none at first protested the scale of reparations imposed by the peace conference.[4] Only the Presbyterian publications urged sound reasons against allied punishment of war criminals.[5]

All of the publications viewed the creation of a League of Nations favourably, and there even seemed to be general agreement that such a league should have the power to impose its decisions on recalcitrant nations.[6] However, Henry Moyle had a difficult time interesting the Baptist church in Ontario and Quebec on the question.[7] Chown, as Methodist superintendent, urged that a unit of the League of Nations Society be established in each congregation. There is no record of this becoming a widespread practice,[8] but on the view that the League was part of the gospel of the kingdom, such a unit had a rightful place in congregational structure.[9] A buoyant belief among Protestant editors that President Wilson would triumph in the contest with the Senate over ratification was shattered in dismay.[10] Some progressive churchmen had proposed to bring a degree of Canadian influence to bear on the scales. Moyle was in touch with the Methodist Board, urging heavy general church propaganda to this end.[11] Methodists responded to the extent of asking the

3 26 Sept. 1918, pp. 279–80; 7 Nov. 1918, p. 417

4 CG, 11 Sept. 1918, p. 5; 25 Sept. 1918, p. 5; 27 Nov. 1918, p. 3. *Presbyterian Witness*, 5 July 1919, p. 1; 24 Jan. 1920, p. 1. *Christian Messenger*, Dec. 1918, p. 4. *Western Methodist Recorder*, March 1920, p. 8

5 *Presbyterian and Westminster*, 12 Feb. 1920, p. 162; *Presbyterian Witness*, 3 Nov. 1921, p. 5

6 *Hamilton Spectator*, 17 Oct. 1918; CG, 11 Dec. 1918, p. 5; *Canadian Churchman*, 16 Dec. 1920, p. 816

7 *Canadian Baptist*, 10 April 1924, p. 3. Maritime Baptists, by contrast, were remarkably international in outlook.

8 CG, 8 Nov. 1922, p. 19

9 *Ibid.*; *Presbyterian and Westminster*, 26 Dec. 1918, p. 587

10 CG, 12 March 1919, 2 April 1919; *Presbyterian Witness*, 26 July 1919, p. 1; 22 Nov. 1919, p. 1; 29 Nov. 1919, p. 1

11 Minutes, Executive, Methodist Board of ESS, 21 Aug. 1921

government for a pamphlet to circulate, and Chown had forcefully argued for the League at the Methodist centenary in Columbus, Ohio, in July 1919.[12] The Anglican Council for Social Service, following the lead of the Lambeth Conference of 1920, devoted the May 1921 issue of the *Bulletin* to lengthy consideration and strong support of the League as an organization which 'applies to international relationships, principles and lines of action which derive their sanction and authority from the truths of Christianity.'

By far the greatest coverage of the League and international questions until 1923 was in the Presbyterian publications. But their interest was at first greater than that of the General Assembly of 1920 which, having taken the trouble to set up a committee on international affairs, perfunctorily passed a motion supporting the League at the end of proceedings. The Assembly was duly rapped on the knuckles and mended its ways in succeeding years.[13] The Presbyterian press probably reflected other denominational viewpoints in urging caution about German membership in the League.[14] But they were the first of the publications to point out clearly that the Allies could not be absolved of all responsibility for the war. No nation, it was argued in June 1920, had seriously attempted to create a new international order before the war. Now some were talking again of preparation for the next war, but surely the last war had punctured the fallacy 'that military preparedness was a guarantee of peace.'[15] In January 1923 the *Presbyterian Witness* was calling for moves in the direction of cancelling war debts.[16] However, all these positions had been anticipated by the liberal church press in the United States by 1919 and 1920.[17]

Although there had been dismay in the church press over the bickering of the Peace Conference and the failure of the United States to join the League, hopes were lifted high by the call to the International Conference on Disarmament, to

12 CG, 30 July 1919, pp. 7, 8, 21–2

13 *Presbyterian and Westminster*, 1 July 1920, p. 6; *Presbyterian Acts and Proceedings*, 1920, pp. 106–7; see also 1921, pp. 100–1; 1922, pp. 20, 23; 1923, p. 105 and Appendix, pp. 305–6; 1924, p. 60. The General Board Report of 1923 was the fullest statement of the assembly, urging joint church support of the League of Nations Society and the formation of a league of Christian churches to back up the League of Nations itself.

14 *Presbyterian and Westminster*, 15 Aug. 1918, p. 147

15 *Ibid.*, 3 June 1920, p. 551

16 25 Jan. 1923, pp. 4–5, echoing proposals of Dr Herbert Gray of Great Britain in a work, *The Christian Adventure*.

17 Miller, *American Protestantism and Social Issues, 1919–1939*, pp. 318–19

meet in Washington in the fall of 1921. The event was followed with great interest. Special prayers and services were offered for its success on the week of 6–11 November.[18] Chown spoke for the reaction of all church leaders to the progress of the conference when, in his New Year's message 1922, he hailed the 'emergence of the principles of Christianity in international affairs as evidenced by the Washington decisions to forsake deeply cherished national ambitions.'[19] The churches could claim to have had a role in initiating the conference. Four large Protestant, Catholic, and Jewish organizations in the United States had urged such a conference the previous spring. They had sent letters to 100,000 congregations asking them to write President Harding and Congress, and called a conference in May to work out plans for an international disarmament conference.[20] The period leading up to the calling of the international conference itself, the months of the conference, and the problem of Senate ratification, were all marked by intense and co-ordinated activity by religious bodies, the church press, and the Church Peace Union, and the World Alliance for International Friendship through the Churches.[21] By and large Canadian church activity reflected this campaign in the United States.[22]

Reactions to the accomplishments of the conference were somewhat diverse among Canadian churchmen. An Anglican columnist, 'Spectator,' in the *Churchman*, saw it as a long step nearer permanent peace, but sentimentally observed that those who had guarded the seas 'may now be summarily dismissed unwept and unsung.'[23] Ernest Thomas wrote to caution against 'too facile an optimism ... Disarmament awaits the resolution of those conflicting interests which lead to national armaments.'[24] The *Guardian* quoted Professor G.M. Wrong's unenthusiastic approval of the conference,[25] and noted, regarding the ban on poison gas, that the Hague Conference of 1907 had done likewise,[26] but that had not prevented German use of poison gas during the past war. This hardheaded response among Methodists was in contrast to the Presbyterian endorsation of both the results and the method of the conference.[27] The enthusiasm of the editor of the *Presbyterian Witness* was heightened by the memory of prewar intrigues of armament manu-

18 *Canadian Churchman*, 27 Oct. 1921, p. 647; 3 Nov. 1921, p. 659; CG, 12 Oct. 1921, p. 12; *Presbyterian Witness*, 20 Oct. 1921

19 *Western Methodist Recorder*, Jan. 1922

20 *Presbyterian Witness*, 26 May 1921, p. 5

21 Miller, *American Protestantism and Social Issues*, pp. 328–9

22 *Presbyterian Witness*, 20 April 1922, pp. 4–5

23 29 Dec. 1921, p. 790

24 CG, 26 Oct. 1921, p. 4

25 *Ibid.*, 8 Feb. 1922, p. 7

26 *Ibid.*, 25 Jan. 1922, p. 3

27 *Presbyterian Witness*, 16 Feb. 1922, p. 3

facturers, whose influence, the conference's success suggested, was at a low ebb.[28] That the Washington agreement contained no means of enforcement seemed no problem to the *Presbyterian Witness*. If anything, the voluntary agreement of the member nations of the conference may have seemed a more hopeful sign than any accord pressed by forces of collective security. Had not the international conference evinced a fundamental change in the world's mind regarding war and armaments? This, certainly, was the level at which the church peace agencies pressed their campaign in the 1920s. No government, it was argued time and again, could act in advance of public opinion. World leaders like Lloyd George called on the churches to create a climate propitious to successful peace negotiations.[29] Thus, while church support for the League did not alter during the decade following the war, this emphasis on their peculiar task led to uncritical enthusiasm for voluntary accords outside the framework of collective security. It followed that Locarno, for instance, was 'a very significant triumph of goodness and of real Christian spirit.'[30] This approach was not altogether wrong. Voluntary agreement was better than none, and not all nations were members of the League. But the churches were too optimistic about the significance of such successes. There were not many during the decade; and none was as significant in its accomplishment or hope as that of 1921. Certainly no later conference prior to 1928 elicited a response equal to that of the Washington Conference.

Anxiety for the peace of the world, however, was not long assured by the Washington Conference. In early 1922, C.W. Gordon, moderator of the Presbyterian Assembly, wrote from Europe to the Inter-Church Advisory Council that international distrust and bitterness were rife and likely to cause the failure of the Genoa Economic Conference, meeting to deal with European economic problems.[31] The conference did fail in its purpose, although, in a development not pleasing to the allies, German and Russian representatives reached an accord embodied in the Treaty of Rapallo. The internal derangement of European political life was evinced by Mussolini's bloodless coup of November, although only the *Guardian* detected a serious threat in the fascist movement,[32] and by military revolt in Spain the next year, which ended constitutional government there. Tension rose to a new height in early 1923 with the French occupation of the Ruhr. In the church press, only the

28 *Ibid.*, 24 Nov. 1921, p. 6
29 To the Copenhagen conference of the World Alliance for International Friendship through the Churches, *Presbyterian Witness*, 5 Oct. 1922, pp. 4–5
30 *New Outlook*, 28 Oct. 1925, p. 3
31 Minutes, Inter-Church Advisory Council, 4 May 1922
32 CG, 8 Nov. 1922, p. 3. *Presbyterian Witness*, 4 Aug. 1922, p. 4; 9 Nov. 1922

Western Methodist Recorder with characteristic anti-Germanism blamed German duplicity for this event.[33] The *Witness* saw the whole sequence of action and counter action in the Ruhr as evidence of the self-defeating character of insistence upon payment of excessive reparation demands.[34] Paradoxically, however, as postwar international relations moved from crisis to crisis in Western Europe, Turkey, China, the Balkans, and the near East in the years following 1921, comment on such questions went into a decline in all publications except the *Christian Guardian* and the *Canadian Student*.

On the basis of the wartime and the postwar record, Creighton's leap to the van of Canadian pacifism was hardly to be expected. It must be said in his defence, however, that both he and his paper exhibited pacifist inclinations prior to the war. As his church had been since 1884, he was a proponent of international arbitration. He had attacked arms makers and urged Canada to withdraw from the arms race and become an advocate of 'a broader and more Christian internationalism.'[35] A 'climax of national folly' had been his comment in August on the outbreak of war. His early reluctance to support a defensive war, however, soon evaporated. In 1918 he was prepared, editorially, to read any dissent regarding the war entirely out of the pulpits of the church.[36] Now, in 1924, was a time for regretting all that. But the tragedy lay not so much in the need for regret as in the failure of the experience to produce a more penetrating re-examination of the ethics of war.

When Creighton came to make his 'reasoned statement' as to the basis of his pacifist declaration, his reply left much to be desired. Honest to the point of being unjust to his own past, he was also forthright in declaring that not so much theological or political considerations as 'the disillusioning process going on since the war' had led him to his position. All that the war had not been, rather than 'a study of Jesus' attitude and teaching as to non-resistance,' had persuaded him. Despite the foregoing, apparently, he could say that it was in the confrontation of the 'whole issue of war' with Christian teaching, especially with 'the great idea of the founding of the Kingdom of God on earth ... that convictions have been formed that cannot be laid aside.'[37] The new orthodoxy of the social gospel, apparently,

33 Sept. 1923, p. 8   34 26 July 1923, p. 1

35 CG, 28 Jan., 15 April 1914. For Methodist attitudes to the war see Bliss, 'The Methodist Church and World War I,' pp. 213–33; on the war and after, Schwartz, 'Samuel Dwight Chown,' pp. 207–18; and for a more extended commentary on the history of Methodist international attitudes, see Royce, 'The Contribution of the Methodist Church to Social Welfare in Canada.'

36 See above, p. 49   37 CG, 9 April 1924, pp. 4–5

obviated the need to wrestle with the difficult problems which vexed the 'whole issue of war.'

As the controversy developed, however, Creighton was forced to refine his thinking further. Later in the year, confronted by defenders of the past war and the wisdom of preparedness, he argued that these traditional concepts were outdated and could only be defended in the most general and academic way. Modern war 'ended nothing that was evil but it did make everything that was good more difficult of achievement.' Hence to talk of preparedness and defensive wars was futile. Furthermore, painful experience had taught himself and others that war had the 'facility ... of making itself look like what it isn't,' and they refused to let it 'paint black white for them' again.[38]

A year later Creighton repeated the same argument.[39] Whether he clearly saw its logical conclusion of passive resistance may be doubted, for he shortly was impressed by a cogent article in the *Christian Century* criticizing absolute pacifism, first, because it was impossible for any person to separate himself completely from complicity in the actions of the state; second, because the writer could not argue that it would be wrong to fight for the oppressed, for justice, or for the defence of one's country; and third, because in a democracy the proper way to deal with a bad law and the surest way to reform was not by personal or collective disobedience but by educating the public mind.[40] His lack of commentary in a lengthy editorial may well betray the unsettling effect of the article. As a social gospeller he could hardly deny the first point. The second he let pass without comment, although it was the one on which he had said most to date. The third, on the priority of the educational process, drew his complete assent. Introducing long excerpts from the article, he had stated the alternatives before those agonizing about their proper response should another great war face them – whether to adopt absolute pacifism 'even going to the length of passive resistance,' or to co-operate in the defence of one's country 'while seeking peaceful measures for the recognition of national rights and the settlement of international disputes.' Having posed the alternatives himself, Creighton clearly was not choosing passive resistance – although just as clearly he was not admitting this in so many words. It may be significant that he did not repeat his resolution again in the 1920s, but the trend of his recent thinking – even within the editorial itself – was away from the appropriate response to a hypothetical war and toward the best means to avert any future war. Whether or not he had come to recognize that in their own way they were as academic as the thesis of the just war, repeated declarations in the manner of February 1924 would hardly of

38 *Ibid.*, 3 Sept. 1924, p. 4   39 *New Outlook*, 9 Sept. 1925, p. 3
40 *Ibid.*, 7 Oct. 1925, p. 4

themselves avert war if the public at large were not persuaded. For that task education was the prime necessity. Creighton was convinced that, at least in part, war was a state of mind, and was probably impressed with evidence that educators were now earnestly undertaking to educate the public mind for peace.[41] Believing in the efficacy of education and trusting a responsible system of government to faithfully reflect the public mind, he simply slipped away from his declaration, undoubtedly holding the support of any future war in as much repugnance as ever and quietly persuaded that the course of passive resistance would never be necessary.

Creighton was not alone, of course, in his disillusionment. His superior, S.D. Chown, soon after the war had undergone a considerable shift in thinking, no doubt partly in response to the needling of his cousin, Alice Chown, who became president of the Women's League of Nations Association in Canada. 'I hold you culpable for ignorance of the facts in this war,' she had written a month after the war had ended, 'but now there is no excuse for you.'[42] Chown, unlike Creighton, however, did not come so close to embracing outright pacifism.

More, however, than the context of disillusionment over the war explains Creighton's route to his position of February. More subtle in its effects, but every bit as significant was the frustration of his prophetic fervour in the realm of industrial relations.[43] The flood of the social passion was not to be so easily dammed. The channels for its diversion into resurgent pacifism were built, however, not simply out of disillusionment, but out of the ongoing pacifist tradition itself. The great pacifist movement prior to 1914 had not entirely died with the onset of war. The Canadian Peace and Arbitration Society died out in the course of 1916–17, but Alice Chown with Laura Hughes had been founding members of the Women's International League for Peace and Freedom in 1915, and by 1918 a few branches were scattered across the country.[44] A solemn pact between the pacifist chaplain to the Kaiser and an English Quaker in Cologne in 1914 grew four months later, in Cambridge, into yet another pacifist organization, the Fellowship of Reconciliation. It crossed the Atlantic to the United States in 1915,[45] and, in 1922, one of its founders, Dr Richard Roberts, came to Canada to take up the influential pulpit of American Presbyterian Church in Montreal.[46] Pacifist organization, apart from the

41 See below, p. 338
42 Alice Chown to Samuel Dwight Chown, 17 Dec. 1918, Chown Papers, cited in Schwartz, 'Samuel Dwight Chown,' p. 214
43 See above, pp. 179, 180
44 I am indebted to Professor Donald Page for this information.
45 *Forty Years for Peace, 1914–1954*
46 Wallace, *The MacMillan Dictionary of Canadian Biography*, p. 634

historic peace churches, remained relatively undeveloped in Canada prior to the 1930s, but Roberts and others became ideological centres of the cause. No sooner had he arrived than he was invited to address the annual conference of the Student Christian Movement, in September 1922,[47] and then the forthcoming national conference of students called by the SCM.[48] From then on he was to figure prominently in the movement's roster of speakers.

Roberts' arrival in Canada coincided with the revival of international discussion in the student movements around the world. The General Council of the World Student Christian Federation, meeting in Peking in October 1922, called on its forty national units to face 'fearlessly and frankly in the light of Jesus' teachings the whole question of war.'[49] In the same month the *Canadian Student*, with a special international issue, broke a silence on international questions which had prevailed since the domestic crises of 1919. Study of the peace question became general in the Canadian and American movements in 1923, and became a central issue of debate at the Indianapolis Student Convention of December 1923.[50] Pacifism was not the predominant view to emerge from these studies, but pacifists were numerous, well-placed in the movement, and often provided the focal point of debate.[51] The editor of the *Canadian Student* had been among those who had tried to fan the 'smouldering coals' into a flaming pacifism at Indianapolis, and was much depressed at its final admonition that, whatever their lights on the subject, students should study and work for peace.[52] N.A. (Larry) Mackenzie, Maritime secretary of the SCM and later a Canadian authority on international law, confirmed the aggressiveness of pacifists at Indianapolis, noted the reaction of some senior participants – 'Generals and such folk' – but the point was to convince enough young people 'of the invariable futility of war [so they] will refuse to fight.'[53] J. King Gordon, SCM delegate to the European Student Relief Conference near Prague in 1922, similarly opined that the students of the world provided the real hope of international brotherhood.[54] Escot M. Reid, although not likely a pacifist but a determined internationalist, destined to become one of Canada's most distinguished ambassadors at

47 CG, 11 Oct. 1922, p. 21   48 *Ibid.*, 17 Jan. 1923, pp. 11–12
49 Cited in Gifford, *The Christian and War*, pp. 208–9
50 *Canadian Student*, Jan. 1924, p. 99
51 *Ibid.*, March 1924, p. 181
52 *Ibid.*; CG, 30 Jan. 1924, pp. 14, 23
53 *Canadian Student*, Jan. 1924, p. 118; Feb. 1924, p. 151
54 *Ibid.*, Oct. 1922, pp. 21–3. Gordon was the son of C.W. Gordon, in the mid-1930s became national secretary of the Fellowship for a Christian Social Order, later editor of the *Nation*, and an officer of the United Nations organization.

mid-century, was in charge of SCM study programmes in 1925.[55] Mary Craig Mac-Geachy, who from her position in charge of the Canadian section of the Information Division of the League of Nations Secretariat in the later 1920s provided a constant flow of encouragement and information to persons and organizations devoted to the cause of peace, likewise first developed her international concern in the context of the SCM.[56] Not only had international concern revived and pacifism become a salient force in the SCM after 1922 but, in the opinion of W.A. Gifford in *The Christian and War*, the student world had become one of the two social areas (with labour) in which internationalism was most firmly established.[57]

The student movement was very much in Creighton's mind as he moved toward his conversion to pacifism. From late 1922 on his paper carried an unusual number of articles on student developments.[58] He seems to have attended the Canadian student conference in early 1923, as did Chown, and may well have been at the Indianapolis convention.[59] He appeared to be testifying to the impact of the student movement, among whom were many who had seen service, when he wrote that 'the convictions and conclusions that the great majority of the young men who were themselves in the war have arrived at ... have largely been influential in bringing this matter home to many of us who are older.'[60]

Whatever the sources of Creighton's new pacifism, however, by and large, in the first half of the 1920s, Canadian pacifism drew its inspiration from American sources, with a larger debt being incurred to the English movement later in the decade. In 1923 one hundred and fifty pacifist pastors in the United States issued a plea that Christians 'abolish war by refusing to share in it, thereby compelling the national authorities to adopt methods of reason rather than physical force.' The

55 *Ibid.*, Oct. 1925, p. 25; see also March–April 1927, p. 174

56 Miss MacGeachy has since become president of the International Council of Women. For the information about Miss MacGeachy, I am indebted to Professor Donald Page who bases it on interviews with several surviving figures of the time, including Miss MacGeachy.

57 See p. 207

58 CG, 11 Oct. 1922, p. 21; 27 Dec. 1922, p. 5; 17 Jan. 1923, pp. 11–12; 10 Oct. 1923, p. 11; 30 Jan. 1924, pp. 14, 23; 7 May 1924, p. 5; 14 May 1924, p. 4; 11 June 1924, pp. 7, 16. Such articles were accompanied by a similar number on various aspects of higher education.

59 *Ibid.*, 17 Jan. 1923, pp. 11–12. It was not unusual for ranking clergymen to attend major student conferences.

60 *Ibid.*, 9 April 1924, p. 5

plea, printed in the *Christian Century*, was passed on to Canadian readers by *Social Welfare*.[61] The Social Service Council invited Kirby Page, pacifist secretary of the Fellowship for a Christian Social Order, an American organization, to address its annual meeting in January 1924.[62] Page's recent book on war was apparently being widely read.[63] When four American peace organizations held a lengthy consultation in Columbus, Ohio, in April 1925, T. Albert Moore and another, perhaps Ernest Thomas, were in attendance.[64] An incalculable amount of pacifist thought was transmitted to Canadian ministers through the *Christian Century* which, although numbers of Canadian subscribers at the time are unknown,[65] seemed to be well on its way to becoming an essential tool of the progressive and ecumenically minded preacher in Canada. Its famous editor, Clayton C. Morrison, long persuaded of the social gospel, had more recently become a champion of pacifism. References to his publication in the Canadian church press were frequent.[66] Morrison was invited to address the first General Council of the United Church in June 1925. He complimented the Canadian churches for taking the lead in abolishing sectarianism and hoped that they would be as successful in 'the great task [of] the abolition of war.'[67] The force of this outspoken minority in American Protestantism undoubtedly gave Canadian pacifists a sense of considerable support as they took their stand after 1922.

Creighton's announcement initiated a heavy controversy on the pages of the *Guardian*, which carried over into its successor, the *New Outlook*. The controversy revealed that he had considerable support both in the ministry at large and among ranking officials of the church. John Coburn of the Department of Evangelism and Social Service, and F.W. Langford, head of the Religious Education Department, immediately declared themselves.[68] The conferences of the Methodist church across

61 sw, April 1923, pp. 137–9

62 *Ibid.*, Dec. 1923

63 *Canadian Baptist*, 6 March 1924, p. 11

64 cg, 6 May 1925, pp. 5, 10; 27 May 1927, p. 19

65 An attempt to secure Canadian subscription figures from the *Christian Century* met with failure.

66 On the subject of peace, see sw, April 1923, pp. 137–9; *Presbyterian Witness*, 8 Jan. 1925, pp. 2–3; *New Outlook*, 7 Oct. 1925, p. 4

67 *New Outlook*, 1 July 1925, p. 7

68 cg, 30 April 1924, pp. 21–2; 28 May 1924, p. 14; 7 May 1924, p. 17; 14 May 1924, p. 18; 25 June 1924, p. 21; 2 July 1924, p. 16

the country in June expressed themselves in terms that indicated that the issue of peace had become a vital one.[69] The subject provided the most stirring debates of several of the conferences. Strong anti-war resolutions were adopted, although all of them stopped short of a pacifist position. None of the resolutions dealt with causes of war. All of them affirmed their confidence that all international conflicts could be settled by conference and conciliation, and urged wider support for and strengthening of international agencies embodying that approach.[70] The Board of Evangelism and Social Service, meeting in November, in effect observed that these resolutions hid a division in the mind of the church as to whether war was in fact a case of unmistakable opposition between the state and the demands of Christianity. The board charged the department with responsibility for helping the church think this issue out and for arousing public opinion in favour of ending 'present international anarchy.'[71]

It was not the department, however, so much as the *Guardian* which attempted to arouse public opinion. And despite the problems with Creighton's own position, it was the *Guardian* which pressed church members to think about the issue. In May and June, Archibald F. Key wrote a series of articles surveying the history of peace movements, the growth of pacifism, the role of international conferences, and hopeful lines of advance. It was significant that he rejected the path of international conferences and societies on the ground that these represented impersonal governments bound by traditions and laws of past ages. A sound observation by Key on the nature of relations between collective groups was obscured by the dream of a new age. The goal was not simply peace but the personalizing of collective relationships. Hence the hope for the future lay in the 'gradual internationalization of the people' by education, open diplomacy, and control through treaties. It was the peace movements which seemed to offer the best hope of progress toward these goals. A measure of growing activity that inspired such a hope was that in England alone there were thirteen branches of international peace movements and twenty-five different peace societies, with a No More War Society attempting to unite them all.[72]

But Key's articles were not hard-hitting enough for the more radical pacifists, and in July R.E. Fairbairn began a series of articles which were to mark him as one of the most able and certainly the most contentious pacifist writer in the church. The

69 See above, pp. 257–8
70 CG, 18 June 1924, p. 20; 2 July 1924, p. 14; 6 Aug. 1924, p. 28; 13 Aug. 1924, p. 12
71 Ibid., 3 Dec. 1924, pp. 17–18
72 Ibid., 28 May 1924, p. 5; 4 June 1924, p. 6; 11 June 1924, p. 6; 18 June 1924, p. 7

engagement over his writing continued for over a year and a half. It wearied some readers, and was wearing upon Fairbairn, who wrote in December 1925:

I did hope and believe that I had earned the right to keep silent on this war question. I have never yet touched it except under compulsion. I bitterly resent the moral pressure it puts upon me. I loathe the controversial atmosphere associated with it. I hate it! ... I hate it! I would give a sigh of relief if the editor will relieve me of responsibility by rejecting this manuscript. But so long as I see something which ought to be said, and which so far as I know, is not being said, I cannot refuse to give it utterance.[73]

Fairbairn came to Canadian Methodism from England via Bermuda and Newfoundland. He was a prolific writer of articles, which appeared in many church journals. Some of these were published in a collection entitled *The Appeal to Reality*, probably in 1927. Weary as Fairbairn might become of this particular issue, he was not to find release from it in the 1920s – or the 1930s either. And neither he, nor protesting readers, could expect relief from the editor, W.B. Creighton, who refused to discontinue articles on the subject simply because it 'provokes strong and unsettling and very diverse sentiments.'[74]

Fairbairn's radicalism was apparent with his first article. Terrifying predictions of the nature of future war did not move him. There was no point in waging war, he said, unless it were done with thoroughness and efficiency. The fundamental problem was the whole war system in which western nations were enmeshed. Arguments about unprovoked aggression were meaningless in this context, and were really part of 'the great confidence trick played upon [the people] over and over again.' Furthermore, 'once the war system has made a conflict inevitable ... it is impossible that the tension should be dissipated without suffering and loss somehow and somewhere.' Pacifism was not a painless way out. It might mitigate the suffering implicit in a military response, but this was not a major point in Fairbairn's argument. Pacifism was the frontal attack on the war system itself.[75]

Postwar revelations about prewar secret diplomacy, the role of commercial expansion and competition in precipitating the war, and the bankruptcy of the hopes engendered by war propaganda, all had persuaded Fairbairn of the existence of the 'war system' and led him to take his stand. The roots of the system lay, he said, in the virtual state of war created within western nations by industrial exploitation of the common people. The expansion of these powerful industrial and commercial interests abroad and their demand for protective guarantees by national power was

73 *New Outlook*, 23 Dec. 1925, p. 5   74 CG, 7 Jan. 1925, p. 4
75 *Ibid.*, 23 July 1924, p. 5

the major cause of modern war. These interests themselves felt no particular loyalty to the nation, however. As a case in point, Fairbairn cited the merger of French and German iron interests shortly after the French annexation of the Ruhr.[76] For him, the struggle against war and that against competitive capitalism were one and the same battle.

But did the struggle against war require pacifism? Was this not a condemnation of war in abstract, a rationalistic procedure which Fairbairn had inveighed against in other articles and one which threw up a false wall against 'life's buoyant realities?'[77] His answer was to argue that in the 'plunge into life's contingencies,' pre-eminent among the facts that were encountered were the historic Christ and personal Christian experience. The argument that Jesus recognized war as part of the human situation and made no general condemnation of it, Fairbairn could not accept. 'Christ condemned war not less emphatically than if he had made a formal pronouncement on it.' It was woven into his whole attitude. The Jews rejected him 'precisely' because of his refusal to lead them in a messianic war.[78] But did this imply a denial of all war on principle and sanction a struggle to remove war as such from the world? There were statements of Jesus which seemed to suggest a pessimistic attitude to such a possibility. What seemed to clinch the argument in Fairbairn's mind, as in Creighton's, was the bedrock belief of the social gospel in the immancence of the kingdom of God in history. For most of Christian history salvation had been viewed as escape from a hopeless race, he said, but 'today we see that Jesus really did propose to secure the redemption of humanity as such.'[79]

Edis Fairbairn's social gospel affinities separated his pacifism from that of most of the historic peace churches,[80] and his view of national rulers as pawns of commercial interests marked him off from pacifists like C.C. Morrison of the *Christian Century*, who would cultivate peace but leave the door open to being taken in once again because 'some other nation is "wantonly attacking" somebody, or "oppressing the helpless." '[81] It was not clear what Fairbairn would propose as protection for actual cases of such injustice. He seems to have endorsed the idea of a League of Nations, but considered it of little value until honest and open diplomacy was

76 *Ibid.*, 7 Jan. 1925, pp. 6, 23
77 Fairbairn, *The Appeal to Reality*, p. 11
78 CG, 30 May 1925, pp. 4, 5
79 Fairbairn, *The Appeal to Reality*, pp. 184–5
80 See, for instance, Dobson Papers, B. 7, F, the typescript article for the League of Nations Society in Canada (1928) by A.G. Dorland, author of *A History of the Society of Friends (Quakers) in Canada*.
81 *New Outlook*, 23 Dec. 1925, pp. 5, 11

established.[82] Nor was it apparent what his attitude was to such features of industrial conflict as strikes. His pacifism was vigorous and radical, but what it gained in force it seemed often to lose in relevance.

Fairbairn's articles stirred a host of critics. All were for peace according to their lights, but that was not the issue. Some questioned the soundness of his interpretation of the origin of the war.[83] The folly of the prewar arms race was contested by the folly of prewar pacifism.[84] Others argued the necessity of recourse to war on the analogy of police restraint of crime, never doubting who would represent the interest of justice most fittingly.[85] These assured the editor that the pew would not respond to Fairbairn's 'misguided apostleship.'[86] However, Fairbairn did get some strong support from fellow ministers,[87] notably from Alberta parsons Charles Bishop and C.H. Heustis. And T. Jackson Wray, presenting the pacifist case to the Lumsden Beach summer school in Saskatchewan in 1925, found more support than he expected.[88] Surveying the problems of the past year, Creighton in the *New Outlook* believed the peace movement to be gaining ground in all churches in the English-speaking world.[89] The following year his swelling satisfaction with the Canadian peace movement could only have increased with the publication of the most thoughtful pacifist statement of the decade.

In 1926 the only Canadian book-length exposition of Christian pacifism to appear in the twenties was published under the title *The Christian and War*. While its major author was W.A. Gifford, professor of ecclesiastical history at United Theological College, Montreal, the book was not his alone. Its initiators had been the Protestant Ministerial Association of Montreal, which six years earlier had rejected capitalism as a vehicle of a Christian social order.[90] A committee was struck to begin the enquiry, and in the light of differences of opinion in the association and of urgency of time, the committee was authorized to complete the work in its own way and accept responsibility for publication. Gifford's original draft was the subject of a number of group conferences over several months on the part of some of Montreal's most notable Protestant clergy: the Revs. T.W. Jones of Calvary Congrega-

82 CG, 3 Dec. 1924, pp. 5, 22
83 *Ibid.*, 8 Oct. 1924, p. 14; 7 Jan. 1925, p. 13
84 *Ibid.*, 14 Jan. 1925, p. 16
85 *Ibid.*, 13 Aug. 1924, p. 13; 5 Sept. 1924, p. 7
86 *New Outlook*, 20 Jan. 1926, pp. 22–3
87 CG, 20 Aug. 1924, p. 13; 4 Feb. 1925, p. 15
88 *New Outlook*, 26 Aug. 1925, p. 29
89 *Ibid.*, 1 July 1925, p. 5   90 See above, p. 156

tional Church, M.F. McCutcheon of First Baptist Church, W.D. Reid of Stanley Presbyterian Church, Richard Roberts of American Presbyterian, and Canon A.P. Shatford of St James the Apostle Church.[91] The finished manuscript, although in Gifford's hand, was the consensus of the group.

The book appeared to have wide appeal. The *Canadian Student* crowed: 'Here is the book on war for which we have been waiting,' while the *Canadian Churchman* commended it to all thoughtful persons.[92] Its argument did not hasten to assign guilt in the origins of the war, although Britain emerged less scathed than the other powers. There was almost an inevitability presented in the interaction of events leading to the war, yet war itself was not simply rooted in human instincts. Economic imperialism, limited loyalties, national fears, policies of 'preparedness,' secret diplomacy, and beyond these, belief in the 'moral efficacy of force,' and in 'war as a school of virtue,' accounted for this human perversion. Such phenomena could be changed; none were ultimate in human nature. Gifford was restrained in recounting the nature and impact of the war: 'It is ... well that we should imitate the fine reticence of those who saw most and say least.'[93] Neither state nor church could escape complicity, yet the important thing was to determine one's duty to the future, 'to those who after him must conduct the business of life.' The Christian's problem, however, lay in the failure of the church, for many reasons, to work out the Christian ethic of war.

Unlike the absolute pacifist, Gifford admitted the use of force which, as long as it was exercized in such a way as not to obscure the ends in view, could be made to 'serve the ends of love, reverence, and service.' War, by definition, was the exercise of force outside such controls, and not only could be productive of no good end but debased the whole moral coinage of civilization. Gifford therefore departed from Fairbairn in strongly supporting the developing agencies of international order to the point of sanctioning international police action. The inadequacies of the social, political, and economic orders of the nations were not so much grounds for suspecting the motives of such agencies and actions as for recognizing their necessity. One might cherish a faith in ultimate efficacy of a moral international order alone, said Gifford, but a great work of domestic and world reconstruction lay between the present and that day. The programme was large, and the battlefront of Christian men and institutions bent on the ever-increasing manifestation of the kingdom of God in the affairs of men ran through homes, schools, libraries, churches, corporations, and legislatures. Concerned persons should arouse the public conscience

91 Gifford, *The Christian and War*, Preface
92 *Canadian Student*, Dec. 1926, p. 88; *Canadian Churchman*, 30 Dec. 1926, p. 865
93 Gifford, *The Christian and War*, p. 25

against economic imperialisms, and should shame those whose special knowledge had made them unwitting accomplices in the destruction of mankind. Political democracy must be extended 'until there can be no decision of the State on the question of war that is not the decision of the Nation itself.'[94] Add to the programme association with one of the many emerging peace organizations and sound knowledge of international affairs and institutions—and the discipline of the Christian life in the twentieth century was a rigorous one indeed! For the church itself, it should make all governments aware that it must oppose such wars as come when arbitration has not been sought or the decision of arbitrators refused. It must proclaim the message that the world, apparently, had not yet heard, 'that Christianity has a gospel for all humanity, and looks out upon the Reign of God in human society.'[95]

In conclusion, Gifford and his group declared, like Creighton, that 'we who make this appeal cannot conceive any future war in which Christian men can participate.' Ignorance and innocence could not be pleaded, for 'men may now know how wars come, how they end, how divorced from right they are.' Let them 'think out the great human issues in advance of mankind, and endure the reproach of dissent ... and thus become creative factors in progress.' However, the future was doubtful, and if any should have to stand alone, counselled Gifford, 'the "City of Man-soul" has but one citizen,' and 'in the day of destiny it rests with him alone to keep its walls intact.'[96]

It was a moving appeal and a substantial contribution both to the current debate and to intelligent action for peace. It was not optimistic in the usual sense of the word – nor, indeed, were Creighton or Fairbairn, but their statements did not exhibit the same intellectual poise or discretion of thought. Yet it had its inadequacies. The declaration that all the knowledge was in for a judgment upon war was only true with respect to past wars. The hinging of opposition to any specific war on the rejection of the mechanics of arbitration presumed that those mechanisms would remain intact. Gifford's casuistry held no word for states should the instruments of international order collapse.[97] Failing in this, the apparently clear word for individual action in the face of war itself became less than limpid. The efficacy of his suggestion that all decisions respecting war should be made by the nation at large presumed the equal march of all nations toward democratic processes, just as his proposal that abandonment of secret diplomacy required only the relinquishing of

94 *Ibid.*, p. 204
95 *Ibid.*, p. 19
96 *Ibid.*, pp. 220–1
97 The word 'casuistry' is used in its proper sense as the science of applying general moral rules to specific situations.

unworthy motives presumed too much on an even progress among men and nations toward the 'Reign of God in human society.'[98] The contrary case, of course, tended to accede to a tragic spiral of escalating suspicion, and the appropriateness of the dramatic rejection by the pacifist of the world of force and counterforce with all its accoutrements might well be argued. But that would be to call for the rigorous presentation of the case for non-violence, which only Fairbairn came at all close to doing. Gifford, rather, was basically concerned 'to set men thinking about the Kingdom of God,'[99] not simply as a spiritual realm, but as the dawning of an historical order of things, in the light of which conviction men and institutions would put aside old thoughts and old ways.

For Gifford, too, the last court of appeal was the social gospel, and for all his care, he shared the elements of gnosticism that permeated the movement. The gnostic sense of special knowledge of the coming of the ultimate order of history, even without the naming of the day, inevitably obscured the tragic ambiguities of social alternatives and the ambivalences of human decisions. To be sure, the social gospel sense of the complicity of all in social guilt tended toward the tragic, but the tensions entailed in accepting that view were assuaged in the activities that seemed appropriate to the coming of the kingdom. The difficulties which had overtaken social gospel programmes, however, and the divisions which had rent the movement might well have suggested that, at the least, the route to the kingdom was neither so singular nor so certain as had been imagined. But to accept the full meaning of the experience of the social gospel crisis was to lose the very means of living with complicity in social guilt which the social gospel prescribed. To be sure, the tragic choices of a decade later were not yet upon Canadians in or out of the social gospel, but the sublimation of the crisis of the social gospel in the resurgence of pacifism inhibited the development of a more profound Christian ethic of war or of peace to bequeath to the following decade of international conflict. Such a judgment was not only appropriate to the social gospel pacifists, but to the broader Canadian peace movement as well.

98 Gifford, *The Christian and War*, p. 204
99 *Ibid.*, p. 19

21

The Eschatology of Peace

No pacifist movement similar to that based largely in the Methodist church and the SCM arose in the other Canadian churches, yet they, too, reflected the changing temper with respect to the issue of peace. The editor of the *Canadian Churchman* noted progress during 1926 in demobilizing 'the battalions of hate.' He criticized those who were trying to put churches and peace agencies in an impossible pacifist position, but he skirted the difficult question of the ethics of the use of force, declaring all such discussion was beside the point. The basis of church action, he believed, was that war was 'inhuman and un-Christian,' and the only way to eradicate it was to create a new spirit by promoting friendship, eradicating animosities, and working for 'agencies, courts and leagues which will gradually bring the world to think of itself as one community.'[1] This was essentially the position of the International Peace Congress in London, July 1922, to which the Presbyterian General Assembly had sent Principal John Mackay as a representative.[2] It was also the heart of the programme of the World Alliance for International Friendship through the churches. Many of those who thought about the goal and tactics of peace, like the editor of the *Presbyterian Witness*, repeated to themselves the belief that the appalling nature of modern weapons and the expense of military preparation made future war unlikely.[3] Such hopes made it easier to reject the old adage, 'In time of peace prepare for war,' and to place greater faith in the mobilization of public opinion than that tactic warranted. That may well have been the only role open to the churches or to a broadly based peace movement, but rather than recognize the limitations of their situation, the proponents of this tactic were certain that 'the Church of Christ in its united capacity, has the power to end war.'[4] Skeptics were pointed to the elimination of deeply rooted systems of evil, such as slavery, by 'the operation of a force more powerful than war.'[5] Encouragement was derived

1 *Canadian Churchman*, 21 Jan. 1926, p. 36
2 *Presbyterian Witness*, 31 Aug. 1922, p. 8
3 *Ibid.*, 6 March 1924, pp. 2–3
4 *Ibid.*   5 *Ibid.*

even from generals, like Bliss in the United States or Haig in Britain, who declared, 'It is the business of the churches to make my business impossible.'[6] In time of peace, therefore, the churches counselled prepare for peace. And preparing for peace meant internationalizing the public mind, demobilizing militaristic influences, and, apparently, refusing to discuss the ethics of force.

Actual church activities and organization for peace in Canada remained at a fairly primitive level during the 1920s. In 1921–2 there was some discussion among Methodists of creating a council of peace.[7] Two conferences, Alberta and Saskatchewan, gave particular attention to the subject in June 1922. They viewed the 'military menace and industrial crisis' as 'two aspects of one world-wide condition.' In response to a few such representations, the General Conference of 1922 proposed the formation of a council of peace incorporating all churches and related to a wider international organization,[8] a proposal supported by the Presbyterian General Assembly in 1923.[9] Slowly the conditions for joint action seemed to be emerging. On the local level, groups like the Brotherhoods of the city of London organized peace rallies variously representing Protestants, Catholics, Jews, labour groups, service clubs, and city councils.[10] Under an apparently short-lived No More War Society, Canadian churches, Protestant, Catholic, and Jewish, together with labour followed similar groups in some twenty other nations in holding a 'no more war' demonstration on 29 July 1923.[11] Systematic church association with world peace organizations, however, began in 1924–5 when the Inter-Church Advisory Council engaged in correspondence with British sources on the question of establishing in Canada a national committee of the World Alliance for International Friendship through the churches.[12]

Roots of the World Alliance went back to 1905 in the United States and to 1907 in Britain. Various ventures by the churches in promoting international goodwill led to an important conference on the subject at Constance, Switzerland, 2 August

6 *Ibid.*, 12 April 1923, pp. 2–3

7 *Annual Report*, 1921–2, Methodist Department of ESS, pp. 18–19, 97–100, 102

8 UCA, Methodist General Conference Papers and Reports of Committees, 1922

9 *Presbyterian Acts and Proceedings*, 1923, Appendix, pp. 305–6

10 *Minutes of Canada Yearly Meeting of the Society of Friends*, 1924, p. 20

11 *Presbyterian Acts and Proceedings*, 1923, Appendix, pp. 305–6; *Canadian Churchman*, 26 July 1923, p. 469; *Presbyterian Witness*, 26 July 1923, p. 2; Stewart and French, *Ask No Quarter*, p. 140. In Toronto the day was marked by a march to Queen's Park and a public meeting addressed by the Rev. Fr Minehan, the Rev. Dr Pidgeon, Rabbi Brickner, the Rev. E. Henderson, the Rev. G. Stanley Russell, Agnes McPhail, and James Simpson. A similar event was staged in Vancouver.

12 Minutes, Inter-Church Advisory Council, 18 Dec. 1924

1914. Before the month's end returning British delegates had established an organization to carry forward the work, but the guns had begun to roar, and further development awaited the war's end. By 1922 the alliance had twenty-six national branches, and was holding its fourth international conference in Copenhagen.[13] Some 300 Canadians had by that date associated themselves with the alliance and officers of the organization contacted the prominent Canadian Quaker, Arthur G. Dorland, requesting him to organize a Canadian branch of the Alliance.[14] Correspondence and contacts of Dorland with both British and American councils of the alliance led to more formal approaches to Canadian churches and the Inter-Church Advisory Council. Quite independently, under the leadership of one Sir Richard Lake, a local chapter had become active in Victoria, attracting Quakers, among others, to its activities.[15] Finally, on 17 November 1926 a Canadian Council of the World Alliance was formed representing all the major Protestant denominations, the Society of Friends, and the Salvation Army.[16] Dorland's role in the fostering of the alliance in Canada was typical of the peace activities of the Society of Friends in the 1920s which preferred to promote the co-operative action of others than to act directly itself. One consequence of this tactic was that its members figured prominently in the resulting organization. Four Friends found their way onto the executive of the alliance, including Dorland as a vice-president.[17] However, the Anglican chairman of the Canadian council, Professor C.V. Pilcher of Wycliffe College, took pains to point out that the alliance was not pacifist in orientation, but that its great aim was to complement the work of the League of Nations by fostering the will to peace and the spirit of international friendship.[18]

Despite these promising beginnings, there remains little evidence of direct activity

13 *Bulletin of the Council for Social Service,* no 73, June 1925; *New Outlook,* 12 Jan. 1927, p. 5. This conference would seem to have been timed to take advantage of the larger congress held in July, the previous month, in London.

14 *Minutes of Canada Yearly Meeting of the Society of Friends,* 1922, p. 7

15 *Ibid.,* 1923, pp. 20–1; 1924, p. 20; 1926, p. 12. I am indebted to Professor Donald Page for the information regarding the roles of Dorland and Lake in promoting the alliance in Canada.

16 *New Outlook,* 12 Jan. 1927, p. 5

17 *Minutes of Canada Yearly Meeting of the Society of Friends,* 1927, pp. 19–20. Others were A.S. Rogers (treasurer), Marion D. Cronk, and Fred Haslam. Friends were also chairman and treasurer of the arrangements committee for the Toronto visit of the representatives of the Washington Congress of the Women's International League for Peace and Freedom in 1924 (*ibid.,* 1924, p. 20).

18 *Canadian Churchman,* 20 Jan. 1927, p. 36; 3 Feb. 1927, p. 74; *New Outlook,* 12 Jan. 1927, p. 5

of the alliance in Canada. Members were urged to live in accord with the aims of international goodwill, and to join the League of Nations Society.[19] Among the local chapters, only the Victoria local's sponsorship of an essay contest in high schools in 1926 has been recorded.[20] Nationally, the alliance seems to have bent its efforts in the direction of Canadian-American relations. On the initiative of the American Council, a Canadian-American Liaison Committee was set up in 1927 and a plan of action developed involving the publication of a pamphlet stressing the importance of friendship between all English-speaking peoples, the arrangement of an exchange of pulpits along the international border, and the suggestion of a large conference for late 1928.[21] The impact of liquor on Canadian-American relations may well have been the stimulus for such a development – at least that is one possible interpretation of the enigmatic comment of the editor of the *Bulletin* that 'the need for such work, in view of certain recent tendencies of sinister import, is too obvious to require explanation.'[22] This limited range of activity by the Canadian branch of the alliance may be explained by an early policy decision to work through existing church agencies and in co-operation with the League of Nations Society.[23] However, on at least one major issue, that of military training in the schools, the Canadian council would seem to have defaulted because of disagreement between its pacifist Quaker and non-pacifist Anglican membership. As a result, the Canadians broke ranks with the rest of the World Alliance and remained silent on a subject of considerable agitation in the later twenties.

Protest over cadet training in the schools was not new in Canada in the 1920s. As early as 1909 the Women's Christian Temperance Union had introduced resolutions against such programmes in the schools. Then there had been some 10,000 cadets in Canadian schools, but now, by the mid-twenties, they had multiplied tenfold. Concerned that 'the forces of militarism were never stronger in this Dominion than they are now,' the WCTU, with the Women's International League for Peace and Freedom, extended the range of their peace activity, and in particular took up the campaign against cadets.[24] The Society of Friends in its enthusiastic response to the organization of the League had taken pains to reaffirm its opposition to military

19 *Bulletin of the Council for Social Service*, no 81, May 1928
20 *New Outlook*, 30 June 1926, p. 8
21 *Bulletin of the Council for Social Service*, no 81, May 1928
22 *Ibid.*
23 *Ibid.*
24 *Report of the Twenty-third Convention of the Canadian* WCTU, 1925, p. 135; Women's International League leaflet outlining a plan of work for the Canadian section (Vancouver nd)

training in the schools.[25] In 1925 it was alarmed to observe the 'recrudescence of the agitation for cadet training' and renewed its protest.[26] The society was encouraged the next year to note the growth of a similar concern in other churches as one of several indications of a greater sensitivity to peace issues among Canadian Protestants.[27] Early in the decade the World Alliance had established a committee to investigate and campaign against militaristic attitudes in school texts, and when a World Alliance conference of peace leaders was held in Chicago in 1926, one of several major objectives agreed upon was the abolition of military training in the schools.[28] This Chicago decision merely intensified a campaign which was already well under way in both countries. Pressure from the conferences of the United Church brought the creation by the General Council of 1926 of a commission to study and report on Cadet and Officer Training Corps. The occasional delinquent conference, like the London Conference which approved the moral and physical effects of cadet training, was lectured by the *New Outlook* on the views of the best authorities as to the inadequacies of military drill as a form of physical exercise.[29] The farm organizations had joined the hue and cry, and in 1926 the United Farmers of Ontario urged the diversion of all provincial funds for cadet training to bona fide physical education programmes.[30] The next two years only saw the campaign intensify. Great was the outcry, therefore, when the United Church commission reported to General Council that 'the evidence accumulated should allay fear that the Cadet Corps as present organized, fosters militarism in Canadian youth, ... or any feature against which the Christian conscience must protest.'[31] The report of the General Council Committee had been drawn up under the chairmanship of Newton Rowell, a prominent Liberal who had been secretary of state in the Union government, in which capacity he had been deeply involved in Canadian external relations during and after the war. Rowell's report had been enthusiastically and unanimously endorsed by the General Council of 1928.[32] The finding on the cadet question, however, was immediately exploited by the advocates of military training for youth, a development which alarmed even non-pacifists in the church.[33] Pacifist critics decried its 'hackneyed idealism' as being 'as innocuous as would be a tirade against intemperance by the liquor interest.'[34] By December the editor of

25 *Minutes of Canada Yearly Meeting of the Society of Friends*, 1920, p. 21
26 *Ibid.*, 1925, pp. 16–17; 1926, p. 13; 1927, p. 20
27 *Ibid.*, 1926, p. 12
28 *New Outlook*, 14 Jan. 1926, p. 16   29 16 June 1926, p. 13
30 *New Outlook*, 7 April 1926, p. 14   31 *Ibid.*, 19 Sept. 1928, p. 2
32 *Ibid.*, p. 12   33 *Ibid.*, 26 Sept. 1928, p. 2
34 *Ibid.*, 10 Oct. 1928, p. 17; 3 Oct. 1928, p. 28

the *New Outlook* confessed he had far too many letters on the subject to publish. Diversity in background and argument marked the flood.[35] Campaigns abroad in which tens of thousands committed themselves to refuse service in any future war, declarations in the secular press, decisions of student organizations, and further church conference debates kept the issue alive until the next general council.[36] Optimistic pacifists believed that they were demonstrating a strength of public opinion that would deter any government from expecting church support in a future war.[37] The best, however, that they could accomplish at the General Council of 1930 was not a condemnation of cadets as such, but a statement discouraging 'all military preparations for war in schools and colleges.'[38] Throughout the campaign the Canadian Council of the World Alliance had stood on the sidelines watching the action.

This campaign was not conducted apart from more general issues of the peace. The church press continued support of the League, although the *New Outlook*, which combined the *Guardian*, the *Witness*, and the *Congregationalist*, had no real competition from the Anglican publications in the field of international questions. Optimism was heightened in 1926 with the entry of Germany into the League,[39] and the United States into the World Court.[40] Concern, however, continued to be expressed over national arms programmes. When the Geneva Conference on Disarmament failed in mid-1927, the *New Outlook* thundered that the nations were attempting 'to solve problems that have no solution: how to make adequate preparation for an unthinkable war ... in short, how to keep the war mind and at the same time go on a peace footing.'[41]

While comment on international questions rose in Anglican, United, and Baptist papers with the signing of the Kellogg Pact in 1928, the *New Outlook* found the agreement difficult to reconcile with current arms production.[42] Nevertheless, there was much enthusiasm over its ratification. The test of the Kellogg Pact should have been success in disarmament negotiations, in progress since 1925. It was with hopes and prayers that the churches received news of an International Conference on Naval Armaments to begin in January 1930.[43] Little did they know the long

35 *Ibid.*, 19 Dec. 1928, p. 5

36 *Ibid.*, 10 April 1929, p. 39; 4 Dec. 1929, p. 1253; 1 Jan. 1930, p. 6; 18 June 1930, pp. 594, 601

37 *Ibid.*, 18 June 1930, pp. 594, 601 38 *Ibid.*, 8 Oct. 1930, p. 986

39 *Ibid.*, 13 Feb. 1926, p. 18 40 *Ibid.*, 10 Feb. 1926, p. 15

41 *Ibid.*, 24 Aug. 1927, p. 13 42 *Ibid.*, 15 Aug. 1928, pp. 12, 13

43 *Ibid.*, 8 Jan. 1930, p. 27; *Canadian Baptist*, 30 Jan. 1930, p. 3

months of alternating hope and despair that would elapse before final failure of the General Disarmament Conference in 1934. Church editors participated in a consultation called by the American Friends Service Committee to discuss informally under such leaders as Oswald Garrison Villard of the *Nation*, Bruce Curry of Union Theological Seminary, Paul Hutchison of the *Christian Century*, and Augustus T. Murray, President Hoover's pastor.[44] Canadian church leaders participated in institutes of international relations such as that at Haverford College in June 1930.[45] On a still larger scale, the churches looked forward to the culmination of four years of careful organization in the 1930 Universal Religious Peace Conference in Geneva.[46]

Canadian Christians at large concerned about peace found a number of avenues of expression open to them quite apart from church sponsored functions. Women's Institutes across the country early exhibited an interest in peace issues,[47] as did the Women's International League for Peace and Freedom. The World Congress of the latter, meeting in Washington in May 1924, held one of its sessions in Toronto under the chairmanship of Agnes McPhail.[48] The Women's Christian Temperance Union, recovering from the diversion of its members' energies during the war years,[49] re-established its Peace and Arbitration Department in 1920.[50] At first slow in picking up the work, and then thrust again into battle for the prohibition cause they thought they had virtually won, the 584 units of the WCTU[51] across the nation in the last years of the decade could report an impressive list of activities, fostering study groups, sponsoring lecture series, requesting clergy for peace sermons, organizing goodwill days, and petitioning governments.[52] Nova Scotia, Saskatchewan, and Alberta, especially, sent in notable accounts over the years.[53] In 1925 the organization became a corporate member of the League of Nations Society, a move that was perhaps not surprising since the national president, Mrs Gordon Wright, was the sister of the founder and first chairman of the society, Newton Rowell. After a grim account of the renewed slavery of the nation to drink in 1927, Mrs Wright, in her

44 *New Outlook*, 25 Dec. 1929, p. 1319
45 *Ibid.*, 2 July 1930, pp. 637–52
46 *Ibid.*, 10 Oct. 1928, p. 6; 14 July 1926, p. 16
47 SW, May 1919, pp. 200–2, and following items in the series, 'For Women's Thought'
48 CG, 4 June 1924, p. 3
49 *Report of the Twenty-first Convention of the Canadian* WCTU, 1920, p. 54
50 *Ibid.*, p. 42
51 *Ibid.*, 1922, 'Statistical Report,' p. 97
52 *Ibid.*, 1929, pp. 151–5
53 *Ibid.*; see also 1922, pp. 165–7; 1925, pp. 133–7

biennial presidential address could turn, at least in part, in 1929, to the great international hope, 'for unless all signs fail, we cannot be far from the time when ... "men shall learn war no more." '[54] Women's groups not infrequently undertook joint action for peace. In Regina the associated women's organizations invited John W. Dafoe, editor of the *Manitoba Free Press* to present a public address on disarmament.[55] In Saskatchewan and Alberta, under the influence of women like Louise C. McKinney and Viola MacNaughton, the WCTU and the Women's International League merged memberships and were both closely allied with the women's sections of the provincial farm organizations. It can hardly be doubted that they in turn put their husbands and the larger farm movement under pressure on the subject of peace. The labour movement was also making its voice heard, and in the view of the *Presbyterian Witness* the solidarity of labour throughout the world would make it one of the most powerful agencies in the overthrow of militarism.[56] A series of international education conferences, meeting in San Francisco in 1923, Edinburgh in 1925, and in Toronto in 1927, stressed the theme of education and peace. Canadians especially attended the first and last of these in considerable numbers.[57] The Religious Education Association, meeting in 1926 in Canada for the first time, similarly devoted itself to studying the role of religious education in furthering international peace and goodwill.[58] So many conferences had there been even by mid-decade that one writer was prone to ask whether the endless stream of contemporary conferences would do more than deoxygenate the air, suffocate the attender, and possibly pollute him with the knowledge of facts undreamt of.[59] It may well have been to the relief of many that the upward curve of the Canadian peace movement after 1922 brought with it at least a change of conference fare. Not everyone, of course, was on the conference circuit, but every community could celebrate its hope with a goodwill day or a ritual hanging of a copy of the Kellogg Peace Pact in the local school.

Standing above the general welter of peace activity in the 1920s, and probably the single most influential agency of its kind in Canada at the time, was the League of Nations Society. Like most groups at work in the field it was heavily manned by Christians giving social expression to their faith. Promoters of the projected society,

54 *Ibid.*, 1927 and 1929   55 *Ibid.*, 1922, p. 166
56 *Presbyterian Witness*, 11 Dec. 1924, p. 1
57 *New Outlook*, 24 Aug. 1927, p. 12
58 *Ibid.*, 24 March 1926, p. 8. Kirby Page, editor of the American pacifist periodical, *The World Tomorrow*, Newton Rowell, Professor W.A. Gifford, and Dr J. Endicott gave keynote addresses.
59 CG, 3 Sept. 1924, p. 6

like Vincent Massey, R.M. McIver, and Robert Falconer, were not untouched by the social movement in the churches. In none, perhaps, was this more evident than in the man most responsible for the organization and early development of the society, Newton Rowell. Like James Simpson in the labour movement, though without such radical results, Rowell had figured prominently in the Epworth League, a movement designed to throw the energies of Methodist young people into the evangelical and social tasks of the church.[60] The prohibition campaigns had claimed a large part of his time, but as a lawyer and as leader of the Liberal party in Ontario he confronted a much wider range of social problems. In 1920, when he took the initiative in pressing the projected League of Nations Society into organizational shape, he was the government minister in charge of the slowly emerging Department of External Affairs. When the society was formed at an impressive gathering in Ottawa, 31 May 1921, Rowell was made chairman of the central executive committee. Although later in the decade he became less active in the society's affairs, he remained the church's chief contact with the society. In the formation of the society he had provided an organizational vehicle for the enthusiasm for the League and a continuing agency for fostering intelligent public discussion of the League and international affairs.[61]

It was across a broad front of groups and activities that churchmen were deployed in their concern for peace in the decade following the war. A few were pacifist, most were not; some were extending their social gospel commitments, others were internationalists of a more traditional stamp. Among them all were many differences in outlook, tactics, and objectives. The movement in the first few years after the war had not been a prominent concern of the social gospel. Only in some pacifists like Woodsworth and Ivens, or in a few non-pacifists like Chown, were the two closely conjoined and they were preoccupied with other tasks at the time. However, as the industrial, political, and religious programmes of the social gospel became jaded on impact with the intractability and complexity of social reality, and as the international world evinced need of zealous cultivation, the social hope of the

60 The most accessible distillation of his thinking in this area is in his Burwash Memorial Lectures of 1921 published as *The British Empire and World Peace* (Toronto 1922), especially chapters XII–XV on the church and international relations, industrial relations, national ideals, and the changing religious order.
61 Page, 'Hon. Newton Rowell and the Founding of the League of Nations Society in Canada.' For a full discussion of the history of the society see Page's forthcoming doctoral dissertation, 'Canadians and the League of Nations before the Manchurian Crisis' (University of Toronto).

social gospel fused with the world hope of pacifists and a broad range of inter-nationalists.

This development was evident in the United States where the broadening social programme of the pacifist Fellowship of Reconciliation in 1928 absorbed the pacifist-tinged, but essentially social gospel organization, the Fellowship for a Chris-tian Social Order.[62] However, it was quite apparent with the rise of the peace issue in such different but nevertheless social gospel minds as Creighton, Fairbairn, Gifford, and Thomas in and after 1924 that a similar process was under way in Canada. This fusion froze in place for a time a number of tensions between the social gospel and both the pacifist and non-pacifist wings of the peace movement. That the tension was endurable through the late twenties and the first few years of the thirties was due both to the character of the international and national scene, and to the crisis through which the various wings of the social gospel had travelled.

If one of the crucial problems of peace was, as most pacifist and non-pacifist proponents of the social gospel believed, the influence of a competitive economic system and its chief beneficiaries upon national policies, was not political and economic reform a pre-condition of peace? For those for whom peace was not simply a social goal but a way of life here and now, these objectives of national and international life were inseparable from tactics which incorporated the goal – the tactics of non-violence. Not for them the measured use of force in the strategy for a new social order. Would not the sanctioning of such means corrupt the very end that was sought? Yet, while the social gospel taught love, not violence, it also asserted that all men were implicated in social guilt. How then could the social gospel pacifist preserve the purity of his means in a corrupt world? The repression of this problem with respect to international issues was perhaps one consequence of the frustration of the social gospel encounter with industrial reality in the first half of the decade. The revival of prosperity later simply glossed over the repression. In the renewed attack upon capitalism in the 1930s, some social gospel pacifists were able to sanction the strike as a non-violent weapon, but when the struggle passed into that upon fascism, the tension became a live one, and the parties split.

Yet another fundamental problem of the peace was that of the use of force by such an agency as the League to restrain aggressive nations. Fairbairn's skepticism about the usefulness of the League prior to the destruction of the 'war system' seemed due in part at least to an inability or unwillingness to credit the possibility of a world of international peace in which peace was simply the absence of outright war. This problem did not seriously afflict Canadian pacifists in the 1920s. How-ever, it was not simply a problem of the pacifist. It afflicted the broader church-

62 Meyer, *The Protestant Search for Political Realism, 1919–1941*, pp. 50–2

based peace movement as well. Consistent church support of the League was accompanied by the belief that the peculiar contribution of the churches was the creation of a spirit of goodwill among people of all lands. To view the latter tactic and the activities that arose from it apart from League support is not to do justice to the mind of the church in this subject. However, there was a tension between the 'world' for which the League was preparing and that implied in this church tactic. In large measure the tension was a consequence of social gospel attitudes. When churchmen praised the League as an institution of the kingdom of God,[63] when they saw the Disarmament Conference of 1921 as a sign of the adoption of Christian principles in international affairs, or when they countered the early wartime argument that the war implied the failure of Christianity with the reply that Christianity had never been tried,[64] they were betraying a view of international life in which ultimate hopes were fulfilled, where the lion would indeed lie down with the lamb, where each man would indeed sit under his fig tree and none make him afraid. This outlook did not contrast sharply with some of the general rhetoric about the League, but it did with the world of the League in which the mechanics of collective security would be a continuing necessity. Creighton cautioned that the League did not stand for absolute departure from war, but to restrain it.[65] Awareness of this tension was apparent in the articles on 'War and Peace' by the Rev. Selby Jefferson in the *New Outlook* in 1928. Jefferson was both enthused by United States insistence on a multilateral treaty to outlaw war and concerned that it might be a means to renounce the covenant of the League. The League, he observed, did not call for renunciation of war as an instrument of policy, but for pledges to wage war against any disturber of the peace. Jefferson resolved the problem by viewing the new proposal as 'crowning evidence of a new sense of confidence the League has inspired.'[66] In other words, church strategy was not simply to make the task of the League easier, but to change the whole quality of international life so as to make the mechanics of the League unnecessary. Thus the church progressives transferred the essentials of their approach from industrial issues to the world of international relations. It was not insignificant that the rise of interest in peace action followed sharply on the heels of the disillusionment of the progressives in the industrial realm. The transfer of social hopes to a fresh field of endeavour, in effect, cancelled the real significance of that encounter with reality. Thus the day of reckoning for the progressive social gospel was postponed. In large measure, as a consequence, the church-based peace movement, despite its protestations of League support, bore

---

63 CG, 8 Nov. 1922, p. 19; *Presbyterian and Westminster*, 26 Dec. 1918, p. 587
64 *Presbyterian Witness*, 8 Dec. 1921, p. 3
65 *New Outlook*, 15 June 1927, p. 13   66 *Ibid.*, 25 April 1928, pp. 7, 25

marks of irrelevance, and with the best of motives may have contributed to the failure of collective security between 1919 and 1939. But the failure of the League cannot be laid at the door of these movements of Christian internationalism when continued exclusive nationalism, isolationism, imperial expansion, military growth, and ideological strife prepared yet another holocaust for the children of the twentieth century. Yet the social gospel was not without guilt.

It may have been coincidence, but it was a notable fact, that the founding of the Canadian Council of the World Alliance for International Friendship through the Churches occurred in 1926, one year after church union, and the same year as the defeat of the Ontario Temperance Act and the decline of the Progressive party. On the one hand, the social purpose of church union meshed with that of the World Alliance, and on the other hand, the conservative wing of the social gospel, in crisis over the defeat of their campaigns to 'possess the land' for righteousness, may have found in the alliance's stress on a strategy 'through the Churches' a ready agency for the diversion of their passion. Visitors like C.C. Morrison in 1925 and 1928 linked church union with the peace issue.[67] And stalwarts of the prohibition movement who were also on or near the conservative wing of the social gospel, such as James Endicott, S.D. Chown, John Coburn, George Pidgeon, the editor of the *Presbyterian Witness*, and many members and leaders of the WCTU, were to be found in considerable numbers in this phase of the peace movement in the later twenties.[68] The prohibition movement had been international, and prohibition in North America had aroused touchy issues in Canadian-American relations. It is not surprising that the Canadian Council of the alliance should have turned so readily to activities in the latter field.

As with the resurgence of pacifism, the thrust of the churches into peace activity came at a time when other avenues of social reform seemed to be closing off. Thus it may be reasonably suggested that the rise of the peace movement in the 1920s was, in one of its major aspects, a function of the crisis of the social gospel in Canada. It was at the same time, and partly by that token, an expression of the social gospel. As a consequence, the peace movement was burdened with a religious function it was doomed to betray. Roughly speaking, it became part of the tactics of the pure end of the kingdom of God conceived as an imminent world order, and of the pure means signifying the presence of the kingdom within the pacifist believer. If there was a tension between the social gospel and pacifism, it was for a

---

67 *Ibid.*, 1 July 1925, p. 7; 21 March 1928, p. 14
68 *Ibid.*, 16 Feb. 1927, pp. 26–7; 11 May 1927, pp. 15, 21; Grant, *George Pidgeon*, pp. 119–21; Schwartz, 'Samuel Dwight Chown,' p. 215

time obscured, not simply by external circumstances, but by the similarity of their belief that the absolute was immanent in real means or real ends in history. In the relatively low key of social and international problems of the later 1920s, the tactics of the pure end and those of the pure means could shift from one to the other with relative ease. In either case, a religious force which had so conceived its religious hopes in immanent terms called for social action to assuage the extra anxiety world problems placed upon its followers.

One of the few in the social gospel who demonstrated a notable sense of realism in his attitude to international questions was Ernest Thomas. When the Methodist Department of Evangelism and Social Service undertook to educate the church on the subject, Thomas seems to have been selected as its chief spokesman. In conference addresses and in numerous articles from 1924 on, he presented a lucid and sensitive view of foreign relations in the light of Christian theology and ethics.[69] Only in him did there seem to be no attempt to resolve the frustrations of earlier crises in an international crusade informed by real if unacknowledged inadequacies in the social gospel.

Almost a year before Fairbairn's articles, Thomas had penned a strong critique of pacifism, which at the same time rejected simplistic arguments validating defensive war or assuming the power of good will in itself. The objection to war was not its toll of life, nor resort to force, but, he said, the impatient and faithless reversion to a self-determined 'short-cut' to national objectives rather than reliance on the more involved way of 'social determination.' The former attitude was the standing temptation of national interests. Talk about defensive war and defence of the oppressed was, he said, too easy a rationalization of such interests, and the 'good will' thesis ignored both their power and its rationalization.[70]

The difference between his view of such interests and that of Fairbairn's 'war system' was not so much in the identity of many of the economic and political forces involved, but in his use of the idea. For Fairbairn, the 'war system' had become an *a priori* means of judging situations and international relations in general, whereas Thomas was particular in his examination of each case. Hence, to counter Fairbairn's interpretation of the origin of the war, and that of Harry Elmer Barnes in articles in the *Christian Century*, Thomas wrote four articles in 1925–6 showing the complexity of the origins of the war and the complicity and the apprehension of

69 *Annual Report*, 1923–4, Methodist Department of ESS, p. 27; *Western Methodist Recorder*, Oct. 1924, pp. 4–5
70 CG, 15 Aug. 1923, p. 5

all parties in the years before its outbreak. He pleaded the necessity of refraining from censuring statesmen who failed to master the situation, and urged general acceptance of responsibility.[71]

Fairbairn was not easily put off and cited chapter and verse to show apparent duplicity of British leaders over understandings entered into in the Triple Entente. Unless such information was available to the people, he observed, there seemed little point in Thomas' argument for the need of informed people with wide sympathies.[72] To this counter-attack Thomas replied that Fairbairn was chiefly reviewing well-known facts. It was one thing to argue the grave inadequacy of the policy of the entente, he said, and another to say a specific arrangement was made and denied. The question was a crucial one, because upon it hung different strategies in promoting peaceful world organization.[73] Not the 'war system' thesis with its panoply of lying leaders but the inherent problems of exclusive nationalism directed by fallible men generated the engines of war. In an observation which might later have been called Niebuhrian, Thomas suggested that 'we may will peace and at the same time adopt policies which make for war.' Such were the ironies of history. This was what lay behind 1914, and no one's passionate revolt against the evil of war would guarantee the prophetic insight which might have avoided it.[74]

Fairbairn's analysis implied distrust of such instruments as the League as long as the 'war system' was intact, but presented no feasible course of action for overcoming the system. It was a strategy that resembled an engine for which no adequate transmission could be devised. It could chiefly stand, pistons plunging and crankshaft turning, as pure potentiability of function. Thomas' analysis, and in this he was joined by Gifford, indicated a slow process of building international institutions of 'social determination' by which the hazards of nationalism could be overcome. He was reminded again how slow the process might be by the celebration of the religion of nationalism in Canada in 1927.[75] But war, in the interval – or in spite of international political organization – might still rise up to confront Christians with conflicting loyalties and difficult decisions. Fairbairn, and Gifford, too, in the last analysis, had a clear and heroic word for such. Thomas, they might have suggested, seemed simply to leave them in confusion and at the mercy of traditional loyalties, and hence of *raison d'état*.

Thomas did not develop any full answer to this question in the twenties, but he encouraged and laid down guide-lines for reflection on the subject, which suggested

71 *Ibid.*, 14 Jan. 1925, p. 6; 21 Jan. 1925, pp. 7, 9; *New Outlook*, 2 Dec. 1925, pp. 7, 29; 6 Jan. 1926, p. 22

72 *New Outlook*, 23 Dec. 1925, pp. 5, 11   73 *Ibid.*, 6 Jan. 1926, p. 22

74 *Ibid.*, 12 Aug. 1925, pp. 5–6   75 *Ibid.*, 27 July 1927, pp. 5, 23

an answer to which he inclined. All Christians could agree that war had no place in a Christian world order. In an imperfectly ordered, competitive world order, however, it was possible that circumstances might prove war to be a lesser evil. However, the church and its members might under certain conditions defy the state. But simply to say that war was war (or business was business) and was external to Christian duty or was the overriding Christian consideration – whether said by statist or pacifist – was to revert to a 'crude polytheism.'[76] A full answer to the problem of Christian duty should war occur could not be given to Canadians in the 1920s, for the context of decision was not yet apparent. The hard decision of Fairbairn was, in fact, the easy one. But its evasion of social reality, the last thing he wished, made this easy decision potentially more tragic than the more difficult course counselled by Thomas.

There were, of course, other thoughtful Christians who took a similar position of international realism. Canon H.J. Cody, rector of St Paul's Anglican Church, Toronto, was one.[77] Newton W. Rowell was another. Rowell was chairman of the 1928 General Council Sessional Committee on War and Peace, which gave a ringing summons to the United church to consider her chief task to be that of peace. While it acknowledged 'the evidence of a new and better day,' it refused to blind its eyes to 'the existence of conditions among the nations which contain the threat of war.' The committee called for active support of international agencies and a broad programme of Christian propaganda and education to create a Christian public opinion and understanding of the causes of war and the problems peace proposals created. With such a world citizenry, 'governments would feel that they could not proceed to war, except on the most unchallengeable grounds of freedom and of right.' The report as a whole was an articulation of the thesis that while every engagement in war was not evil, every war had its roots in evil. This was the foundation of the 'new crusade' to which the committee called the church.[78]

The report was a statement both the supporters of the World Alliance and Thomas could accept. Both, however, dissented from the failure of the committee to condemn cadets in schools. Both were more prone to look ahead to the 'new day.' Thomas had hopes that the 'new type of Christianity' prefigured by church union would bring about 'the transcendence of national patriotism in a truly Catholic Christian society.'[79] But it was just at this point in a matter of attitude and of substance that he departed from the World Alliance position and went beyond the General Council report. In contrast to the former he treated the hope of a new

76 *Ibid.*, 12 Aug. 1925, pp. 5–6
77 *Canadian Churchman*, 16 Sept. 1926, p. 597
78 *New Outlook*, 19 Sept. 1928, p. 2   79 *Ibid.*, 12 Aug. 1925, pp. 5–6

social order with fine discrimination. He did not read his hopes wantonly into the very course of contemporary history, nor mistake his critical standpoint vis-à-vis the social order for the social process itself. And he went beyond the World Alliance and the General Council report both in his analysis of the social conflict within the nation and in the content of social democracy he poured into the mould of the Christian social order for which he worked. These were the signposts of the gulf in the peace movement between the progressive and radical wings of the social gospel, and between the General Council type of realism and radical social gospel realism.

Thomas' position on the vital issues of war and peace seemed to strike a new note in the social gospel chorus in the degree to which it rang true to the demands of social reality and of responsible Christian ethics. It was essentially the new note of a social gospel schooled in the crises of 1919 to 1928. The note had not been altogether absent from Thomas in the earlier years. The discreet character of his thought had always inhibited him from the prophetic passion of such a person as Salem Bland and from the pacifism of Woodsworth, with whom he otherwise shared a great deal. There had never been much doubt as to whether Thomas had his social hope firmly in hand, or whether the passion of the new social order held him in its grip. In the post-war situation of the later 1920s he was, therefore, one of the few who were able to re-present the social hope to a social gospel generation whose eschatology had gone awry, but who, rather than recognize that fact, had invested their hope in yet another cause for the realization of the kingdom of God on earth.

Thomas, in fact, represented the social gospel in transition. The new form of the social gospel was not to be clear until the acids of depression and international crises more severe than the twenties had known had done their corrosive work. But in the midst of a perilous prosperity which tempted church extension departments to make hay while the sun shone and which hid festering sores of industrial Canada, an agonizing reappraisal of the social gospel was under way and a new social gospel, or as its later proponents preferred to call it, a radical Christianity, was in genesis.

22

The Social Gospel and the Crisis in Progressivism

The crest and crisis of the social gospel in Canada between 1914 and 1928 was in one respect a series of crests and crises in the various expressions the movement had evolved, and in another more fundamental respect a crest and crisis in the conceptions commonly held across the front of progressivism which the social gospel had so largely informed. In 1914 the movement was marked by slight polarities of outlook and association. However, as the late wartime crisis was followed by the agrarian revolt, labour unrest, and depression, and as social gospellers became more closely allied with various groups in conflict in Canadian society, differentiation within the movement was pressed into tension and even antagonism. This growing differentiation marked at the same time a new degree of influence for the social gospel. As in its position within the churches, so in its association with the movements of revolt and reform, the social gospel did not exist simply as an outside opinion regarding their role and place in the social process, but as an internal factor in their development. Hence, the crest and crisis of the social gospel was intimately bound up with the fortunes of the farmer, labour, and social work, as well as of the churches and interdenominational organizations, just as to a lesser or greater degree the fortunes of these groups were influenced by the adequacy of the concepts of the social gospel.

It was no mere coincidence that the culmination of the crisis in the social gospel was contemporary with the final crisis of the Progressive party, which seemed destined in 1921 to take its place as a major force in Canadian political life. From the beginning, however, the party lacked unity, not only in terms of the scale of social reform envisaged but also in terms of the tactics it should adopt. Those who aimed at a revivified Liberal party sat beside those who wished the Progressives to become a major party in their own right. These in turn were seated with Progressives who wished to see an end to partisan politics as such. Joined with them were the radical exponents of 'group government,' chiefly UFA representatives, and working closely with them were Irvine and Woodsworth whose ideas on political reform were tied in with a socialist programme of social and economic reform. It was a shaky alliance. From the beginning it had been subject to the persistent wooing of

Mackenzie King, leader of the minority Liberal government. It arrived on Parliament hill at a time of economic depression and lowered resources, when farmers were turning again to co-operative economic action for relief. All of these problems affected the course of Progressive politics, but none of them, nor all of them together, is an entirely satisfying explanation of the Progressive decline.

Explanations of the decline of the party in terms of 'a new surge of nationalism and the revival of prosperity' have rightly been rejected in favour of an explanation based on the passing of the reform movement at large.[1] That in turn, however, raises questions. It is probably true that one reason for the loss of élan in the larger movement was simply its success, and that 'public opinion had absorbed about all the reform it could in one generation.' It has also been argued that reform had been cut short by the war and the issues that arose out of it, but in many respects the war promoted reform as much as it detracted from it. Among reform successes, prohibition and extension of the franchise were hastened by it, while government intervention in social and economic matters was rendered more acceptable. Most of the issues of labour radicalism and political fragmentation were in the making as much in spite of the war as because of it. Furthermore, in considerable measure radicalism was a concomitant and extension of the progressive impulse, rather than an independent phenomenon compromising reform. Neither success nor external interference was the primary cause of the decline of reform at large, but rather a more fundamental crisis in the source or sources of the élan of reform. It is necessary, therefore, to turn to the ideology which unified and gave meaning to reform activity. In short, while the problems which confronted the Progressive party reflected those of the reform movement at large, the fate of both was heavily intertwined with the crisis of the social gospel.

The mingling of the fortunes of the social gospel and Progressive politics was a complex affair. The fortunes of the social gospel in non-political realms was bound to have repercussions for the political movement, and vice versa. In this connection, like the social gospel at large, it was not all of one piece in politics, and the question of the correlation of the major wings of the social gospel and the various factions of progressivism inevitably arises, whether it can be satisfactorily demonstrated or not. Finally, the social gospel in politics provides its own particular instance of crest and crisis in these years.

The significance of the experiences of the social gospel at large for the Progressive

1 Morton, *The Progressive Party*, pp. 266–8. The other important interpretations of the crisis in Progressive politics are to be found in McNaught, *A Prophet in Politics*, Graham, *Arthur Meighen*, Cook, *J.W. Dafoe*, and Neatby, *William Lyon Mackenzie King*.

party after 1922 is easier to suggest than to document with any precision. The causes which had marked the association of the conservative social gospel with the Progressive party were not propitious ones in the twenties. Prohibition had ranked high in the priorities of the Progressive constituency, but prohibitionists were being steadily outflanked from 1920 to 1926. That Progressives in the House were the most ardent proponents of prohibitive legislation as devices of moral and social reform has frequently been noted. When W.C. Good, for instance, introduced a bill to curb race-track gambling, 80 per cent of the Progressive MPS supported it, although it was defeated in the House as a whole.[2] The moral earnestness of Progressives was to become the primary condition of their dilemma in 1925–6, when a liquor-corrupted Liberal administration weighed in the balance with Conservative tariff iniquity.

The welfare legislative programme favoured by progressive social gospellers of the Social Service Council made headway by contrast with that of conservatives, but the crises which beset their industrial affinities and programmes and led to the taming of social service enthusiasm for labour and to a new interest in the 'socialized businessman' increased the susceptibility of moderate Progressives to the blandishments of Mr King. It is difficult, also, to doubt that the disenchantment of social service and the secularizing of social work bore some relation to the decline of the divinities which had surrounded the farmers' movement in politics. Furthermore, the Progressive party had been the one party to give unanimous support in 1925 to the parliamentary bills enabling church union.[3] While this was not an experience of defeat, it was not one likely to encourage political separateness. Although difficult to document in detail, the loss of social gospel élan after 1923 inevitably affected both the parliamentary Progressive party and the constituency to which it appealed. The decline of the social passion could hardly have any other effect than to make the Progressive party appear more and more exotic as the months passed.

While conservatives and progressives of the social gospel were slowly accepting a new orthodoxy, the radicals were experiencing increasing alienation in church and state. It is not surprising that their crisis experiences had the effect not of eroding identity but of sharpening it. The decline of the Labor church accompanied the formation of the Ginger Group under Woodsworth in 1924, and shifted something of the zeal and the burden of the religious hope still more fully into politics itself. It is not surprising that this was in turn a contribution to the disintegration of the Progressive party after 1924.

2 'Social Service Committee Report,' *Year Book of the Congregational Union of Canada*, 1923, p. 43

3 Grant, *George Pidgeon*, p. 99

But the decline of the Progressive party was more than a reflection of the crisis in the other reform movements informed by the social gospel. It was, in essentials, the same crisis, a crisis in fundamental concepts brought on by the encounter with social reality. The ambiguities of the situation of the Progressives in Parliament in the years 1922–6 were due in no small measure to the religious hope of the social gospel, in whose 'light' the congeries of interests which made up the Progressive movement was 'obscured.' Its dedication as a broad movement for justice tended to prevent Progressives from seeing the hard core of self-interest driving them toward the establishment of new balance of power relationships within the nation. A new balance of power might provide a more just society, but when Progressives spoke of a new social order, they spoke not in the accents of power and interest, but in the tones of moral earnestness, good will, social righteousness, and brotherhood. The propensity to see the politics of the Progressive movement as a new, non-partisan politics and as a harbinger of a qualitatively different society was to ignore the whole history of politics. This was not entirely a liability for a protest movement. The partisans of reform have always had to find their justification in some measure outside the established framework of politics and beyond the categories of history. But the problems created for responsible politics were evident in Salem Bland's formulation of the Progressive task: 'To destroy the old social order is not enough. What we want is to see the new social order built up inside or alongside the old, so that all shall not be for even a little while homeless.'[4]

When the Progressive party refused to accept the role of official opposition to which its numbers entitled it, it was attempting to act 'inside or alongside the old,' while rejecting the ways of the old. This left it a more easy prey to the machinations of those who accepted the old, and more readily subject to eruptions of the internal divisions which had been sublimated in the 'non-politics of hope.' With the assembly of the fourteenth Canadian Parliament in 1922, the stage had been set for yet another encounter of the social gospel with social realities, and the curtain rose upon one of the most fascinating dilemmas in Canadian political history. The test of Progressive political hopes and tactics was also a test of the social gospel.

Only among the radical Progressives, which is virtually to say among the radical social gospel, did the non-politics of hope survive almost unscathed from the fiery furnace of 1926. Because this religious demand of the social gospel was more insistent in Woodsworth and many in his group, and because the programme of reconstruction it entailed was clearer, more radical, and comprehensive than was the case with the bulk of the Progressives, the Ginger Group survived the gruelling crisis of

4 Bland Papers, 'The Call of Canada to the Farmers,' *The Farmers' Sun* [ca Oct. 1921]

1926 to become the nucleus of a farmer-labour party, built on traditional party lines, but still imbued with many of the conceptions of the social gospel. For another six years, however, they were just to be a nucleus – not even that, but a group, small, able, trenchant in analysis, and bold in social proposals, gaining in respect, but for all that a small group left high and dry by the retreat of the Progressive tide – a sign of the crest of the social gospel in politics before its ebb.

Hence, for the social gospel at large, the first significance of the decline of the Progressive party was the withering of the belief that immense power for social regeneration would accompany the progress of democratic movements like those of the farmers' organizations. This would only be true, Henry Wise Wood had pointed out, if the movement remained devoted to its principles and subject to the spirit of Christ. Progressives generally thought of themselves in that light, but found, in their excursion into federal politics, that they had to mix the evil with the good like any other party. They had failed to force either a complete realignment of political parties, or any extensive reform of the political system itself. The price of Progressive support for the Liberals in the session of 1926 had entailed the end of Alberta's semi-colonial status, and the bare beginnings of a federal social welfare state. Ironically, these were more concessions to the radicals who survived the Progressive debacle of 1926 than to those who returned to the Liberal fold. Generally speaking, the populism of the western Progressives fused once again with the Whig tradition, and in the sequel, the Progressive party was no more.

The non-politics of hope of moderate Progressives did not easily die, but lived on in a muted form in the Liberal party. When Mackenzie King piped a populist tune in the constitutional crisis of 1926, it was possible to sublimate the Progressive encounter with political reality in the defence of the people against the power of the crown. But this was old liberalism, not new politics – the spurious, but highly successful expedient of a cornered politician. Despite the explosion of King's interpretation of the issue in later years, erstwhile Progressives had difficulty making a rational response to the argument.[5] It was too much to think that political innocence might have been sacrificed in vain. But the Liberal régimes which followed in the later 1920s and the 1930s gave little evidence of having received a transfusion of reformist blood in 1926.

In the political aftermath of the crest and crisis of the social gospel and progressivism alike, the standards of hope were giving way to the standpoint of pragmatism. The fact may have been obscured by widespread appropriation of the language of the social gospel and of progressivism, which had begun during the war. By the end of the twenties the currency of reform had so depreciated that even

5 See, for instance, Cook in *J.W. Dafoe*, pp. 165–6

Ku Klux Klan leaders in Saskatchewan could take a spurious place in the progressive procession by calling themselves social reformers, even winning a few erstwhile Progressives of some prominence to their cause.[6] Perhaps even this was some evidence of the influence of the progressive tradition in general, and of the social gospel in particular. It also suggested that the new Canada to which the social gospel had tried to respond – and which in another sense it had tried to create – had overtaken most of the categories in which the social gospel had conceived its task. The ranks of all movements stood fractured. All had accomplished something; none had realized its hopes. Some, not accepting the crisis, continued to affirm old approaches. Others called for reorganization. A few who could hear what the spirit was saying through the events of the previous decade began to engage in fundamental reconsiderations. But the salient fact was that by 1928 crisis had overtaken all major phases of the social gospel.

What the precise nature and degree of the social gospel's influence upon Canadian society was during this period of its crest is difficult to assess. It would be too much to say that it won any of the churches fully to its concept of social reality or its interpretation of the social implications of the gospel. Yet after 1914 no major church could ignore its force in the formulation of social policy. Whether accepted fully by the churches or not, it underscored the need for an adequate social ethic for the new Canada. In this respect, it brought a broad range of social reforms within the sanctions of Canadian Protestantism, and in so doing was probably the medium by which the multitude of social programmes making up the Canadian welfare state first found their way into the main channels of Canadian social attitudes. Some of the agencies of the social gospel had been prominent in winning legislation of aid to the underprivileged or the overpowered, while others had played a notable role in developing more adequate programmes of social work and in promoting the national organizations of social workers themselves. To ask the proper weight to assign the social gospel in the policies and actions of many agrarian labour leaders would be an impossible demand, yet that it was a fundamental motivation in their various campaigns for what they believed to be a more just social order cannot be doubted. Although it would take much research to prove the contention, it almost seems that to scratch a progressive in most endeavours from 1914 to 1928 was to find a social gospeller, either avowed or implicit. In short, to write a history of this period in Canada without allowing the social gospel a significant place would be to miss one of the most creative, if sometimes intangible, movements of the time. If its

6 Calderwood, 'The Rise and Fall of the Ku Klux Klan in Saskatchewan,' chap. VIII, 'The Klan and the Political Parties'

ambiguities brought conflict between wings of the movement, that apparent defect perhaps served to enlarge, rather than diminish, the range of social gospel impact.

The task of deliberate social change is so formidable that it would seem to require not only a real interest to serve and a body of ideas by which to order action, but also a sense of a more ultimate significance than the temporary gain of an ephemeral social group. The history of reform movements is replete with the intimate association of religion and reform – and hence also with instances of the confusion of this religious dimension of reform and the immediate interest it serves. Over the centuries the most constant ingredients of the tradition of reform and revolt in the West have been, on the one hand, a great vision of the end, the consummation of the meaning of history, and on the other, a desire to live in that meaning now.[7] In the mainstream of Christian theology the vision and the desire have been kept under tight control, maintaining a critical tension between the real world and the world of hope that shone so brightly. The ancient civilizations had not known, or at least failed to embody, such a tension in their social orders, and it had been the great work of Augustine in the fifth century to overcome the compact unity of the political and religious orders, which had been a mark of the old empires, in his conception of the City of God and the City of Man. The City of Man – the world of politics – did not derive its values from or within itself and could only secure proximate realizations of the understanding of the good it derived elsewhere. The City of God – the world of religious faith, of hope, and love – could never become the City of Man in time, but it provided the true measure of political or social accomplishment.[8]

Augustine's conception is equally relevant to the political religions of the fifth and the twentieth centuries, and in one form or another has been normative for most of the subsequent history of western civilization. Yet it has been normal for political and religious movements to break away from the norm in such a way as to lose the creative tension for themselves, although not necessarily for society itself. Conservative Christians tended to sanctify the established order while isolating it from judgment by interpreting the Kingdom of God in an entirely supra-historical sense. Their radical counterparts tended to reject the established order in its entirety in the name of a thoroughly historical conception of the consummation of God's

---

7 See Morris, *The Christian Origins of Social Revolt*, for a brief, suggestive, but rather partisan review of the subject; also, from another perspective, Lowith, *Meaning in History*.

8 See the very impressive volumes of Voegelin's still uncompleted study, *Order and History*. His central argument is presented in *The New Science of Politics*.

rule, but usually in the interest of a particular group, class, or nation.[9] There may be few nobler uses of religion than breaking the bonds of the captive, but the fusion of religion and politics creates problems of its own for any political order. Whether this is an inevitable concomitant of the genesis, generation, and culmination of reform may be debated, but that it was often so with the social gospel has been clear in this account.

To raise this large question is to pose the religious problem that lay at the heart of the crisis of the social gospel in Canada from 1914 to 1928. The essence of the religious problem is that man, a creature of time yet able to transcend it, is satisfied with nothing less than eternal significance. The essence of the problem of the relation of religion and social order, therefore, is that man cannot leave his ultimate desires in heaven, nor refrain from colouring his temporal constructions with ultimate meaning. It may have been no accident that Bland's title, *The New Christianity*, was the same as one of Saint-Simon, one of the precursors of Comte's positivism. In a culture, many of whose intellectual constructs were strongly influenced by positivism, there was a greater likelihood of the religious hope being diverted into the drive for worldly accomplishment, with the corresponding heightening of the temptation to read social reality in terms of religious wish-fulfilment. Although the social gospellers spoke often of justice, society was approached by the social gospel more from the point of view of the fulfilment of love than from the point of view of justice. Educating, campaigning, even politicking for good will took the place of nice calculation of power relations and proximate goals. Absolute ethics and tactics became confused.

The Brotherhoods, and many in the social service departments, reacted against autocracy in industry in the name of personality. If they were aware of the fact of power relations, they did not really credit their reality, and clothed their social tactics in the appealing garments of an ultimate brotherhood. The Labor church, on the contrary, was fully aware of power, having grown out of such a confrontation. Part of its expression was a political programme to overcome the power of capital. This strategy was realistic, but the task itself was looked upon as a religious task in the belief that human alienation in society would be overcome within history. However, the formally religious aspect, the Labor church itself, died from an essential failure to distinguish between the religious and the political and economic concern. The New Christianity struck something of a mean between the Brotherhoods

9 On the interesting subject of the relation of this phenomenon to conceptions of history, see Tillich, 'Historical and Non-historical Conceptions of History,' *The Protestant Era*, pp. 16–31. See also Niebuhr, *The Social Sources of Denominationalism*, chaps. II and III, 'The Churches of the Disinherited'

and the Labor churches. Bland and Thomas were ready to credit the reality of the struggle for power, but were kept from accepting this as a normal human condition by believing in an immanent God working out a society of brotherhood. Public ownership was indeed, for them, a movement of divinity in the modern world. The new evangelism treated the figure of Jesus in terms of the historical records of his life, but at the same time accepted him as a pan-historical absolute. While in some ways this made the gospel more immediate, it opened it to a demythologizing and remythologizing process in terms of a heroic personal ethic and an immanent evolutionary eschatology. Thus the partisans of the theology of radical reform in the Student Christian Movement believed that in their repetition of the sacrifice of Jesus as they understood it, the new social order would ensue. The internationalism of the peace movement of the 1920s, similarly, could perhaps be better described as 'inter-personalism.' Their formulations were hardly designed for a world of principalities and powers.

The hopefulness of all the phases of the 'religion of the new age,' indeed, of the Progressive tradition itself, was based on belief in an immanent principle of meaning. Thus, for instance, it was only necessary that labour be brought to a knowledge of what it already was, making the social gospel role analogous to that of the Communist party in historical materialism. With consciousness of evolution came, it seemed, both a knowledge of destiny and a sense of control. Because of this immanent principle it seemed reasonable to anticipate a society in which all human relationships would be free and open and loving – and at the same time disciplined. But love, like truth, is both a very personal and a trancendent reality in which man lives but which he cannot programme. It could be aided by social arrangements, and its forms of expression might affect the social order. But in another sense it was irrelevant to it. Nor could any social arrangement guarantee love. The practitioners of the 'religion of the new age' somehow recognized this in urging the necessity of religion. But could religion guarantee love? They all readily acknowledged that religious interests had crucified their Jesus – had crucified the very personification of love. Religion, too, served finally to point beyond itself to those reaches of man incapable of incorporation in the social order – or in the religious order either.

The religious problem underlying the crisis of the social gospel in Canada was barely being formulated in 1927 and 1928. At times Bland could write that Christianity was not sociology, the gospel was not politics, and religion was not ethics, but preoccupation with these things and intoxication with the new wines of the 'real Jesus' and evolution led to an underplaying of the insight. Helen Nichol was asking her difficult questions of the Student Christian Movement. Canadian Christians who attended ecumenical conferences in Europe in the course of the decade were aware of the new force in Protestant theology of Karl Barth and his uncompromising reassertion of the 'wholly otherness' of God, with the radical judgment it entailed upon all social accomplishment.[10] Canadians could not be expected to know that in 1928 a young Dutch scholar, Visser't Hooft, was finishing the first penetrating analysis of the intellectual background of the social gospel in America, but he, too, was voicing skepticism of the continuity of cultural progress and the will of God.[11]

It was not surprising, however, that, as the social problems of a growing industrial urban society multiplied and as new currents of social thought developed, the urgency of the evangelical concern to save this man now, should have been transferred to the social sphere and social action become virtually a religious rite. Nor is it astonishing, although it was hardly intended by social gospellers, that the social gospel represented Canada in mid-passage from a society that was jealous of the status of its churches to one that comfortably wore the habillements of secularism. The social gospel's heavy emphasis on the immanence of divinity in the social process, for better or for worse, encouraged the development of a secular society, and at the same time imparted, at least for a time, a sense of meaning to that development that was essentially religious. But the immanence of divinity cannot be long sustained, and the new orthodoxy of the mid-twenties (one of social service and business efficiency, the radicals said), entailed not simply temporary compromises but a degree of disengagement with the divine vision and the decline of the social passion. A new religious experience and a genuine sense of divine transcendence, or a comfortable complacency were the primary alternatives of the new situation of the latter 1920s. Both could be readily observed.

Here was an end to enchantment. The orthodox might have foretold it, but most of them had not taken up the whip of cords against the defilement of the temple. In their righteousness they had nothing to say. In the search for a valid Christian ethic for industrial Canada, they were irrelevant. In its application they were often at the centre of the problem. But was the process of reconsideration, evident in the writing of Ernest Thomas and stirring in the struggles of the Student Christian Movement with such themes as 'Man at Odds with His Society,' a ground of hope that a new, more adequate social conscience than that fostered by the social gospel was being formulated for the day when again 'an angel would trouble the waters'? To answer that question would be to begin another story. The epilogue of the social gospel is the prologue of the Radical Christianity of the years of the great depression.

10 This would be especially true of delegates to the World Conference on Faith and Order held at Lausanne, August 1927. See series of six articles by D.L. Ritchie in the *New Outlook*, beginning 19 Oct. 1927.
11 Visser't Hooft, *The Background to the Social Gospel in America*

Bibliography

The extent and nature of the sources, both primary and secondary, upon which this study is based are apparent in the citations which accompany the text, but it may be useful to indicate briefly in a single place the proportions of the research which underlies it, and provide a list of works cited for more complete bibliographical information than appears in the footnotes to the text.

For its general context the book rests upon extensive reading in the literature of modern social thought and social movements in general, of Christian social thought and movements in particular, and of Canadian history. This study is especially indebted to the deservedly well-known literature on some of the Canadian social movements the social gospel became part of – works associated with such names as Morton, Sharp, Lipset, Masters, MacPherson, Irving, Clark, and McNaught, most of whom recognized the presence of the social gospel but, except for McNaught, did not pursue it.

The slight secondary literature in article, book, and thesis form relating to the Canadian social gospel, and the small but significant body of books and pamphlets produced by the movement in Canada, were thoroughly examined. Much more valuable among the published sources for ferreting out the history of the Canadian social gospel was the church press of the Protestant denominations. In the proportions in which it was of use it is cited above. However, virtually every publication of this kind was carefully examined for the years in question: the *Canadian Baptist*, the *Canadian Congregationalist*, the *Canadian Churchman* (Anglican), the *Canadian Friend*, the *Canadian Student* (Student Christian Movement), the *Christian Guardian* (Methodist), the *Christian Messenger* (after 1922 the *Canadian Disciple*), the *New Outlook* (United Church), the *Presbyterian Record*, the *Presbyterian and Westminster*, the *Presbyterian Witness* (Halifax), the *Presbyterian Witness* (Toronto), the *Western Methodist Recorder* (after 1925 the *Western Recorder*, United Church, in British Columbia), *Youth and Service* (Methodist).

For editorial comment and further reporting on specific events of significance, the daily press was regularly consulted. The value of an occasional daily such as the *Toronto Daily Star*, however, went far beyond that limited purpose. Progressive, farm, and labour papers and journals proved to be an especially rich source, and long runs of the following were consulted: the *Alberta Labor News*, the *Alberta Non-Partisan*, the BC *Federationist*, the *Canadian Forum*, the *Confederate*, the *Edmonton Free Press*, the *Grain Growers' Guide*, the *Industrial Banner*, the *Nutcracker*, the OBU *Bulletin*, the *Searchlight*, the *Single Taxer and Direct Legislation Bulletin*, *Social Welfare*, the *Western Independent*, the *Western Labor News*, and the *Voice*.

The official records and reports, published or otherwise, of the highest councils of the Protestant denominations, together with those of the relevant subordinate boards, departments, and committees, have, for the most part, been consulted, the most extensive and valuable being those of the Methodist and United churches. The minutes of the General Committee of the Student Christian Movement and those of the Social Service Council were examined, as were the proceedings of the conferences sponsored by them, where available. Reference was also made to the minutes of the Board of Directors and of the Executive of the Board of Wesley College, Winnipeg, of the Winnipeg Methodist Ministerial Association, and of the Board of Directors of the Saskatchewan Grain Growers' Association.

The following collections of papers proved useful: the Salem G. Bland Papers, the George Pidgeon Papers, Papers and Correspondence of the Methodist Court of Appeal, Papers and Reports of Committees of the Methodist General Conference, Papers on the Attitude of the Methodist Church to War, and Papers on Methodist Industrial Relations, 1920–2 (all examined at the United Church Archives, Toronto) ; the Hugh Dobson Papers (United Church Archives, BC Section, Vancouver) ; the RCMP Papers, the Papers of Charles Frederick Hamilton, and the Papers of James Shaver Woodsworth (all at the Public Archives of Canada) ; the William Ivens Papers (Provincial Archives of Manitoba) ; and the Papers on the Alberta School of Religion (Archives of Saskatchewan).

A small body of correspondence and a number of interviews, including two days with William Irvine, complete the general documentation of the book.

BOOKS

The Baptist Convention of Ontario and Quebec. *Baptist Year Book for Ontario and Quebec and Western Canada.* Toronto 1907–30

Berger, Carl. *The Sense of Power: Studies in the Ideas of Canadian Imperialism, 1867–1914.* Toronto 1969

Bland, S.G. *James Henderson,* D.D. Toronto 1926

– *The New Christianity, or the Religion of the New Age.* Toronto 1920

Booth, General William. *In Darkest England and the Way Out.* London 1890

Campbell, R.J. *The New Theology.* Rev. ed., London nd [1909]

Canada. *Report of the Royal Commission on Industrial Relations.* Ottawa 1919

– *Royal Commission on Customs and Excise. Interim Report.* Ottawa 1928

Carter, P.A. *The Decline and Revival of the Social Gospel, 1920–1940.* Ithaca 1956

Case, S.J. *The Social Origins of Christianity.* Chicago 1923

Cleverdon, C.L. *Woman Suffrage Movement in Canada.* Toronto 1950

Cohn, N.R.C. *The Pursuit of the Millennium.* New York 1961

The Congregational Church, Canada. *The Canadian Congregational Year Book.* Toronto 1916–25

Connor, Ralph [C.W. Gordon]. *To Him that Hath.* New York 1921

Cook, Ramsay. *J.W. Dafoe and the Politics of the Free Press.* Toronto 1963

Crysdale, S. *The Industrial Struggle and Protestant Ethics in Canada.* Toronto 1961

Dawson, R.M. *William Lyon Mackenzie King: A Political Biography.* Vol. 1, Toronto 1958

Defence Committee. *The Winnipeg General Sympathetic Strike, May–June, 1919.* Winnipeg nd [1920]

Denison, M. *The People's Power.* Toronto 1960

Dorland, A.G. *A History of the Society of Friends (Quakers) in Canada.* Toronto 1928

Eby, Charles S. *The World Problem and the Divine Solution.* Toronto 1914

Fairbairn, Robert E. *The Appeal to Reality.* New York 1927

Ferns, H.S. and B. Ostry. *The Age of Mackenzie King: The Rise of the Leader.* Toronto 1955

Follett, M.P. *The New State.* New York 1920

Forty Years for Peace, 1914–1954. New York 1954

French, Doris. *Faith, Sweat and Politics.* Toronto 1962

Gandier, Alfred. *The Son of Man Coming in His Kingdom.* New York 1922

Gifford, W.A. *et al. The Christian and War.* Toronto 1926

Goodwin, C.D.W. *Canadian Economic Thought.* Durham, NC 1961

Gordon, C.W. *Postscript to Adventure.* New York 1938

Graham, Roger. *Arthur Meighen: a Biography.* 3 vols., Toronto 1960–5

Grant, John W. *George Pidgeon.* Toronto 1962

Grant, W.L. and C.F. Hamilton. *Principal Grant.* Toronto 1904

Harnack, A. *History of Dogma.* Trans. Neil Buchanan. 7 vols., London *ca* 1900

Hart, E.J. *Wake Up! Montreal! Commercialized Vice and Its Contributors.* Montreal 1919

Hofstadter, Richard. *The Age of Reform.* New York 1955

Hopkins, C.H. *The Rise of the Social Gospel in American Protestantism, 1865–1915.* New Haven 1940

Hopkins, J. Castell. *The Canadian Annual Review.* Toronto 1902–30

Hutchinson, Bruce. *The Incredible Canadian.* New York 1953

Inglis, K.S. *Churches and Working Classes in Victorian England.* London 1963

Irvine, William. *Farmers in Politics.* Toronto 1920

Kidd, Benjamin. *Social Evolution.* London 1894

King, W.L.M. *Industry and Humanity.* Boston and New York 1918

Leete, F.D. *Christian Brotherhoods.* Cincinnati 1912

Lipset, S.M. *Agrarian Socialism: The CCF in Saskatchewan.* Los Angeles and Berkeley 1950

Lower, A.R.M. *Colony To Nation.* Toronto 1946

Löwith, Karl. *Meaning in History.* Chicago 1949

MacDougall, John. *Rural Life in Canada, Its Trends and Tasks.* Toronto 1913

MacGregor, F.A. *The Fall and Rise of Mackenzie King.* Toronto 1962

MacInnis, Grace. *J.S. Woodsworth: A Man to Remember.* Toronto 1953

Masters, D.C. *The Winnipeg General Strike.* Toronto 1950

May, H.F. *Protestant Churches and Industrial America.* New York 1949

McCurdy, J.F. *The Life and Work of D.J. Macdonnell.* Toronto 1897

McNaught, K. *A Prophet in Politics.* Toronto 1959

Mechie, Stewart. *The Church and Scottish Social Developments, 1780–1870.* London 1960

Methodist Church of Canada. *The Doctrine and Discipline, 1914.* Toronto 1915

– *Methodist Year Book.* Toronto 1914–25

– General Conference. *Journal of Proceedings.* Toronto 1894–1922

Meyer, Donald B. *The Protestant Search*

for Political Realism, 1919–1941. Los Angeles and Berkeley 1960

Miller, R.M. American Protestantism and Social Issues, 1919–1939. Chapel Hill, NC 1958

Milner, Viscount Alfred. Speeches Delivered in Canada in the Autumn of 1908. Toronto 1909

Morgan, H.J. Canadian Men and Women of the Time. Toronto 1912

Morris, W.D. The Christian Origins of Social Revolt. London 1949

Morton, W.L. The Progressive Party in Canada. Toronto 1950

– Manitoba, A History. 2nd ed. rev., Toronto 1961

National Council of Social Work (USA). Proceedings of the National Conference (held in Toronto). Chicago 1924

Neatby, H. Blair. William Lyon Mackenzie King: A Political Biography. Vol. II, Toronto 1963

Nichols, J.H. History of Christianity, 1650–1950. New York 1956

Niebuhr, Richard. The Social Sources of Denominationalism. New York 1929

Plewman, W.R. Adam Beck and Ontario Hydro. Toronto 1947

Presbyterian Church in Canada. Acts and Proceedings of the General Assembly (containing the annual reports of the Board of Social Service and Evangelism, and after 1916, the Board of Home Missions and Social Service). Toronto 1913–25

– Pre-Assembly Congress. Toronto 1913.

– The War and the Christian Church. np nd [ca 1917]

Rauschenbusch, Walter. The Social Principles of Jesus. New York 1916

– A Theology for the Social Gospel. New York 1917

Reid, J.H. Stewart, Kenneth McNaught, and Harry S. Crowe. A Source Book of Canadian History. Toronto 1959

Reports of the [National] Conventions of the Canadian Women's Christian Temperance Union. np 1919–29

Riddell, J.H. Methodism in the Middle West. Toronto 1946

Roberts, Richard. The Christian God. New York 1928

– The New Man and the Divine Society. New York 1926

Robin, Martin. Radical Politics and Canadian Labour. Kingston 1968

Robinson, F.A. Religious Revival and Social Betterment. Boston 1918

Rodney, William. Soldiers of the International. Toronto 1968

Rolph, W.K. Henry Wise Wood of Alberta. Toronto 1950

Ross, Murray G. The YMCA in Canada. Toronto 1951

Rowell, Newton W. The British Empire and World Peace. Toronto 1922

Sandall, Robert. The History of the Salvation Army. 3 vols., London 1958. III, Social Reform and Welfare Work

Schweitzer, A. The Quest of the Historical Jesus. Trans. W. Montgomery. 3rd ed., London 1954

Semmel, B. Imperialism and Social Reform. Cambridge, Mass. 1960

Sharp, Paul. The Agrarian Revolt in Western Canada. Minneapolis 1948

Silcox, C.E. Church Union in Canada. New York 1933

Smith, A.E. All My Life. Toronto 1949

Smith, T.L. Revivalism and Social Reform in Mid-Nineteenth Century America. New York 1957

Social Service Council of Canada. The Social Service Congress of Canada, 1914. Toronto 1914

Society of Friends. Minutes of Canada Yearly Meeting of the Society of Friends. np 1916–27

Spence, Ruth E. Prohibition in Canada. Toronto 1919

Stapleford, F.N. *After Twenty Years: A Short History of the Neighborhood Workers' Asociation*. Toronto nd [1938]

Staples, M.H. *The Challenge of Agriculture*. Toronto 1921

Stewart, Margaret and Doris French. *Ask No Quarter: A Biography of Agnes McPhail*. Toronto 1959

Student Christian Movement of Canada. *Building the City of God*. Addresses delivered at the first National Conference of Canadian Students. Toronto 1923

– *Man at Odds with His Society*. Toronto 1926

– *Some Canadian Questions*. Toronto 1920

– *This One Thing*. Toronto 1959

Sutherland, A. *The Kingdom of God and Problems of Today*. Toronto 1898

Tawney, R.H. *Religion and the Rise of Capitalism*. London 1926

Tillich, Paul. *The Protestant Era*. Chicago 1948

Troeltsch, E. *The Social Teachings of the Christian Churches*. Trans. Olive Wyon. London 1931

The United Baptist Convention. *The United Baptist Year Book of the Maritime Provinces of Canada*. Truro, NS 1918–30

United Church of Canada. *The Message of the Basis of Union*. Toronto 1926

– *Minutes of the Conferences*. Toronto 1926–30

Visser't Hooft, Willem Adolph. *The Background of the Social Gospel in America*. Haarlem, Holland 1928

Voaden, Thomas. *Christianity and Socialism*. Toronto 1913

Voegelin, Eric. *The New Science of Politics*. Chicago 1952

– *Order and History*. 3 vols., Baton Rouge 1956–

Wallace, W. Stewart. *The Macmillan Dictionary of Canadian Biography*. 3rd rev. ed., Toronto 1963

Walsh, H.H. *The Christian Church in Canada*. Toronto 1956

Ward, William. *The Brotherhood in Canada*. London nd [1912]

Weber, Max. *The Protestant Ethic and the Spirit of Capitalism*. Trans. Talcott Parsons. London 1930

Woodsworth, J.S. *My Neighbour*. Toronto 1911

– *Strangers Within Our Gates*. Toronto 1909

PAMPHLETS

Bureau of Municipal Research. *What is the Ward going to do with Toronto?* Toronto 1918

Canada. Commission of Conservation. *Conference of the Civic Improvement League*. Ottawa 1916

Canadian Brotherhood Federation. *Constitution* (and list of officers and General Council). Toronto nd. UCA

Church of England in Canada. Council for Social Service. *Bulletin*. Toronto 1917–30

Denison, L.E. *Facts and Figures*. A Reply by Toronto Typographical Union, No 91, to Advertisements Published by Toronto Typothetae, Appearing in the Public Press of Toronto during May and June 1921. np, nd. MIR, UCA

A Group of Presbyterians. *The Need of the Presbyterian Church*. np, nd. MIR, UCA

International Typographical Union. *Facts About the Forty-four-hour Week*. np, nd. MIR, UCA

Kew Beach Presbyterian Church Association. *Official Organ of Methodists Denies the Atonement*. np, nd [ca 1923]

Master Printers' Association. *Five Facts.* Ottawa nd [1921]. MIR, UCA

Methodist Church of Canada. *Intensive Evangelism.* How to Organize and Conduct Group Studies of the Actual Experiences of Jesus, with Testimonies to Results Achieved. Toronto 1922

– and Presbyterian Church in Canada. *Reports of Investigations of Social Conditions and Social Surveys* (Vancouver, Regina, Fort William, Port Arthur, London, Hamilton, Sydney). Toronto 1913–14

– Department of Evangelism and Social Service. *Annual Reports.* Toronto 1914–25

– Department of Evangelism and Social Service. *Christian Churches and Industrial Conditions.* Toronto nd [1921]

– Department of Evangelism and Social Service. *Christian Hope.* Toronto nd [1922–3]

1921 Negotiations Between Committees Representing Toronto Typothetae and Toronto Local, No 91 of the International Typographical Union. np, nd [1921]. MIR, UCA

Presbyterian Church Association. *An Open Letter to the Members and Adherents of the Presbyterian Church.* Toronto 1924

Silcox, J.B. *Social Resurrection.* Montreal 1895

Social Service Council of Canada. *A Résumé of Labour Legislation in Canada, 1922.* Toronto nd

Toronto. *Report of the Social Survey Commission.* Toronto 1915

United Church of Canada. Board of Evangelism and Social Service. *Annual Report.* Toronto 1925–30

– Joint Committee of the Board of Evangelism and Social Service and the

Board of Religious Education. *Fellowship Studies.* Toronto nd [1928]

Woodsworth, J.S. *The First Story of the Labor Church.* Winnipeg nd [1920]

– *Organized Helpfulness.* Report of All-People's Mission, 1911–12. np, nd

ARTICLES

Albaugh, Gaylord P. Themes for Research in Canadian Baptist History. *Foundations*, VI, Jan. 1963

Allen, Richard. The Social Gospel and the Reform Tradition in Canada, 1890–1928. *Canadian Historical Review*, XLIX, 4, Dec. 1968

– The Triumph and Decline of Prohibition. Bumsted, J.M., *Documentary Problems in Canadian History.* 2 vols., Georgetown, Ont. 1969

Baker, W. John Joseph Kelso. *Canadian Welfare*, XLII, 6, Nov.–Dec. 1966

Bliss, J.M. The Methodist Church and World War I. *Canadian Historical Review*, XLIX, 3, Sept. 1968

Ernst, Eldon G. The Interchurch World Movement and the Great Steel Strike of 1919–20. *Church History*, XXXIX, 2, June 1970

Fox, Paul. Early Socialism in Canada. Aitcheson, J.H., *The Political Process in Canada.* Toronto 1963

French, Goldwin. The Evangelical Creed in Canada. Morton, W.L., *The Shield of Achilles: Aspects of Canada in the Victorian Age.* Toronto 1968

Gutman, H.G. Protestantism and the American Labor Movement: The Christian Spirit in the Gilded Age. *American Historical Review*, LXXII, 1, Oct. 1966

Irvine, W. The Labor Church in Canada. *The Nation*, 1 May 1920

Jackson, F. Ivor. Howard Falk. *Canadian*

Welfare, XLI, 6, Nov.–Dec. 1965

Johnson, Gilbert. James Moffatt Douglas. *Saskatchewan History*, VII, 2, spring 1954

Judd, Rev. Canon W.W. The Vision and the Dream: The Council of Social Service – Fifty Years. *Journal of the Canadian Church History Society*, VIII, 4, Dec. 1965

Knotman, R.N. Volstead Violated: Prohibition as a Factor in Canadian-American Relations. *Canadian Historical Review*, XLIII, 2, June 1962

Magney, William H. The Methodist Church and the National Gospel. *The Bulletin* (United Church Archives, Toronto), XX, 1968

Maines, Joy A. Through the Years in C.A.S.W. (Canadian Association of Social Workers). *The Social Worker*, XXVII, 4, Oct. 1959

McCormack, Thelma. The Protestant Ethic and the Spirit of Socialism. *The British Journal of Theology*, XX, 3, Sept. 1969

Morton, W.L. The Social Philosophy of Henry Wise Wood. *Agricultural History*, XXII, April 1948

Spafford, D.S. Independent Politics in Saskatchewan Before the Non-Partisan League. *Saskatchewan History*, XVIII, winter 1965

Watt, F.W. The National Policy, the Working Man and Proletarian Ideas in Victorian Canada. *Canadian Historical Review*, XL, 1, March 1959

UNPUBLISHED WORKS

Allen, A. R. Salem Bland and the Social Gospel in Canada. MA thesis, University of Saskatchewan 1961

Barker, R.W. The United Church and the Social Question: A Study of the Social and Theological Outlook of the United Church of Canada after Thirty-five Years. THD thesis, University of Toronto 1961

Buck, John M. The 'Community Church' and Church Union. MTH thesis, McGill University 1961

Butcher, Dennis L. Rev. Dr Salem Bland: A Study of His Activities and Influence in the Politics, Reform, Church and Society of Manitoba and Western Canada, 1903–19. Honours paper, University of Manitoba 1970

Calderwood, W. The Ku Klux Klan in Saskatchewan. MA thesis, University of Saskatchewan, Regina Campus 1968

Christie, E.A. The Presbyterian Church in Canada and its Official Attitude towards Public Affairs and Social Problems, 1875–1925. MA thesis, University of Toronto 1955

Forsey, Eugene. Labour and the Lord's Day Act, 1888–1907. Typescript nd

Grantham, R.G. Some Aspects of the Socialist Movement in BC, 1898–1933. MA thesis, University of British Columbia 1935

Page, Donald. Hon. Newton Rowell and the Founding of the League of Nations Society in Canada. Typescript nd

Pierson, Stanley. Socialism and Religion: A Study of their Interaction in Great Britain, 1889–1911. PHD dissertation, Harvard University 1957.

Pratt, D.F. William Ivens and the Winnipeg Labor Church. BD thesis, St Andrew's College, Saskatoon 1962

Rhodes, D. Berkeley. The Star and the New Radicalism: 1917–1926. MA thesis, University of Toronto 1955

Royce, M.V. The Contribution of the Methodist Church to Social Welfare in Canada. MA thesis, University of Toronto 1940

Schwartz, E.R. Samuel Dwight Chown; Architect of Church Union. PH D dissertation, Boston University 1961

Stolee, Lief. The Parliamentary Career of William Irvine. PH D thesis, University of Alberta 1969

Summers, David. The Labour Church. PH D dissertation, University of Edinburgh 1958

Wood, Charles R. The Historical Development of the Temperance Movement in Methodism in Canada. BD thesis, Emmanuel College, Toronto 1958

Index

This book

was designed by

WILLIAM RUETER

under the direction of

ALLAN FLEMING

and was printed by

University of

Toronto

Press